Why is the relationship between inequality and democracy so compelling to the contemporary social scientist? This volume addresses questions that were raised as early as the time of Aristotle and through Marx to the present. Theoretical lacunae are explored, as are major current policy concerns. The book focuses on the sources of democracy, the relationship between economic development and thresholds of democracy, and finally responses to democratization. Of course, definitions of democracy have varied over an extraordinarily wide range, as have conceptions of inequality, and the reader will find such variations reflected in the contributions to this volume. Descriptions of democracy vary from an emphasis on equality of participation for all citizens in decision making, to more complex indices emphasizing competitiveness and civil liberties. The contributors to this volume provide the kind of multidimensional analysis which is essential to a comprehensive treatment of the relationship between inequality, democracy, and economic development.

Inequality, democracy, and economic development

Inequality, democracy, and economic development

edited by

Manus I. Midlarsky

Moses and Annuta Back Professor of International Peace and Conflict Resolution at Rutgers University, New Brunswick

CAMBRIDGE
UNIVERSITY PRESS

PUBLISHED BY THE PRESS SYNDICATE OF THE UNIVERSITY OF CAMBRIDGE
The Pitt Building, Trumpington Street, Cambridge CB2 1RP, United Kingdom

CAMBRIDGE UNIVERSITY PRESS
The Edinburgh Building, Cambridge, CB2 2RU, United Kingdom
40 West 20th Street, New York, NY 10011–4211, USA
10 Stamford Road, Oakleigh, Melbourne 3166, Australia

First published 1997

Printed in the United Kingdom at the University Press, Cambridge

Typeset in Monotype Plantin 10/12 pt. [wv]

A catalogue record for this book is available from the British Library

Library of Congress Cataloguing in Publication data

Inquality, democracy, and economic development / edited by Manus
    I. Midlarsky
        p.   cm.
    Includes bibliographical references and index.
    ISBN 0 521 57191 X. – ISBN 0 521 57675 X (pbk.)
    1. Democracy.   2. Equality.   3. Economic development–Political
aspects.   I. Midlarsky, Manus I.
JC423.I485   1997
321.8–dc21   96–40356
                                                                                       CIP

ISBN 0 521 57191 X hardback
ISBN 0 521 57675 X paperback

This volume is dedicated to my family who generously allowed additional time away from home to plan the conference and edit the volume, and to the memory of Ned Muller who made such an important contribution to the conference proceedings and more generally to the fields of political science and sociology.

Contents

Contributors

KENNETH A. BOLLEN is Professor of Sociology at the University of North Carolina, Chapel Hill

STEVE CHAN is Professor of Political Science at the University of Colorado, Boulder

MICHAEL COPPEDGE is Associate Professor of Government and International Studies at the University of Notre Dame

EDWARD CRENSHAW is Assistant Professor of Sociology at Ohio State University

GUISEPPE DI PALMA is Professor of Political Science at the University of California, Berkeley

CAROL R. EMBER is Executive Director of the Human Relations Area Files in New Haven, Connecticut

MELVIN EMBER is President of the Human Relations Area Files in New Haven, Connecticut

MARK J. GASIOROWSKI is Associate Professor of Political Science at Louisiana State University

BÉLA GRESKOVITS is Deputy Head of the Department of Political Science at the Central European University, Budapest College

RAYMOND V. LIEDKA is Assistant Professor in the Department of Sociology at the University of New Mexico.

ELIZABETH MIDLARSKY is Professor of Psychology and Education at Teachers College, Columbia University

MANUS I. MIDLARSKY is the Moses and Annuta Back Professor of International Peace and Conflict Resolution, Rutgers University, New Brunswick

EDWARD N. MULLER was Professor of Political Science and Sociology at the University of Arizona

VICTOR NEE is the Goldwin Smith Professor of Sociology at Cornell University

PAMELA M. PAXTON is a Ph.D. candidate in Sociology at the University of North Carolina, Chapel Hill

BRUCE RUSSETT is the Dean Acheson Professor of International Relations and Political Science at Yale University

MILES SIMPSON is Professor of Sociology at North Carolina Central University

Introduction

Manus I. Midlarsky

This volume emerged from a conference entitled "Inequality and Democracy" held in New Brunswick, New Jersey in February 1994, under the auspices of the Center for International Conflict Resolution and Peace Studies at Rutgers University. An important impetus for the conference was the empirical finding, so far not contravened, that democracies seldom, if ever, war against each other, certainly not in the contemporary period. This finding is of critical importance for international relations theory, as it suggests that an increasing number of democracies will perforce decrease the prevalence of international warfare. A universal peace, as Kant implied, might be the consequence of a universal democratization.

Equally important as a basis for the conference is the constant presence in the literature of the nexus between inequality in its various manifestations and democracy. From the time of Aristotle through Marx and the present systematic literature, claims for a relationship between inequality and democracy have been strong and direct. Of course, formulations of democracy have varied over an extraordinarily wide range, as have conceptions of inequality. Indeed, one finds such variations in the contributions to this volume as appropriate reflections of this earlier variety. Democracy varies from an emphasis on equality of participation in decision making of all citizens, to the more complex indices emphasizing competitiveness and civil liberties. Inequality also varies from an emphasis on individual landholdings or income, to societal sectors. A comprehensive treatment of the relationship between inequality and democracy requires such a multidimensional analysis.

Why is the relationship between inequality and democracy so compelling to the contemporary social scientist? In addition to the theoretical lacunae, examined in the succeeding chapters, there are major current policy concerns as well. Strong differentiations in wealth are emerging both between and within nations. As much of the Third World, especially in Africa, descends further into poverty and disorder, the European Union (EU) and North American Free Trade Association

1

(NAFTA) proceed further in their mostly successful economic and political efforts. The vast majority of the world's poor are found in Third World countries, with India, China, Bangladesh, and Brazil, in descending order, having the greatest numbers of poor.[1] But the problem of North–South international divisions is compounded by inequalities within societies. Countries such as India with a large proportion of poor also house a large middle and even a sizeable upper class that contrast sharply with the remainder. Even Western countries with a far greater GDP/CAP have clear divisions between rich and poor that, on the whole, appear to be widening.[2] This fault line between rich and poor (or simply between middle class and poor) is reinforced by the convergence between economic inequalities and primordial descriptors such as race, religion, or ethnicity. In the United States, the fault line is essentially a racial one where the confluence between economic status and ascriptive characteristics appears most strongly between those of African–American and European descent. In France, Muslim Arabs, principally from North Africa, constitute such a group, while in Germany the ascriptive characteristic also denoting economic marginality is Muslim Turkish. What are the implications of such reinforced inequalities for the future of Western democracy, not to mention the potential consequences of similar inequalities in fledgling democracies both in Eastern Europe and the Third World? Issues of this type are addressed, if only obliquely, in the subsequent chapters.

More directly to the theoretical point, are inequalities of various types necessary conditions for the destruction of democracy or are they quite the opposite, namely necessary conditions for the emergence of democracy, at least in its early stages? A vast literature has emerged, referenced heavily in subsequent chapters, that asserts the inimical effect of inequalities on democracies. Certainly, the argument is eminently plausible, as suggested above. Yet in at least one chapter in this volume, with indications in a second, there is evidence that land inequalities may be necessary for the emergence of democracy in its earliest manifestations. Thus, certain fundamental theoretical questions are addressed in this book: the nature of democracy as manifested in various definitions and practices, the necessary conditions for its early emergence, and the institutionalization of democracy are treated here.

Organization of the conference was intentionally interdisciplinary. Leading scholars in the fields of anthropology, economics, political science, psychology, and sociology were assembled to discuss their respective papers, and the general relationship between inequality, democracy, and economic development. Each of the individual chapters in this volume clearly reflects the author's particular point of view. The differing, yet at times convergent perspectives drawn from several disciplines is almost invariably richer in both conceptual and empirical detail than a viewpoint drawn from a single discipline.

The book is divided into three parts corresponding approximately to these central concerns. The first deals with the historical record concerning some of the earliest societies, or those that have not changed substantially for many centuries. The second section examines various pathways to democracy, with an emphasis on economic development, while in the third we consider various responses to democratization.

In the first of these, Kenneth Bollen and Pamela Paxton compare the Athenian democratic experience with those of three hunter-gatherer societies. Their conception of democracy is essentially an egalitarian one, viz. democracy refers to the extent to which political power is evenly distributed in society. Structural barriers to participation in the system such as the exclusion of some persons from citizenship, or the concentration of power in the hands of the few, will lessen the degree of democracy. This definition allows Bollen and Paxton to measure the extent of democracy using Lorenz curves and Gini coefficients. These are measures used initially by economists to describe the extent of inequality (or equality) in income distributions; anthropologists, political scientists and sociologists have also used these measures that are now applied to inequalities in the distribution of political power, in turn defined as participation. Bollen and Paxton carefully describe the construction and use of these measures. Their findings are gleaned from three hunter-gatherer societies – the !kung of Sub-Saharan Africa, the Agta of the Philippines, and the Pintupi of Australia. The findings are clear-cut. Based on the identification of democracy as participation, the hunter-gatherer societies demonstrate greater democracy than did Periclean Athens.

My own contribution also emerges from a concern with Athens as a benchmark for democratic development. But here, instead of a comparison between Athens and other societies, the emphasis is on using the Athenian experience as a possible guide to the development of democracy. At the time of Solon, the emergence of differential wealth based on land ownership became the basis for a departure from the traditional tribal hereditary aristocracy and for the beginnings of an incipient democratic government. This early departure from tribe and heredity as a leadership principle laid the basis for later democratic development. At the same time, however, the effects of aridity and the threat of war as twin environmental threats to human civilization led to rigid controls in the form of political autocracy. Four ancient societies, Sumer, Mesoamerica, Crete, and China are compared as to their early, likely pre-historical experience with democracy. Additionally, in early modern Europe, war, or the threat of war had an impact on the diminution of land inequality which in turn, is associated with the decline of representative institutions. In the quantitative analysis of contemporary societies, democracy is measured by the Gastil political rights index that emphasizes principally freedom of election. Land inequality, rainfall, and the minimized threat of war are strongly associated with political rights, in addition to variables such as economic development and European location which have been found to be associated with democracy in prior studies. A variable that was also found to be significant, agricultural density, will have echoes in the succeeding chapter.

A third study that explores conditions for the early emergence of democracy is that by Edward Crenshaw. He begins by examining theories of modernization and dependency and points to their failure to predict democracy in preindustrial social development. In contrast, he develops the theory of technoecological heritage as a means of understanding the rise of democracy in societies that did not benefit from the modern accoutrements of economic development or other facilitators of democracy in industrial society. Crenshaw looks back to Spencer who asserted that high population density leads to an increase in the complexity of the division of labor. Social differentiation and complex interdependence also can put pressure on states to recognize the individual as a possessor of certain political rights. Using agricultural density as a measure of technoecological heritage and holding modernization and dependency constant, he finds significant associations between agricultural density and an index of political democracy. He also finds a positive, although non-significant association between land inequality and democratization, consistent with that found in chapter 2.

Two points are noteworthy. First, these findings of a positive association between agricultural density and land inequality, on the one hand, and democracy, on the other, were found using a very different theoretical framework than in the preceding chapter. Second, the index of democracy, instead of being based almost entirely on freedom of election as in Gastil's index used in that earlier chapter, is a multidimensional one based on participation, inclusiveness, competitiveness, and extent of civil liberties. Thus, there is a certain degree of mutual validation between the two chapters.

In contrast with the narrative treatment of the pre-historical societies found in my own analysis, Melvin Ember, Carol Ember, and Bruce Russett, systematically analyze societies that are not states in the modern sense. Their data base is the ethnographic record used now in a cross-sectional treatment of certain similar issues examined in the preceding two chapters. Consistent with the idea of participation as a form of democracy used in Bollen and Paxton and consistent with my own finding relating the threat of war to the diminution of democracy, Ember, Ember, and Russett find that war tends to diminish female participation in decision making. However, in contrast with at least some of the implications of the preceding two chapters, intensity of agriculture predicts less female participation. Additionally, social stratification as an indicator of land inequality as well as other inequalities, is associated with less political participation, also in apparent disagreement with these two chapters. To be sure, agricultural density and intensity of agriculture are not the same thing. Land inequality and income inequality, here combined in one measure of social stratification, actually have opposite theoretical and empirical implications in my own work.[3] The non-state societies of the ethnographic record are certainly not the same as modern states or even those of pre-history, as the authors clearly indicate. Nevertheless, these different findings and theoretical implications constitute the basis for additional studies to examine in the future.

The second section examines pathways to democracy emphasizing economic development. These take the form of causal sequences or specifications of particularly crucial variables necessary for democratic development, common pathways among regions, or specifics to given countries. Edward Muller asks the important question: why do countries at intermediate levels of economic development have difficulty in sustaining stable democracies? Certain larger South American countries, such as Argentina and Chile, immediately come to mind. Muller's answer is given as the result of a careful examination of the oft-found relationship between economic development and democracy, while at the same time examining income inequality as an intervening variable. He finds that the relationship between economic development and democracy constitutes a U-curve, with declining democracy at the intermediate levels, but increasing at the higher levels. This relationship is explained by his finding that income inequality, prevalent at the intermediate levels of economic development, is a direct cause of a decrease in democracy at this level of development. This is an important finding, for it suggests mechanisms of equalization through which countries must traverse prior to achieving stable democracy. Note that this negative relationship between income inequality and democracy is consistent with that found in prior research, but in no way reflects on the consequences of land inequality that are found to have opposite effects from that of income.[4]

Miles Simpson asks a related question. Given the many findings of a relationship between economic development or modernization and democracy, what is it *specifically* about these processes that most strongly affects democratic development. He develops a theory that places literacy at the center of the development process. Theoretically, this view is consistent with the earlier chapters in Part I that emphasize democracy in pre-modern societies. Clearly democracy was able to exist, if not flourish in certain of those societies, and so modern economic development, although important in contemporary democratization, was not a necessary condition for early democracy. The emergence of modern representative democracy after the invention of the first printing press offers a clue as to the importance of literacy in larger societies where the written word was now critical to communication, instead of the largely oral political communication prevalent in small city-states such as Athens. Information and communication also were found to be important in earlier societies, but Simpson is the first to develop a full-blown theory and extended empirical test of the role of literacy. After controlling for variables such as economic development, Simpson finds that literacy predicts changes in democratization between 1965 and 1990 no matter how democracy is measured, whether by Gastil's political and civil rights indices or Vanhanen's indicator of democratization. His analysis also shows how dramatically literacy affected the move towards democratization and the break-up of the Eastern bloc. This finding is of extreme importance, for it suggests that the trend towards increased democratization worldwide will be further facilitated by increases in literacy.

A question remains after examining the preceding two chapters, namely, how generalized are these findings of economic development mediated by income inequality or literacy affecting democracy? Michael Coppedge addresses this overall issue by means of a careful examination of transitions from one scale score to the next on a polyarchy scale. Here, as in Simpson's chapter, education – a correlate of literacy – appears as one of six critical variables to the democratization process. Economic development appears once again, as in earlier chapters, as do measures of modernization such as the percentage of non-agricultural population and the Gini coefficient of sectoral inequality. Coppedge finds that overall, the relationship between polyarchy and socioeconomic modernization is different at different thresholds of polyarchy, but that the model works just about equally well for all regions of the world. This two-fold finding is important not only in addressing the issue of universality of the path to democracy, but also in distinguishing between different processes occurring at different scale levels. Importance attributed to economic development or literacy does not mean that they will affect all countries equally. The differential impact will be far less dependent on region than on the particular stage of democratization at which the country is situated. This general conclusion is consistent with that of the preceding chapter; economic and social modernization are suggested here to empower citizens at the upper half of the polyarchy scale. Literacy also is a basic form of empowerment and so the findings of the two chapters nicely complement each other.

The role of markets and institutional arrangements then is examined by Victor Nee in the transition from state socialism. He focuses especially on the impact of the market on inequality in China as state socialism, in redistributing wealth, gives way to the more anarchic distribution mechanisms of the market. From this perspective, the state is examined as its influence recedes and another, far more inchoate in its structure, assumes the dominant role. Nee contrasts the sociological literature deriving principally from Marx that predicts vast market induced inequalities, with the economic literature that increasingly is based on Kuznets' early suggestion of an inverted U-curve between per-capita GNP and inequality. In this view, as per-capita GNP rises, income inequality increases through the intermediate stages of development, but at the highest levels of industrial economies, income distribution tends to be more equalized. Note the similarity in functional form between this U-curve (albeit inverted) and the one examined by Muller in chapter 5 concerning economic development and democracy mediated by income inequality. Certain of the mechanisms also may be similar.

A detailed and intensive empirical analysis yields a rich set of findings. In the rural, non-coastal provinces, the shift to a market economy increases income inequalities examined by Nee. The greater the reliance on markets, the more inequality increases. However, the strongest record of maintaining growth with equity is found in the corporatist provinces where governmental redistribution moderates the effects of economic growth inducing increased inequality, thus demonstrating that the Kuznets inverted U-curve is not inevitable. State intervention can redistribute income progressively even in an increasingly market-dominated economy.

Our final part examines various responses to democratization in the form of the influence of democracy on inequality, the consequences for industrial wages of transitions toward or away from democracy, a treatment of recent processes in Eastern Europe in comparison with those of Latin America, and the development of democratic institutions in the new democracies. Steve Chan asks how the initiation of a democratic opening is likely to affect policy choices influencing inequality, here treated as expenditures in several categories of public welfare.

Employing a quasi-experimental research design, Chan compares his "experimental" cases, Taiwan and South Korea which experienced democratic transitions, with a "control," Singapore, that did not. Using an innovative form of multiple regression analysis, Chan finds that Taiwan and South Korea both increased spending on education and social security after their respective democratic openings. Singapore, on the other hand, only increased spending on social security during the same period. And education is probably a more certain leveler of income inequalities than a safety net such as social security. Although Chan does not allude to this example, we know that Wilhelmine Germany hardly experienced a democratic transition of the Taiwanese or South Korean type, yet was a world leader in the innovation of social security programs. Perhaps the introduction of safety net legislation is an effort to *forestall* the demand for more open and democratic politics instead of being a consequence of a recent democratic opening.

We turn now to Mark Gasiorowski's examination of the impact of democratic or authoritarian regimes on industrial wages. Here one asks for more subtle consequences of authoritarian or democratic governance than the obvious curtailment or expansion of political and civil rights. Do authoritarian regimes use labor repressive measures to drive down industrial wages to stimulate economic growth? In answering this question, despite his emphasis on the consequences of transitions toward or away from democracy, Gasiorowski arrives at some surprising findings reflecting on possible causes of such transitions. After a detailed analysis, he finds that real wage growth fell sharply two to four years before transitions away from democracy, suggesting an economic source of such transitions. High inflation or slow economic growth (or both) may have facilitated these transitions. After the transitions toward authoritarian regimes, wages tended to be flat, increasing only after several years in power of the new regimes. There may have been a reluctance of these regimes to depress wages further and, in doing so, depress demand that could exacerbate a recession. A possible source of destabilization for new democracies worldwide is specified here.

Béla Greskovits compares the recent Eastern European experience with that of Latin America and arrives at some interesting, even counterintuitive conclusions. His general survey of post-communist Eastern European societies reveals that on the whole, they compare favorably with those of Latin America. The Eastern European transformation process included the peaceful takeover of power. The relative absence of riots and other forms of violent protests may, according to Greskovits, be attributable in part to the far more level income distributions in an Eastern Europe recently emerged from communism in comparison with the gross inequalities of Latin America. New political institutions may have played the role of a safety valve in channeling social discontent into the democratic process. Voting may have emerged as the weapon of choice, instead of the riot, violent protest, or guerrilla movement. Theoretically, this argument is rooted in Hirschman's well-known distinctions between exit, voice, and loyalty. Here it is voice that is being expressed in the ballot box, but as a consequence of the relatively underdeveloped state of Eastern European democratic institutions, perhaps it is a muted voice. Whether these favorable circumstances in comparison with Latin America will continue, of course, will be decided within the next decade or two.

In the last chapter of this section, Giuseppe Di Palma summarizes his view that a well-rooted constitutional state is the essential agent of a democratic civil society. Although the market may be necessary for such a civil society, it is not sufficient. There must be a compromise between the reproduction of capital and the reproduction of popular consent; the constitutional state offers the best means for peacefully channeling individual freedoms into the competitive exercise of citizenship. Interestingly, DiPalma independently agrees with Greskovits on the more sanguine prognosis for post-communist societies in comparison with those of Latin America. In the latter region, the break with the past has been less sharp thus allowing the continuation of older inequalities, political parties and statist ideologies having agendas that are inconsistent with successful modernization within a democratic framework. A swiftly reformed state of the post-communist variety may have a better chance of establishing a sustainable national economy, probably essential to a stable democratic future. Institutional innovation is the key, for without it democracy may ultimately founder. Finally, a concluding chapter examines the inequality and democracy nexus with a special emphasis on paradoxes of democracy which emerge from that analysis.

What do these studies have in common? First, they share a concern with causality or the consequences of democratization. How did early democracies evolve and what are some of the pathways to democracy and institutions that can either stabilize or undermine the processes of democratization? Second, they ask important questions concerning the most significant variables that have impact on democracy or its consequences, and when variables are specified such as economic development, they ask further questions concerning the most important "kernels" within such complex variables, or how the impacts of these variables on democracy are mediated. Finally, they show a deep and abiding concern for conceptual and empirical rigor. Concepts are defined and examined in a rigorous fashion both theoretically and empirically. At the same time, the results presented here are far from definitive. Even controversies related to the consequences of certain types of inequality for democracy have not been resolved. Nevertheless, many important questions associated with the nexus between inequality and democracy have been examined and the findings presented. Certainly, there should be much grist in this mill for scholars to examine in the future, both analytically and empirically.

NOTES

1 This rank order is based on the absolute numbers of poor, not proportions of populations. See *The Economist* (1994, p. 110).
2 For the United States, the gap between the most affluent and everyone else is now wider than at any time since the end of World War II (Holmes, 1996; Peterson, 1994). In cases of still developing countries such as Mexico, the situation is even worse (De Palma, 1996).
3 See Midlarsky (1992a, p. 468)
4 *Ibid.* Also see the debate between Muller (1995a, b), on the one hand, and Bollen and Jackman (1995), on the other.

Part I

The early bases of democracy

1   Democracy before Athens

Kenneth A. Bollen and Pamela M. Paxton

For over a decade, the world has been in the midst of a global demo-cratization movement. All regions of the world have felt the impact of this movement as the number of countries under liberal democratic rule has grown. The trend has renewed attempts by scholars to explore the meaning of democracy. In their efforts to understand the concept, schol-ars have sought a vision of ideal democracy and many have turned to the origins of democracy as a source of inspiration.

The starting point for such inquiries is often Athens during its demo-cratic period of 507 to 322 BC.[1] During that period, major decisions were made by a simple majority of thousands of citizens who assembled for long discussions of issues. Selection to many important positions was by lot and there was considerable freedom of speech and association. All of this occurred in a city-state that existed centuries before the industrial liberal democracies of the contemporary world began to take shape.

It is hard to overestimate the importance of Athens to the develop-ment of contemporary representative democracies. Hobbes, Locke, Mill, Jefferson, Tocqueville, and other political philosophers who helped crystallize the concepts of representative democracies were deeply influenced by Athenian democracy.[2] This, despite the fact that Athens was a *direct* democracy. Though direct democracy was not feasible in industrial societies with their larger populations, Athenian democracy inspired the attempt to have many citizens play a role, albeit an indirect role, in the governing of a society.

Yet, Athenian democracy is also an antecedent to the exclusionary tendencies found in representative democracies, particularly their earl-iest forms. Athens had an exclusionary political system, even during its peak democratic period. A large population of slaves had no say in Ath-enian politics. Women, even those married to citizens, were denied the right to participate in decision making. Metics (resident foreigners) were also blocked from participation. Athens was a democracy for male citi-zens but a system outside the control of the majority of the city-state residents.

Early representative democracies also excluded portions of their population. Some called the United States at independence in 1776 a democracy, yet it would not end slavery till nearly a century later. Women, including those who were not slaves, were denied the vote until 1920. Other European democracies delayed political rights to women even longer. Belgium waited until 1948 to grant the female franchise and Switzerland did not allow women to vote in national elections until 1971. The female franchise has not meant equal representation in governing positions, either. Today women are only a small percent of legislative representatives in the United States and other liberal democracies of the West (Sivard, 1985; Paxton, 1995). Similarly, race and class continue to influence opportunities for political participation in modern liberal democracies.

The coupling in Athens of a highly democratic system for some, with the exclusion of others established a vision of democracy that allowed the same disjunction in early representative democracies. To the extent that Athens dominates our conception of democracy, its discriminatory legacy can continue. We can widen our vision of democracy by considering other direct democracies that are more inclusive than Athens. Hunting and gathering societies are the main candidate, since they were generally more democratic than Athens.

Many writers recognized the democratic nature of hunting and gathering societies. Marx and Engels saw equality in "primitive" societies and it influenced their vision of the democratic communist society (Hunt, 1984). Rousseau too, was inspired by the freedom in "savage" societies when constructing his concept of democracy (Masters, 1968). Anthropologists recognize that hunting and gathering (henceforth H & G) societies exhibit political equality that is not present in other societal types.[3] Yet Athens still dominates most discussions of ideal and direct democracy.

The degree of democracy in H & G societies arguably surpasses that in contemporary democracies. One obvious difference is that, like Athens, democracy in H & G societies is direct rather than representative. Most would agree that power is more evenly spread in direct democracies. In a representative democracy only a minute fraction of the population sits in positions of power while in direct democracies every eligible member can directly influence decisions.

Part of Athens' appeal is its age; it is considered the historical root of democracy as well as its ideal. However, Athens is more closely aligned with the development of the West while H & G societies represent the historical roots of all contemporary societies. Athens' close association with Western tradition has led people to associate the democratic tradition with the West and to view democracy as a foreign import to other regions. The geographical dispersion of H & G societies suggests a democratic history shared by a broader spectrum of regions and traditions. Additionally, H & G societies precede Athens and their span of human history dwarfs the Athenian period.

The above comments assume that Athens' political system was less democratic than those found in many H & G societies. Much of the remainder of this chapter addresses the validity of that assertion. First, we compare democracy in Athens and in H & G societies using descriptive accounts of their societies. Based on these reports, we introduce a method to quantify the descriptions and to allow a numerical comparison of the degree of democracy in these direct democracies. This provides a new perspective on the difference in democracy that is not available from the verbal descriptions. To the best of our knowledge, the quantitative approach that we take to comparing democracy has not been tried before and may apply to other societies as well. Finally, we explore the ramifications of our discussion for the manner in which we regard Athens and H & G societies with respect to the origin and vision of democracy.

Democracy

It would be foolhardy to suggest that we can provide a definition of democracy with which all or nearly all would agree. However, it would be just as foolish to proceed without explaining our use of the term. We use democracy to refer to the degree to which political power is evenly distributed in a society. Political power concerns the ability of individuals and groups to influence the decisions of the society. By ability we do not mean the physiological and psychological capacities of individuals or their oratory skills. These will vary over individuals in democratic and non-democratic societies alike. Rather, we refer to structural barriers to participation in the political system, such as excluding some groups from citizenship or concentrating power in one or a few individuals and restricting access to such positions. Our definition highlights the groups included and excluded from participation and/or positions of leadership.

To clarify our concept of democracy, it is useful to describe the two endpoints of the continuum. The lowest level of democracy would occur when all decision-making power resides in one person. Decisions such as whether a society should move or stay, fight or have peaceful relations with neighboring groups, build or destruct shelters, or other such society-wide actions would be determined by a single individual.[4] At the other extreme, the highest level of democracy, all individuals would have equal say in such decisions. No structural barriers would exclude any member of the society from participating and expressing his/her views. Of course these two points of the continuum are ideal types for which no actual societies exist.

The direct democracies of our contribution differ from the representative democracies that are the subject of the other contributions in this volume. Liberal or political democracies are the primary form of representative democracies. As with other large-scale political systems, they have a political elite that has primary responsibility for governing. What distinguishes liberal democracies from other political systems are electoral rights and political liberties (Dahl, 1971; Bollen, 1980, 1993). Electoral rights refer to the elite accountability that occurs through free and fair elections with universal adult suffrage. Political liberties include the freedom of the mass media, free speech, and the freedom to politically organize.

For the bulk of the citizens in a liberal democracy, the primary form of participation is being exposed to multiple sources of political information, contributing time or money to political organizations, and voting. A smaller proportion of the population plays more active roles in political parties or political organizations. Some may run and be elected to local government. In direct democracies, a wider proportion of the population is more immediately involved in societal decisions. Though leaders exist in direct democracies, most adults have direct access to them. In addition, individuals can directly express their concerns rather than having a representative do so.

We limit our research to direct democracies rather than representative democracies because representative democracies raise some difficult questions about the distribution of political power. One problem is calibrating what happens to political power when representatives replace the face-to-face interactions and decision making that occurs in direct democracies. In the direct democracies of Athens and the H & G societies we have information on the group gatherings at which decisions are made and we can consider who is entitled to participate and who is excluded from these collective governing events. The division of political power is less clear when representatives intervene between the population and decision makers.

We examine the distribution of political power in three different settings: (1) Athens (507–322 BC), (2) H & G societies in general, and (3) three specific H & G societies – the !Kung of Sub-Saharan Africa, the Agta of the Philippines, and the Pintupi of Australia. For each, we extract qualitative descriptions of the distributions of political power from the relevant literature. Based on these accounts, we then roughly quantify the distribution of power in each as another means of contrasting their degrees of democracy. We use Lorenz curves and Gini coefficients in this task.

Athens (507–322 BC)

Kleisthenes initiated the Athenian democracy in its most primitive form in 507 BC and it lasted until 322 BC when the Macedonians conquered Athens. Outside of one eight-year lapse (411–403 BC), democracy prevailed in Athens throughout that time. The period from 460 to 330 can be viewed as the peak period for democracy since, beginning in 460, a series of reforms made the democracy more accessible to all citizens (Webster, 1969).

The three major social groups in Athens were slaves, metics (foreign residents), and citizens. We can further subdivide each group into children/adults and males/females. Within each subgroup, male adults had the greatest power with females and children having the least. Among the subgroups, citizens held almost all the power within the society. Metics and women married to citizens could occasionally influence citizens to gain political power but held no power themselves. Slaves had virtually no political power.

Thus, the Athenian "democracy" was a democracy only for adult male citizens. Women, metics, children, and slaves were not included. Though thousands were eligible to participate in ruling Athens, many thousands more were excluded. Indeed if the Athens city-state of this period existed today, the practice of slavery alone would make it a pariah state in the international community much as South Africa was during the 1970s and 1980s.

The democratic legacy of Athens originates with the political system that existed for adult male citizens. The democratic system had six components: (1) the assembly, (2) the nomothetai, (3) the people's court, (4) the boards of magistrates, (5) the council of five hundred, and (6) ho boulomenos (individual citizens) (Hansen, 1991).[5] The most outstanding feature of the system was the assembly. All adult male citizens could participate in the assembly, which had a quorum of 6,000 men. The assembly met about 40 times a year for the citizens to listen to proposals and vote. A simple majority determined the outcome (Finley, 1985, p. 19).

The nomothetai consisted of 500 men, chosen by lot (from the jurors), who served for a single day. Their task was to consider and vote on changes in law. In contrast, the assembly could only pass decrees. Decrees that conflicted with laws were invalid (Sealey, 1987, p. 32). Thus, the nomothetai role was more powerful than the assembly's.

Six thousand citizens over 30 years old made up the people's court. Jury members for a particular case were chosen by lot from those 6,000 and varied in size (Hansen, 1991). The court met frequently during the year and though the cases included some private suits, most were political trials, sometimes concerning control of the assembly, the council, the magistrates, and the political leaders. The court's power derived from its judicial influence over the other major political institutions.

The magistrates were the men who implemented the decisions of the assembly. They were selected by lot (from those who put their names forward), held office for one year only, and could not hold the same office twice (military commanders excepted). Over a thousand magistrates were needed each year and these men were divided into boards that oversaw particular sections of Athenian society (Hansen, 1991).

The council of five hundred was the most important board of magistrates. Members were selected by lot and could only serve a total of two, non-consecutive yearly terms. The council met daily and had the right to set the agenda for the assembly. Additionally, it controlled a great deal of public administration and prepared proposals for the nomothetai (Hansen, 1991, p. 259). Although the council of five hundred could influence the agenda, it was not the major decision-making body; the assembly made all vital decisions (Jones, 1957, pp. 118–19).

Though the work before a decision and the responsibility for the execution of a decision lay with the magistrates, the matter had to be raised by an ordinary citizen to start the process. Ho boulomenos, meaning "he who wishes," was a member of the assembly who took that initiative. "Is there anyone who wishes to speak?" was asked at the beginning of the assembly meeting (Hansen, 1991). Ordinary citizens could seize this opportunity to propose the initiative for laws, decrees, and legal cases.

Many features of this system encouraged political equality among adult male citizens. Selection by lot, rotation of positions, and payment for public service all contributed to balanced distributions of political power. Of course, all men do not have the same speaking or administrative skills and this created some political inequality. Also, the wealthy may have been better able to afford to participate. Although there was monetary compensation for political participation, the wealthy had more money and leisure for intense political involvement. In addition, even though it is impressive that 6,000 citizens participated in the assembly to vote on proposals, they did not comprise the entire population of eligible adult males.

As mentioned above, when we contrast the power of the adult male citizens with the slaves, metics, women, and children in Athens, the political inequality between adult male citizens seems minor compared with the far greater power differential between citizens and the other members of the city-state. Those in other categories had no direct role in the governing of Athens.

Women did not share in any of the freedoms, public or private, that men enjoyed. Women were severely restricted in all of their activities. They were not allowed to make contracts or wills and had to have a guardian all of their lives. They were given from their first guardian, their father, to their second, their husband, through marriage. An example of the position of women in Athenian society is that the laws treated the rape or seduction of a man's wife as the same act; the woman's wishes were not important (Sealey, 1987, p. 10). For most purposes, women were considered minors in Athenian society. Women were citizens only to the extent that they bore citizen sons, and thus had no direct political power.

Additionally, only a minority of the men enjoyed the liberty of citizenship. Outstanding foreigners or metics were occasionally granted citizenship as a reward for good service but most remained politically powerless. Metics doing business with citizens may have tried to use persuasion to further their interests but had no other way to influence decisions. Slaves, as a whole, had no political rights or liberties. Many served in mines or agriculture and had little to no contact with citizens. A few slaves served as aides to magistrates and might have had a small amount of influence on that office. Those influences were generally negligible in relation to the whole population of slaves, however. Overall, women, metics, slaves, and children were relatively powerless segments of Athenian society.

Measuring democracy in Athens

Translating descriptive accounts into numerical measures of democracy is the challenge to this analysis. We propose to use Lorenz-type curves and Gini coefficients to quantify and compare Athens with hunting and gathering societies. Lorenz curves are common in sociology and economics as a way of representing income inequality in a particular society. The first step in constructing one is to rank people by their income from lowest to highest amount. Then for each cumulated population figure record their cumulated income. The next step is to plot both columns of figures on a graph. Mark the horizontal axis with the cumulative number of people and show their corresponding cumulative income on the vertical. Connecting the resulting points leads to a curve that shows the proportion of people holding a particular proportion of the wealth. Perfect equality results in a straight 45 degree line from the lower left corner to the upper right corner of the graph. The greater the deviation of the actual curve from the 45 degree line, the higher is the inequality in the society.

Following our working definition of democracy, we measure democracy as the distribution of political power in a society, using the notion of political units. For ease of quantification, we assume that the total number of political units available to a society equals the number of adults in that society. Thus, in a perfectly equal society, each person would have one unit of political power and the Lorenz curve would be a straight line with a Gini coefficient of zero. Since no society is perfectly equal, some people have more than one political unit while others have less than one. As the Lorenz curve departs from perfect equality, the Gini coefficient increases. To determine the amount, we need to provide estimates of what groups in a society have more or less political power than their share.

To make our calculations, we need (1) divisions within the society between groups of people who might have more or less political power, and (2) estimates of the population size. It is clear from the above description of Athens that there are six groups within the society with major differences in power.[6] These are male citizens, female citizens, male metics, female metics, male slaves, and female slaves. (Children are assumed to have no political power and are not included in the analysis.) In the Athenian political system, some of these groups had much more political power available to them than others.

From the description above, we can make reasonable assumptions about the relative political power of the different groups in Athens. Based on the qualitative descriptions of Athens, a case could be made that the only people with political power in Athens were the male citizens. Thus, 100 percent of the power would reside in them with zero percent held by the other groups. If we allow that women, metics, and slaves might have had indirect influence on decision making through their connections with male citizens, the 100 percent figure appears too high. It is clear that the males had the overwhelming majority of the power in Athens. Our reading suggests that any figure below 75 percent of the power for males is inconsistent with the qualitative accounts of Athens and that even 75 percent is low. Our moderate estimate is that male citizens held 85 percent of the political power in Athens (although, as will be seen below, they only made up 20 percent of the population). Male metics are assumed to hold 5 percent of the power with male slaves and all females each also holding 5 percent of the power.

Male citizens can be further divided in terms of political power. Male citizens between 20 and 30 were not eligible for as many political offices as those above 30. For example, only males over 30 could be jurors (and therefore nomothetai). Since those positions held a political advantage, we assume those above 30 hold 75 percent of the male citizens' power, while those between 20 and 30 have only 25 percent of the power.

Additionally, among the women of the society, we assume that 70 percent of the women's power is held by the female citizens,[7] 20 percent by the female metics, and 10 percent by the female slaves. Since the only political power available to women was through influence, we assume that most of the potential power of women was concentrated in citizenship. None of these assumptions is absolute. Later we vary the assumptions on power distributions to assess their impact on the Lorenz curves and Gini coefficients.

To calculate the Lorenz curves and Gini coefficients we also need the population size of each group. The exact size of the population of Athens and the relative size of the different groups within it are unknown. There are a number of good estimates, however, based on historical information. Since there are a number of possible combinations using the available evidence, we begin with one that is a well-accepted estimate.

Gomme (1967) uses historical evidence to piece together the population of Athens. He uses a number of accounts, including numbers from Herodotus, Thucydides, and various inscriptions to determine how many people lived in Athens for various years. We use his estimates for the year 431 BC as our moderate, well-informed estimate. Later we demonstrate the effect of varying the population estimates on the measures of inequality.

Gomme estimates approximately 43,000 male citizens in 431 BC with about an equal number of female citizens. His estimates of male and female metics are 9,500 each. The figure for male slaves is 80,000, and for female slaves, 35,000. This moderate estimate is somewhat conservative because the number of estimated citizens is higher than the average for other years. We represent all of the information and assumptions in table A1, which is in appendix A.

Combining the estimates of the size of Athens with the power differential estimates gives all the information necessary to construct the Lorenz curve and Gini coefficient. The results are shown in figure 1.1.

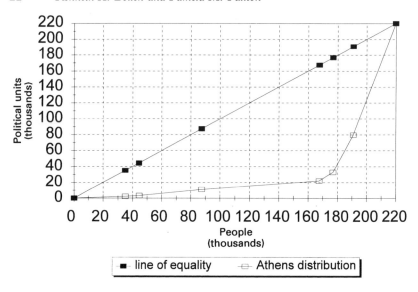

Figure 1.1 Lorenz curve for Athens
Note: Gini coefficient of 0.71.

Because the actual population of Athens is unknown, it is beneficial to change some of the estimates to reflect a possible range of political power that existed in the society. The number of slaves provides the most extreme changes to these numbers. Different sources place the number of slaves anywhere from 20,000 to 400,000. Both of these estimates are considered to be very extreme by scholars of Athens, although they are mentioned in some historical sources. We therefore utilize two more reasonable slave population estimates. Utilizing 60,000 slaves creates an estimate of Athenian democracy that can be considered "low inequality." Utilizing 150,000 slaves creates a "high inequality" estimate. We additionally change the assumptions about differences in power to represent more extreme examples. In the extreme equality case it will be assumed that male citizens only have 75 percent of the power and in the extreme inequality case male citizens have 95 percent of the power. It will be assumed that the rest of the groups in the society have the same proportions of the remaining power relative to their size.[8] These assumptions are represented in the table A2 and A3 in appendix A. Although other changes are possible, such as changing the number of citizens or varying the sex ratio in a particular group, we have chosen estimates to represent a reasonable range of possibility for Athenian democracy.

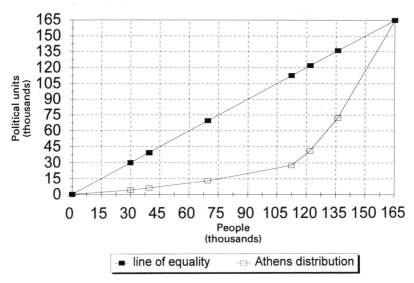

Figure 1.2 Athens with low inequality
Note: Gini coefficient of 0.57.

These estimates produce slightly different Lorenz curves and Gini coefficients, as shown in figures 1.2 and 1.3. We consider these estimates to give the possible range of democracy in Athens with the moderate estimate being the one in which we have the greatest confidence.

Hunting and gathering societies

As mentioned above, social and political theorists consider hunting and gathering societies extremely democratic. This view is generally upheld in the anthropological literature. Woodburn (1982) asserts that greater equality of wealth, power, and prestige was achieved in certain hunting and gathering societies than in any other type of society. He looks at five hunting and gathering societies and states that this equality is an option because hunting and gathering societies have direct, individual access to resources, means of coercion, and mobility. All of those factors limit the imposition of control by one individual on another.

The following quotes by anthropologists further illustrate the overall democratic nature of hunting and gathering societies:

Here, then was a land where . . . there were no social classes or castes, and where men could not be tyrannized by well-organized central governments. (Strehlow, 1970, p. 130 on the Aborigines of Australia)

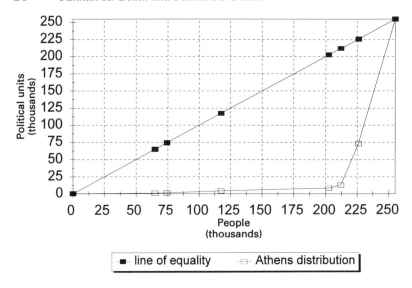

Figure 1.3 Athens with high inequality
Note: Gini coefficient of 0.81.

The freedom to live as one chooses, to move when and where one pleases, and to schedule, order and arrange one's life as one wishes . . . the people stress individualism, anti-authoritarianism, and independence. (Ridington, 1988, p. 104, quoting Savishinsky, 1974, on the Hare, a Subarctic people)

Positions of leadership are, on the other hand, plentiful . . . since the leader is unable to compel any of the others to carry out his wish, we speak of his role in terms of influence rather than authority. (Begler, 1978, p. 575 on hunting and gathering societies in general)

The basic principle of egalitarian band society was that people made decisions about the activities for which they were responsible. Consensus was reached within whatever group would be carrying out a collective activity. (Leacock, 1978, p. 249 on hunting and gathering societies in general)

While all foraging societies are egalitarian within sexual boundaries, not all are egalitarian across sexual boundaries. (Begler, 1978, p. 571)

These quotes emphasize the egalitarian nature of modern hunting and gathering societies in general. It must be understood, however, that although there is a general conception of H & G societies as egalitarian they are quite diverse. Recently, the notion of H & G societies as similar and interchangeable has come under attack (Wilmsen, 1989). Some have stressed the diversity among H & G societies and have suggested that rather than denying difference it should be studied (Kent, 1992). Thus, although all H & G societies have many things in common, it would be faulty if we did not recognize that variation can exist in their political systems. For that reason, we choose three societies to study more intensely. These three societies provide a range of democracies within H & G societies. We do not claim that these societies are the most or least democratic of all H & G societies, only that they represent considerable breadth in the degree of democracy within this type of society. So, where as for Athens we had different estimates of size and the relative power of groups as our basis for obtaining democracy estimates, H & G's have different societies.

We examine three groups: The !Kung, the Agta, and the Pintupi. These three societies were chosen for a number of reasons. All three have available information on their political systems, which was necessary in making assumptions about the distribution of political power. In addition, for two of the societies, we had an expert to evaluate our assumptions about political power.[9] We also wanted the societies to come from different regions of the world and represent variation in power differentials between the groups in their society. We can consider these groups a spectrum, with the !Kung representing the middle level of democracy, the Agta the highest level, and the Pintupi the lowest degree of democracy. Nearly all the other H & G societies we are aware of would fall within the levels of democracy represented by these cases.[10]

One source of variation among H & G societies involves the status of women. Researchers generally agree that overall, H & G societies are egalitarian. When the question of women is raised, however, the issue becomes more muddled. The dispute lies mainly with the access of women to the supposedly egalitarian political process. For this analysis, we have made sure that women's status also varies among these three H & G societies. (In comparison to Greece, however, hunting and gathering societies allow much more participation of women. The issue of women's status is qualitatively different from that in Athens, since in Athens women were completely excluded from the decision-making activities.)

The !Kung

The !Kung have no formal political system. Decisions are arrived at mainly through discussion and there is no permanent, established leader. Experts in certain areas of life influence discussions related to their area of expertise but their influence does not extend to other areas. Like the assembly in Athens, all members of the group can present an opinion in any discussion and attempt to sway the other members through persuasion. A leader in a particular situation may have more weight given to his or her opinion but he or she does not have any formal authority and cannot force the other members of the group to comply with his or her wishes.

The only potential stratification in political life is through age and sex. Regarding age, it is the older members of the group who often have more influence in informal discussions. Older members (over 40) have the suffix n!a added to their name and if a member is referred to as n!a by other older members of the group it is an indication of leadership (Lee, 1979, p. 344).

Regarding sex differentials, Lee (1982) notes that women participate less than men in group discussions, with men usually doing two-thirds of the talking. He also notes that although men and women are relatively equal in decision making, men do appear to have more influence in public matters. This observation is corroborated by Shostak (1981). Additionally, there is some violence against women in the society and that might curb women's political participation (Lee, 1982, p. 44). Women are able to take a leadership role, however (Lee, 1982, p. 46; Shostak, 1981) and there is no conspicuous male solidarity within the society.

To determine the distribution of political units, it is necessary to know the size, age distribution, and sex ratio of the !Kung population. Lee (1979) provides the necessary information. Children are 30 percent of the population. Adults (aged 15–59) constitute approximately 60 percent of the population and those classified as old (over 60) approximately 10 percent. The sex ratio is 90 for the adults and 63 for those over 60. The mean size of an individual !Kung group is about 20.

From the descriptions of !Kung bands, we introduce three divisions that may determine political power slightly – age, sex, and leadership. Involving age, we assume that all those over 60 are leaders. This distinction is due both to the possibility of them being viewed as wise by other members of the group and to their greater likelihood of being a !Nore owner. Owning a !Nore is an economic distinction in which a person has control of a particular area of land. !Nore ownership could lead to more political power (Hitchcock, 1993, personal communication). The age and sex composition of the society indicates that in an average group of 20 people, there would be one older women and one older man. (The six children indicated by the age composition are not included in the analysis.) Additionally, we assume that leaders constitute 10 percent of each sex among the adults. Again, the result in a group of 20 is one adult male leader and one adult female leader. Thus, there are a total of four leaders, a reasonable assumption for a group of that size.

Since leaders have little power outside of influence, in dividing up the power we assume that leaders have 40 percent of the total power (they make up 30 percent of the group). Their ability to influence gains

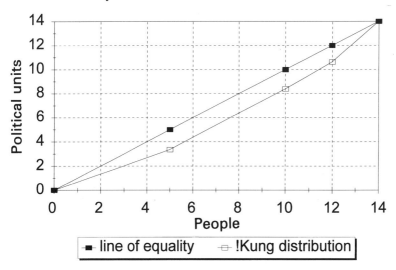

Figure 1.4 Lorenz curve for the !Kung
Note: Gini coefficient of 0.17.

them some extra power but not much. Four of them therefore share 5.6 units (40 percent of the total political units) instead of the four units they would share under a perfectly equal distribution. Additionally, the qualitative descriptions indicate that though men and women do not share power equally (50/50), they are relatively close. To allow for power differences due to sex, we have allowed men 60 percent of the influence for each group, leaders or non-leaders. Since the !Kung exhibit little inequality, no group has more or less than ten percentage points above or below what it would have under a system of complete equality. These assumptions can be seen more clearly in table A4 in appendix A. The Lorenz curve and Gini coefficient for the !Kung are shown in figure 1.4.

Clearly the Lorenz curve for the !Kung shows far less inequality than any of those for Athens. This impression is reinforced by the Gini coefficient of 0.17 for the !Kung compared to 0.71 for the moderate estimate of inequality in Athens. Even the set of assumptions that leads to the most equal distribution for Athens has a Gini coefficient of 0.57, a value considerably larger than that for the !Kung.

The Agta

The Agta are a hunting and gathering society of Eastern Luzon in the Philippines. Like the !Kung, their political system is open to all adults.

There are no formal leaders and all individuals can present opinions during discussion. Members with better oratory skills or who are considered to have wisdom may have more influence in informal discussions. Individuals are able to do as they wish, however, in that social control is very weak (Headland, 1993). No member can force another to do anything.

One interesting facet of the Agta is the extremely weak division of labor. Women participate in hunting and sometimes women hunt with bow and arrow themselves (Estioko-Griffin, 1985). There are very few activities (weaving, washing clothes, spearing fish in deep water, and climbing trees for honey) that are divided on the basis of sex (Headland, 1992). Additionally, there is little or no physical violence against women in Agta society (Headland, 1993). These facts indicate that women may enjoy a higher status position in this society than in other H & G societies. This is confirmed by the political presence of women in Agta society. Women participate equally with their husbands in decision making and can take an equal role in leadership during discussions (Barbosa, 1985).

The power differentials in Agta society are thus very weak. According to Headland (1993) there are no political power differentials between men and women. The only differentials that exist are between single and married individuals of different ages. Thus, adult society can be divided into the following groups, young single adults, young newly married adults (married less that one year), young ever-married adults (married more than one year), ever-married adults 30–9, and older ever-married adults (40+). Members of the society who have been married more than one year usually have at least one child and have more power. However, the power differentials between these groups are very weak.

Besides power differences, we require demographic information to form the Lorenz curves. Within the Agta, a typical camp consists of 23 people. The sex ratio is basically equal and the age distribution indicates that children (0–14) make up 35 percent of the population, adults (15–39) make up 45 percent, and older members (40+), 20 percent (Headland, personal communication). Among the adults we assume that 60 percent are 15–29 and 40 percent 30–9. Within the young adult category (15–29) we assume that one-third are single, one-third are newly married, and one-third have been married over one year. Thus, for a typical Agta band, there are two single adults, two young newly married adults, two married adults, four married adults aged 30–9, and five older adults.

Single adults have the least power with newly married adults having the next most power. Individuals who have been ever-married for more

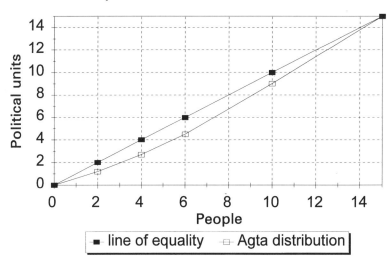

Figure 1.5 Lorenz curve for the Agta
Note: Gini coefficient of 0.12.

than a year increase their power with age. The Agta do not show any particular respect toward white or gray haired individuals (Headland, 1993) although wisdom and charisma are important factors and can be perceived to increase with age (Barbosa, 1985). If an older Agta loses his or her hearing or becomes senile, his or her power drops. The exact assumptions about power differentials are represented in table A5 in appendix A. The very small differentials reflect the equality evident in the qualitative descriptions compared with the !Kung; there is no difference between men and women in the Agta and all adult groups are within approximately five percentage points of the power they would have under a system with complete equality.

The Lorenz curve and Gini coefficient are in figure 1.5. As expected, the Agta have even less inequality than the !Kung. The Gini coefficient of 0.12 reinforces this impression. Though the difference between the !Kung and Agta is far less than that between either of these groups and Athens, we find that the Agta have less inequality than do the !Kung.

The Pintupi

The Pintupi are an aboriginal society in the Western Desert of Australia. Within the society there is great value placed on individual autonomy (Myers, 1986). No one is willing to be told what to do and people do not attempt to force others to their will. No individual has authority in him or herself; they must instead defer to an outside power, an autonomous code called "the dreaming." There is no formal political leadership within the traditional community, suggestions are based on knowledge of the dreaming.

Women in this society appear to have less power than may be true in other H & G societies. Women and men believe that there is a sharp division between their activities and are segregated a great deal of the time (Gratton, 1992). Marriage is polygynous and women are at times exchanged along with other objects of value (Myers, 1986, p. 111). Women do have some autonomy and can attempt to refuse marriages which are distasteful to them. Men control all elements of violence in the society, however, and there is violence against women in the society. This negatively influences women's power. Women basically conduct their own affairs within what is considered their realm but they do not influence what is considered men's business. Their value or activities are considered a social surplus to the social value of maleness, however. Women's power is simply not equal with that of men (Myers, 1986, p. 252).

Besides inequality on the basis of sex, there is also political inequality due to age. Older members of the group are considered to have more experience with the dreaming and can interpret its dictates more often. This enables them to mediate disputes and provide guidance. Pintupi social structure contains the idea of "holding," which is like the relationship of a senior to a junior. One member of the community may "hold" or "look after" another. Generation is the general determinant of who holds another with a rough equivalency within a generation (Myers, 1986, p. 214) For these reasons, there is a deference to the opinion of older people and older members get priority in discussion (Myers, 1986, p. 219)

From the above description, it appears that there are a number of power divisions. Since the sexes are often segregated, this differential will be noted first. It is assumed that females hold 25 percent of the power and males 75 percent. This large division in power is utilized to reflect the lack of power available to women in this society.[11] (Comparably, the women of Pintupi society have less power relative to men than the women of !Kung society – where !Kung women had 40 percent of the power, Pintupi women only have 25 percent.) Within each sex there are four divisions. For the males, these correspond to four significant stages within the lifecourse. After circumcision, males are allowed to marry although they do not usually do so until after a period of wandering. Later, males become novices in Tingarri (the dreaming). This allows them some power but they are considered inexperienced. After a male has completed his Tingarri instruction, he has more experience and can interpret the dreaming more often. Finally, middle-aged men are considered to be older and wiser than others.

The female lifecourse can also be divided into fourths. Young, unmarried women have the least power. Women with new children are considered inexperienced, have less power than women with older children who have more experience. Finally, older women, as with the men, have the most power.

The size of a Pintupi group can vary greatly due to mobility. It will be assumed, however, that a typical group around a waterhole consists of 200 people. Children make up 30 percent of the population and the sex ratio is assumed to be around one. There are therefore 140 adults, 70 males and 70 females. Within each group ten members are assumed to be young, 25 are assumed to be inexperienced, 25 are assumed to be experienced, and ten considered older. Within each group (males and females) the older group holds 25 percent of the power, the experienced group holds 39 percent, the inexperienced group holds 30 percent, and the youngest group, 6 percent. This power distribution is an attempt to model the hierarchy of "holding" within the society, which allows the older members to hold much more than their share of power. In the moderate estimate for the !Kung, the most powerful group, the male leaders, have 1.7 times the power they would under complete equality. Since the Pintupi are more extreme, their most powerful group, older men, have closer to three times the power they would have under equality. They should have at least this amount of power since they can influence the younger groups but we would not expect them to have more power since autonomy is valued and younger members are not required to obey the older members. The assumptions about the power of these groups are shown in table A6 in appendix A.

The Lorenz curve and Gini coefficient in figure 1.6 show that the Pintupi have greater political inequality than either the !Kung or the Agta. Although they can be considered an extremely unequal H & G society, when comparing their Gini coefficient of 0.35 with that of Athens, it is readily apparent that they still have a more democratic political system. Thus, even hunting and gathering societies with more inequality are more democratic than Athens.

Conclusion

We began the chapter with the assertion that hunting and gathering societies are generally more democratic than the city-state of Athens during its democratic period. Our analysis contains evidence that sup-

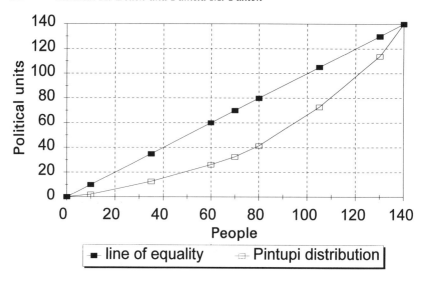

Figure 1.6 Lorenz curve for the Pintupi
Note: Gini coefficient of 0.35.

ports this contention; the descriptive material we reviewed is consistent
with this view as are the Lorenz curves and Gini coefficients that derive
from the qualitative material. Table 1.1 summarizes the evidence for
the Gini coefficients.

Our lowest Gini estimate of political inequality in Athens is 0.57 and
the highest is 0.81. For the H & G societies our extremes are 0.12 and
0.35. Thus, even under conditions that lead to the highest inequality
for H & G societies and the lowest inequality for Athens, we find that
Athens has less democracy. Since our results are linked to our assumptions garnered from qualitative descriptions, in appendix B we perform
a sensitivity analysis on the assumptions that lead to the Gini coefficients
and find that a range of alternatives leads to the same conclusion:
Athens is less democratic (i.e., has a higher Gini coefficient) than the
H & G societies.

Table 1.1 *Comparison of Gini coefficients*

	Athens	Hunting and gathering societies
Low inequality estimate	0.57	0.12
Moderate estimate	0.71	0.17
High inequality estimate	0.81	0.35

One plausible explanation for H & G's high democracy is based on the smaller size of H & G societies relative to Athens and other societal types. The H & G societies typically have fewer than 100 members whereas societies based on other technologies have thousands or, in the case of industrial societies, millions of members. The Pintupi, who we describe as the H & G society with the lowest democracy, is also the largest H & G society in this analysis. Smaller size can lead to the possibility of face to face interaction for all individuals in a society and H & G societies often split into smaller groups if they grow too large (although this is often a result of resource pressure).

However, size cannot be the only explanation. Currently, many societies far larger than Athens do not totally exclude women from the political system and virtually all societies forbid slavery. In addition, the degree of democracy varies even in large societies, so that England, for example, is more democratic than China. Outside of the ability to support a large population, mass communication, transportation, and the possibility of closer contact between individual and group made possible by industrial technology are likely to be contributing factors toward greater democracy. Greater communication can also enhance the spread of a democratic ideology across the globe.

The mode of production is a related factor that is likely to shape the political system. In H & G societies no group monopolizes the means of production. The technology does not provide a dependable and lasting surplus for which members might compete. Thus, economic inequality is low and this contributes to democracy in the political system. Athens was a city-state that thrived on mining and agriculture. Private ownership of property and the economic exploitation of women and slaves was conducive to an exclusionary political system. Though Athens was extraordinarily democratic for male citizens, the rest of its population faced repression that was commonly associated with an agrarian technology and a mode of production that included private ownership (e.g., Lenski and Lenski, 1987, chapter 7). Again, however, this cannot be the whole explanation. Further industrialization shifts the class structure of a society, often giving more power and resources to the middle and working classes. This new-found power enables these classes to demand and receive some say in the political system.

Outside of explanations, we must remember that part of the appeal of an "origin" of democracy, such as Athens, is its age. Thus, the results we obtain by investigating contemporary H & G societies take on additional significance when we consider the degree that their democracy is similar to the levels of democracy that characterized the first H & G societies. H & G societies were the earliest forms of human societies. If we consider the various technology bases for societies such as horticultural, agrarian, pastoral, industrial, etc., humans have spent more time living in H & G societies than all the other types combined. Lenski and Lenski (1987) estimate that H & G societies were the dominant type for the first four million years of hominid history. Limiting ourselves to *homo sapiens*, H & G societies dominate for the first 70,000 to 80,000 years of *homo sapien* existence. Conversely, industrial societies have only been around since 1750. This period of about 250 years is only a small fraction of the time that *homo sapiens* have spent in H & G societies. The 200-year period in which democracy flourished in Athens is an even smaller fraction of the H & G era. To the degree that the first H & G societies had political structures similar to the ones studied here, the bulk of human existence has been spent in democratic societies. H & G societies provide a historical root of democracy that extends back much farther than the Athenian legacy.

The assumption that contemporary H & G societies provide insight into past H & G societies is based on the concept of "analogous peoples" (For more information on the idea of "analogous peoples" see Lenski and Lenski, 1987; Clark and Piggott, 1965 or Renfrew, 1979). Modern hunters and gatherers are assumed to have much in common with pre-historic hunters and gatherers. For example, knowledge gained from modern H & G societies has been used to explain puzzling archeological evidence. The primary argument against the analogous peoples assumption is that modern H & G societies have inevitably had contact with other societies based on more productive technologies. In addition, modern H & G societies have been pushed to more and more marginal lands by more technologically sophisticated groups. These contacts could alter modern H & G society's structure from what it would be in a world that consisted only of other H & G societies (see Wilmsen, 1989).

Even if we accept these critiques of the analogous peoples assumption, the key question is whether contacts with other societal types would lead to more or less democracy in the contemporary H & G societies. It is easier to come up with hypotheses concerning how such interactions could lessen rather than increase democracy in modern H & G societies. For instance, other societal types are likely to have a more hierarchical political form and may promote such a form in the H & G society by choosing to interact with only certain individuals, by serving as a model, or by demanding that the H & G political structure change to match their own. Such contact might also create greater wealth differences in a H & G society which could accentuate differences in political power.

Thus, the world's democratic heritage is far more geographically dispersed than the impression gained by relying only on Athens as a point of reference. Dictators sometimes justify their hold on power

by describing democracy as a creation of the West that is inappropriate for their region of the world. H & G societies, though rapidly
diminishing, have been present throughout the world and, as we have
argued, these societies in general had high levels of democracy. So
the suggestion that democracy of all forms is "foreign" to certain
regions is hard to defend. Indeed, the most impressive democracies
built by humans are found in the societies that relied on the simplest
technologies and these societies were found throughout the globe.
Hunting and gathering societies may have set the limits for minimizing political inequality. Whether new technologies will enable us to
reach similar democratic levels or will move us in the opposite direction remains to be determined.

Appendix A: Numerically measuring democracy in Athens and hunting and gathering societies

Athens

Tables A1, A2, and A3 illustrate the quantification of the qualititative
accounts. In each, the divisions of the population are in separate columns. Under each group, the first number is the amount of people in
that category, with their percentage of political power in relation to the
total group. Underneath is the number of political units that the people
in the category share. With the tables, it is easy to see which groups have
more than their share of power and those that have less. For example, in
table A1, the three columns illustrate the increasing inequality when we
consider different groups. The far left column illustrates the political
power available to all individuals. The middle column illustrates how
dividing the population into male and female reduces the political units
available to females and male slaves while increasing it for male metics
and male citizens. The further divisions in the third column illustrate
further inequalities so that in the last group, the 29,000 male citizens
over thirty share 140,250 units of political power – about five times what
they would have under a system of complete equality.

Hunting and gathering societies

In developing the assumptions for hunting and gathering societies, we
asked various experts for aid. Two professors of anthropology with extensive experience with the !Kung and Agta checked our assumptions about the
distribution of political power for the society in which they had expertise.

Table A1 *Moderate estimates for Athens*

All individuals	Division 1 Females, male slaves/ metics/citizens	Division 2 Female slaves/metics/citizens, male citizens 20–30/30
		Female slaves 35,000 share 20% of 5% of the power 35,000 share 2,200 political units
	Females 87,500 share 5% of the power 87,500 share 11,000 political units	**Female metics** 9,500 share 10% of 5% of the power 9,500 share 1,100 political units
		Female citizens 43,000 share 70% of 5% of the power 43,000 share 7,700 political units
All individuals 220,000 have 100% of the power 220,000 share 220,000 political units	**Male slaves** 80,000 share 5% of the power 80,000 share 11,000 political units	**Male slaves** 80,000 share 5% of the power 80,000 share 11,000 political units
	Male metics 9,500 share 5% of the power 9,500 share 11,000 political units	**Male metics** 9,500 share 5% of the power 9,500 share 11,000 political units
		Male citizens (20–30) 14,000 share 25% of 85% of the power 14,000 share 46,750 political units
	Male citizens 43,000 share 85% of the power 43,000 share 187,000 political units	**Male citizens (30+)** 29,000 share 75% of 85% of the power 29,000 share 140,250 political units

Professor Robert Hitchcock is specifically interested in politics in hunting and gathering societies and specializes in the !Kung. Professor Thomas Headland, an anthropologist who spent over twenty years living with the Agta, provided information about their society. We were unable to find an expert to check our assumptions about the Pintupi but we had some helpful discussions with Professor Fred Myers, who is the author of the book, *Pintupi Country, Pintupi Self.*[12] We listed some of the assumptions about the

Table A2 *Extreme inequality estimates for Athens*

All individuals	Division 1 Females, male slaves/ metics/citizens	Division 2 Female slaves/metics/citizens, male citizens 20–30/30
		Female slaves 65,000 share 20% of 1.7% of the power 65,000 share 867 political units
	Females 117,500 share 1.7% of the power 117,500 share 4,335 political units	**Female metics** 9,500 share 10% of 1.7% of the power 9,500 share 433 political units
		Female citizens 43,000 share 70% of 1.7% of the power 43,000 share 3,035 political units
All individuals 255,000 have 100% of the power 255,000 share 255,000 political units	**Male slaves** 85,000 share 1.6% of the power 85,000 share 4,080 political units	**Male slaves** 85,000 share 1.6% of the power 85,000 share 4,080 political units
	Male metics 9,500 share 1.7% of the power 9,500 share 4335 political units	**Male metics** 9,500 share 1.7% of the power 9,500 share 4335 political units
		Male citizens (20–30) 14,000 share 25% of 95% of the power 14,000 share 60,562 political units
	Male citizens 43,000 share 95% of the power 43,000 share 242,250 political units	**Male citizens (30+)** 29,000 share 75% of 95% of the power 29,000 share 181,688 political units

three H & G societies in the individual hunting and gathering society's section. The information contained in those sections and additional information about power differentials are in figures A4, A5, and A6.

Appendix B

Calculation of the Gini coefficient and robustness of the results.

Table A3 *Extreme equality estimates for Athens*

All individuals	Division 1 Females, male slaves/ metics/citizens	Division 2 Female slaves/metics/citizens, male citizens 20–30/30
		Female slaves 30,000 share 20% of 12.7% of the power 30,000 share 4,191 political units
	Females 82,500 share 12.7% of the power 82,500 share 20,955 political units	**Female metics** 9,500 share 10% of 12.7% of the power 9,500 share 2,095 political units
		Female citizens 43,000 share 70% of 12.7% of the power 43,000 share 14,669 political units
All individuals 165,000 have 100% of the power 165,000 share 165,000 political units	**Males slaves** 30,000 share 4% of the power 30,000 share 6,600 political units	**Male slaves** 30,000 share 4% of the power 30,000 share 6,600 political units
	Male metics 9,500 share 8.3% of the power 9,500 share 13,695 political units	**Male metics** 9,500 share 8.3% of the power 9,500 share 13,695 political units
	Male citizens 43,000 share 75% of the power 43,000 share 123,750 political units	**Male citizens (20–30)** 14,000 share 25% of 75% of the power14,000 share 30,937 political units **Male citizens (30+)** 29,000 share 75% of 75% of the power 29,000 share 92,813 political units

The Gini coefficient

The Lorenz curve is a pictorial representation of inequality. In addition, we can form numerical measures to concisely represent the amount of inequality. The most widely used single measure of income inequality is the Gini coefficient. The coefficient is a measure of the ratio of the area between the Lorenz curve and the line of perfect equality to the area beneath the line of perfect equality. Thus, the higher the Gini coefficient,

Table A4 *!Kung*

All individuals	Division 1 Non-leaders/leaders	Division 2 Females/males
		Female non-leaders 5 share 40% of 60% of the power 5 share 3.4 political units
	Non-leaders 10 share 60% of the power 10 share 8.4 political units	**Male non-leaders** 5 share 60% of 60% of the power 5 share 5.0 political units
All individuals 14 have 100% of the power 14 share 14 political units		**Female leaders** 2 share 40% of 40% of the power 2 share 2.2 political units
	Leaders 4 share 40% of the power 4 share 5.6 political units	**Male leaders** 2 share 60% of 40% of the power 2 share 3.4 political units

Table A5 *Agta*

All individuals	Division 1 Single/married, age
	Single adults 2 share 8% of the power 2 share 1.2 political units **Young, newly married** 2 share 10% of the power 2 share 1.5 political units
All individuals 15 have 100% of the power 15 share 15 political units	**Young, married** 2 share 12% of the power 2 share 1.8 political units **Married, aged 30–9** 4 share 30% of the power 4 share 4.5 political units **Older** 5 share 40% of the power 5 share 6 political units

Table A6 *Pintupi*

All individuals	Division 1 Females/males	Division 2 Age and experiance
		Young women 10 share 6% of 25% of the power 10 share 2 political units **Inexperienced mothers** 25 share 30% of 25% of the power 25 share 10.5 political units
	Females 70 share 25% of the power 70 share 35 political units	**Experienced mothers** 25 share 39% of 25% of the power 25 share 14 political units **Older women** 10 share 25% of 25% of the power 10 share 9 political units
All individuals 140 have 100% of the power 140 share 140 political units		**Young men** 10 share 6% of 75% of the power 10 share 6 political units **Novices** 25 share 30% of 75% of the power 25 share 31.5 political units
	Males 70 share 75% of the power 70 share 105 political units	**Completed Tingarri instruction** 25 share 39% of 75% of the power 25 share 41 political units **Older men** 10 share 25% of 75% of the power 10 share 26 political units

the greater is the inequality in a society. Since our analysis will allow us to draw a Lorenz curve, we can calculate the Gini coefficient with the following formula (Nygard and Sandstrom, 1981, p. 292, equation 8.10)

$$R_L = p_{k-1} - \sum_{i=1}^{k-1} L(p_i)(p_{i+1} - p_{i-1})$$

In the equation, R_L is the Gini coefficient and p_i is the proportion of the population in a particular category. Categories, i, range from 1 to k. $L(p_i)$ is the cumulative share of political units for a category.

The Gini coefficient is a lower bound since it, like the Lorenz curve, assumes equality within groups. Additionally, the coefficient reflects the number of categories used to calculate it. The more categories utilized, the more exact we can draw the curve and the more inequality represented. A society with fewer categories than another but a similar power distribution would result in a smoother curve and a score indicating less inequality. Related to the number of categories, how close the last category of people is to 100 percent (its percentile) can also influence the Gini coefficient. Lorenz curves that include a last group in a high percentile might indicate more inequality simply because that distinction is available.

The robustness of our results

Since the societies utilized in the analysis do differ on the number of categories and the highest percentile, we provide the following analysis to show that variance on those factors is not large enough to make a discernible difference in the scores. We experimentally change some of the features of the societies utilized in this analysis. Looking at table B1 indicates that Athens, as modeled under conditions of inequality in the text, has seven categories and a top percentile of 11 percent (meaning, the last category of people in Athens, male citizens over 30, constitute 11 percent of the population). We can collapse the number of categories by lumping all male citizens together and all females together. This destroys the deviation within those groups and reduces the number of categories. If we change the features of Athens by collapsing its categories to four, its Gini coefficient is only lowered by 0.01.

Like Athens, the number of categories in the Pintupi analysis was also collapsed, while for the Agta, the number of categories was increased. The number of categories was increased for the Agta by splitting the top percentile of individuals into two parts. None of these drastic changes in number of categories or highest percentile affect the Gini coefficients by more than 0.04, however.

The lack of change in table B1 indicates that our results are robust to variations in the way that different qualitative information is incorporated quantitatively. For example, although the information on Athens led us to divide it into seven categories with a top percentile of 11 per-

Table B1 *Comparison of Gini coefficients for original and collapsed categories*

Society	Original # categories	Original % in top category	Gini	Changed # categories	Changed % in top category	Changed Gini
Athens						
(unequal)	7	11%	0.81	4	26%	0.80
Pintupi	8	7%	0.35	4	43%	0.31
Agta	5	33%	0.12	6	13%	0.12

cent, if we had instead chosen four categories with a top percentile of 26 percent our results would not be different. The results also show that our findings are robust across societies. One might argue that the equality shown in the Agta is a reflection of the presence of only five categories compared with Athens' seven. This analysis shows that this is not the case; Athens still shows much more equality than the Agta even if Athens is forced into fewer categories and the Agta into more. We invite readers to test other plausible assumptions. Any reasonable assumption about these groups would produce the same result.

NOTES

We thank Barbara Entwisle, Thomas Headland, Charlie Hirschman, Robert Hitchcock, Gerhard Lenski, Manny Midlarsky, Jim Moody, Fred Myers, and Buck Schieffelin for their helpful comments on earlier drafts of this paper. Professors Headland and Hitchcock provided evaluations of our assumptions regarding the Agta and !Kung societies. We are responsible for any errors. Partial support for this research comes from the Sociology Program of the National Science Foundation (SES-9121564) and the Center for Advanced Study in the Behavioral Sciences, Stanford, California. An earlier version of this paper was presented at the Inequality and Democracy Conference, February 4–6, 1994, Rutgers University, New Brunswick, New Jersey.

1 Athens also serves as an ideal for the "rule of law." This refers to a society where law has more power than any individual and laws cannot be arbitrarily changed at the whim of a ruler. Rule of law can be found in some authoritarian systems as well as in democracies. Our primary concern is not with Athens as a model of the rule of law, but rather with Athens as a model of ideal democracy.

2 One reason that scholars choose Athens as a starting point for democracy is that written documentation is available. Aristotle, Plato, Thucydides, and others left us a record of the political system in the Athenian city-state. Obviously a written record enhances the survivability and dispersion of infor-

mation relative to an oral tradition. Indeed, if there were no written historical accounts of Athens during this period, it would not play such a prominent role in the study of democracy.

3 By highlighting the democratic nature of hunting and gathering societies, we run the danger of idealizing all aspects of such societies. Though we are impressed by the degree of democracy in such societies, we also recognize other aspects that are less enviable (e.g., generally lower life expectancy and the scarcity of basic necessities compared with industrial societies).

4 We focus on society-wide decisions rather than day-to-day, more technical, or familial decisions. Specialized areas might have "experts" making the decisions. For instance, a family's decisions on child-rearing could be dominated by one person with decisions on weapon construction by another. We attempt to focus beyond these microdecisions and limit ourselves to broader decisions that affect the entire society. Furthermore, we do not treat egalitarian societies as equivalent to democratic ones. "Egalitarian" connotes an even distribution of economic and social resources while our use of democracy concentrates on the distribution of political power. Clearly the two are related, but our focus is on the latter.

5 Hansen includes a seventh category, the Areopagos, which was a remnant of an earlier form of government and played only a minor role in Athenian democracy for much of the period. Its role can be considered somewhat like an advisory magistrate board.

6 It is difficult to represent the full complexity of power relations in this society (or any society) with just a few divisions. There are a variety of ways that people can individually gain power, such as through kinship or charisma. These methods are very individual, however, and therefore impossible to measure. For the purposes of this study, we attempt to outline the broad power divisions within society that hold in general.

7 Female citizens were referred to as citizens even though they did not hold citizen privileges. They needed to be called citizens since a new citizen could only be born by two citizens.

8 This means that in the extreme equality case male slaves have less power since their numbers are proportionately lower than in the other two cases. Additionally, females in the extreme equality case are given proportionately more power since their numbers have increased proportionately.

9 Our many thanks to Professor Thomas Headland and Professor Robert Hitchcock for commenting on our assumptions and to Professor Fred Myers for extensive telephone conversations.

10 Some exceptions involve cases with debatable H & G status. For instance, some American Indian tribes on the Pacific Northwest coast (Haida, Tlinget) may have had less democracy than the Pintupi due to the presence of pronounced social inequality and slavery. Their subsistence technology is not solely the traditional one that we associate with H & G societies, however, since their use of rich fishing areas led to a far greater surplus than in other H & G societies. This abundance of resources made a dense population possible and the acquisition of property and wealth important. These societies were not nomadic and lived in permanent villages of close to 1,000 individuals. In fact, these societies might have as much in common with

simple horticultural societies as they do with hunting and gathering societies (see Drucker, 1965; Lenski and Lenski, 1987, p. 211; Woodcock, 1977). Lenski and Lenski (1987, p. 211) suggest that these societies are not H & G societies but rather a specialized societal type which they refer to as fishing societies. Thus, though we can find some H & G societies with democracy levels that fall outside the democracy range of the !Kung, Agta, and Pintupi, these will be the exceptions and may utilize technologies that fall outside the usual H & G techniques.

11 Bell (1993) asserts that women in aboriginal society have more actual power than most anthropologists have allowed them. She emphasizes the separation of male and female spheres and the presence of female rituals. Although she studies societies to the northwest of the Pintupi, her argument is worth noting. To affect our results, her evidence would need to apply to the Pintupi and the existence of female power in rituals and the separation of spheres would have to give women more power in societal decision making than we assume. The net impact would be a range of inequality among H & G societies that is even narrower than we find. This would lend even further support to our argument that H & G societies are far more democratic than Athens.

12 The assumptions we make for the Pintupi are based on our reading of the accounts of this group in the anthropological literature.

2 Environmental influences on democracy: aridity, warfare, and land inequality

Manus I. Midlarsky and Elizabeth Midlarsky

A conundrum surrounds the origins of ancient autocratic empires (Eisenstadt, 1963, 1986). Why did they originate in the East in places such as Mesopotamia and not in Western Europe that has experienced such a fluorescence of civilized activity both of the aggressive and contemplative variety? Few, if any definitive answers have been given to this question. One approach will be suggested here in the form of environmental influences that can increase or decrease the probability of democratic development.

Macroinfluences of the environment of course had venerable antecedents in the theories of Mahan and Mackinder on the respective influences of sea and land on national power. And Harold and Margaret Sprout (1962) later expanded several of these into a more coherent theory of environmental influences on international relations. A nexus between environmental change and violent conflict is found in the recent work of Homer-Dixon, Boutwell, and Rathjens (1993). However, there are still few outstanding general theories on the impact of environmental change on societal conditions.

One of the few theorists who did offer a general theory of environmental influences on domestic societal concerns was Karl Wittfogel (1957). Although often interpreted as a theory of the origins of the state (Haas, 1982, p. 146), his was actually a theory of the rise of Eastern autocracy. This chapter will empirically examine his theory of hydraulic civilization that presumably gave rise to autocracies in hydraulic civilizations such as ancient Mesopotamia. This treatment also will "reverse the causal arrow" in examining the effects of war on democracy instead of the converse as has been done recently. In doing so, an important environmental influence on democracy will emerge, that of sea borders. Additionally, and most importantly, the occurrence of warfare will be associated with the diminished influence of land ownership on political rights. And land inequality, in itself, will be demonstrated to have a positive influence on political rights.

Because Wittfogel's theory is well known, it will not receive extensive

45

presentation here beyond the elements needed to advance the argument. On the other hand, the effects of war on democracy are little known and so will receive a more developed exposition. As we shall see, both aridity and the threat of war implied by many land borders constitute twin environmental threats to human civilization that historically have led to rigid controls in the form of political autocracy. At the same time, sufficient rainfall and a maximum number of sea borders constitute two dimensions of minimized environmental threat that allow the growth of democracy without the need for despotic control of irrigation systems, food distribution, or the mobilization of sedentary populations to confront invading hostile forces.

Hydraulic civilization

Karl Wittfogel enjoyed enormous influence on social scientific treatments of the origins of the state. Researchers such as Sanders and Price (1968) and even theorists such as Carneiro (1970, 1987) based much of their earlier thinking on Wittfogel's theory. Briefly, the theory stipulates that early autocracies arose as the result of human need to manage irrigation waters in arid zones. A bureaucratic-despotic organization was needed to manage the water drained from rivers and streams, hence the term hydraulic civilization coined by Wittfogel and its intimate connection with autocracy.

As Wittfogel (1957, p. 70) puts it:

The fact that work on the public fields was usually shared by all corviable adult males indicates the power of the hydraulic leadership to make everyone contribute to its support. The establishment of a money economy goes hand in hand with greater differentiations in property, class structure, and national revenue. . . . Comparison shows that in this respect it was much stronger than the governments of other agrarian societies.

Or elsewhere:

Demonstrative and total submission is the only prudent response to total power. Manifestly, such behavior does not gain a superior's respect; but other ways of proceeding invite disaster. Where power is polarized, as it is in hydraulic society, human relations are equally polarized. Those who have no control over their government quite reasonably fear that they will be crushed in any conflict with its masters. (Wittfogel, 1957, p. 154)

Although several studies have disputed the relevance of Wittfogel's theory to the origins of the *state* (Adams, 1966; Chang, 1986), none to my knowledge has in a systematic way, empirically addressed the issue of hydraulic civilization in relation to the issue of autocracy, or its logical and empirical obverse, democracy.

Perhaps one reason for the failure to test Wittfogel's hypothesis in relation to autocracy or democracy is its overused and misinterpreted application to the origins of the state *per se*. Another may be the difficulty in statistically analyzing a small number of historic hydraulic civilizations. This problem may be solved by viewing it from an obverse standpoint. Rainfall and the need for hydraulic agriculture can be seen as flip sides of the same coin, or as mirror images. As we have seen, arid regions, as well as sources of irrigation are required for hydraulic civilization. Zones of sufficient rainfall (as in Northern Europe), on the other hand, by definition, are not arid and also do not require irrigation. Wittfogel (1957, pp. 15–16) himself recognizes this duality when he states that "the stimulating contradiction inherent in a potentially hydraulic landscape is manifest. Such a landscape has an insufficient rainfall or none at all; but it possesses other accessible sources of water supply. If man decides to utilize them, he may transform dry lands into fertile fields and gardens."

Further, we can examine the effect of rainfall on autocracy as well as democracy by using as the dependent variable a scale that reflects a continuum of political rights from the most complete to the most restricted. This scale will be introduced shortly.

Interestingly, the connection between hydraulic civilization and autocracy is not only found in ancient civilizations. Arid landscapes that also have sources of water supply in the contemporary period can furnish illustrations. Spain, for example, has many arid regions that require irrigation for successful agriculture. And it was the Spanish dictator, Primo de Rivera in the 1920s, the precursor of later Spanish fascism, who made the most concentrated efforts until that time to emphasize hydraulic agriculture. Indeed, according to Malefakis (1970, p. 284), "Primo de Rivera . . . emulated Mussolini in deriving the maximum publicity from his hydraulic projects."

There is another reason to identify rainfall as a relevant factor in the rise of democracy or diminution of autocracy. That is the need for centralized distribution systems in arid climates. Just as a bureaucratic-despotic regime can arise as a consequence of the need for centralized irrigation control, so too the need to store food and redistribute it in times of drought-induced famine can lead to a centralized autocracy. Food and water are functionally interchangeable in this context. Bureaucracies necessary to administer the distribution of water in arid zones would be equally necessary to store and distribute food in time of drought. Decisions to distribute each of these commodities require centralized political control.

Spain offers another illustration of centralized decision making in response to aridity, and here it is in the area of food redistribution. As in many other countries with arid climates, the monarchy took it upon itself to require the storage of food and its redistribution in times of scarcity. As Herr (1989, p. 32) remarks on such activities in eighteenth-century Spain, "The first response of the crown to the growing threat of grain shortages was to expand an institution long familiar in Spain. Beginning in the Middle Ages, Spanish authorities had established public granaries (pósitos) as a defense against bad harvests." Clearly a central authority, and one likely given to autocratic methods in response to desperate human need would be required. The quotation from Wittfogel concerning the polarization of power in hydraulic societies (see p. 46) is equally applicable here in the instance of food redistribution in arid climates. In extreme cases of aridity and drought, warlordism as an extreme form of despotism, can arise or be intensified, as we have seen in Somalia.

A third reason for identifying rainfall as a potential source of democracy is the ability of individual persons to escape from a despotic authority and begin to establish a more egalitarian and democratic society. In arid climates dependent on bureaucratically managed irrigation or food redistribution, people would not have that option. The desert in Egypt or Mesopotamia could not support large numbers of human beings if they chose to dissent from the prevailing despotic authority. (Carneiro [1970] identifies this situation as circumscription and ties it to the origins of the state.) In zones with large amounts of rainfall, on the other hand, escape to "open" villages as in England, offered a reprieve, respite, and potential source of opposition to the regime. These were areas that were not clearly tied into the dominant British political or social system and hence could serve as breeding grounds for dissent of various types and a further democratization of British society. Wrightson (1982, pp. 171–2) describes it in the following way:

As for the inhabitants of the "open" parishes, certainly they were often poor and they were not immune from government, but the different conditions of their existence and the more egalitarian structure of their communities helped preserve to them what their social superiors saw as a worrying degree of independence of spirit which they did not trouble to hide.

In general, rainfall is an *enduring* feature of the environmental landscape (as are sea borders to be introduced shortly), in contrast to the vicissitudes of personal despotisms that can vary considerably over time. Environmental variables of this type provide a constant backdrop to the political arena and constrain it to move in one or another direction.

Warfare and democracy

Our second environmental concern emerges from another societal process, that of warfare. Just as bureaucratic-despotic political organizations can arise in response to the twin needs for irrigation and food redistribution as the result of limited rainfall, so too can they arise in response to the threat of war. Indeed Wittfogel was concerned with the problem of war but more in the nature of conquest and expansion by hydraulic civilizations as a consequence of the control exercised over large, submissive populations. As he put it, "Organized control over the bulk of the population in times of peace gives the government extraordinary opportunities for coordinated mass action also in times of war" (Wittfogel, 1957, p. 59). Here, however, we are concerned with the *origins* of despotism, not its consequences for success in war and territorial expansion. As a result, the theoretical orientation differs from that of Wittfogel and in fact emerges from a different literature concerned with war and democracy.

In recent years, the relationship between democracy and war has begun to receive full exploration. The early philosophical development of the concept of "perpetual peace" by Kant has been expanded by scholars such as Doyle (1983). Direct empirical examination of this relationship has led to the generally accepted conclusion that democracies seldom, if ever, fight each other, at least not in the contemporary period (Rummel, 1983; Chan, 1984; Maoz and Abdolali, 1989; Ember, Ember, and Russett, 1992; Schweller, 1992; Maoz and Russett, 1993; Mintz and Geva, 1993; Russett, 1993; Ray, 1995).[1] This chapter asks a different but ultimately related question, namely, what happens when the causal arrow is reversed? What is the impact of war on democracies, especially in their earliest stage of development when they are only embryonic and clearly vulnerable? This question is of obvious importance in light of the large number of new democracies emerging from the former Soviet Union as well as those in Latin America and now increasingly, Africa. To answer this question, we will need to turn to the early history of state formation to discover the impact of warfare on early democracies, or at least societies that exhibited evidence of political rights for their residents. This analysis will set the stage for more systematic analyses of the modern period.

In fundamental ways, the treatment here differs from that of Tilly

(1990, pp. 16–28). Whereas Tilly points to the role of accumulated coercion and capital formation within states as a path to war, the analysis here emphasizes extreme threats to societies (states, chiefdoms, or other organized social forms) that can lead to autocracy as a mobilized response to the external threat. Early democracy can be easily vitiated in this fashion.[2]

There are three elements of democracy that are emphasized here. First, in any democratic polity, or even one that has only retained the vestiges of democracy, there are limitations on executive or monarchical authority. Of course, this was the basis of English democracy as expressed initially in the *Magna Carta* and carried forward in history until the present. Second, is the matter of representation in which societal units of whatever form (congressional districts or Chinese *kan* as we shall see later) are represented within the governing unit(s). Finally, and perhaps most important in the modern period is freedom of election as a basis for fair and impartial selection of the representatives that will govern.

The last of these, although critical in contemporary history especially in light of the political depredations of the twentieth century, is less salient for early societies. Simply the massive size of modern political units when compared with their early predecessors requires a fair method of selection among so many potential candidates. Indeed, in early city-states, the population was small enough so that all free men (and in some instances, women) could participate in the Assembly. Additionally, in ancient societies smaller groupings such as lineages likely had standard methods (e.g., age) for selecting among relatively few possible candidates so that the issue of selection itself was not of central concern. As we shall see, political representation and limitations on monarchies will be found in one form or another in virtually all of the cases in pre-history considered here. Later, in the systematic analysis for the modern period, we will use the political rights index as a measure of early democracy, based principally on freedom of election.

Early developments

Four ancient societies will be examined for whatever evidence they may offer on the nexus between democracy and war. They are ancient Sumer, Mesoamerica, Crete, and China. The first two are widely acknowledged by anthropologists and archaeologists to be "pristine" states meaning that they arose *sui generis* and not through any external influence from earlier established polities (Fried, 1967). The second two are not acknowledged to be "pristine" having been exposed to some

Near Eastern influences in both cases, and, in the instance of Crete, Egypt. But as I argue elsewhere (Midlarsky, forthcoming), the coercive state as it developed in later Mesoamerica and Egypt was a model not to be emulated but to be escaped from. As such it would not likely be imitated by observers. In any event, Renfrew (1972), a preeminent analyst and chronicler of the ancient Aegean, and Chang (1986), perhaps the dean of American archaeologists of China, argue respectively that, in both instances the continuous development of indigenous cultures mostly overshadowed any external influences. At most, adjacent settlements may have learned from each other in what Renfrew (1982) calls peer polity interaction. Any serious external influences also appeared well after the native civilizations had taken on their unique forms. These societies also are examined here well *before* an increased population density led to the widespread use of centralized irrigation systems and consequent autocracy.

Sumer

Evidence for the early development of what has been called "primitive democracy" (Jacobsen, 1943) comes from one of the earliest written documents, the Gilgamesh epic. Perhaps it is best to allow Kramer (1963, p. 74) to summarize:

In early days, political power lay in the hands of these free citizens and a city-governor known as *ensi*, who was no more than a peer among peers. In case of decisions vital to the city as a whole, these free citizens met in a bicameral assembly consisting of an upper house of "elders" and a lower house of "men." As the struggle between the city-states grew more violent and bitter, and as the pressures from the barbaric peoples to the east and west of Sumer increased, military leadership became a pressing need, and the king, or as he is known in Sumerian, the "big man," came to hold a superior place. At first he was probably selected and appointed by the assembly at a critical moment for a specific military task. But gradually kingship with all its privileges and prerogatives became a hereditary institution and was considered the very hallmark of civilization.

Elsewhere, Kramer (1981, pp. 30–5) refers to a bicameral "congress" consisting of a "senate" of elders and an "assembly" of fighting men. Recently disclosed archaeological evidence emerging from Mashkan-shapir in Mesopotamia supports this view. As Stone and Zimansky (1995, p. 123) put it, "The overall organization of Mashkan-shapir suggests that textual sources have not misled us about the broad involvement of Mesopotamian city dwellers in shaping their local power relationships."

This, in a nutshell, is the basic argument. The early state evolves in a democratic or quasi-democratic fashion, including as in this instance, bicameralism, but the threat of war intervenes in the form of hostile city-states or predatory nomadic herdsmen. The influence of the latter on early state formation has been singled out especially by Cohen (1978). As a result of these threats, the "big man" becomes necessary to confront the external danger by his or her (cf. the Old Testament heroine Deborah) examples of bravery or organizational skills. When the threat of war persists, as it frequently does, the temporary military leader can, over time, easily become the hereditary monarch.

As late as the Old Babylonian period (early second millennium BC), the office of *rabianum* or "mayor" of a small city rotated every year among the "Elders." By this time, the Assembly had been reduced to an organ of local administration but it "could nevertheless write letters to the King, make legal decisions, sell real estate and assume corporate responsibility for robbery or murder committed within its jurisdiction" (Oates, 1977, p. 476). Even the later Mesopotamian city, according to Oppenheim (1977, p. 11), is characterized by a "lack of status stratification" suggesting the continuation of the earlier essentially egalitarian and democratic practices.

We even have a record of a likely transition from the earlier democratic period to the later monarchical one in the Gilgamesh epic. Gilgamesh himself very probably was a ruler of Uruk in the Early Dynastic I period (mid-third millennium BC). At the beginning of the poem, Gilgamesh tells how he had to suppress the people of the city in order to build a city wall (Nissen, 1988, p. 95). Here we now have the nexus between the necessity for fortifications to counter the threat of war and coercive action against the population that is characteristic of the end of democracy and the rise of autocratic rule. Additional evidence for the gradual emergence of autocratic leadership, likely stemming from temporary war leadership, is given in Crawford (1991, p. 170).

The transition from democracy in the other instances is less clear. Nevertheless there is evidence of what I call vestigial democracy in all three cases to follow.

Mesoamerica

The Maya are a literate people that left various records in the form of glyphs and stone carvings. Although they were exposed to other Mesoamerican cultures, probably the Olmec and certainly Teotihuacan, again whatever influences were decisive occurred well after the Formative period and the consolidation of the indigenous culture. A sequence of events occurring between 200 BC and AD 200 basically transformed the culture (Adams, 1991, p. 128).

An explicit model for rotation of political and religious offices by Maya leaders has been put forward by Vogt (1971). Theoretically, every man in Maya society was eligible for such offices. Successful fulfillment of lesser political and religious offices qualified someone for higher offices, that would then rotate among the eligible persons. Although Vogt suggests that the model may even fit the Classic period, Adams (1991, p. 189) remarks that "the model might well fit the Middle and late Formative societal picture but not the later Classic period." This is because of the "increasingly aristocratic principle" (Adams, 1991, p. 189) that later developed and became associated with considerable warfare among the Mayan city-states or regional polities (Hammond, 1988). It was this warfare, among other factors, that has been suggested to have led ultimately to the Maya collapse, at least in the Lowlands (Culbert, 1973).

Warfare also very likely intensified elite control of Mayan society. We know that the Maya aristocracy must have gained increasing control not only from evidence of the increasing distance between elite and commoner (Sabloff, 1990, p. 143), but also by the spurt in Maya construction by the elite especially at Tikal during the Terminal Classic period prior to the collapse (Blanton *et al.*, 1981, p. 208). Such large-scale construction must have required the mobilization of large numbers of commoners probably by force, or at least the threat of severe sanctions. The democratic or quasi-democratic practices suggested by Vogt gave way to the increasingly emergent aristocracy, as competition and warfare began to become prevalent in the Maya civilization.

An interesting perspective is provided by research on the island of Cozumel off the Yucatan coast. The island began flourishing in the Terminal Classic period through the Late Post Classic, well after the heyday of the Lowland Maya and their frequent internecine wars. As such, the island may have escaped much of that warfare by virtue of its temporal development and island status. Many of the island sites have been found inland, suggesting the avoidance of raids by tribesmen and others from the mainland. Of greatest interest is the large number of sites and the dense population of the island. At the same time, there was an increasing egalitarianism in the holding of goods by the commoners in the population (Sabloff, 1990, pp. 133–4). This possible association between increasing density of agricultural population and their increased political rights, in the absence of war, will have strong echoes in the subsequent analysis.

Evidence of a vestigial nature also comes from another somewhat unexpected area of Mesoamerica, Teotihuacan. Long thought of as an absolutist theocracy, recent research has suggested perhaps a decentralized element of its rule. Cowgill (1983) focuses on the Ciudadela, a great structure in Teotihuacan that is generally believed to have been the residence of the rulers of that city-state. The basic question that he raises is why, in light of the monumental aspects of that structure, are there apartments within it that cover so small an area. Centralization of political authority would require much larger space. As Cowgill (1983, p. 331) puts it, "the most important point is that the Ciudadela does not seem to provide enough facilities for much of the day-to-day government of either the city or the state of Teotithuacan." He then identifies several possible political loci outside of the Ciudadela that could have fulfilled administrative functions. The importance of this structure apparently resides in its symbolic significance as a home of the political elite. The building of it likely "represents the relatively orderly intensification of long-term trends" (Cowgill, 1983, p. 336) of increased autocracy. If so, then there should exist earlier periods of outright decentralized rule, if not a rudimentary democracy that gradually came under greater centralized and autocratic control. It is noteworthy that the Ciudadela remained constructed pretty much as it had been for approximately 350 years, with changes in its architecture occurring only at a time close to the fall of the city. High-level centralized political management may have been required at the time of external threat to the city, consistent with the hypothesized relationship between increasing external threat and autocratic rule.

Crete

The evidence in the case of Crete is not abundant partly because of the absence of translation of Linear A, apparently the language of Minoan Crete. Linear B, an early ancestor of classical Greek also was discovered on the island and has been translated. It is likely that the Linear B script was introduced after the Mycenaen conquest of Crete from the Greek mainland (after 1400 BC, Graham, 1987). Nevertheless, despite these difficulties, there is evidence for at least a vestigial democracy in Minoan Crete. This vestigial democracy likely occurred in the absence of war, for prior to the Mycenaen conflict there is no evidence of fortifications on the island. This is one of the remarkable features of Minoan society that distinguishes it from the remainder of the ancient Aegean and even from the vast majority of the world (Renfrew, 1972; Willetts, 1965; Cadogan, 1976; Matz, 1973; Branigan, 1970; Finley, 1981; and Cherry,

1986). We can now examine the kinds of political arrangements that attended the growth of this island civilization.

Initially, the society was egalitarian as suggested by the equal status of individuals interred in the Early Minoan tombs (Branigan, 1970). Later, as in most other societies, stratification occurred, but the consequences for leadership tenure appear to differ from the hereditary status of leadership in societies in which warfare, or at least the threat of war is prominent. As Branigan (1970, p. 119) tells it:

In Early Minoan II and Early Minoan III as overseas trade grew and towns began to emerge from villages, the importance of the man who produced and controlled the main commodities of trade would increase greatly. Such men would naturally rise to prominence and be elected to office. It seems not unlikely that the period of tenure would be eight years. The legends which relate the octennial offering of Athenian youths to the Minotaur and the octennial departure of Minos to converse with Zeus are thought to indicate that this was the period of tenure during the palatial era and such an important tradition would very probably have its roots in the origins of the system, which seem to be in the Early Bronze Age.

Thus, leadership tenure apparently was limited. This limitation is consistent with another limitation that also distinguishes ancient Crete from other ancient societies. In comparison with other cultures of the same period, there is little that is royal or majestic about the political presence in the palaces. Even the throne is not especially impressive in the largest palace at Cnossos. No pictures exist that depict historical events or "which reveal administrative or judicial activity or any other manifestation of political power in action" (Finley, 1981, p. 41). There is an absence of monumentality that Finley (1981, p. 42) associates with the absence of war but that also could easily be associated with the absence of hereditary monarchs who would seek to augment their own status as did the Pharaohs of Egypt and other leaders of that period.

China

Here the evidence is also suggestive of a vestigial democracy that existed earlier. I rely here on Chang's (1980) analysis, for it is most complete in the instance of the first Chinese civilization for which we have written records, the Shang, particularly in the form of a king list. Other writings in English exist (e.g., Keightley, 1983), but the majority of analyses are in Chinese and indeed many of them are reviewed by Chang (1980, 1986).

Members of the ruling clan actively involved with the kingship were segmented into ten categories called *kan* units. These units had both ritual and political significance. In turn, *kan* units were affiliated with two divisions, A and B, that constituted two large aggregate groupings. There were two rules of succession for the kingship. "First, it could not stay within the same *kan* unit and second, when the kingship stayed within division A or B, it had to be assumed by an heir from another *kan* unit from within the same generation as the former king, but if it went over to the other division, it had to go to an heir of the next generation" (Chang, 1980, pp. 180–1). Put another way, when the kingship passed to another generation, it was forced to move to the opposite division. An alternation in power between two political groupings, not terribly dissimilar to that of a two-party system, is found here. Further, the king's principal official advisor was the chief of a *kan* unit from the opposite division. Thus, no individual *kan* unit was allowed to dominate politically, in addition to the alternations between divisions A and B.

Certainly these rules do not constitute democracy, but they do establish political rights for other political and religious units (*kan*) in Shang society. And this vestigial form of democracy, expressed as political rights, existed well after warfare became fairly endemic both within the more civilized portion of China and between the settled villages and invading nomads from the north and west that in fact necessitated the building of the Great Wall of China during the first dynasty to unify China, the Ch'in (Hucker, 1975, p. 44). Without such incursions, it is possible that the earlier, possibly more egalitarian form would have persisted, instead of the more vestigial version that we find in Shang society.

One pattern emerges clearly. That is the increasing aristocratic control of these ancient societies, usually associated with increasing incidence of war. One can therefore infer the existence of early, less autocratic, or more democratic control, at least in the form of representational arrangements for clans, kinship groups, and the like. We turn now to a systematic examination of environmental components of the theory. Measuring the minimization of external threat, an operation not immediately obvious, will emerge from the following treatment.

Land inequality and war

These considerations are to be combined with an earlier model that emphasized domestic societal variables in the genesis of democracy (Midlarsky, 1992a). All of the hypothetical sources of democracy (or autocracy) should be examined simultaneously to ascertain the extent of independent influence of each on democracy.

The domestic model was built up from various elements of the Athenian democratic experience as a historical prototype. Foremost among them is land inequality that would allow some with more land and a greater agricultural yield to break through and overcome the hereditary entitlements of others to govern in traditional tribal settings.

Indeed, the Solonic reforms (c. 594–3 BC) did precisely that. As a result of overpopulation and the sale of smaller, uneconomical plots of land to larger landowners, debt burdens increased for the now landless peasants. Only through an emerging land scarcity as the result of growing population (as in all of Greece during this period) could such a large number of farmers become indebted to their neighbors or other larger landowners. The Solonic reforms relieved these burdens, but also established the right of the larger landowners to govern in place of the traditional tribal, largely hereditary elite. Four categories of citizens were created with graded formal influence on the political process based on wealth (Finley, 1973, 1981; Grant, 1987). Each of these groups had various rights and responsibilities varying from eligibility for the highest offices for those in the most wealthy category, to election to a new council of state, the Boule, for members of the next two categories, and rights to attend and vote in the Assembly for those in the last category. Although this was not democracy, as Finley (1981, p. 125) remarks, "later Athenians looked back to Solon as the man who set them on the road to democracy."

Although the impact of land inequality on democracy was discovered independently, this relationship is consistent with that implied in Wittfogel's work. He emphasized the contrast between early modern Europe and despotic hydraulic civilization. As Wittfogel (1957, pp. 84–5) puts it:

In late feudal and post-feudal Europe the state recognized a system of inheritance for the landed nobles which favored one son at the expense of all others. And in the modern Western world the state by and large permitted the individual to dispose over (sic) his property at will. The hydraulic state gave no equivalent freedom of decision either to holders of mobile property or to the landowners. Its laws of inheritance insisted upon a more or less equal division of the deceased's estate, and thereby upon a periodic fragmentation of property.

Thus, as a result of continual subdivision, a basic land inequality was prevented from emerging in hydraulic society. A nobility with large holdings and in consequence an independent power base to challenge despotic authorities could not come into being, in contrast to the Northern European experience.

This argument takes a different perspective from works such as Russett (1964), Dahl (1971), Lindblom (1977), Lijphart (1984), Vanhanen

(1990), Hadenius (1992), or Rueschemeyer, Stephens, and Stephens (1992) who directly or indirectly imply that inequalities of various forms are inimical to democracy. However, the emphasis here is on the *early* development of democracy in the form of rudimentary political rights. Most or all of the preceding works are directed to the *maintenance* of democracy once established, and especially the stability of such democratic development. These issues, although important in themselves, are not within the purview of this study. And as we shall see, certain differences in findings between Rueschemeyer *et al.* and the present study concerning land inequality can be attributed to the more restricted sample of their analysis. This empirical difference will further reflect on the differing purposes of the present study in comparison with others.

A related variable is agricultural density which acts as a progenitor of land inequality. Increased density yields increased inequality as the result of the increased land scarcity attendant upon population increase (Midlarsky, 1988). In descriptive terms, one assumes a relatively equal distribution of land parcels at some early point in time. As population grows, there is a geometric subdivision of the land so that at a later point in time, an exponential distribution describes the landholdings. The greater the scarcity of land either due to circumscription, or to population growth (or both), the steeper the exponential curve and the greater the inequality in holdings. Later, an independent effect of agricultural density will be demonstrated, consistent with certain earlier treatments (e.g., Crenshaw, 1992).[3]

Historically, warfare has demonstrated a significant impact on land inequality, in fact decreasing its material advantages in influencing politics. As Duby (1968, p. 297) tells us concerning the consequences of war:

> But of course it was the lords' dwellings, more exposed because relatively richer, which suffered most, together with their appurtenances, mills, bakehouses, enclosures, orchards, in short all the luxury capital of the countryside. The fact that war struck the manorial economy harder is worth remembering. Damaging the rich more than the poor, it helped to level down the differences in rural wealth. At all events the capital losses it caused were very unequally distributed.

However, it was not all of the nobility that suffered equally.

> [The] manors belonging to princes and the great families, as well as those belonging to the church, suffered less. . . . As for the princely manors, they benefited first from the concentration of compulsory powers. This process protected them and also facilitated their restoration; the all-embracing taxation strengthened them by providing a constant stream of liquid funds and a part of this capital at least helped to stimulate the manorial economy. Lastly, the top ranks

of the lay aristocracy were everywhere reduced in numbers and power lay in fewer hands. . . . the present state of research certainly shows that the most obvious signs of malaise revealed themselves in the middle ranks of manorial wealth. (Duby, 1968, p. 316)

Thus the authority of princes, in contrast to lower levels of nobility was increased by war, while that of the lower levels of nobility was decreased. This process was to have its most extreme consequences in virtually landlocked Germany, with its extraordinary experience of warfare in the sixteenth and seventeenth centuries.

Prior to the Reformation and the continual warfare associated with it, the princes of Germany and the various estates, including the nobility, had reached an accommodation. In the fourteenth century, they shook off the superior control of the emperor and reduced the empire to a collection of principalities. At the time, the individual princes acted to assert their authority over their subjects and destroy the privileges of the feudal classes (Barraclough, 1984, p. 321). In this they were largely successful, having forced the "estates" consisting of knights, cities, and often church prelates to participate in States-General or territorial assemblies (*Landtage*) instead of the provincial ones. In this fashion, the authority of individual nobles was reduced, but the nobility as a whole as well as the towns and elements of the church were required to be consulted in matters of taxation by the princes governing a particular territory.

These States-General were not unlike the British parliament in their financial roots but also were used to ventilate grievances and to begin reforming activity (Barraclough, 1984, p. 350). The nobility, among other classes, were able to exert their influence in the various *Landtage*. But the religious wars of the sixteenth century followed especially by the Thirty Years War of 1618–48, were to transform German society. "The weakening of all classes in town and country, which was the inevitable consequence of generations of strife, the effect of war on commerce, industry, and agriculture, brought about, with the religious changes, a further rise in the power of the princes, which ushered in the period of princely absolutism" (Barraclough, 1984, p. 373).

The Reformation had the consequence of increasing the power of the princes as the result of Luther's need for their support in furthering the spread of Protestantism. In particular the Peasants' War frightened him and led to his increased support of princely power. This process was mirrored in the Counter-Reformation, in that Catholic princes also sought to tie the territorial church to the particular secular ruler. Hence religion was subordinated to the dictates of the princes. Afterwards, however, as Barraclough (1984, p. 377) observes, "Once they had bound the territorial churches to the secular power, the princes sought to drive home their advantage by attacking the nobility and the towns and freeing themselves from dependence on the States-General."

As early as the sixteenth century, the Bavarian *Landtag* was in decline and in Austria, the Catholic rulers destroyed the power of the *Landtag* by driving out the nobility, the vast majority of whom were Protestant at the time. The principle of *cuius regio eius religio* emerging out of the Peace of Augsburg in 1555 and reinforced by the Peace of Westphalia in 1648 was not only a means of assuring religious uniformity between rulers and ruled, but was a major step in the creation of German absolutism. No longer could a largely Catholic population have a Protestant noble at its head and so the power of the nobility was substantially reduced. Here in the German case, we see some of the dynamics by which the destruction of a nobility or at least its political prerogatives results in the diminution of political rights. As the result of war, the power of land ownership is reduced and whatever land inequality remains is rendered largely impotent politically. We turn now to a systematic examination of environmental components of the theory. Measuring the minimization of external threat, an operation not immediately obvious, will emerge from the following treatment.

The model

Our two principal variables for empirical testing are rainfall and minimization of the threat of war. Average rainfall for a country is measured by the annual average experienced by all major cities in that country for the period 1931–60 (Bair, 1992).[4] The use of all cities is simply a means of obtaining a geographical dispersion for a country. Smaller countries have a smaller number of cities associated with this measure.

The minimized threat variable also is to be understood within an environmental context, namely the number of sea borders. First, excepting Crete, all of the preceding illustrations of eventual autocratic empires – Mesopotamia, Mesoamerica, and China – were land based. And Crete, as we have seen, never really evolved into an autocratic empire comparable to the others. Second, we know that several studies found a significant positive relationship between the number of land borders a country has and that country's war experience (Richardson, 1960; Starr and Most, 1978). Thus, the number of sea borders constitutes one element of a country's minimization of the threat of war and also does not suffer from difficulties in interpretation that a direct measure of war experience would incur.

Whereas it is clear that democracy cannot cause geography in the form of sea borders, no such certainty exists in the case of autocracy and actual war experience. Autocracies may begin more wars as is implied by much of the earlier research cited. On the other hand, autocracies may be a consequence of these wars as is suggested here. Correlations, even within a multivariate setting as will be done shortly, cannot distinguish between these two possible interpretations. Aside from this inherent flaw, there is another that is equally troublesome. That is that the available war data during the past several centuries do not reflect on the earlier experiences of nation-states that may have laid the foundations for democratic development many centuries ago, as in the instances of England and Iceland. Minimization of the threat of war and especially invasion from abroad may have occurred in early national history, thus allowing for a slow democratic development not hindered by a constant military preparedness. The existence of a large military establishment, of course, increases the probability of military intervention against democratic rule, as understood by the Costa Ricans nearly a half century ago.

Democracy in ancient Athens, in fact, may be a consequence of the minimization of external threat as the result of a peninsular setting. We know that Athens is one of the few ancient Greek city-states that was distinguished by continuity even through the dark ages (Warren, 1989), perhaps as a result of its semiprotected position as a city in Attica, a peninsula. Equally to the point is the evolution of democracy in portions of the Cyclades and other islands in the Aegean not far from Attica off the Greek coast. Renfrew (1982) emphasizes the interaction among various Aegean polities that likely led to the spread of democracy among the Ionian dominated islands. It is likely that similar geographic protection from war among these islands and peninsulas allowed for a continued democratic development that simply was not experienced by communities in the interior subject to the threat and actuality of war.

A fourth argument for use of the sea borders variable emerges from an exacting test of an earlier model of democracy (Midlarsky, 1992b). In an examination of residuals from prediction, those countries that were least well explained by domestic variables to be introduced shortly, were those that were either islands or peninsulas. Sri Lanka, Papua New Guinea, Jamaica, Malaysia, Ireland, Dominican Republic, and Greece were underpredicted by the model. They had levels of democracy that were simply too large to be explained by the variables then constituting the model. These countries also had levels of international violence that were very low or non-existent relative to the international norm.

Finally, in order to assess the validity of sea borders as a measure of minimum threat, it was correlated with changes in military force size. Clearly force size alone is a function of many domestic and international factors, not the least of which may be political and bureaucratic inertia stemming from earlier historical experiences. (Both Austria and Hungary had officers with the rank of Admiral in their military establishments during the interwar period when both countries were landlocked.) But changes in such force sizes, even in the short term, can reveal feelings of security or insecurity associated with geographical position. The sea borders variable (0–4) was constructed by assigning a zero to countries with no sea borders, 1 to those with one sea border, and so on through islands which had four sea borders. The source was Lye and Carpenter (1987).

Change in military force size is measured by the increase, decrease, or no change in the number of military personnel per thousand working age persons between 1965 and 1975 (Taylor and Jodice, 1983, I, pp. 37–9).[5] A reduction or no change between the two years was coded as 1 while an increase was coded as 0. The number of sea borders and change in military personnel size correlated $r = 0.35$ ($N = 113$, $p > 0.001$), suggesting a highly significant relationship between them. Given the many reasons for changes in military personnel size including purely bureaucratic ones, this relationship between a large number of sea borders as reflecting a fair degree of security, on the one hand, and decline or no change in military personnel size over a ten-year period, on the other, is noteworthy. Later we will see that the geographical variable performs better in explaining democracy than changes in military personnel size, likely due to the additional extraneous influences (e.g., bureaucratic) on those changes.

Other variables include economic development, trade, age of the polity, and domestic violence. Economic development is suggested as an important variable leading to political democracy by the arguments found in several works such as those of Lipset (1959), Lenski (1966), and Dahl (1971). Trade/GNP is included to examine the impact of external commercial contacts so important to the Athenian economy, while controlling for the overall size of the economy. Although admittedly an international variable, it was examined here more in relation to Athenian economic development and Finley's (1982) account of the distinctiveness of Athenian society, hence its democracy. Age of the polity is incorporated to control for maturation processes, while domestic violence is included to test for the possible effect of violence processes on democracy as suggested in Moore (1966). Both variables are logged to control for outliers. Data sources for these variables and countries included in the analysis are found in the appendix. These are all countries with market economies during the period 1973–87.

The dependent variable is the political rights index for 1973–87 developed by Gastil (1988). It emphasizes freedom of election. The concept of right of participation as in the election of political officers is critical to the beginning stages of democracy. Later of course, as Dahl (1971) indicates, participation can be broadened in a variety of ways to bring about the more variegated version that we now associate with political democracy. Clearly, it is the more basic, primitive notion of political rights that must be explored in an analysis of the origins of democracy. More complex indices such as that of Bollen (1980) would not be appropriate for an examination of the roots of democracy.

Gastil's political rights index is averaged over a 15-year period, 1973–87, which allows (1) for the correction of errors if they crept in for an earlier year and (2) gives a fairly long "window" of measurement in contrast to virtually all other measures of this type which are given at one year only, and (3) allows for greater variability in the dependent variable by adding a decimal point to the yearly data that in the data source are given only in single digit form (1–7). The averaging process for the dependent variable yields 1980 as the median year.[6] As the most complete data for the independent variables are circa 1970 and 1975 (see the appendix), a desirable five- to ten-year lag is effectively introduced to allow for the impact of the societal variables on political rights. The mean scores on this political rights index also are for a later period than other measures. For example, one of the best of these, Bollen (1980), is given only for 1960 and 1965.[7] Given the rapid changes that can and do occur internationally, this is not a trivial advantage. The average scores are from 1 to 7 taken to one decimal place, thus effectively yielding a scale from 1 to 70 (1 = most political rights, 70 = least political rights). The scale criteria are given in Gastil (1988, pp. 29–35).

Prior to the empirical analysis itself, it might be useful to consider a contrast between two potential historical candidates for democracy, England and Prussia. England may be the archetypical example of a country that experienced very early democratization and that also embodies the four principal variables examined here. Average rainfall is consistently high. As an island nation, especially after the subjugation of surrounding peoples such as the Irish, Scots, and Welsh, she was relatively free from the threat of war. At the very least, she had leeway in choosing her time of entry into Continental wars and with force sizes pretty much at her own discretion. The English economy, of course, industrialized earlier than any other, leading to a very high GDP/CAP and consequent impact on democracy. And land inequality, especially in terms of landholdings by the nobility, was substantial. As Spring (1977, p. 6) put it, "no Continental landed elite owned so large a part of its nation's territory as did the English." His explicit comparisons are with the French, Spanish, Prussian, and Russian elites, all of whose societies, of course, democratized at much later dates than did the English.

One of the closest counterparts to the English landed elite in terms of residence patterns, political dominance of the local countryside and thence of the state, and inheritance laws that tended to maintain entire estates intact over time, was the Prussian. And here, this basic similarity that might have led to a similar democratic evolution is vitiated strongly by the Prussian military tradition. Whereas the English landed elite opposed standing armies and evolved a strong libertarian tradition, it was said of the Prussian, "what they loved best next to their estates was an army and all that went with it – splendid uniforms, military pomp, and chivalric codes of honor" (Spring, 1977, p. 17). All of this stemmed directly from the extensive militarization of Prussian Junker society with potential enemies on three sides and the incessant warfare that attended the rise of the Prussian state. Of course the Junker role in preventing the rise of early democracy in Prussia is crucial (Stern, 1977). Here we now see the critical role of the maximization of the threat of war by many land borders and its diminution of the positive impact of other variables on the evolution of democracy.

Three more variables are included, principally as controls. These are British colonial heritage, European location, and population. Many of the islands that have democratized such as Sri Lanka, Jamaica, and Ireland were British colonies and so, to avoid an artifact of democratic rule simply as the result of diffusion at the hands originally of the British navy, British colonial heritage (0, 1) is included. A similar argument holds for the inclusion of another variable, European location (0,1).[8] The possibility of a diffusion of democracy especially under the impetus of the EC should be controlled. A possible artifact of rainfall associated with democracy because of a European locus, but not elsewhere, also should be controlled. With regard to the third of these variables, population, island countries tend to be small size so that an artifact of size could be introduced. Smaller countries could more easily be governed democratically as suggested by Dahl and Tufte (1973). Population size as a variable (logged to control for outliers) is introduced to control for this possibility.

Table 2.1 *Regression of the political rights index on the explanatory variables*

Variable	Correlation (r)	Partial	b	Tolerance	t	Sig. t
Rainfall	0.001[a]	0.280	0.011	0.812	2.606	*0.005[b]*
Sea borders	0.488	0.420	0.442	0.773	4.140	*0.000*
GDP/CAP	0.784	0.539	0.001	0.328	5.724	*0.000*
Europe	0.582	0.200	0.779	0.509	1.818	*0.036*
Agricultural density	0.001	−0.168	−0.0001	0.479	−1.520	0.066
Log age	0.495	0.273	10.434	0.445	2.536	*0.007*
Bricol	0.060	0.231	0.620	0.668	2.120	*0.019*
Log deaths	−0.331	−0.013	−0.006	0.502	−0.120	0.453
Log population	0.174	−0.024	−0.031	0.413	−0.218	0.414
Trade/GNP	0.013	0.034	0.002	0.331	0.300	0.383
Constant			72.101		2.308	*0.012*

$R^2 = 0.756$, $R_a^2 = 0.725$, $N = 91$

Notes: [a]Positive signs (implied by no indication of sign) denote positive impact on the political rights index while negative signs have a corresponding interpretation.
[b]Italics denote significance at least at $p < 0.05$. These are one-tailed tests because of the directional hypotheses tested here.

Testing the model

A simultaneous inclusion of all independent variables in a multiple regression equation will lead to an assessment of the independent impact of each on the dependent variable, the political rights index. Economic development as measured by GDP/CAP, for example, is a central predictor of democracy in many treatments as we have seen, and so must be included if only as a control variable. All of the included independent variables effectively act as controls on the others. The significance level is chosen as $p < 0.05$ (one-tailed), because of the directional hypotheses tested here.

Table 2.1 presents the first assessment of the impact of the independent variables in explaining the political rights index. In order to maximize the number of cases, agricultural density is used here without land inequality that has significant amounts of missing data. In order to fully demonstrate the extent of explanation and face validity of the individual variables, a fair amount of information is included in the table. First, consider the rainfall variable in its impact on the political rights index. As one would expect, the simple bivariate correlation coefficient ($r = 0.001$) between the two variables is very near zero. The amount of rainfall should not demonstrate any evident effect on democracy, especially when one considers the impact of economic development as an overall modern influence on democracy that can conceal more subtle historical influences. Yet when all other variables are included, the partial (controlled) correlation rises considerably and the regression coefficient (b) is significant at $p = 0.005$, using the t ratio.

Given the very small bivariate correlation between rainfall and political rights, it is likely that there are both positive and negative elements in the association between the two variables. Positive impacts of rainfall on political rights were enumerated in the theoretical portion at the outset of this chapter, namely absence of dependence on the state for irrigation or food distribution and the ability to establish autonomous farming communities removed from state control. These communities tend to demand greater political rights than others more accustomed to reliance on the state with all the limitations on autonomy and other political rights implied by that dependence. The negative impact of rainfall on political rights likely proceeds via the increase in pathogens from high levels of rainfall that can decrease productivity thus lowering GDP/CAP and in turn, political rights. Certain Latin American and Sub-Saharan African countries provide illustrations of this effect. Controlling for GDP/CAP therefore should elevate the impact of rainfall on political rights, and this is what was found here.

Turning to the second environmental variable, the positive impact of the number of sea borders on democracy is significant at $p = 0.0001$. Interestingly, it is one of the few variables that has its zero order correlation affected hardly at all by the other variables of the multiple regression analysis. As expected, economic development demonstrates the strongest single relationship with political rights. Also, as expected, age of the polity influences democracy in a positive direction; the older the polity, the more democratic. That relationship however, may be a function of more fundamental societal variables, as will be shown later. Both British colonial heritage and being a European polity are significant. Agricultural density is not significant here, although if the more industrialized countries are removed, leaving the most agrarian, agricultural density is found to be significant as in Midlarsky (1992a). Evidence of sign reversals from the bivariate relationship as well as from the prediction of a positive relationship between agricultural density and democracy suggests collinearity problems that will be addressed shortly. Trade/GNP is not significant in the table nor in the analysis in table 2.2, suggesting that there is no evidence here for a possible alternative interpretation of sea borders as maximizing trading patterns, thereby leading to a commercial route to democracy.

Tolerances can reveal much about the structure of explanation and shed light on its face validity. (The tolerance is defined as $1-R_i^2$, where R_i^2 is the maximum explained variance in one independent variable by all of the others. Another widely used measure of collinearity is the Variance Inflation Factor [VIF], which is the reciprocal of the tolerance; thus it contains precisely the same information. Because of the more direct interpretation of the tolerance, it is reported in tables 2.1–2.3.) The higher the tolerance, generally the lower the multicollinearity or extent of overlap among the several explanatory variables. To that extent, the tolerance tells us how genuinely "independent" each variable is from all of the others taken simultaneously. With the exception of agricultural density, none of the independent variables exhibit the symptoms of multicollinearity, nor are there high intercorrelations among them. (The highest correlation among the independent variables is that between European location and GDP/CAP [$r = 0.62$], but both variables are well behaved in the regression equation, and both are found to be significant, suggesting that one variable did not "edge out" the other as in many highly collinear settings.)

Rainfall and sea borders have the two highest tolerances, as one would expect given their environmental status, in contrast to the remaining purely societal variables. They should have the greatest degree of "apartness," and do so in this context. On the other hand, GDP/CAP, the most complex societal variable, exhibits a lower tolerance than do the environmental variables. This finding is consistent with the suggestion that GDP/CAP is a surrogate for related variables such as human well being that demonstrates a higher correlation with political rights (Diamond, 1992). A thorough treatment of the complex and multidimensional effects of economic development on democracy is found in Huntington (1991). The fact that all of the values are above 0.30 suggests that multicollinearity overall is not a problem. The highest value of VIF, correspondingly, is 3.051 for GDP/CAP, a relatively low value by most standards (Kleinbaum, Kupper, and Muller, 1988, p. 210; Fox, 1991, p. 13). The extent of overall explanation is considerable, as shown by the amount of explained variance R^2, and its counterpart adjusted for sample size and other specifics of the analysis, R_a^2.

Findings shown in table 2.2 are similar to those in table 2.1, with the exception of log age and British colonial heritage. Here land inequality is introduced and now demonstrates a significant relationship with the political rights index. The remaining variables, formerly significant in table 2.1, also are strongly significant here. The three variables with the highest tolerances are the two environmental elements and land inequality, once again suggesting a high degree of face validity to the

Table 2.2 *Regression of the political rights index on the explanatory variables plus land inequality*

Variable	Correlation(r)	Partial	b	Tolerance	t	Sig.t
Rainfall	−0.103[a]	0.363	0.014	0.686	2.937	*0.002[b]*
Sea borders	0.456	0.406	0.384	0.746	3.353	*0.001*
GDP/CAP	0.774	0.598	0.001	0.318	5.634	*0.000*
Europe	0.570	0.369	1.326	0.433	2.999	*0.002*
Land inequality	0.226	0.376	0.026	0.614	3.059	*0.002*
Agricultural density	−0.040	−0.076	0.000	0.398	−0.577	0.283
Log age	0.541	0.133	5.407	0.305	1.013	0.158
Bricol	0.086	0.209	0.549	0.573	1.612	0.056
Log deaths	−0.298	0.016	0.007	0.456	0.123	0.451
Log population	0.175	−0.042	−0.046	0.388	−0.315	0.377
Trade/GNP	−0.044	−0.047	−0.002	0.281	−0.352	0.363
Constant			32.850		0.804	0.212

$R^2 = 0.804$, $R_a^2 = 0.766$, $N = 69$

Notes: [a]Positive signs (implied by no indication of sign) denote positive impact on the political rights index while negative signs have a corresponding interpretation.
[b]Italics denote significance at least at $p < 0.05$. These are one-tailed tests because of the directional hypotheses tested here.

outcome of this analysis. Now that land inequality is introduced, the constant term is not significant as it was in table 2.1, suggesting a more complete model specification. The effect of introducing land inequality is not only to have another significant variable and more complete model specification, but also to render age not significant as a predictor of political rights, in contrast to the results of table 2.1.

Log age and land inequality are correlated positively ($r = 0.26$); the effect of land inequality is apparently that of introducing a more fundamental structural variable that obviates the effect of age as a surrogate for these basic processes.[9] Some further implications of this finding will be developed in the following section. The number of cases differs from table 2.1 because of the absence of data for certain cases in the source for land inequality (Muller and Seligson, 1987).

As a further check on the role of the number of sea borders as a measure of minimization of the threat of war, change in military personnel size was inserted into the regression equations of tables 2.1 and 2.2. This more proximal variable (in the sense of a more direct measurement of the threat of war) was expected to demonstrate a stronger relationship with political rights than the more remote sea borders as a geographical condition. And this indeed proved to be the case for the bivariate correlations, with change in military personnel size demonstrating a higher correlation with political rights than sea borders, as can be seen by a comparison of the first columns of tables 2.2 and 2.3. However, when controlling for the remaining independent variables, sea borders has a higher partial correlation and level of significance. As is the case in the preceding tables, the partials reveal that the variable, sea borders, is little affected by the other variables. This is not true for change in military personnel size.

What is interesting to observe in table 2.3 is the extent to which the introduction of this variable tends to heighten the positive correlations and significance levels of the already significant variables, especially rainfall, European location, and land inequality. Perhaps even more important, it apparently resolves the collinearity problem involving agricultural density. Now, in table 2.3, it is positively related to political rights as predicted theoretically (Midlarsky, 1992a) and there are no sign reversals. The tolerance for agricultural density is much higher when compared with values reported in tables 2.1 and 2.2. This consequence most likely derives from the fact that Singapore, with by far the highest value for agricultural density among countries analyzed in tables 2.1 and 2.2, is not included in the multiple regression of table 2.3 because of the absence of data on military personnel size for 1965 (see table 2.1A in the appendix). At the same time, the highest value for trade/GNP is for Singapore, thus yielding a positive collinear bias between agricultural density and trade/GNP that is now removed ($r = 0.66$ reduced now to $r = 0.11$). The independent effect of this variable even when controlling for land inequality will be discussed in the following section.

Implications for the future

Now we can understand the rapid failure of democracy in Eastern and Central Europe after World War I. As land-locked countries or nearly so, they always were prone to the threat of war. This was especially salient after World War I with its large numbers of military trained and combat-experienced personnel. Especially important would have been the existence of a military leadership in these newly independent countries that had served in the armed forces of the former empires, Austria-Hungary, Russia, and Germany. The existence of both a rank and file cohort and a leadership prone to autocratic or at least hierarchical mili-

Table 2.3 *Regression of the political rights index on the explanatory variables plus land inequality and substituting military personnel size*

Variable	Correlation (r)	Partial	b	Tolerance	t	Sig. t
Rainfall	−0.105[a]	0.419	0.015	0.741	3.422	*0.001*[b]
Military personnel	0.508	0.365	0.853	0.733	2.908	*0.003*
GDP/CAP	0.775	0.625	0.001	0.318	5.936	*0.000*
Europe	0.566	0.457	1.673	0.426	3.813	*0.000*
Land inequality	0.215	0.446	0.031	0.596	3.695	*0.000*
Agricultural density	0.194	0.270	0.001	0.718	2.084	*0.021*
Log age	0.534	0.045	1.745	0.310	0.331	0.371
Bricol	0.116	0.264	0.679	0.607	2.028	*0.024*
Log deaths	−0.287	0.128	0.055	0.476	0.959	0.171
Log population	0.186	−0.164	−0.189	0.358	−1.232	0.112
Trade/GNP	−0.012	−0.139	−0.007	0.524	−1.044	0.150
Constant			6.145		0.152	0.440

$R^2 = 0.816$, $R_a^2 = 0.780$, $N = 67$

Notes: [a]Positive signs (implied by no indication of sign) denote positive impact on the political rights index while negative signs have a corresponding interpretation.
[b]Italics denote significance at least at $p < 0.05$. These are one-tailed tests because of the directional hypotheses tested here.

tary control likely made it far easier to assume military control of countries such as Poland in 1926 by Marshal Pilsudski, than if such war experience were absent.

On the other hand, the prognosis for democracy in many of these countries is somewhat better now than in that earlier period. Although still subject to the threat of war, the absence of very recent experience in major armed struggles using large numbers of armed personnel, may make it more difficult for current military establishments to intervene. However, there is a probable covariation between the increasing tendency toward military violence in Eastern Europe and the threat to democratic development. To the extent that the communal conflicts in those countries fester, the greater is the likelihood of some political intervention by military personnel accustomed to autocratic methods of resolving political disputes. Their central role in these societies acculturated to this new war experience also might facilitate intervention of military personnel into the affairs of new democratic polities.

Of course, failures of economic development also are suggested as potential pitfalls for these new democracies, as suggested by the importance of GDP/CAP for democratic development.

Agricultural density demonstrated a significant relationship with political rights apart from any connection with land inequality, as shown in table 2.3 when collinearity effects were minimized. This finding suggests an independent effect for agricultural density that is consistent with the findings of Crenshaw (1992; chapter 3 of this volume). His work has emphasized the role of agricultural density as a progenitor of social and institutional complexity that, in turn, generates democracy as an end-product. Greater density yields greater social and structural differentiation; political democracy is surely one illustration of such complexity. Thus, as density on the land increases, the likelihood of democracy increases. Currently, some of the least democratic countries also have some of the lowest population densities, as in the Middle East. With rapidly growing populations, this situation is likely to change quickly, if it has not already done so.

The importance of land inequality has been reinforced over and above earlier findings (Midlarsky, 1992a). This has come about because of the introduction and control of variables such as European location, that had the effect of comparing Latin America with much of Africa and parts of the Middle East. A major difference of course, is that Latin American countries were conquest states that for centuries had a conquering elite that not only ruled the subject population but, in the process, seized much of the land, generating a considerable inequality with much of the subject population. (England, of course, is a much earlier case in point.) In Africa, on the other hand, the colonial conquest was not so thorough as in Latin America and of much shorter duration. As a result, there was no homogenizing influence of a long-term conquest elite and little land inequality that could be used as a secure basis of economic and political control that would allow a gradual introduction of more political rights at a later time, but a continuation of tribal politics that limited democracy and in many cases, as we have seen, led to tribal warfare that even limited state governance itself, let alone democracy.

This is a fundamental reason for the difference in findings between Rueschemeyer *et al.* (1992) and the present study. That study, although non-quantitative, is still based on a careful examination of advanced capitalist societies and Latin America. African countries are excluded. Yet it is precisely in the comparison between African and Latin American countries that we can see the differences in early democratic development dependent on emergent inequalities that can provide leadership independent of tribe or heredity. Clearly, African democracies have foundered on tribal animosities at least as much as on any other cause. In much of Latin America, it is probably the very gradually liberalizing consequence of a fairly secure long-term conquering elite unchallenged by any serious competitor and hence less likely to block rudimentary, hence unthreatening, democratic development that is captured by the land inequality variable. Alas, it is difficult to institutionalize such a process, if that is even desirable, and so limitations on democracy in Africa can be expected for the foreseeable future.

On the other hand, the institutionalization and diffusion of democracy in Europe appears to be robust. European location is significant in all of the analyses, suggesting the important role of the European Community (EC) in providing a carrot and stick approach to democratization emanating from the core countries of the older European Economic Community (EEC). Those countries who would not democratize would not be allowed the benefits of membership that increasingly became desirable for European countries. At the same time, a successful model for stable government was provided by the core countries. A culture of democracy (Putnam, 1993) may have evolved over time that encouraged the growth and spread of democracy in Europe. British colonial heritage, on the other hand, is not significant in table 2.2 and has much lower partial correlations in comparison with European location, suggesting that a temporary colonial heritage including parliamentary rule is not sufficient for democratization to take hold. Additional institutional efforts along the lines of an EC probably are required.

From a policy perspective, it would appear that there is little that can be done politically to promote democracy in this context, as geography is a "given" of international life. The number of sea borders enjoyed by a country is extraordinarily difficult to change, if at all, and so it would appear that "all is lost," as it were. Yet it is the threat of war and its minimization that we are directly concerned with and here, of course much can be done to effect such minimization. A major change in the international political climate can yield dramatic results as, for example, in the instances of three conflict prone countries, Afghanistan, a land locked country, and Syria and Egypt, with at least two land borders each. Yet despite this apparently immutable quality of international geopolitical life reflected by the number of land borders, these countries also were affected strongly by the global system. The economic and political strains of the Soviet Union and its impending collapse, already apparent, forced its withdrawal and the removal of Afghanistan from major international conflict. Syria and Egypt were strongly influenced by the new US diplomatic inroads into the Middle East after the 1973

Yom Kippur War. Thus, major power influences can make a keen difference in the threatening aspect of a nation's activities, whatever its particular geopolitical environment. Both Syria and Egypt have modulated their stances considerably on several key Middle East issues while Afghanistan has been removed from international political violence. Other countries with many land borders can be affected in a similar fashion as the US and the EU powers have been attempting to do in the case of Yugoslavia, Bosnia, and Croatia. Put another way, environmental influences are constraints. Here, they constrain potential enemies from attacking the polis and so act to minimize the threat of war. In general, these constraints condition the structures of political life and in some sense provide broad limits to what can be done, but in no sense are they deterministic.

Rainfall also does not exert a deterministic influence on democracy as we have seen from the findings reported in tables 2.1–2.3. Yet, here, in contrast to sea borders, there may arise future changes in this environmental variable. Global warming may increase rainfall in some parts of the world and diminish it in others. To the extent that this process yields increased aridity in some countries, the prospects for democratic development may diminish. African countries have thus far demonstrated the strongest tendencies toward drought and famine with a concomitant increase in warlordism as a form of centralized control within regions. Somalia, of course, is a case in point.

Conclusion

Perhaps the major contribution of this chapter in addition to confirmation of the positive impact of land inequality on political rights, has been to emphasize the important influence of environmental factors on the genesis and sustainability of early democracy. Hostile environments can generate autocratic responses, either subverting an early democratic development or preventing its organization altogether. Wittfogel (1957) singled out one such threatening source in the form of aridity and a bureaucratic-despotic response in the form of hydraulic civilization. This theory has been generalized to include the influence of rainfall on democracy and has found empirical support.

The second threat takes the form of political invasion by hostile peoples and the consequent need for military preparedness that can lead to autocracy in countries with many land borders. In contrast, countries with many sea borders, while not immune from such threats, nevertheless enjoy at least a modicum of security. In this sense, both aridity and many land borders share a common dimension – a threatening environment for human populations that can give rise to rigid controls in the form of despotic political organization.

Another contribution of this chapter has been to emphasize an international dimension in understanding the origins and survivability of early democracy. The international venue is robust when compared with other antecedents of democracy such as rainfall, economic development, and land inequality. Minimization of the threat of war is an important condition for the emergence of a durable democracy as indicated by the evidence pertaining to four ancient societies and the early modern period in Europe, and the systematic analysis of the contemporary period.

Although not directly examined here, it is likely that there is a reciprocal, and over time, reinforcing influence between the threat and actuality of war, and democracy. A portion of the literature cited earlier strongly suggests the inhibiting effect of democracy on war between democracies. This combined with the finding here that minimizing the threat of war enhances democracy's chances of survival strongly suggests this reciprocal relationship. Over time, the continued absence of first the threat and then the actuality of war reinforces the burgeoning democracy and in turn this even stronger democracy further inhibits the likelihood of war, at least with other democracies.

These findings also explain a historical anomaly. Why have democracies apparently been so rare in human history (excluding pre-history)? It clearly does not require a modern economy to initiate and maintain democratic practices as the ancient Athenians so clearly demonstrated. Why then was prototypical modern democracy confined to this and later, relatively few others, such as the English, Icelandic, and American examples in the medieval and early modern periods? Two answers, as we have seen, are (1) insufficient rainfall that requires autocratic control systems, and (2) the ubiquity of warfare in countries with many land borders that would destroy the early attempts at democracy due to the need for war leadership and mobilization. But another answer is the relative isolation of polities with many sea borders, especially islands and peninsulas. Only the nearby Cyclades and as a consequence, Ionian polities on the Anatolian coast could be directly influenced by Athens, and only a colonial offshoot such as the United States could be directly influenced by the English model. Interestingly, another isolated instance, Switzerland, this time not due to the protection of the sea, but the protection of the mountains also evolved as an early democratic polity. These countries were relatively well protected from the threat of war, but also were somewhat confined in their day to day interactions with other polities that could have yielded the spread of democracy to additional political units.

We also have an answer to the question posed at the outset, namely why the earliest despotic empires arose in Mesopotamia. The combination of minimal rainfall requiring irrigation and the absence of sea borders contributed in their separate ways to the rise of autocracy in imperial form. It is likely that the *combination* of the two influences had a far more pronounced effect on this unique historical outcome in comparison with each of the two sources of autocracy having occurred separately.

Appendix: The remaining independent variables, their data sources and countries included in the analysis

The basic strategy was to obtain as many cases as possible, consistent with the time span of the political rights index and a time lag between independent and dependent variables. This was understood to be necessary to allow some time for the socioeconomic variables to affect the political rights index, especially in the instance of more "remote" variables such as agricultural density and land inequality. Thus, most of the data for these variables center on 1970, while those with perhaps some more immediate impact such as economic development, are circa 1975, hence allowing for an approximate five- to ten-year lag for most variables until the median year of 1980 for the dependent variable. The actual lag is not crucial, as these variables do not change rapidly in time. Indeed, an earlier "pilot" analysis revealed many of the significant effects reported here, with a shorter or non-existent lag among variables, but with a smaller impact of independent on dependent variables.

Agricultural density is reported for the year 1970 in Taylor and Jodice (1983, I, pp. 102–4) while for the Gini index of *land inequality*, circa 1970, the data in Muller and Seligson (1987, pp. 445–7) were used because this is perhaps the most comprehensive recent list of such data available. *Age* of polity is introduced as the year of independence to control for maturation of democratic processes and is found for most countries in Taylor and Hudson (1972, pp. 26–8), and where missing, is supplemented by values in Lye and Carpenter (1987).

Economic development is measured by *GDP/CAP* to allow for the impact of purely domestic processes and is found in Summers and Heston (1984) for the year 1975. This makes it consistent with *trade/ GNP* for 1975 (Taylor and Jodice, 1983, I, pp. 226–8). Here, the entire economy, not only its domestic component, should be controlled in relation to the international variable, trade. The variable *deaths due to*

Table 2.1A *Countries included in the analysis*

Country names	Countries included in table 2.1 ($N = 91$)	Adding land inequality (tables 2.2 & 2.3, Ns = 69 & 67)
Afghanistan	X[a]	
Algeria	X	X
Angola	X	
Argentina	X	X
Australia	X	X
Austria	X	X
Bangladesh	X	
Bolivia	X	
Brazil	X	X
Burma	X	
Cameroon	X	X
Canada	X	X
Central African Republic	X	X
Chad	X	X
Chile	X	
Colombia	X	X
Congo	X	X
Costa Rica	X	X
Denmark	X	X
Dominican Republic	X	X
Ecuador	X	X
Egypt	X	X
El Salvador	X	X
Ethiopia	X	
Finland	X	X
France	X	X
Germany, West	X	X
Ghana	X	X
Greece	X	X
Guatemala	X	X
Haiti	X	X
Honduras	X	X
India	X	X
Indonesia	X	X
Iran	X	X
Iraq	X	X
Ireland	X	X
Israel	X	X
Italy	X	X
Ivory Coast	X	X
Jamaica	X	X
Japan	X	X
Jordan	X	
Kenya	X	X
Korea	X	X
Liberia	X	X
Madagascar	X	

Table 2.1A (*cont.*)

Country names	Countries included in table 2.1 ($N = 91$)	Adding land inequality (tables 2.2 & 2.3, $N\text{s} = 69$ & 67)
Malawi	X	X
Malaysia	X	X
Mali	X	X
Mauritania	X	
Mexico	X	X
Morocco	X	
Mozambique	X	
Nepal	X	X
Netherlands	X	X
New Zealand	X	X
Niger	X	
Nigeria	X	
Norway	X	X
Pakistan[b]	X	X
Papua New Guinea	X	
Paraguay	X	
Peru	X	X
Philippines	X	X
Portugal	X	X
Senegal	X	
Sierra Leone	X	X
Singapore[b]	X	X
Somalia	X	
South Africa	X	X
Spain	X	X
Sri Lanka	X	X
Sudan	X	
Sweden	X	X
Switzerland	X	X
Syria	X	X
Tanzania	X	X
Thailand	X	X
Togo	X	X
Trinidad and Tobago	X	X
Tunisia	X	
Turkey	X	X
Uganda	X	
United Kingdom	X	X
United States	X	X
Uruguay	X	X
Venezuela	X	X
Zaire	X	X
Zambia	X	X
Zimbabwe	X	

Notes: [a]X denotes presence in this category.
[b]Omitted from the regression analysis of table 2.3 because of the absence of data on military personnel size for 1965.

political violence was drawn from the numerical listing of the 1948–77 series as found in Taylor and Jodice (1983, II, pp. 48–51). Later years (1976 and 1977) were deemed to be part of the entire political violence process and so were included. Population size for 1975 is found in Taylor and Jodice (1983, I, pp. 91–4).

Countries included in the analysis are found in table 2.1A.

NOTES

Portions of this chapter appeared in the June 1995 issue of the *Journal of Conflict Resolution* with the kind permission of that journal. Hochul Lee and Susan Craig are acknowledged here for their excellent research assistance.

1 For arguments that support at least some propensity for democracies to fight each other, especially prior to the contemporary period, see, for example, Layne (1994), Spiro (1994), Mansfield and Snyder (1995), and the correspondence concerning these issues (Russett *et al.*, 1995).

2 After completing the analysis of the impact of external threats on early democracy for its first presentation at the 1992 American Political Science Association meetings under the title of "Reversing the Causal Arrow" (Midlarsky, 1992b), I became aware of Downing's (1992) treatment of a similar theme concerning the decline of representative institutions in central Europe as the result of war during the early modern period. Of course, a major difference between the two treatments, among others, is the much longer time span and geographical scope incorporated here.

3 Crenshaw's (1992) finding is of a negative relationship between agricultural density and income inequality. As prior studies have found a negative association between income inequality and democracy (e.g., Midlarsky, 1992a, p. 468), one can infer a positive association between agricultural density and democracy as, in fact, is found by Crenshaw in chapter 3.

4 This is the period for which reliable time series data exist, as given in the latest edition of the data source (Bair, 1992). For our purposes here, the fairly substantial time lag between the independent variable, rainfall, and democracy is an advantage, for it is clear that an environmental variable such as aridity or rainfall existing as a societal backdrop would require a long time to affect the structure of politics.

5 Payne (1989) uses a similar force ratio. Additionally, he finds no relationship between "political freedom" and his military force ratio (Payne, 1989, p. 182), but his causal arrow is reversed from that hypothesized here. Whereas his dependent variable is his military force ratio, that employed here is the political rights index.

6 This averaging process does not distinguish between stable and unstable democracy, in that countries with consistent scores are combined with those having fluctuations over the length of the time period. As the objective here is to examine conditions for the emergence of early democracy, not its stability, the comparison of countries with scores averaging at one point on the continuum with those averaging at another, yields the desired outcome of overall variation in the dependent variable. On the whole, the scores tend

toward consistency for most countries during this period and the fluctuations, where found, are not extreme. Another advantage to the averaging process is found in the potential minimization of systematic error found by Bollen (1993). Random error was found to be non-existent in the Gastil data set for 1980 and the validity was found to be 93 percent, the highest of all the data sets examined by Bollen, but still leaving 7 percent for "method" or systematic error (Bollen, 1993, p. 1220). If judges' ratings tend toward bias in one year or two, then it is possible that averaging over a 15-year period may minimize such method bias because of some compensation against that bias in succeeding years.

7 A more recent treatment by Bollen (1993) gives estimates for 1980, but for liberal democracy as a multidimensional composite measure including openness of selection processes, freedom of the press and other media, and civil liberties, among others. This does not capture the essence of early democracy as basically concerned with the electoral process as found in Gastil's measure.

8 The variable, British colonial heritage, controls for countries such as Australia, New Zealand, and others who would have been directly affected by the European experience with democracy.

9 The other possibility is that the introduction of land inequality affected the British colonial heritage variable, rendering it non-significant in table 2.2. However, because the correlation between land inequality and British colonial heritage is $r = -0.02$, the introduction of land inequality could not have had a direct effect on the now non-significant British colonial heritage.

3 Democracy and proto-modernity: technoecological influences on the growth of political and civil rights

Edward Crenshaw

Introduction

The relevance of political democracy to the social sciences stems from a broader concern for individual civil and political rights around the world. The growing consensus that individuals ought to have such rights is the legacy of Western philosophy, and particularly the doctrines of classical liberalism. In a nutshell, classical liberalism holds that the individual is sovereign over his or her own person, that society is an "emergent property" arising from the voluntary market transactions between self-owned, self-interested individuals, and that the state is a contractual instrument that is best devoted to preserving the individual's right to engage in self-interested behavior. Foremost, preservation of liberty means protecting both private lives and private property from all parties that threaten them, with particular emphasis on the state's abusive potential (MacPherson, 1962). Democracy is thus viewed as the governmental form most favored by rational, market-oriented individuals who require many civil and political freedoms in order to maximize their social transactions, the ultimate outcome of which is the "invisible hand" of the market that brings the greatest good to the greatest number over time. This perspective is quite explicitly *utilitarian*, a notion to which we will return.

Using this perspective, the emergence of political democracy can be clearly subsumed under modernization theory. As societies urbanize and achieve higher levels of wealth, mass literacy and access to the mass media become possible for the first time (Lipset, 1959). Just as important, larger and larger segments of a national population become "modern" (Inkeless and Smith, 1974), boosting feelings of self-efficacy and mastery, social psychological forces that reinforce the macrosocial pressures to forge pluralistic, representative government. Even if an extreme diffusionist position is taken on this issue, like that proposed by Gastil (1985), we cannot escape the hypothesized linkages between sociocultural modernization and the emergence of democracy, at least so long as we embrace the logic of classical liberalism. Although the diffusionist stance views political democracy as a Western import rather than any kind of spontaneous outgrowth of internal structural processes sprouting here and there across the globe, one of the most important factors in the success of any diffused cultural artifact is compatibility between the sending and receiving social structures (Rogers, 1983). This suggests that whether or not the growth of democratic values is an indigenous process, the nature of empirical tests probably will not be affected. Either way, political democracy should appear to be a creature of modernization.

Recently, however, many scholars look to global political economy and the capitalist world system as crucial determinants of democracy. In essence, these theorists either reject the idea that modernization breeds democracy in developing countries (O'Donnell, 1979), or believe that the "dependent development" occurring in the Third World hampers socioeconomic progress, which in turn retards democratization (Timberlake and Williams, 1984; Evans, 1979). In general, these arguments hinge on the social inequalities that are allegedly bred by an alliance of foreign investors, national elites, and indigenous governments that exploits national populations. Therefore, economic and political dependency enforced by the systems logic of capitalism and the military might of capitalist core nations "short-circuits" the process of socioeconomic development in non-core nations, generating high inequalities, intense class conflicts, and repressive, non-representative governments. Indeed, some scholars view the lack of democracy and concomitant civil and political rights as an essential prerequisite to national mobility in the world system. As Chirot notes (1986, p. 128):

But when a peripheral society moves toward semiperipherality, or when a semi-peripheral society seriously attempts to attain core status, lack of democracy is not a disadvantage. On the contrary, nondemocratic governments are more likely to keep down consumption (thus freeing funds needed for investment), and they are also more likely to repress discontent powerfully and ruthlessly.

These arguments suggest that if democratization is a political form evolved or borrowed to match an increasingly pluralistic, complex set of market relationships, then political democracy may come late or not at all to peripheral and semiperipheral populations due to the distorting influences of the capitalist world order. An extreme strand of this school of thought would insist that developed countries can afford the "luxury" of political democracy only because of the ongoing surplus extraction from periphery to core.

Many cross-national studies of democratization, regime repressiveness, political conflict, and social inequality have been couched in this type of language, pitting modernization theory against this more recent, critical theory (Bollen, 1983; Timberlake and Williams, 1984; Boswell and Dixon, 1990), but at a very abstract level both theories posit the same expected relationship: equalization of economic resources breeds demands for representative government. While this is essentially Vanhanen's (1990) point (i.e., that the system of power relationships mirrors or is dependent on the distribution of power resources), Vanhanen's evolutionary account based on a Darwinian model misses a fundamental difference between classical social evolutionary theory and modern formulations stressing class conflict and power politics. Although Vanhanen posits that democracy arises when resources are well dispersed (which disallows single-group domination of governments), an evolutionary-functionalist account would note that social stratification is a function of *social differentiation and integration,* and therefore social complexity should be a crucial predictor of political democracy (Parsons, 1977). This is to say, under a revised evolutionary theory it is possible that the relationship between social stratification and the growth of political and civil rights may owe much of its strength to a mutual correlation with social complexity. Undoubtedly patterns of social inequality do influence national polities, but we must not ignore the probability that such phenomena as regime repressiveness, rebellion or political violence, and other forms of conflict are conditioned by the degree to which populations are integrated into numerous, interdependent institutions and groups. This is the social cement based on mutual need, and whether we label it "organic solidarity" (Durkheim, 1893 [1964]) or "gesellschaft" (Tonnies, 1963), the fact remains that *mutual* dependency should be a powerful force in securing expanded civil, political, and economic rights. Of course, this mutual dependency is highest among small groups of people, and this probably accounts for the very high levels of democracy observed in hunting and gathering bands and other very simple societies (see Bollen and Paxton or Ember, Ember, and Russett, this volume). Nonetheless, it should also be remembered that very advanced agrarianism is characterized by complex interdependencies, interdependencies that eventually give birth to such social phenomena as industrialism, modernity, and individual political and civil rights. This advanced agrarian heritage should therefore be recognized for what it is: *proto-modernity.*

What follows then is a call for a theoretical reformulation of the question of democratization, with emphasis on ecological-evolutionary theories past and present. Although we will return to the question of resource distribution, the theoretical discussion and empirical tests that follow will highlight structural differentiation and social complexity as the major engines of democratization, along with a few other hypotheses that have been suggested in the theoretical development of this topic.

Theory

Most theories of democratization explicitly acknowledge either class formation or class conflict as the impetus behind changes in political and civil rights. Various strands of thought that can be roughly grouped under modernization theory assert that industrialization entails urbanization, and such concentration "exposes" an increasingly large portion of a country's population to literacy, mass media, and class formation. This of course gives the citizenry both the ability to pursue representative government and the desire for it (Lerner, 1958; Lipset, 1959). As the forces of modernization mobilize the masses, classes form around different sectors of the rapidly changing economy and grow in power, eventually contesting the traditional elites' hold on government (Bollen, 1983). It is important to understand that modernization theory as stated does not rely on structured inequalities to explain democratization. Most of the crucial assumptions made by this model are implicit: (1) that "modernization" involves increasing differentiation and social complexity; (2) that subgroups are connected to differing socioeconomic functions that entail self-interest; and (3) that pluralism dictates political activism, although not necessarily political unrest or armed conflict (the "mass society" hypothesis). In short, modernization theory is a class formation theory asserting that, holding social inequalities constant, higher levels of socioeconomic differentiation lead to higher levels of civil and political rights.

The assumption that democratization is linked to stratification and overt inequalities can be traced from Aristotle's day to the Enlightenment. More recent efforts to understand democratization usually include some notion linking inequalities to the likelihood of political democracy, even when it is only one factor among many (Dahl, 1971; Huntington, 1984). Whether we term this the "distributive justice" school (Rawls, 1971), "relative deprivation theory" (Gurr, 1968; Huntington, 1968), or simply "class analysis", theorists in this tradition emphasize relationships between gross social inequalities, the overt class conflict and political violence they may engender, and democratization.

Research of this type has become very popular in recent years, and none more so than investigations of how international economic, political, and social relationships impact internal developments. Such studies are generally conducted under the rubric of dependency theory and world-systems theory, sharing the common assertion that, whether through the inherent logic of capitalism or through coercion, less-developed countries have been "underdeveloped" (Frank, 1967; Wallerstein, 1974). That is, underdevelopment is a status that has been imposed on less-developed countries by the forces of global capitalism through such mechanisms as colonialism, foreign investment, indebtedness, unequal exchange, and military/political dependency. Of course, the influence of international capitalism on any particular nation will depend on the type, rate, and depth of the interaction, but the general premise is that a nation's internal social organization (and most particularly its stratification system) is a direct by-product of its "position" in the world economic order (Wallerstein, 1974; Evans, 1979; Timberlake, 1987).

It is here that modernization theory and dependency/world-systems theory sharply differ. While modernization theory is fairly clear about the impact of modernity on democratization, few theorists in this school have spent much time elaborating on why the pace of modernity varies around the globe. Although there has been the recognition that "traditional" group affiliations, social psychologies and production techniques hinder the process of technological diffusion and concomitant modernization (Rostow, 1960), it is painfully apparent that older modernization writings depict the preindustrial, non-Western world as a mass of essentially similar societies dedicated to custom and married to subsistence economies. In this theoretical near-vacuum grew dependency/world-systems theory. The answer was simple: differentials in the pace and timing of development can be explained by examining a nation's relationship to global capitalism. That is, external factors play a far larger role in socioeconomic and political change than do any particular internal characteristics of non-core nations.

Although it is beyond the purpose here to delve into the "deep logic" of dependency and world-systems theorizing, essentially this "family" of theories assumes that capitalism is an inherently antagonistic, exploitative political economy, and as such requires severe social inequalities at all levels in order to function. Such inequalities include income inequality, sectorial inequality, severe spatial disarticulation (urban bias and rural underinvestment), and of course international disparities in wealth, stocks of information, and military might. Therefore, whereas modernization theory emphasizes internal characteristics as determining a society's stratification system, dependency and world-systems theories point to a society's relationship with the forces of international capitalism as the prime determinant of social inequalities (Evans and Timberlake, 1980; Timberlake, 1987).

Two of the more persuasive variants of these arguments involve the inequalities generated by the legacy of colonial land policies and those springing from foreign investments in national economies. According to world-systems theory, land ownership concentration can be directly linked to colonization, the production of export crops, and agrarian social systems. In Latin America, for example, very large estates were granted to individuals to promote export production while protecting landowners from the vicissitudes of the world market (Furtado, 1970). The resulting *latifundio–minifundio* system is therefore quite pronounced in some parts of this region. As an example, between 1950 and 1960 the largest Chilean estates represented only about 7 percent of all farms yet occupied over 80 percent of the land area, while the smallest farms occupied only 1 percent of the land area while comprising a full third of all farms (Furtado, 1970). Given that exploitation of land is a principal source of wealth and basic subsistence in most developing countries, severe inequalities in land ownership should directly shape national stratification systems.

Another major argument concerns the deleterious influence of foreign capital penetration on less-developed societies. Although original formulations of dependency theory emphasized colonialism and export dependency (Baran, 1957; Galtung, 1971), these have generally been replaced by *dependent development theory* (Evans, 1979; Cardoso and Faletto, 1979). The notion here is that direct private foreign investment has replaced colonialism and commodity/trade partner concentration as the primary means whereby core nations exploit the less-developed world. Once again, the primary influence of foreign capital on national developments of all kinds (including democratization) is through the creation of severe social inequalities. First, foreign investment encourages capital-intensity, which causes gross sectoral disparities in productivity, the formation of labor aristocracies with loyalties to multinational firms, and the underabsorption of labor. Second, multinationals may monopolize indigenous sources of credit and invest locally derived capital either in their "home" countries or in other concerns in different parts of the world, practices that may starve native entrepreneurs of capital. Finally, governments in less-developed countries may engage in global competition for MNC investments, and this competition may lead to stringent controls over labor or over-lenient taxation policies toward such firms (Cardoso and Faletto, 1979; Evans, 1979; Todaro, 1969; Bornschier and Chase-Dunn, 1985).

The final outcome of these processes is economic growth in non-core nations that is bereft of most of the beneficial side-effects extolled by modernization theory. In place of native, politically active bourgeoisies are small elites with international ties that lack legitimacy (Roberts, 1985). Rather than dynamic, interdependent economic sectors that provide occupational mobility for growing numbers of people, dependent development offers narrow employment opportunities for the lucky few and informal economies for all others (Evans and Timberlake, 1980). Although the list of alleged social problems attached to peripheralization in the global economy is potentially quite long, the ultimate point is that global capitalism and its structures of international exploitation disallow what O'Donnell calls Lipset's "optimistic equation," which is that socioeconomic progress can be translated into political democracy (O'Donnell, 1979).

Although dependency/world-systems theory does provide a powerful and cogent explanation for differentials in the timing and pace of development around the globe, this family of critical theories has been almost as ahistorical as modernization theory. Why are some nations more heavily penetrated by foreign capital? Why did colonization result in severe land inequality in one society but not in another? Why does mobility in the interstate system exist at all? It is fair to say that dependency/world-systems theorists have difficulty supplying *generalizable* answers to such questions, the same difficulty modernization theorists have had in explaining why one nation achieves "take-off" quite rapidly while another languishes for decades.

What will be suggested below is that both major theories of development overlook the technological/ecological histories of developing societies, and this omission erects a significant stumbling block in our attempt to understand democratization. The key to removing this block is to somehow operationalize *preindustrial social development*, or that set of initial social conditions that influences both economic and political development as well as a nation's position in the global economy.

Technoecological heritage and democratization

To foreshadow this discussion, the concept of *institutional inheritance* plays a crucial role in the discussion of a nation's past developmental history. This idea is simply that those nations that possess more of the precursors of modern social institutions will be more quickly "integrated" into the modern world than those societies or nations that possess only a modest institutional inheritance. To apply this idea specifically to democratization is quite simple: *Political democracy is more likely to arise (or, as a diffused cultural artifact, more likely to take root) in societies or nations that enjoy a more complex institutional inheritance.*

As mentioned above, most proponents of modernization theory and dependency/world-systems theories have had an unfortunate tendency to label preindustrial systems as "traditional" societies, and to assume that real social change began only with either the English Industrial Revolution or the commercial capitalism characterizing the early modern period of European history. As an alternative to this narrow view of recent social change, however, new variants of ecological-evolutionary theory point out that "development" is a process that spans all of human history (and pre-history). As Lenski and Nolan (1984) note, the technoeconomic heritage of a society at the beginning of industrialization is a critical determinant of its subsequent development trajectory. In their formulation, adoption of plow agriculture is the single most important technology that shapes past development and sets constraints on contemporary world societies. Specifically, the use of the plow has lent old agrarian societies a developmental advantage by providing higher levels of economic surplus, which allowed for larger and more densely settled populations, the early emergence of city-states, occupational specialization, literacy and formal education, governmental bureaucracies, monied economies, and so forth (Lenski and Nolan, 1984; Nolan and Lenski, 1985). Conversely, *horticultural societies* (those that lacked plow agriculture) and *new agrarian societies* (formerly horticultural societies that have been "jump-started" by early colonialism) begin modernization with far fewer social, economic, and political resources, a fact that tends to retard their development relative to other societies.

The central concept of ecological-evolutionary theory is its emphasis on *social carrying capacity* and the social structure which is created in response to it. Although different versions of evolutionary theory stress technology as a cause of demographic characteristics (Lenski, 1966), or, the reverse, that demographic pressures dictate the creation of technology (Boserup, 1965), it is really the *social organization* that emerges from this technological/demographic interaction that is theoretically relevant.

To denote this shift in emphasis from older ecological-evolutionary models, the term *technoecological heritage* seems most appropriate. Climates, disease regimes, and the social environment (e.g., war) in addition to technology allow larger and more densely settled populations, so technoecological theory might be viewed as putting the ecology back into evolutionary theory (see Midlarsky, this volume, for another essentially "technoecological" account of political development). This formulation of technoecological heritage owes much to older models of social evolution. Specifically, Spencer (1852 [1972]) asserted that high population density leads to an increase in the complexity of the division of labor. In a refinement, Durkheim (1893 [1964]) suggested this complexity is attributable to socioeconomic competition and the need for individuals and groups to reduce direct competition with others through innovation and differentiation (occupational specialization). In essence, growing differentiation and innovation (i.e., growing social complexity) are functions of demographic pressure and the need to obtain sustenance in highly competitive environments. One could almost say that the more intense Hobbes' "struggle of all against all" has been in the past, the more complex and adaptable the contemporary society.

Vanhanen (1990, p. 48) apparently advocates a similar evolutionary scheme, noting that "we live in a world of scarce resources where competition and struggle are the major ways to distribute those resources. Thus the evolutionary roots of politics lie in the necessity to solve conflicts over scarce resources by some method." To Vanhanen, market-driven economies are important only because they "presuppose the distribution of economic power and resources among many competing and independent groups" (1990, p. 168), which is perfectly consistent with modernization theory's emphasis on the differentiation incumbent on industrialization. Nonetheless, Vanhanen draws a sharp contrast between his theory and modernization theory, stating that "It [socioeconomic development] is only an intervening variable that correlates positively with democratization because various power resources are usually more widely distributed at higher levels than at lower levels of socioeconomic development" (Vanhanen, 1990, p. 195). Therefore, embracing Vanhanen's theory suggests a heavy emphasis on scarce resources, competition, and social inequality.

Technological theory differs substantially from the theory discussed above. First, innovation and differentiation are older than formal politics, and constitute human populations' first line of defense against internecine conflict and anarchy. The technoecological perspective stresses how competition leads to innovation, differentiation, and interdependency rather than conflict, and in turn how interdependency creates conditions suitable for social change (which include stratification systems and their attendant polities). Second, although Vanhanen apparently rejects simplistic socioeconomic formulations of democratization, his theory really provides no *systematic* explanation for resource distribution independent of socioeconomic modernization. Therefore, what is needed is an ecological-evolutionary theory that constitutes more than just relabeling or even synthesizing older notions about the relationships between democratization, modernization, and stratification.

The broad outlines of such a theory can be stated briefly. The influence of technoecological heritage on a nation's division of labor and stratification system can be traced from the most macrosocial of phenomena to microsocial environments that create social psychologies and individual motivations. Specifically, technoecology's influences can be examined at the world-system level, the national/regional level, and at the individual level.

Although dependency/world-systems theorists have written innumerable words on the deleterious influences of international stratification on social development, these theorists have virtually ignored the strong impact of technoecological heritage on a nation's integration in the world's division of labor. True centrality in the world economy without a large, densely settled population and the complex social organization this requires is highly unlikely; technoecological advantage may be the "price of admission" into the semiperipheral and core groups of nations. On the other hand, thinly populated nations, especially those that had lacked other "modern" institutions in the past (e.g., states, monied economies) are not likely to be central players in the world economy any time soon. To give an example, we could claim that Chad's peripheral status is attributable to the colonial past and the current state of the global economy, but that would be both ludicrous and inefficient when the evidence for technoecological handicaps lies there in Chad's soil/climate interaction, its few cities, and its religious/ethnic divisions.

Furthermore, even the colonial experiences of developing nations were strongly conditioned by their technoecological legacies. For instance, European colonization of horticultural societies usually entailed large land grants and the importation of labor (both slave or free) due to labor shortages, whereas the experiences of high-density societies involved greater utilization of native labor and land tenure systems. A contrast between the experiences of Korea and the Philippines, for instance, or between most Asian countries and Latin American countries clearly demonstrates this tendency (Furtado, 1970; Geertz, 1963; Nemeth and Smith, 1985). The social consequences of this differential in developmental histories is reflected in higher land ownership concentration, the higher likelihood of racial/ethnic divisions due to the fragmentation typical of horticultural societies as well as to the importation of non-native labor, and the severe stratification that emerges as a result. This is because the relative poverty of their institutional inheritances made horticultural societies excessively fragile, and although their transformation into new agrarian societies has been fairly swift, we should not expect that transformation to be particularly well balanced. On the other hand, old agrarian societies have been far more resistant to acculturation. Kelly (1984) provides a small but telling example. The French educational systems of Indochina and West Africa differed in curriculum, coverage, and orientation. French schools in Indochina offered all levels of schooling and taught advanced courses in mathematics, science, and written language, while the same colonizers in West Africa educated only tribal elites and offered only primary education that stressed simple mathematics and spoken French. Moreover, in Indochina the French emphasized the inherent inferiority of native institutions, whereas in West Africa this same government taught the essential equality of French and African institutions. In both systems, the ultimate aim was to use education as a tool to acculturate the colonial peoples. The differences in curriculum, coverage, and orientation sprang from the differences in the two regions: in Indochina, the French were in competition with well-established Buddhist schools that trained civil servants for the Vietnamese bureaucracy. This forced the French to offer more people a better education, while belittling the competition. In West Africa, on the other hand, all that seemed necessary was to coopt the tribal leadership, and to do that the French offered primary education and flattering comparisons between French and West African societies. The point is that *a complex institutional inheritance confers resistance to exploitation and has a lasting influence on a society's mobility in the global division of labor.*

It is at the national/regional level, however, that technoecological heritage has its most profound effects. In terms of stratification, access to land has traditionally been the single most important scarce resource that determined the fates of individuals and groups. In old agrarian societies, as populations grew, labor became the only flexible source of wealth as land and capital became dear. As elites substituted labor for scarcer factors of production, the problem of hoarding labor power forced powerful groups to distribute subsistence more evenly, a feat usually accomplished through lenient forms of tenant-farming and food-for-labor customs. Moreover, increasing scarcities of land over generations compelled elites to continually subdivide their assets among their offspring, a dynamic that eventually eroded land ownership concentration and produced flatter distributions of income or its equivalent, particularly in societies that did not practice *primogeniture* (Nolan and Lenski, 1985).

Technoecological heritage also influences both social and spatial articulation, meaning that the levels of socioeconomic and political interdependencies are influenced by a society's institutional/demographic inheritance. First, technoecological-advantaged societies usually exhibit highly articulate, complex systems of villages, towns, and cities *prior to contact with "modern" societies.* Densely settled land naturally contains more permanent settlements, and this difference is striking when old and new agrarian societies are compared. Second, it is logical to assume that these advanced village/town systems are supported by rural infrastructure, and roads in particular. Although the fact has seldom been brought up in the literature, preindustrial societies tend toward spatial disarticulation due to poor transportation and communication technologies. Nonetheless, high-density societies experienced the need for more advanced rural infrastructure in the past, and given that historically they have enjoyed more complex political organization, this demand has generally been met well before nascent industrialization (Boserup, 1990, p. 71). Third, a direct relationship exists between population density and farm size, with density forcing subdivision as discussed above. This is significant because, all else constant, smaller farms are more productive than large estates and, furthermore, even large farms in *high-density societies* tend to be more productive than their counterparts elsewhere (Berry and Cline, 1979, pp. 34–49). This in turn allows for higher levels of *non-farm employment* and more complicated divisions of labor in rural areas (Boserup, 1990, p. 86; World Bank, 1978; Epstein, 1971).

This proto-modernity directly influences a society's political heritage. According to Lenski (1966), old agrarian societies have long histories of centralized, bureaucratic governments. Although the view of these historical empires and kingdoms as repressive and autocratic prevails in the literature (Wittfogel's (1957) "hydraulic societies"), it is nevertheless true that advanced agrarian societies are complex, and this complexity challenges rulers and their agents. Rulers who are confronted by complex society are forced to diffuse their authority in order to more perfectly exploit their territories' resource bases (e.g., populations and revenues) (Tilly, 1990, p. 24). This diffusion of authority usually weakens what Levi (1988; p. 17) terms a ruler's "relative bargaining power," or the ability to gain compliance from the autarkic centers of power within the state.

The political/institutional influence of proto-modernity does not end there. The more complex a society, the stronger has been the *institution of bargaining* between the state and its people, in that rulers of complex societies have been forced throughout history to gain "quasi-voluntary compliance" (Levi, 1988; pp. 52–67), or the exchange of political and civil rights for compliance with tax and military levies. Logically, the more complex the society, the more complex this bargaining process, and the more differentiated the deals made among cross-cutting affiliations (e.g., occupational groups), interest groups (e.g., the clergy) and regional/local centers of power (e.g., the nobility). Once this dynamic begins, the demand for equal treatment and better terms leads to a heritage of bargaining and rent-seeking from the state that better prepares a population for democratic institutions, behaviors, and attitudes than would otherwise be the case. Finally, if we consider that rural populations living in highly stratified, complex societies are in better communication with one another, are less likely to be splintered into many hostile ethnicities due to centuries of intermarriage and warfare, and are far more likely to play an integral role in the complicated interdependencies tying cities, hinterlands, and governments, it seems likely that peasants in advanced agricultural societies possess more political leverage than their counterparts in horticultural societies, a fact borne out by the long histories of compromise between rural and urban areas found in many of these societies (see European and Japanese examples in Hilton, 1978; Davis, 1974). Thus, the notion that densely settled agrarian societies might be more prone to democratization is not as strange at it might first appear.

Through its macrosocial consequences, technoecology also shapes the microeconomic environments in which socioeconomic and political forces play themselves out. For instance, although the social psychological dimension of modernization theory is not as popular as it once was (e.g., Inkeles and Smith, 1974), if "modern" psychologies are necessary to modernization then technoecological considerations will probably be important. Individuals functioning in complex social environments are much more likely to engage in the "economic calculus" that supposedly typifies the "modern" individual. Both private property and wage labor emerge well before industrial capitalism, and both come in response to the erosion of communal land tenure and labor-sharing customs in the face of population pressure (Fogg, 1971, pp. 576–7; Boserup, 1990, p. 19; Hayami and Kikuchi, 1981, p. 27). Moreover, a bit of purely sociological wisdom has remained buried in classical texts, to the effect that *individualism is a product of the structural–functional differentiation of populations* (Simmel, 1971, pp. 251–93). As populations grow and are forced to differentiate economic, political, and social activities, role segmentation occurs, the number of transactions per person increases, and individual resources and attendant interests naturally emerge. Therefore, it is likely that human beings in high-density environments exercise economic rationality, move in relatively more complicated microeconomic environments, and engage in role segmentation in dealing with other economic actors. In short, possessive individualism arises in these preindustrial populations, as do the cross-cutting affiliations so important to the theories of Lipset and others. Given these macro- and microsocial dynamics, it is probable that, prior to nascent industrialization, technoecologically advantaged societies are in fact *proto-modern* societies.

The relationship between technoecological heritage (or institutional inheritance) and democratization can therefore be linked to a utilitarian view of society. Technoecologically advantaged societies are social environments that are relatively "transaction-rich," which is to say that social differentiation and complex interdependencies tend to individuate human beings and increase their market exchanges, and this in turn puts pressure on states to recognize the individual as an inherently valuable possessor of civil, political, and economic rights. Two important considerations separate this idea from either modernization or dependency/world-systems theory. First, the assumption of modernization theorists that industrialization creates differentiation and enriches the transaction environment is true, but their implicit assumption that all preindustrial societies are therefore poorly differentiated or "transaction-poor" is false. There is a type of differentiation and interdependency that is not necessarily dependent on national wealth or industrialization that nonetheless encourages democratization (or leads to the acceptance of democracy as a diffused "artifact"). On the other hand, while the assumptions of dependency or world-systems theorists (among others) that severe inequalities hinder democratization and that these inequalities are the by-product of the systems logic of global capitalism do merit consideration, technoecological theory reminds us that both intranational and international stratification systems are by-products of the complexity of societies, and that this speeds their integration into the world economy. Moreover, simplistic formulations that focus on the relationships between raw inequalities, power politics, repression, and political change fail to note that complex interdependencies probably condition these relationships. *Mutual need* probably leads to a higher degree of bargaining and compromise in politics, which is to say that interdependency provides the non-elite with *leverage,* and elites are far more likely to grant civil, political, and economic rights when they profit from doing so. Therefore, technoecological theory would grant that conflict plays a role in political change, but would also add that complex interdependencies engender processes of exchange between elites and the masses that are essentially non-conflictual.

This discussion leads to two general hypotheses:

H_1: Holding modernity constant (industrial labor force and educational enrolments), technoecological heritage (agricultural density) will be positively related to the growth of democratic rights.

H_2: Holding economic, ethnic, or international inequalities constant (sectorial and land inequality, ethnic dominance and linguistic fractionation, foreign capital penetration and world-systems position), technoecological heritage (agricultural density) will be positively related to the growth of democratic rights.

Design and variables

Given that democratic rights are granted by national governments, the unit of analysis should be the nation. For this reason, cross-national research is ideal for assessing the impact of modernization, stratification, and technoecology on democratization. I conduct two sets of analyses, one using all countries for which data are available, and the other using only non-core countries as defined by Snyder and Kick (1979) and as modified by Bollen (1983). The reasons for this strategy are two-fold. First, dependency theorists sometimes argue that social processes fundamentally differ between the core and non-core groups of nations (Bornschier and Chase-Dunn, 1985). For instance, world-systems theory focuses on the alleged parasitic relationship between core and non-core nations, so it would be illogical from this perspective to look for similar processes in the two groups. Second, Midlarsky (1992a) argues that nascent democratization will occur in predominately non-industrial or agrarian societies, and that the processes that influence early democratization in these societies may be replaced later on by such forces as urbanization and mass communications. This argument in conjunction with dependency arguments warrants using two samples in this study. Countries included in the samples are reported in appendix A.

Many past investigations of democratization have been limited to cross-sectional analysis (e.g., Bollen, 1983), averaging some measure of democracy over a number of years (e.g., Midlarsky, this volume), or combinations of cross-sectional analysis over time (e.g., Vanhanen, 1990). With the exception of the contributions made to this volume (see also Crenshaw, 1995), only Arat (1991) apparently provides *bone fide* longitudinal analysis, but her dependent variable is democratic instability (or the "choppiness" of democratization), and her tests involve only zero-order correlations and very simplistic regression models that are undoubtedly underspecified. What is needed are longitudinal tests that pit competing theories of democratization against one another in single equations in order to sort out the unique influences of variables.

To accomplish this, the results below are based on panel regressions of the level of democratic rights in 1980 regressed on its lagged value in 1965 and other pertinent variables. The dependent and lagged dependent variables are adapted from Arat (1991). This index of political democracy incorporates four related dimensions of representative government: (1) participation, or the degree to which the executive and legislative organs are selected by the population and in fact constitute separate governmental bodies; (2) inclusiveness, or the coverage of the voting franchise in the national population; (3) competitiveness, or the degree of real choice presented to the electorate; and (4) civil liberties (government coerciveness), or the extent to which government sanctions (e.g., marshal law) exceed what might be considered legitimate given the level of unrest (see Arat, 1991, pp. 23–31 for more specific details). While indices of political systems are always subject to criticism, Arat's operationalization of democracy is similar in construction to Bollen's (1980) POLDEM index, and in fact correlates highly with it as well as a number of other indices used in past studies (Arat, 1991, p. 28).

The growth of democratic rights from 1965 to 1980 is modeled on ten different equations, five for the world sample and five for the non-core sample. Modernization theory is represented by two fairly standard development indicators: the percentage of the labor force in industry in 1965 and secondary school enrolment ratios in 1965 (World Bank, 1980). Although the percentage of the labor force working in industry is generally accepted as compatible with other measures of national wealth, this indicator has been selected in the belief that it may provide better face validity as a measure of the interface between economic systems and populations. That is, among the assertions of the "logic of industrialism" hypothesis is the idea that industrialism generates economic complexities which require elites to recruit new technical and management workers from the working classes, thus forming new middle classes (Kerr et al., 1960). Given that the labor force in industry is a direct measure of how penetrated the workforce is by industrialism, it seems ideally designed to help separate the economic complexity bred by industrialism from complexities that arise from preindustrial or non-industrial sources.

The use of the secondary school enrollment ratio as a modernization indicator is more problematic from a theoretical standpoint. Specifically, it might be argued that literacy and school enrollments constitute political variables given their linkages to public institutions (Simpson, 1990,

1993a). Of course, if we do consider schooling essentially political, then it might be interpreted as a form of institutionalized inequality, and the differentiations that flow from differentials in education are really just forms of stratification. Nonetheless, the secondary school enrollment ratio is used as a modernization indicator in this analysis for a variety of reasons. First, modernization theorists view education and industrialism as inextricably linked, going so far as to label education "the hand-maiden of industrialism" (Kerr *et al.*, 1960). Systems of stratification are by-products of the complex interplay of economic development and education, and the assumption that the influence of education on strati-fication is mediated by class conflict and political mobilization or activ-ism is somewhat dubious (Crenshaw, 1992). Many of the influences of education on stratification are *economic* in nature, including the social mobility engendered by higher-order skills, the strong interaction between educational payoffs and the level of development, the influences of literacy on rural-to-urban migration, and the rapidity of com-munication in literate societies, all of which argue for using education as a modernization indicator (Psacharopoulos, 1973; Bairoch, 1988). Add to this the emphasis that Lipset or Lerner placed on literacy and mass communications as facilitators of democratization, or the strong correlation between educational measures and development (see table 3.3), and the use of educational measures as adjuncts to the influence of industrialism on political change seems more than warranted.

The number of military personnel per 1,000 population in 1965 is included in the basic model as a proxy for the role of war and state building on democratization (see Midlarsky, this volume, for a good discussion of this dynamic). Given the potential relationship between military might and the coercive capacities of government (Zwick, 1984), indicators of military strength have generally been used from a conflict perspective (e.g., Cutright, 1967; Arat, 1991). Others note that a high degree of military participation may broaden the franchise over time as well as lower inequality through human capital formation (Lenski, 1966; Weede and Tiefenbach, 1981c). Also, military mobilization has been an important part of evolutionary-functionalist thought since the inception of that paradigm. For instance, Spencer posited that high levels of exter-nal and internal threat breed militarism, and this in turn leads to more centralized (less democratic) government (Turner, 1993, p. 140). Although there are likely to be relationships between threat, stratifi-cation, militarism, and democratization, the great diversity of theories applied to this topic necessarily muddies any interpretation. Moreover, while military establishments are public institutions, they also tend to be the most organized entities in many nations and enjoy quasi-independence as a result. For this reason, it is not clear whether military mobilization represents repressive class structures, the hostility of social environments, or something about the institutional configuration of societies. It is therefore best to err on the side of caution; although the expectation is generally for a negative relationship between militarization and the growth of civil and political rights, the exact reasons underlying it are debatable.

The central focus of this analysis is technoecological heritage, which is represented in the equations below by the log of rural population density. The variable is calculated by dividing the non-urban population in 1960 by arable land in square kilometers in that same year (World Bank, 1984b; Taylor and Jodice, 1983). The resulting ratio is then logged to correct for skewness. Although similar indicators have been used in the past as proxies for either agricultural adversity (Firebaugh, 1979; London, 1987; Chan, 1989) or land ownership concentration (Midlarsky, 1992a; Simpson, 1992), this is probably a severe underestimation of the variable's meaning or worth. The use of agricultural density or its analogues as either a basic needs indicator or a measure of stratification is rooted in the Ricardian view of high-density rural districts as impoverished, stagnant backwaters where "agricultural involution" leads to diminishing returns to labor (see Geertz, 1963). This view ignores the high degree of social "scaffolding" required to maintain high densities: dense networks of villages and towns, collective building and use of infrastructure, more extensive divisions of labor, and other dynamics discussed above. Indeed, regions that suffer from thin populations, inadequate or non-existent infrastructure, and truncated labor and consumer markets are the ones that tend to experience more severe agricultural adversity (e.g., many areas of Africa). Luckily, the central tenet of technoecological theory, that social complexity is (proximately) driven by demography, leads to expected relationships between agrarian density and such topics as democratization, income inequality, and economic growth that are diametrical to those posited by more conventional approaches. In other words, we are fortunate to have a critical experiment in this instance.

The modernization indicators, the lagged dependent variable, the control for militarization as well as the log of rural density are retained in every equation, while other variables that have been used by stratification theorists are entered independently.[1] This was done for two reasons. First, both modernization and technoecological theories key on differentiation, interdependency, and social complexity as their primary explications of social change, although differing on the source of this complexity (industrialism versus demography). Because this affinity means that modernization theory is the most viable alternative explanation to findings that support technoecological theory, it is desirable to pit these two competing explanations against one another in every equation to more sharply differentiate their influences. Second, distinguishing between interdependency- and inequality-oriented models is clearly policy relevant. As Vanhanen notes, it is not likely that public policy can make poor countries rich in the near future, but the distribution of resources may be more easily manipulated by policy interventions (1990 p. 195). Therefore, many social scientists and policy makers may consider the differing measures of inequality more relevant. Entering each inequality indicator independently maximizes its chance to co-vary with the dependent variable and, more importantly, allows us to retain much larger sample sizes than would be the case if all the inequality measures were entered simultaneously.

Two variables represent the first dimension of stratification considered here: land inequality. In the world sample (core and non-core), I adapt Vanhanen's (1990) measure of the percentage of farms that are family owned (or leased where dependency is not the result) due to its greater availability. Of course, the logic is that land confers economic and therefore political power, and societies that have a high proportion of owner-operators are also likely to have well-dispersed agricultural resources. The Gini coefficient of land inequality is used for the non-core sample (Muller and Seligson, 1987). Some past research links land inequalities with income inequality and political violence (Russett, 1964; Midlarsky, 1988; Prosterman and Riedinger, 1987; Boswell and Dixon, 1990; Simpson, 1993a; Crenshaw, 1992). It is also worth noting that Midlarsky (1992a or this volume) finds a *positive* effect of land inequality on nascent democratization, explaining that demonstrable differences in wealth are necessary for class formation and the beginnings of participatory government. His hypothesis is evidently unique, contributing an interesting variant of the stratification/inequality school of thought on this topic.

The second dimension of inequality is racial/ethnic differentiation. The percentage of the largest homogeneous ethnic group in a country's population is adapted from Vanhanen (1990 p. 111) and is used in the world sample. A more common indicator, ethnolinguistic fractionation, is adapted from Taylor and Hudson (1972) for use in the non-core sample. Hypotheses concerning the relationship between ethnic heterogeneity and democratization tend to be inconsistent. While most scholars working in this area have assumed that sharp ethnic cleavages and rivalries deprive national populations of the cross-cutting socioeconomic ties that might foster political democracy, others note that ethnic differentiation might support a more even spread of resources and might therefore be conducive to democratization. Given that racial, ethnic, or linguistic cleavages often correlate with significant socioeconomic inequality (e.g, South Africa, Northern Ireland), I expect demographic or social heterogeneity to hinder democratization.

The last dimension of inequality is international stratification. In the world sample two indicators have been selected: the Gini coefficient of sectoral inequality in 1970 to represent dependency theory (Taylor and Hudson, 1972) and world-systems position circa 1965 to represent world-systems theory (Snyder and Kick, 1979). The use of sectoral inequality is meant to capture dependency arguments concerning *economic disarticulation*, or the juxtaposition of small modern sectors linked to global capitalism and poor subsistence agriculture where the bulk of the third world's labor force languishes. Essentially this is an argument about economic dualism, the point being that the involvement of international capital has "disarticulated" many national economies (Stokes and Anderson, 1990). Of course, countries suffering from dualism should experience lagging democratization due to poor distribution of economic and political resources. World-systems position is more straightforward. If the cross-sectional findings of Bollen (1983) are borne out in this analysis, net of development we should see negative coefficients for the peripheral and semiperipheral groups of countries due to the multifaceted influences of global capitalism on non-core nations. Although some could argue that the entirety of the world system's influence on democratization is mediated through such variables as development or prior level of political democracy, the theory provides a number of hypothesized relationships (e.g., government sanctions against labor mobilization) that should *directly* affect the process of democratization. Therefore, we are looking for significant coefficients net of modernization effects.

The log of foreign capital penetration in 1967 and political instability from 1948 to 1965 have been selected as the dependency/world-systems proxies for the non-core sample. Studies linking foreign capital dominance with such topics as economic disarticulation (e.g., Evans and Timberlake, 1980), income inequality (e.g., Bornschier and Chase-Dunn, 1985), and political violence (e.g., London and Robinson, 1989) are numerous. As with world-systems position, many of the theorized effects of foreign capital should be mediated through economic complexity, but not all. Moreover, analysts who share this critical outlook on world affairs have usually reported direct relationships between foreign capital penetration and a variety of outcome variables, and this study should prove no different. The indicator is constructed by dividing the dollar value of total direct, private foreign-owned stock in 1967 by the total dollar value of all stock (foreign plus domestic) in 1967 (Ballmer-Cao and Scheidegger, 1979). The variable is logged to correct for extreme skewness.

The logic of modeling political instability or violence stems from the emphasis placed on it in the literature. Political unrest is thought to represent a "crisis of legitimacy" (Lipset, 1959), and as operationalized here might be considered a "heritage of coercion" variable. Many scholars view political violence as stemming from severe economic inequalities in society and, more importantly, they view such unrest as a *proximate cause* of governmental repression and the retardation of democratic processes (Arat, 1991, p. 80). It has been entered into this analysis for precisely this reason: the variable has long been a favorite in the dependency/world-systems literature and should be expected to exhibit a direct effect on democratization. Political violence can be defined in any number of ways, but in this study it is defined as the sum of four different kinds of political incidents occurring between 1948 and 1965: armed attacks, deaths from domestic violence, assassinations, and riots (Taylor and Hudson, 1972). Following the procedure employed by Bollen and Jones (1982), these are summed, divided by four, and then converted to a scale ranging from 0 to 100, the high score representing the largest number of political incidents in the sample. The indicator is logged to correct skewness.

In the analysis to follow, all equations have been subjected to outlier analysis and tests for violations of OLS. Influential cases were identified using studentized residuals, hat matrix, and DFITS diagnostics (Bollen and Jackman, 1985c), and tests for heteroscedasticity included Spearman rank-order correlation and the Breusch–Pagan global test. Variance inflation factors and beta correlation were used to detect the presence of multicollinearity (Johnson, Johnson, and Buse, 1987). Although diagnostics pointed to several outlying cases, removing them did not change the substantive findings of this study (although slight modifications in coefficient strength, significance level, and explained variance did occur, as is normal when deviant cases are removed). In addition, no pervasive evidence of non-constant variance in error terms was found in these equations, but collinearity between the level of political democracy in 1965, labor force in industry in 1965, and secondary school enrollments in 1965 does complicate interpretation of results where noted.

Analysis

Zero-order correlations between most of the modeled variables are reported in tables 3.3 and 3.4. The most notable correlations are those shared by political democracy, labor force in industry, and secondary school enrollment ratios, all measured in 1965. Although only industrial labor force's correlation with secondary school enrollments is exceptionally high ($r = 0.84$ in table 3.3 and $r = 0.77$ in table 3.4), these results explain the confirmation of modernization effects on democracy in cross-sectional studies. Only the prior level of democracy shares a significant zero-order effect with *growth in democracy*, however, meaning that a significant ceiling effect exists; the higher the level of political democracy, the less room for improvement over time, and thus the negative correlation. Therefore, while the panel design adopted in this study will obscure this powerful (but artifactual) relationship, its existence dictates that other effects on democratization must be cleansed of their intercorrelation with the level of democracy if we are to arrive at reliable estimates of the influence of theoretically relevant variables. Panel regression accomplishes this.

Columns 1 through 5, based on all nations for which data exist, are reported in table 3.1. These samples (ranging from 78 to 71 cases) produce remarkably stable results. The influence of labor force in industry and secondary school enrolment ratios fit well with modernization theory; both exert a statistically significant positive effect on the growth of democratic rights between 1965 and 1980. Also, the number of military personnel per 1,000 population in 1965 is negatively associated with democratization, in keeping with a variety of theories. Apparently a high degree of military mobilization is somewhat incompatible with enhancing political and civil liberties, and the consistency of this finding in the face of statistical competition from modernization, technoecological, and dependency/world-systems/conflict variables suggests either unmodeled environmental determinants or, as likely, the institutional independence of militaries in many societies.

The effect of the log of rural density in 1960 on democratization demonstrates that technoecological theory gains real purchase on this research problem. The coefficients in question are consistently positive and statistically significant, regardless of specification or sample composition (cf. Midlarsky, this volume, for differing results based on cross-sectional analysis). Although the magnitudes of rural density's standardized coefficients are slightly smaller than the militarization control variable, and only half as large as either of the modernization coefficients, this pattern conforms perfectly to theoretical expectations. The aim is to demonstrate that a source of socioeconomic differentiation and interdependency exists apart from and side-by-side with industrialization, creating a socioeconomic environment that is conducive to democratization. To illustrate the point quite plainly, technoecological theory is an important adjunct to modernization theory because it helps explain

Table 3.1 *Panel regression of democratic rights (ca. 1965–80) regressed on selected variables (standardized coefficients are in parentheses)*

	Democratic rights, 1980				
	1	2	3	4	5
Intercept	49.62	47.58	52.86	58.40	47.03
Democratic rights, 1965	−0.04	−0.05	−0.03	−0.09	−0.05
	(−0.04)	(−0.05)	(−0.03)	(−0.09)	(−0.05)
Labor force in industry, 1965	0.67**	0.73**	0.70**	0.61**	0.74**
	(0.43)	(0.47)	(0.45)	(0.39)	(0.47)
Secondary school enrol., 1965	0.33**	0.28*	0.35**	0.35**	0.32*
	(0.39)	(0.33)	(0.41)	(0.41)	(0.37)
Armed forces per 1,000, 1965	−0.61**	−0.60**	−0.57**	−0.69**	−0.74**
	(−0.22)	(−0.22)	(−0.21)	(−0.24)	(−0.26)
Log rural density, 1960	2.85**	2.64**	2.79**	2.80**	3.18**
	(0.20)	(0.18)	(0.19)	(0.19)	(0.22)
Percentage family farms	–	0.08	–	–	–
		(0.08)			
Ethnic homogeneity	–	–	−0.07	–	–
			(−0.09)		
Gini sectoral inequality, 1970	–	–	–	−0.12	–
				(−0.09)	
Semiperiphery	–	–	–	–	1.30
					(.03)
Periphery	–	–	–	–	2.25
					(0.06)
N	78	77	78	74	71
R^2	0.55	0.55	0.56	0.54	0.54
R^2	0.52	0.51	0.52	0.50	0.49

Notes: **$p \leq 0.05$, two-tailed test.
*$p \leq 0.05$, one-tailed test.

why countries like India can be both *poor* and *democratic*, a paradox that has been used to criticize socioeconomic theories of democratization many times in the past.

Of note is the poor showing of inequality measures. None of these indicators is statistically significant, and only two have signs that are consistent with theory (family farm percentage and the Gini coefficient of sectorial inequality). Although it is possible that the influence of these measures of land, ethnic, and international stratification might be mediated by the base model, the theories that suggest these variables posit a wide range of influences on democratization, not all of which should be mediated by the variables at the top of the table. Moreover, if we do assume these results are the by-products of inappropriate modeling, what does this say about theories that stress inequality? One interpretation seems fairly clear: the distribution of resources has no influence on demo-cratization outside of its effects on socioeconomic complexities and inter-dependencies. While this analysis cannot provide certitude on this score, the consistent patterns in the data are quite suggestive.

The results produced through excluding core countries are reported in table 3.2. A similar pattern prevails, with a few important exceptions. First, these models exhibit lower R^2 statistics than did those in table 3.1, which can be attributed to a combination of factors. The most import-ant reasons for this are: (1) outlying cases, although not particularly influential, are concentrated in the non-core sample and erode explained variance; and (2) collinearity apparently becomes more problematic in the non-core sample (i.e., the correlations among the prior level of democracy, industrial labor force, and secondary school enrollments). The coefficients in column 6 are consistent with world-sample results, but in column 7 we see the lagged endogenous variable and the edu-cation variable assuming the variance previously explained by industrial labor force. Of note, however, is the very small sample size of this equa-tion ($N = 46$). In columns 8 through 10 industrial labor force verges on statistical significance (as signposted by the superscript), but in all but the last equation secondary school enrollments is clearly the stronger of the two predictors. This suggests that the purely economic aspects of modernization dynamics operate less strongly in non-core nations, and are in fact secondary to educational effects. Nonetheless, the stronger showing of the labor force variable in table 3.1, in addition to inconsist-encies illustrated by column 10, should lend a note of caution to any interpretation in this regard.

Dropping "core" nations from the analysis strengthens the density effect, as we might expect. If we restrict the sample to nations at rela-tively higher levels of agrarianism, we should expect any process of democratization to be even more dependent on preindustrial social complexity. Moreover, if Gastil's (1985) assertions about diffusion and democracy hold any validity whatsoever, we should see that technoecol-ogical differentiation and interdependency more frequently substitute for the complexities attendant on industrialism, urbanization, and mass literacy.

Table 3.2 *Panel regression of democratic rights (ca. 1965–80) regressed on selected variables/non-core nations only (standardized coefficients are in parentheses)*

	Democratic rights, 1980 (non-core nations only)				
	6	7	8	9	10
Intercept	45.79	47.23	46.98	48.17	45.07
Democratic rights, 1965	−0.06	−0.23	−0.08	−0.12	−0.09
	(−0.06)	(−0.22)	(−0.08)	(−0.11)	(−0.09)
Labor force in industry, 1965	0.60**	0.43	0.53^a	0.59	0.61*
	(0.32)	(0.23)	(0.26)	(0.27)	(0.29)
Secondary school enrol., 1965	0.46**	0.71**	0.47*	0.50**	0.38
	(0.44)	(0.66)	(0.35)	(0.44)	(0.27)
Armed forces per 1,000, 1965	−0.64**	−0.75*	−0.60**	−1.09**	−0.75**
	(−0.26)	(−0.23)	(−0.27)	(−0.33)	(−0.31)
Log rural density, 1960	4.12**	4.05**	4.25**	4.46**	4.73**
	(0.28)	(0.27)	(0.29)	(0.29)	(0.32)
Gini land inequality, 1970	–	13.18	–	–	–
		(0.13)			
Ethnol inguistic fractionation	–	–	−0.14	–	–
			(−0.01)		
Log foreign capital penetration, 1967	–	–	–	−0.66	–
				(−0.03)	
Log political instability, 1947–65	–	–	–	–	1.37
					(0.09)
N	65	46	60	56	58
R^2	0.45	0.49	0.33	0.42	0.37
R^2	0.40	0.41	0.26	0.35	0.29

Notes: **$p \leq 0.05$, two-tailed test.
*$p \leq 0.05$, one-tailed test.
$^a p \leq 0.15$, two-tailed test.

Once again, typical stratification/inequality effects fail to gain purchase on the problem; all fail their t-tests. The sign of the Gini coefficient for land ownership concentration is consistent only with Midlarsky's (1992a) account of how land distribution translates into class

Table 3.3 *Zero-order correlations between selected variables used in equations 1 through 5 (sample sizes vary from N = 73 to N = 78)*

	1	2	3	4	5	6	7	8	9
1 Growth of democracy, 1965–80	1.00								
2 Democratic rights, 1965	−0.59*	1.00							
3 Percent labor force ind., 1965	0.06	0.55*	1.00						
4 Log rural density, 1960	0.18	−0.06	−0.08	1.00					
5 Secondary school enrol., 1965	−0.03	0.64*	0.84*	−0.00	1.00				
6 Armed forces per 1,000, 1965	−0.08	0.13	0.27*	0.13	0.29*	1.00			
7 Percentage family farms	−0.09	0.38*	0.24*	0.20	0.48*	0.09	1.00		
8 Ethnic homogeneity	−0.07	0.38*	0.51*	−0.05	0.52*	0.30*	0.13	1.00	
9 Gini sectorial ineq., 1970	0.01	−0.54*	−0.74*	−0.15	−0.65*	−0.22	−0.22	−0.47*	1.00

Note: *$p \leq 0.05$.

politics. Although ethnolinguistic fractionation and the log of foreign capital penetration are appropriately signed, their direct influence on growth in civil and politic rights is minuscule. The log of political violence between 1948 and 1965 displays surprisingly little direct influence, although it has contributed to the replacement of education by industrial labor force as the more powerful modernization indicator in equation 10. One could interpret this as educational attainment leading to rebellion and unrest, except that such an account would reverse the temporal ordering of these variables (political violence *ends* in 1965). Moreover, neither zero-order correlation nor beta correlation suggest any great relationship between these two indicators.

Discussion

It would be premature to dismiss relative equality as a necessary condition for the emergence of political democracy. This analysis suggests only that the influence of social inequalities may have been overemphasized in past theorizing and empirical research on democratization. Although it would be easy to blame Marxist influences on the social sciences as the reason behind this strong focus on stratification and class

Table 3.4 *Zero-order correlations between variables used in equations 6 through 10 (sample sizes vary from a low of N = 40 to a high of N = 65)*

	1	2	3	4	5	6	7	8	9	10
1 Growth of democracy, 1965–80	1.00									
2 Democratic rights, 1965	−0.65*	1.00								
3 Percent labor force ind., 1965	0.15	0.33*	1.00							
4 Log rural density, 1960	0.22	−0.10	−0.16	1.00						
5 Secondary school enrol. 1965	0.03	0.50*	0.77*	−0.09	1.00					
6 Armed forces per 1,000 1965	−0.07	0.10	0.27*	0.11	0.30*	1.00				
7 Gini land inequality, 1970	0.18	−0.01	0.28	−0.20	0.03	0.01	1.00			
8 Ethno-ling fractionation	0.03	−0.24	−0.34*	0.04	−0.42*	−0.30*	−0.52*	1.00		
9 Log foreign cap. pen., 1967	−0.13	−0.01	−0.21	−0.24	−0.35*	−0.39*	0.28	0.10	1.00	
10 Log political instab. 47–65	0.06	0.05	0.13	−0.02	0.08	0.06	0.10	0.06	−0.07	1.00

Note: $*p \leq 0.05$.

analysis, in reality viewing social equality as the *raison d'etre* of representative government goes back to the classical Greeks, and the strong *individualism* of Western civilization makes us value independence over interdependence, which of course skews our view of things. Regardless of its source, however, this heavy reliance on egalitarianism as a necessary condition for the emergence of political democracy requires much more scrutiny. It is possible that the distribution of scarce resources in part determines a society's level of complex economic, political, and social interactions, and these interdependencies are either the proximate causes of democratization or, alternatively, constitute forces that condition the extent of political competition and its outcomes. Another way of saying this is that the greater the interdependencies, the more useful people and groups become to one another, resulting in more cooperation and exchange as opposed to competition and conflict.

Of course, just because the results of these analyses are consistent with certain theories in no way proves those theories, and much depends on how we interpret the rural density variable. It is, after all, only a crude proxy for preindustrial (or non-industrial) social complexity. The case of India has been mentioned as an example of the utility of the technoecological perspective, but ironically it also serves as a prime example of the problem of epistemic correlation. Although India is a densely settled, old agrarian nation, there are structures within its agrarian social organization that militate against complex interdependencies. As Baechler (1988, pp. 54–5) states:

Within the framework of the village there is no market at all [in India], but a clearinghouse – moreover, an unsymmetrical one because economically it works to the advantage of the dominant *jati*, the owners of the land, but not those who work it – for the offer and exchange of goods and services. Between villages exchange is virtually non-existent because the jajmani system ensures the economic autarchy of each one of them. Finally, between villages and towns, the flow is one-way: the towns consume the products of the taxes levied on the villages by the political authority.

Of course, to the extent that this is a true depiction of rural socioeconomic organization of Indian society, it will impoverish (but not eliminate) the complex interdependencies thought to result from population density. This exemplifies the problems associated with proxy variables: No matter how well they seem to fit the need, intricacies of the concept always exist that cannot be captured by proxy and, of course, the epistemic correlation between theory and measurement suffers as a result. Still, it is logical to assume that rural densities reflect some very fundamental dimensions of rural social organization, and these results suggest that the epistemic correlation between the theory and measurement is relatively high, at least by the standards of current cross-national research.

Future research should investigate the relationships between complex interdependency and economic growth, military repression and political unrest. Technoecological theory would lead us to expect that democratic instability should be lower in densely settled societies, primarily because complex interdependencies are more stable over time and should lower the ability and the desire of elites to engage in political repression of different kinds.

Furthermore, another fascinating way to interpret the results reported above is through the lens of diffusion theory. Perhaps democracy was a unique product of the religious sensibilities and political fragmentation of the West. If this is true and democracy is simply something imported from Europe and North America, is contact with (and pressure from) the West conditioned by technoecology, such that Western influences have much greater multipliers in technoecologically advantaged environments (e.g., Japan, Korea, Taiwan, India)? Even more interesting is the notion that global modernization is simply a pattern of Western diffusion, the success of which varies according to the level of *proto-modernity*. Are poor but technoecologically advantaged societies "flies caught in amber" that require external social forces before they can realize their potential? Although this shift in perspective might not change the tenor of empirical research, it might go far in explaining paradoxes in the data.

While these questions can be partially answered by cross-national research, comparative-historians should be sensitive to the *generalizability* of technoecological propositions. Too often in recent years, social scientists have been split into two camps, one consisting of those who believe in fundamental social forces that structure all human societies and therefore can be abstracted, and those who reject such abstractions and instead view social interaction and structure as products of initial conditions and subsequent (specific) historical events. Technoecological theory offers a common ground, however, suggesting ways to capture small differences in initial conditions without losing the explanatory power or elegance of cross-national, quantitative research. It is to be hoped that the essential compatibility between historical context and abstract social forces will be more readily recognized in the future.

Appendix A Sample composition

List of countries used in various equations reported in table 3.1 (N = 78):
Canada, United Kingdom, Netherlands, Belgium, France, Austria, Italy, Yugoslavia, Sweden, Norway, Denmark, Australia, Japan, Haiti, Dominican Republic, Mexico, Guatemala, Honduras, El Salvador, Nicaragua, Costa Rica, Panama, Colombia, Venezuela, Ecuador, Peru, Brazil, Bolivia, Paraguay, Chile, Argentina, Ireland, Luxembourg, Spain, Portugal, Greece, Cyprus, Finland, Iceland, Senegal, Benin, Mauritania, Niger, Liberia, Ghana, Togo, Cameroon, Nigeria, Gabon, Central African Republic, Chad, Congo, Zaire, Somalia, Ethiopia, South Africa, Madagascar, Morocco, Tunisia, Libya, Sudan, Iran, Turkey, Iraq, Egypt, Syria, Lebanon, Jordan, Israel, Afghanistan, India, Pakistan, Sri Lanka, Nepal, Thailand, Laos, Philippines, New Zealand.
List of countries used in various equations reported in table 3.2 (N = 65):
Haiti, Dominican Republic, Mexico, Guatemala, Honduras, El Salvador, Nicaragua, Costa Rica, Panama, Colombia, Venezuela, Ecuador, Peru, Brazil, Bolivia, Paraguay, Chile, Argentina, Ireland, Luxemburg, Spain, Portugal, Greece, Cyprus, Finland, Iceland, Senegal, Benin, Mauritania, Niger, Liberia, Ghana, Togo, Cameroon, Nigeria, Gabon, Central African Republic, Chad, Congo, Zaire, Somalia, Ethiopia,

South Africa, Madagascar, Morocco, Tunisia, Libya, Sudan, Iran, Turkey, Iraq, Egypt, Syria, Lebanon, Jordan, Israel, Afghanistan, India, Pakistan, Sri Lanka, Nepal, Thailand, Laos, Philippines, New Zealand.

NOTES

1 My analysis began with the assumption that the structure of inequality is a crucial determinant of democratization. Specifically, I expected the influence of agricultural density to be mediated by income inequality, in keeping with past research linking density with income distribution (Crenshaw 1992). Unfortunately, adding measures of income inequality to the base equation reported below generates more questions than answers for the following reasons. First, use of the Muller (1988) data on income distribution (as augmented by Simpson (1990)) restricts the sample to 45 cases (even fewer for the Hoover (1989) data on income distribution), and statistically significant differences exist between this group ($N = 45$) and the excluded group ($N = 33$) in terms of level of democracy, labor force in industry, and secondary school enrollment ratios. I attribute this to the relative overrepresentation of developed nations and Latin American nations in the included sample. Second, the equations are plagued by influential cases. Argentina, Chile, Bolivia, and El Salvador (cases of democratic set-back) have to be dropped to find a statistically significant effect of income inequality on democratization, and only the Muller–Simpson formulation of the top 20 percent share exerts a robust influence. Third, with or without entering income inequality into the equation, the log of rural density performs poorly in these small samples. Given the robustness of density in the larger samples reported below, however, I suspect this is attributable to the sample's size and biased composition. The secondary school enrollment ratio is also washed out, although labor force in industry is strengthened, with a magnitude not quite twice that of income inequality. These considerations led me to shift the focus of the research to other dimensions of inequality that have been more widely reported. Although it is hard to reconcile these findings with those of Muller (this volume), using Bollen's formulation of PDI for 1965 and 1980 (Crenshaw, 1995) leads me to suspect that the disparity between this study and Muller's have more to do with specification than with sample composition or formulation of the dependent variable.

4   Inequality and democracy in the anthropological record

Melvin Ember, Carol R. Ember, and Bruce Russett

How are inequality and democracy related? More equality could be a cause of more democracy. Or more democracy could be a cause of more equality. Or both might be joint consequences of something else. Exactly how social inequality is related to political democracy has long been a focus of speculation and research by social scientists in general and political scientists in particular. This chapter is an attempt to look at the anthropological evidence on the matter. To do so, we have to transform the concept of democracy to fit the ethnographic (cross-cultural) record. For example, hardly any societies in that record have contested elections. So, as we describe below, we measure democracy mainly in terms of degree of political participation. We describe how inequality and political participation are distributed cross-culturally, and how they seem to be related cross-culturally.

In the cross-national literature, economic equality, political participation (democracy), and economic development are, with some complexities, positively related. For example, cross-nationally it has long been known (Russett *et al.*, 1964) that both land and income equality are positively related to per-capita income. Furthermore, the cross-national literature agrees that, with some exceptions, political participation is generally greater at higher levels of economic development. It is not entirely clear what the causal relationship is, and the relation between democracy and economic growth over time in the latter half of the twentieth century is problematic. Nonetheless, the correlation holds up throughout a variety of multivariate cross-sectional analyses of nation-states (Helliwell, 1994; Lipset, Seong, and Torres, 1993; Przeworski and Limongi, 1993; Diamond, 1992). Finally, and independent of levels of economic development, economic equality seems related to political participation. For example, a recent complex model suggests that great inequality produces greater state repression as measured by low scores on a political and civil rights index, and higher frequencies of state-enacted sanctions and political deaths (Moaddel, 1994).

The cross-cultural relationship between economic development and both equality and political participation, however, is different. In the ethnographic record – which does not include many industrialized societies – equality decreases with economic development. That should not be too surprising once one remembers that the apparent cross-national linear relationship between development and equality really masks a U-shaped curve whereby equality generally decreases in the early stages of economic growth, but then rises to relatively high levels as the economy reaches a fairly advanced stage of industrialization (reviewed by Lipset, 1994). But since most societies in the ethnographic record are predominantly agricultural, an economically "advanced" society in that record is likely to be characterized by features such as plowing, fertilizers, and irrigation, which make permanent cultivation of fields and permanent communities possible. Such intensive agricultural activity is more conducive to concentrated wealth than is hunter-gatherer subsistence or shifting cultivation (commonly referred to as "horticulture" or "slash-and-burn" agriculture). Hence in the ethnographic record we may be seeing something akin to the decrease in equality that we see over the first part of the U-shaped curve in the cross-national record.

Similarly, among non-industrial societies the cross-sectional relationship between development and participation is negative, as we shall see. Very likely, the same political and social structures associated with intensive (but not industrialized) agriculture strengthen political hierarchy. In terms of conventional measures of economic development, most of these societies are relatively poor as compared with most modern nation-states. So, as with the relationship between development and equality, a U-shaped pattern over the entire range of human societies is plausible (perhaps flattening out at very high levels of economic development, as Muller indicates in his chapter).

The cross-national and cross-cultural (ethnographic) records differ then in how equality and participation relate to economic development; equality and participation are positively related to development in the former (mostly), but negatively related to development in the latter. Given this difference, the relationship between inequality and participation in the societies known to anthropology requires greater scrutiny. Before turning to that analysis, however, we must devote some attention to the ways in which cross-cultural research differs from cross-national research.

Cross-cultural versus cross-national research

Worldwide cross-cultural comparison has two major advantages, compared with other types of statistical comparative research (Ember,

1991). The major one is that the conclusions drawn from a worldwide comparison are probably applicable to most societies, assuming that the sample is more or less free of bias. (For a discussion of sampling in cross-cultural research, see Ember and Otterbein, 1991; see also Ember and Ember, 1993.) In other words, in contrast to the results of a within-region comparison, which may or may not be applicable to other regions, and in contrast to the results of a cross-national comparison, which may or may not be applicable to preindustrial societies, the results of a worldwide cross-cultural comparison are probably applicable to most if not all regions and most if not all types of societies. Thus, other things being equal, the worldwide type of cross-cultural comparison has a better chance than other types of comparison of coming close to the goal of knowing that an observed relationship has nearly universal validity, which is consistent with the general scientific goal of more and more comprehensive explanations.

In addition to the advantage of greater generalizability, the worldwide cross-cultural comparison offers maximum variation in the variables to be investigated. If a researcher uses data from a single society, a single region, or even from the recent historical record for nation-states, there may be relatively little variation to study. Moreover, even if there is some variation, it may be at just one end of the spectrum of variation, so that it is possible for a relationship to be positive (or negative) in one region or cross-nationally and yet be curvilinear in a worldwide cross-cultural sample (Whiting, 1954, pp. 524–5). This is the situation we have with inequality and democracy when either is plotted against degree of economic development in the ethnographic record.

The need for cross-cultural comparison is even stronger if in a cross-national comparison the variation is located in the middle of the spectrum of worldwide cross-cultural variation. We may not notice how that middle range of variation is related to something else. That is, the amount of middle-range variation might not be great enough to show how the variable of concern is correlated with other variables cross-culturally. Thus, we may require cross-cultural research just because it is more broadly comparative than cross-national research. The latter compares only relatively complex societies. The cross-cultural study compares all types of society, from hunter-gatherers with bands of fewer than 75 people and total populations in the hundreds, to large industrial societies dependent on intensive agriculture with cities and populations in the millions. To be sure, as already noted, the typical cross-cultural sample contains few or no modern industrial societies, so even cross-cultural research is typically not as broadly comparative as it could be.

But the focus on societies that are not nation-states has the advantage of providing a check on research using cross-national samples.

The greater variability of the ethnographic record, as compared with the recent historical record, is highly relevant to our particular concern in this chapter. All nation-states have what anthropologists call "class stratification." While countries may vary with regard to degree of inequality, none of them approach the degree of social *equality* that characterizes societies labeled "egalitarian" by anthropologists, where families and other kin groups have more or less equal access to resources and power. If it is hypothesized that more democracy is associated with more equality, whatever the causality of the relationship, it is necessary to look at egalitarian as well as stratified societies. The relationship might obtain only in some types of societies, not across the entire range of recorded cultural variation. Or the relationship might differ in form in different segments of that range.

Cross-cultural research typically uses data – the information in ethnographic texts[1] – that are qualitative to begin with, which means that variables can only be measured ordinally, at best. But this does not preclude sophisticated statistical tests or powerful results. If coding rules are explicitly designed to fit ethnographic descriptions, and data quality controls are used to reduce the likelihood of error, there is no reason to expect more error in cross-cultural measures than in cross-national ones that use numerical survey data (Ember *et al.*, 1991). Moreover, since ethnographers typically live for an extended period of time in the communities they study, ethnographic documents may be superior sources of information about aspects of life that people are unwilling to reveal to strangers and therefore are unlikely to be tapped by surveys. Nevertheless, unlike some possibilities opened up with cross-national data, systematic empirical work with the ethnographic record must usually be cross-sectional. The ethnographic record is rarely detailed enough yet on process or change over time to talk about sequences. (This situation will change as accounts of modern cultures continue to be added to the ethnographic record.)

Finally, the two types of comparative research (cross-cultural and cross-national) differ of course in their typical units of analysis. The type of unit compared usually in a cross-cultural study is the society, a population that more or less contiguously inhabits a particular area and speaks a language not normally understood by people in neighboring societies. Cross-national research typically compares countries or nation-states, each of which is politically unified at least in some formal respects; for example, there is a monarch or president or some other central authority. Thus, in the modern world there are many nations that contain more than one society in the anthropological sense. Nigeria contains scores of societies (e.g., Hausa, Yoruba, Ibo); the former Yugoslavia and Soviet Union also contained many societies, as did all empires in world history.

The cross-cultural distribution of inequality

The sample we refer to here consists of 186 mostly preindustrial societies which are said to represent the culture areas of the world (Murdock and White, 1980). Since most of the societies that anthropologists study had non-commercial or only incipiently commercial economies when they were first described, it is not possible to use measures of inequality that reflect the distribution of monetary income. So, in measuring inequality, we focus on the conventional anthropological classification of social stratification, the presence of some groups with unequal access to resources and wealth. Land is the major resource in most societies known to anthropology, so a highly stratified society probably always has land inequality. Inequality of income is also reflected in our measure.

We use here the scale scores on social stratification devised by Murdock and Provost (1980). They rate societies according to a five-point ordinal scale. The most egalitarian are societies that lack social classes, castes, hereditary slavery, and important wealth distinctions; some 35 percent of our sample cases fall into this category. Examples include: the !Kung Bushmen and Mbuti Pygmies of Africa (as of the 1950s); the Zuni and Copper Eskimo of North America (as of the late nineteenth and early twentieth centuries, respectively); and the Yanomamö of South America in the 1960s. Somewhat more stratified (28 percent of the cases) are societies that lack class distinctions among freemen, but there is hereditary slavery and/or important status differences based on wealth. Examples are the Kikuyu of Kenya as of 1920, the Rwala Bedouin (as of 1913) in what is now Lebanon and Syria, the Manus of the South Pacific in 1929, and the Huron as of 1634. Then there are 10 percent of the cases with two classes of freemen, e.g., nobles and commoners, but no castes or slaves; these cases include the Ashanti of West Africa in 1895, Malinowski's Trobrianders in 1914, and the Samoans in 1829. More stratified are 11 percent of the cases, with two classes of freeman plus hereditary slavery and/or castes; these cases include the Ganda of Central Africa in 1875, the Khalkha Mongols in 1920, and the Natchez in the Lower Mississippi Valley in 1718. Finally, the most stratified cases (16 percent of the sample) have three or more classes or castes. Our sample cases in this highest category of stratification include the Hausa of 1900 (in what is now northern Nigeria), the ancient Egyptians and Hebrews, the Russians in 1955, the North Vietnamese in 1930, and the Aztecs in 1520. For further information on our sample cases, see Murdock and White (1980).

The cross-cultural distribution of democracy

In order to examine "democracy" in the anthropological record, we need to rephrase the concept to fit that record. For example, very few societies known to anthropology have the equivalent of formal, contested elections with secret balloting; and the band or village is the largest political unit in about half of the societies in the ethnographic record. To measure "democracy," then, we focus mostly on local political participation, as we did in a previous study (Ember, Ember, and Russett, 1992). We largely use the framework and coding scales developed by the political scientist Marc Ross (1983). (We use his codes for half the sample societies; we ourselves coded the other half for our previous project – see the appendix here for the coding rules, and see Ember, Russett, and Ember [1993] for our procedures and the coded data.) With Dahl (1971) we identify modern democracy with a responsible executive, wide voting francise, contested elections, and protection of civil liberties. Ross's definitions are appropriate to conditions in non-industrial societies where formal elections rarely occur and full-time political officials are usually non-existent. The variables we use from Ross include: checks on leaders' power (approximating the modern separation of powers); ease of removing leaders from power (approximating elections); extensiveness of participation (approximating extent of the franchise); and lack of fission of the community following a political dispute (approximating civil rights and the tolerance of dissent).

There is often a good deal of political participation in our sample societies, which are located mostly toward the lower end of the scale of social and political complexity. (Ross's (1981) results indicate that concentration of political power, i.e., little political participation, generally increases with political complexity in our sample societies.) In about 59 percent of the sample, leaders can be removed (or ignored) by ordinary members of the community (scale scores 3–4 on Ross's variable 7); and in about 53 percent of the sample, involvement in community decision making is high (scale scores 1 and 2 on Ross's variable 11).

Democracy and equality

How do our measures of "democracy" relate to degree of social stratification (our measure of inequality)? By and large, and consistent with most of the cross-national findings, the more political participation there is, the less the inequality. For most of the variables, the relationship is roughly linear. Checks on leaders' power generally decline with social stratification (Spearman's rho = -0.45, $p < 0.001$, two tails; $N = 108$), as do peaceful ways of removing leaders (rho = -0.53, $p < 0.001$, two tails; $N = 98$), leaders' need to consult (rho = -0.48, $p < 0.001$, two tails; $N = 110$), broad-based councils (rho = -0.37, $p < 0.001$, two tails; $N = 109$), and widespread political participation (rho = 0.30, $p < 0.01$, two tails; $N = 104$; high values on the scale indicate low participation). The only political variable that shows a reverse trend is the presence of community fission following a dispute (rho = 0.26, $p < 0.05$, two tails; $N = 78$). However, this reversal is not unexpected. The likelihood of community fission, which we interpret as the absence of "agreeing to disagree" (see Ember, Ember, and Russett, 1992), generally decreases with inequality. That is, the more inequality, the *less* community fission. But inequality increases with intensivity of agriculture and settled populations, and so it is likely that community fission becomes less likely in more complex preindustrial societies because it may be disadvantageous to leave investments in land, animals, and structures. Alternatively, fission may be less likely in more complex societies because those individuals (slaves, serfs) who are themselves the investments may not be free to leave. Slave-owners and lords with serfs do not look kindly on laborers who flee; neither do governments look kindly on possible soldiers and taxpayers who flee.

Although inequality is associated with less political participation in the ethnographic record, just as in the cross-national record, political participation is not related to economic development cross-culturally as it is cross-nationally. Using the amount and intensity of agriculture as a measure of degree of economic development, we can see how political participation is related to economic development cross-culturally. Societies dependent on hunting and gathering or fishing cannot support many people in one place. Simple agriculturalists have bigger communities but not much surplus. Intensive agriculturalists usually produce surpluses, have substantial investments in land, structures, and equipment, and can support towns and cities. In other words, at the highest end of the economic development scale in the ethnographic record (scale 3 in Murdock and Provost, 1980) are societies that depend mostly on intensive agriculture (with irrigation, plowing, fertilizers); at the lowest end are societies that have no agriculture at all. With the exception of community fission following disputes, which decreases with economic development, all the political participation variables significantly decline with economic development. This fits with the expectation that the relationship between economic development and democracy (viewed as political participation) is roughly U-shaped across the entire spectrum of human societies, assuming that we could measure all societies in the same ways. As noted in our introduction, modern nation-states, particularly the more industrialized ones, are relatively high on political participation, just like the simpler societies in the ethnographic record.

Density, intensive agriculture, or political hierarchy?

In the ethnographic record, as well as in the archaeological record, many traits indicative of social complexity are correlated. These include a hierarchy of political units (smaller units such as villages and then districts nested into larger units), greater population density, and more intensive agriculture, among others. Therefore, it behooves us to ask whether political participation and inequality are causally related (in either direction) or whether a correlation between them is an artifact of some other causal relationship.

In addition to inequality as social stratification, we looked at three of these conceptually related and somewhat correlated variables reflecting social complexity. The codes are from Murdock and Provost (1980); our appendix describes these codes in detail. The first variable is represented by Murdock and Provost's (1980) ordinal scale 3, measuring amount and intensity of agriculture. The second is a straightforward ordinal measure of population density relative to land area. The third is an ordinal measure of political hierarchy above the local level (band, village) in the society. The highest score (4) on this scale is given to a case with three or more administrative levels above that of the local community, as where there is a large state organized into provinces which are subdivided into districts. A case with two administrative levels above the local community, as in a small state divided into districts, gets a scale score of 3. One administrative level above the community gets a scale score of 2. A society with politically autonomous local communities gets a scale score of 1. And a society where political authority is not centralized even on the local level gets a scale score of 0.

The four variables of amount and intensity of agriculture, population density, hierarchy of political units, and social stratification/inequality are all moderately correlated, but there is no problem of multicollinearity according to the Systat tests. The rank-order correlations (Spearman's) range from 0.460 to 0.688.

We computed multiple regressions of the effect of each of these independent variables on each of the measures of political participation. Table 4.1 shows that the results are somewhat different for each depen-

Table 4.1 Multiple regression analyses predicting local political participation variables (standardized coefficients shown)

	1 Checks on leaders' power (var. 6)	2 Removal of leaders (var. 7)	3 Need for consultation (var. 8)	4 Broad-based councils (var. 9)	5 Extent of particip. (var. 11)	6 Community fissions after dispute (var. 30)
Constant	0.000	0.000	0.000	0.000	0.000	0.000
Degree and inten. of agric.	−0.083	−0.065	−0.079	−0.111	0.159	0.095
Density of population	−0.091	−0.177	−0.191	−0.111	−0.146	0.113
Hierarchy of political units	−0.245*	−0.192	−0.205*	−0.148	0.268*	−0.058
Social stratification	−0.147	−0.206	−0.205*	−0.127	0.115	0.187
N	108	98	110	109	104	78
R^2	0.237	0.297	0.330	0.172	0.136	0.080
p value	0.000	0.000	0.000	0.000	0.004	0.122

Note: $*p < 0.05$, one tail.

dent variable, suggesting that different aspects of complexity have varying effects on participation. Only four of the shown relationships are
significant. A low degree of political hierarchy provides the only significant predictor of checks on leaders' power (column 1). In columns 2
and 3 (removal of leaders and need for consultation), political hierarchy
and social stratification (our measure of inequality) have about the same
predictive power, though they are significant predictors only of the need
for consultation. Hierarchy is also significant as predicted for reducing
the extent of participation. Social stratification shows up as significant
only with regard to consultation. In columns 4–6, the only significant
relationship is between political hierarchy and less-extensive participation. Amount and intensity of agriculture (our measure of economic
development) is not significantly related to any measure of participation
in these multivariate equations.

What about Midlarsky's (1992a) suggestion, extrapolating from
classical Athens, that inequality in land may be a predictor of more
democracy in agrarian societies? To test this suggestion cross-culturally,
we redid the multiple regression analyses described immediately above,
restricting the sample to societies that depended largely on agriculture
(scores of 3 and 4 on Murdock and Provost's (1980) scale 3), thus
eliminating amount and intensity of agriculture as a separate independent variable. The results are shown in table 4.2. (As noted above, the
presence of social stratification indicates the presence of land inequality
as well as other inequalities.) Social stratification appears to be the most
important of the indicators of social complexity we looked at, in predicting political participation. Indeed, it is the *only* significant predictor – in four of the six columns. But the relationships are generally
opposite to what Midlarsky suggests. Political participation generally
declines with increasing social stratification; the trend is significant for
checks on leaders' power (see column 1 of table 4.2), peaceful removal
of leaders (see column 2), and leaders' need for consultation (see
column 3). As before, and probably for the same reasons discussed
before, the only variable to show a significant reverse trend is fission
following a dispute; fission is less likely with more social stratification
(see column 6).

Female participation

The highest score on Ross's (1981) measure of extensiveness of political
participation is given to societies where women as well as men participate in political decision making. The next highest score is given to
societies where there is substantial political involvement for certain

Table 4.2 *Multiple regression analyses predicting local political participation variables in societies mostly dependent on agriculture (standardized coefficients shown)*

	1 Checks on leaders' power (var. 6)	2 Removal of leaders (var. 7)	3 Need for consultation (var. 8)	4 Broad-based councils (var. 9)	5 Extent of particip. (var. 11)	6 Community fissions after dispute (var. 30)
Constant	0.000	0.000	0.000	0.000	0.000	0.000
Degree of population	−0.118	−0.224	−0.160	−0.023	−0.178	0.119
Hierarchy of political units	−0.099	−0.039	−0.066	−0.187	0.231	−0.304
Social stratification	−0.318*	−0.339*	−0.414**	−0.096	0.150	0.399*
N	64	54	64	64	64	43
R^2	0.205	0.263	0.298	0.062	0.094	0.064
p value	0.003	0.001	0.000	0.274	0.113	0.235

Notes: * $p < 0.05$, one tail.
** $p < 0.01$, one tail.

groups, but others (e.g., women) are excluded from political life. What predicts female participation? Ross (1986) found that women are included in political life where society emphasizes "female" values in socialization (particularly warmth and affection). He also found that conflict (including war) with other societies decreases female participation but conflict within the society increases it. He was puzzled why different kinds of conflict appear to have different effects.

We looked at female participation in our data, but differently. When Ross analyzed female participation, he included cases where participation was low for both men and women. But we did not want to equate exclusion of women with low participation where both men and women are excluded. Therefore, we decided to look just at the cases with the two highest scale scores on extensiveness of participation (widespread participation including women versus widespread participation excluding certain groups such as women). Below these levels, participation for most individuals (men as well as women) is low. First, we calculated logistic equations (logit) with the dichotomized dependent variable, trying to predict female participation from our four measures of social complexity: amount and intensity of agriculture, population density, hierarchy of political units, and social stratification (inequality), adding also measures of overall war frequency and of warmth/affection. To evaluate the possible effect of war on female participation, we must exclude pacified cases (those forced by external powers to stop fighting). The participation of women in those cases might still be low because of the prior warfare. For overall frequency of war, we use the data provided in Ember and Ember (1992b). For warmth/affection, we use the Barry et al. (1980) measure of socialization for trust, "confidence in social relationships, especially toward community members outside the family, e.g., children are welcome in any home in the village, possessions are left unguarded." This measure of socialization for trust proved to be the most satisfactory indicator of warmth/affection, or high need satisfaction, in a previous study (Ember and Ember, 1992a).

As shown in table 4.3, the logit analysis is statistically significant ($p < 0.02$). Overall war frequency by itself significantly predicts less female participation in the direction we expected ($p < 0.05$, one tail), as does amount and intensity of agriculture ($p < 0.05$, two tails). Table 4.3 also shows the means for each of our independent variables, comparing societies where women are widely included versus societies where participation is fairly widespread but certain categories of people, including women, are excluded. Socialization for trust is not significant by itself, but it tends to predict in the same direction found by Ross (more female participation, more trust). Other measures of complexity

Table 4.3 *Predicting female local political participation by logistic regression in non-pacified societies*

	Fairly wide political participation (score 2 on variable 11)	Women included in widespread political participation (score 1 on variable 11)	(*t*-statistic)
Constant	1.000	1.000	−0.224
Mean on agriculture	3.321	2.100	2.098**
Mean on density	2.571	2.000	−1.680
Mean on political hierarchy	2.643	2.200	−0.984
Mean on social stratification	2.036	1.500	1.388
Mean overall war frequency (5 = constant; 1 = absent or rare)	3.304	2.113	2.014*
Mean socialization for trust (0–9 scale; 9 = highest socialization for trust)	5.214	6.500	−1.386
N	28	10	38

−2 times log likelihood ratio (chi-squared), 6 *df* = 16.238; *p* < 0.02

Notes: **p* < 0.05, one tail.
****p* < 0.05, two tails.

predict less female participation, but these results are not significant in the logit analysis. However, it should be noted that, in bivariate Mann–Whitney *U*-tests (not shown) where the *N*s are larger, two other variables are significant predictors of female participation. These other two predictors are political hierarchy (inversely) and socialization for trust (positively). That is, in the Mann–Whitney *U*-tests, societies with high female participation are significantly lower on political hierarchy and significantly higher on socialization for trust.

We are not surprised at the results regarding certain variables of complexity (particularly intensity of agriculture) predicting low female participation. Variables of cultural complexity generally predict lower status for women cross-culturally across many domains (e.g., religion, domestic authority) in the sample of societies used here (Whyte, 1978). But it is not clear why. We do know that women in intensive agricultural societies, as opposed to horticultural societies, have much more work in and around the home, probably because of the larger number of children they have and because more food-processing work is required, e.g., grinding grain to make cereal crops edible (C. R. Ember, 1983). Given that preindustrial intensive agricultural women are almost constantly working, and most of their work occurs in and around the home, they may have little opportunity to do things outside the home that would allow them to acquire the kinds of information about the larger world which may be required for high participation in political life (C. R. Ember, 1983, p. 300).

Not only does more war overall predict less female participation; similar logit results (not shown) are obtained if we look at the separate frequencies of internal (within the society/language group) and external war – both types of war predict less female participation (but not significantly).[2] Of course, the causality might be in the opposite direction: more women in politics may make for less war. After all, cross-cultural research strongly indicates that young girls are less aggressive than young boys (Ember, 1981), and males are responsible for most of the lethal violence cross-culturally (Daly and Wilson, 1988, pp. 146–8).

Since military decisions probably constitute a large part of political life in most societies, and men are usually the warriors (Adams, 1983), it is perhaps not surprising that women are more likely to be excluded from decision making in more warlike societies. In many societies known to anthropology, war occurs internally or within the society, often close to home and often between communities whose members marry each other. In these circumstances, women are not allowed to handle weapons or go near discussions of war (Adams, 1983). Close-to-home internal war is relatively rare in most contemporary nation-states (particularly the more economically developed ones). So might the absence of such war help explain the relatively high political participation of women in such societies, at least with respect to voting? And might the proportion of women in parliaments be higher in countries experiencing less internal and external war?

In other words, is more democracy (in the sense of more female political participation) causally related to less war? We suspect that it is, but more research (cross-cultural and cross-national) is required. And might more equal economic opportunities for women and other disadvantaged groups (and more achievements by them) produce more democracy (more political participation)? Or is it the reverse? Does more democracy provide the means whereby disadvantaged groups can become more equally advantaged? With recent social and cultural change in many societies, we may soon be able to tell whether more equality makes for more democracy, or the reverse.

Summary and conclusions

In this chapter we have examined the relationship between inequality and democracy (viewed mainly as political participation) in the ethnographic or anthropological record. We find that equality (as measured by less social stratification) does strengthen many aspects of "democracy," just as it does in most of the cross-national record. Although inequality is moderately related to measures of participation in bivariate tests, it is not generally strong in multivariate analyses that also include other aspects of societal complexity as possible predictors of less participation. Inequality does show up as strongly related to reduced participation in the more "developed" societies of the ethnographic record (those mainly dependent on agriculture, but not industrialized). Thus, democracy is especially unlikely in these "developed" societies, which also tend to have dense populations, a hierarchy of political units, and considerable inequality as measured by social stratification. In these agricultural societies, the ruling elites can employ relatively developed technology and political instruments of control, and thereby appropriate greater shares of land and production. Where the population is dense and agriculture is intensive, ordinary laborers have no place to go. They have little alternative source of livelihood. The elites' position at the top of the social and economic hierarchies gives them the resources to suppress political participation by those below – which in turn enables the elites to extract more surplus. In societies sharply divided between rich and poor and developed enough to provide a surplus, the rich control politics as well as the economy (Russett, 1964). Economic and political concentration very likely reinforce each other, with neither having clear "causal" priority.

While social stratification does not account for degree of female participation in political life, some other aspects of complexity – preeminently intensive agriculture – appear to work against female participation. (Female participation is greatest in societies with the highest general level of political participation, in the ethnographic as well as cross-national records.) The frequency of war, which is hardly related to social complexity in the ethnographic record (Ember and Ember, 1994), does significantly predict the participation of females: less war predicts more female participation. We have speculated that both intensive agriculture and more warfare work against women obtaining information and recognition that might increase the likelihood of their participation in political life.

If we are to arrive at a more complete explanation of democracy, we need to investigate all kinds of societies, not just recent nation-states.

We need to take results from cross-national research and test them cross-culturally, as we have done here with regard to the relationship between inequality and democracy. But we have to do the reverse too. For example, does less war predict more female participation cross-nationally?

Appendix

We show here the coding rules used in our research. First, we show the variables involving political decision making at the local level, following Ross (1983); they are numbered as he numbered them (variables 6, 7, 8, 9, 11, 30). Then we show the variables taken from Murdock and Provost (1980).

For the political variables, if the case was in the HRAF collection, we asked our assistants to read the text materials in HRAF categories 621 (community structure), 622 (headmen), 623 (councils), 624 (local officials), 625 (police), and 626 (social control). For those cases not coded by Ross (1983; he coded half the sample), the assistants coded the local political participation variables described below. Unless stated otherwise, the coding rules are taken directly from Ross (1983, pp. 176–7). (The actual codes for each case can be found in Ember, Russett and Ember, 1993.)

Variable 6: Checks on leaders' power

(1) There are few checks on political power in the society or those which exist do not seem to be invoked very often.
(2) There are checks on leaders' power which seem to make them sensitive to popular pressures.
(3) Political leaders in the society are careful to act only after securing substantial support for particular actions.
(4) There are no leaders who act independently, lest they lose their backing in the community.
(9) Not codable.

Variable 7: Removal of leaders

(1) There appears to be virtually no way in which incompetent or disliked leaders can be removed except for rebellion or popular uprisings.
(2) There are institutionalized means for removing leaders which are

invoked from time to time, possibly by other elites in the community.

(3) Leaders are not necessarily removed from office in a formal manner but they may be ignored and come to lose their influence in the community.

(4) Leadership is not formalized so individuals lose power when support disappears or diminishes.

(9) Not codable.

Variable 8: Leaders' need for consultation

(1) Leaders frequently act independently and make authoritative decisions which are then presented to the community.

(2) Leaders seem to make relatively few decisions on their own without consultation with members of the community.

(3) Leaders or influential individuals use persuasion (personal skills as opposed to exercise of authority) to help organize and structure group action.

(9) Not codable.

Variable 9: Decision-making bodies

(1) Most decisions seem to be made by individual(s), perhaps with advice from a few advisors.

(2) Most decisions seem to be made by individual(s) working with an elite council.

(3) Most decisions seem to be made by individual(s) working with a broad-based council.

(4) Most decisions seem to be made by a broad-based community council.

(5) While few explicit decisions are made, those which are seem to be made by the community at large, sometimes meeting together.

(9) Not codable.

Variable 11: Political participation: extensivity of involvement

This dimension of participation concerns patterns of involvement in those areas where collective decision making is present. How widespread or restrictive is adult political participation in a community?

Note that in Ember, Ember, and Russett (1992) and in Russett, Ember, and Ember (1993), the scores for variable 11 were reversed from those shown here. In other words, 4 was 1 and 1 was 4. Here, to facilitate combining scores with others previously published by Ross (1983, p. 177), the meanings of the scores are as Ross originally published them.

Within those areas where community decision making occurs, adult involvement in decision making is best characterized as:

(4) Low or non-existent: leaders make most decisions and involvement of the average person is highly limited or absent.

(3) Moderate: some consultation is present and there is some input from the community, but on the average it is not high.

(2) High for some: substantial political involvement for certain persons or groups, but others are excluded on the basis of gender, age, or kinship status.

(1) Widespread: decision-making forums (formal or informal) are open to all adults and involvement seems relatively great. (Societies with widespread participation for men but not women are scored 3.)

(9) Not codable.

Variable 30: Local political fission

(1) Dissatisfied persons often move to another community following disputes.

(2) Dissatisfied persons sometimes move to another community following disputes.

(3) Dissatisfied persons rarely or never move to another community following disputes.

(9) Not codable.

As we coded variable 30, we interpreted moving to include imprisonment or internal banishment for "political" crimes (such as treason) as well as external banishment for such crimes; but we did not consider imprisonment or banishment for "civil" crimes (such as incest or theft) to be moving after a dispute.

Agriculture

We use scale 3 from Murdock and Provost (1980, p. 148):

(4) Agriculture contributes more to the society's food supply than does any other subsistence activity and is conducted by intensive techniques such as irrigation, plowing, or artificial fertilization.

(3) Agriculture contributes more to the food supply than does any other subsistence activity but is not conducted by intensive techniques.

(2) Agriculture yields more than 10 percent of the society's food supply but not as much as does some other subsistence activity.

(1) Agriculture is practiced but yields less than 10 percent of the food supply.

(0) Agriculture is not practiced or is confined to non-food crops.

Social stratification

We use scale 10 from Murdock and Provost (1980, 150–1):

(4) The society exhibits a complex stratification into three or more distinct classes or castes regardless of the presence or absence of slavery.

(3) The society is stratified into two social classes of freemen, e.g., nobles and commoners or a propertied elite and a propertyless proletariat, plus hereditary slavery and/or recognized caste divisions.

(2) The society is classified into two social classes of freemen but lacks both caste distinctions and hereditary slavery.

(1) Formal class distinctions are lacking among freemen, but hereditary slavery prevails and/or there are important status differences based on the possession or distribution of wealth.

(0) The society is essentially egalitarian, lacking social classes, castes, hereditary slavery, and important wealth distinctions.

Density of population

We use scale 8 from Murdock and Provost (1980, p. 150):

(4) The mean density of population exceeds 100 persons per square mile.

(3) The density of population averages between 26 and 100 persons per square mile.

(2) The density of population averages between 5.1 and 25 persons per square mile.

(1) The density of population averages between one and five persons per square mile.

(0) The density of population averages fewer than one person per square mile.

Hierarchy of political units

We use scale 9 from Murdock and Provost (1980, p. 150), which they label "Level of Political Integration":

(4) Three or more administrative levels are recognized above that of

the local community, as in the case of a large state organized into provinces which are subdivided into districts.

(3) Two administrative levels are recognized above that of the local community, as in the case of a small state divided into administrative districts.

(2) One administrative level is recognized above that of the local community, as in the case of a petty state with a paramount chief ruling over a number of local communities. Societies which are politically completely dependent, lacking any political organization of their own and wholly absorbed into the political system of a dominant society of alien culture, are likewise coded as 2.

(1) The society is stateless but is composed of politically autonomous local communities.

(0) The society is stateless, and political authority is not centralized even on the local level but is dispersed among households or other small component units.

NOTES

Some of the data described here were collected as part of a project, on democracy and peace in the ethnographic record, which was supported by grants from the National Science Foundation (Program in Political Science and Program in Social/Cultural Anthropology) and the United States Institute of Peace. We thank Nate Gallon, Daniel Jacoby, and Kirsten Sadler for coding assistance. Other data came out of the Embers' previous research, on war and aggression in the ethnographic record, which was supported by two grants from the National Science Foundation (Program in Social/Cultural Anthropology) and small grants from the Research Award Program of the City University of New York. We thank the Embers' previous assistants: Alex Cohen, Carolyn Cohn, Gerald Creed, Peggy McGarrahan, Claire Riley, John Roberts, Marie-Jeanne Roche, Joshua Rubin, John Willis, and Robyn Wishengrad.

1 Retrieving and coding information from the ethnographic record is facilitated immeasurably by the annually growing full-text collection known as the HRAF Collection of Ethnography. The HRAF collection provides a collection of ethnographic materials which have been indexed by topic and grouped by culture to facilitate the retrieval of particular kinds of information; the indexing uses a list of 700+ categories for the kinds of information one might find in an ethnographic document. The HRAF collection does not provide coded information on variables; cross-cultural researchers who use the HRAF collection must do their own coding. The HRAF collection is merely a complexly indexed collection of documents, now nearly a million pages in all. Complete and incomplete copies of the HRAF collection, which currently covers more than 350 societies past and present, are located at more than 300 institutions in the United States, Canada, and 24

other nations. Now usually available in microfiche format, the ever-expanding HRAF Collection is being updated and converted to electronic format (CD-ROM and Web) over the next decade (see Ember 1997 for more about HRAF).

2 Note that our results differ somewhat from Ross's (1986) in that we obtained similar results for the two types of war (internal, external), whereas Ross obtained different results for his two types of "conflict." We cannot now explain why. All we can say now is that the differences in results may be due to how we measured female participation and/or the fact that Ross's measures of conflict include more than war.

Part II

Economic development and thresholds of democracy

5 Economic determinants of democracy

Edward N. Muller

Quantitative cross-national research on the economic determinants of democracy consistently finds that a country's level of economic development is associated positively and strongly with the extent to which the political system manifests properties of democracy. Moreover, in multivariate models that take into account numerous economic and non-economic factors, level of economic development (as measured by gross national product or energy consumption per-capita) typically is the single most important explanatory variable.[1] The form of the association is monotonic but non-linear: when level of democracy is plotted by level of economic development, the slope of the relationship ascends sharply from low to intermediate levels of development and then flattens out for countries at high levels of development. This function implies that a given increase in level of economic development produces a greater increase in level of democracy among countries in the low to intermediate range of development than among highly developed countries. The rapid acceleration of the slope from low to intermediate levels of economic development means that most countries reach a relatively high level of democracy after they have moved into a "threshold" region of intermediate development. As countries move beyond this threshold, their levels of democracy should remain high and relatively constant regardless of further increases in economic development.[2] If the positive impact of economic development on level of democracy is most pronounced among less-developed countries (LDCs), then positive economic growth should foster democracy in economically advanced LDCs with relatively low levels of democracy. LDCs with relatively high levels of democracy should maintain stable democracies, given stable levels of economic development. However, this scenario did not occur during the 1960s and 1970s: economic development or "modernization" tended to be associated with *declines* in democracy. Declines in levels of democracy were especially prevalent in Latin American countries (e.g., Argentina, Brazil, Chile, Ecuador, El Salvador, Mexico, Panama, Peru, Uruguay), where, with the exception of Venezuela, even the most economically advanced countries became less democratic as indicated by the repression of dissent (Mexico) or a change from a competitive democratic system to a harshly repressive military dictatorship (Argentina, Chile, and Uruguay). Large declines in level of democracy also occurred in modernizing states in other regions (e.g., Greece in Europe; Lebanon, Tunisia, and Turkey in the Middle East; Malaysia and the Philippines in Asia).

The task for quantitative cross-national research, then, is to explain the apparent contradiction between the robust relationship between level of economic development and level of democracy, which implies that intermediate levels of economic development promote democracy, and the empirical fact that many moderately developed countries experienced substantial declines in level of democracy. I argue that income inequality, a variable that does not explain variation in level of democracy at a single point in time (Bollen and Jackman 1985b), but which has a negative impact on the stability of democracy over time (Muller 1988), is a critical component of the explanation. Income inequality is hypothesized to be an economic determinant of *democratization* (positive or negative change in level of democracy) that is as causally relevant as level of economic development. Furthermore, its negative effect on democratization can counteract the positive influence of economic development. Moreover, the process of economic development initially exacerbates income inequality, which may explain the declines in levels of democracy in moderately developed countries.

Theory

As originally proposed by Lipset (1959), the explanation for the positive effect of economic development on the likelihood of a country establishing and maintaining democracy emphasizes two interrelated intervening variables: political culture and social structure. First, economic development is closely associated with increases in education, which in turn promotes political attitudes conducive to democracy (e.g., interpersonal trust and tolerance of opposition). Second, economic development alters the pyramid-shaped social stratification system, in which the majority of the population is lower class and poor, to a diamond shape, in which the majority of the population is middle class and relatively well-off. This social change moderates the intensity of the "class struggle" by reducing the proportion of the population that is susceptible to anti-democratic parties and ideologies and by increasing the proportion of the population that supports moderate pro-democratic parties. Moreover, because middle-class occupations require an educated population, the middle class will hold political attitudes conducive to democracy that are acquired through formal education. Thus, "the middle class emerges as the main pro-democratic force in Lipset's analysis, and this class gains in size with socioeconomic development" (Rueschemeyer, Stephens, and Stephens, 1992, p. 14).

While increasing the size of the middle class, economic development also expands the size of the urban working class. Rueschemeyer *et al.* (1992) stressed the importance of the urban working class for the establishment of democracy and proposed an interpretation of the correlation between economic development and democracy that differs from Lipset's. First, their analysis was based on a rational-choice model of collective class interest that focuses exclusively on the effect of economic development on social structure – the roles of political culture and education are ignored. Second, they argued that the urban working class has a more consistent interest in democracy than does the middle class. The strong positive correlation between economic development and democracy occurs because economic development changes the balance of class power in favor of the working class: "Socioeconomic development enlarges the size of the working class and it increases the organizational power of subordinate classes generally. At the same time, it erodes the size and the power of the most anti-democratic force – the large landowning classes, especially those that rely on coercive state power for the control of their labor force" (Rueschemeyer *et al.*, 1992, p. 76). The roles of the middle classes – urban professionals, state and private-sector employees, merchants, craftsmen, and farmers – in the balance of class power is pivotal but ambiguous. Their interests are subject to a variety of social interpretations, and their intermediate position in the class structure makes them susceptible to anti-democratic alliances with the dominant classes – the landed aristocracy and the bourgeoisie (owners and managers of capital).

However, one potentially inimical effect of capitalist economic development on democracy was not considered by Lipset (1959) or Rueschemeyer *et al.* – income inequality. The highest levels of income inequality tend to occur among countries at intermediate levels of economic development; income inequality varies as an inverted U-shaped curve in relation to level of economic development. This inverted U relationship between economic development and income inequality holds across a wide variety of data sets (Ahluwalia, 1976b; Bollen and Jackman, 1985b; Bornschier and Chase-Dunn, 1985; Kuznets, 1963; Lydall, 1979; Muller, 1988; Paukert, 1973; Weede, 1980; Weede and Tiefenbach, 1981a; World Bank, 1980). While capitalist economic development increases the size and organizational power of subordinate classes with an interest in democracy, it generates greater inequality in the distribution of income.

When democratic institutions with universal male or adult suffrage are introduced into an extremely inegalitarian society, those among the subordinate classes who resent inequality will seek to reduce the gap between the rich and the poor by using the electoral process to reassign property and income. Political attempts to reassign property and income, through policies like land reform, taxation of personal income, and welfare spending are, in turn, likely to be resented by the dominant, wealthy classes. Although vastly outnumbered by the poor, the rich nevertheless may be able to convert their greater economic resources into a countervailing political influence and prevent significant redistribution. If redistributive policies are blocked in the legislature or are not even proposed, then the belief among the subordinate classes in the legitimacy of the democratic process will be eroded. If these dissident groups turn to non-democratic methods of participation, such as civil disobedience and violence, in order to attain their economic objectives, the rich will probably respond in kind by using military power to suppress rebellious collective action. Therefore, conflict over inequality may substantially increase the likelihood of a breakdown of democracy through civil war, revolution, or a *coup d'état*.

The timing of the establishment of democracy then becomes critical. If inclusive democracy, characterized by universal male or adult suffrage, occurs at a relatively late stage of industrialization when income inequality has begun to decline, then working-class and middle-class support for democracy should be high. Moreover, at a relatively high level of economic development, the power of the dominant class most opposed to democracy – the landed aristocracy – will be relatively low. And although the bourgeoisie will become dominant and its power will be high, its political interest is in limited, oligarchic democracy. Hence this class will tolerate more inclusive democracy only if its own economic interests are not seriously threatened. By contrast, if inclusive democracy is established at a stage of industrialization when income inequality is high or increasing, then the working class will be susceptible to the appeals of revolutionary socialism, which will inhibit the development of a broad pro-democratic coalition of the working class and middle class, and a powerful anti-democratic coalition of the bourgeoisie and the landed aristocracy would be likely.

Thus, there is a plausible theoretical rationale for expecting that the relationship between economic development and democracy may be more complex than a positive monotonic association. Indeed, I argue that the process of capitalist economic development has a positive direct

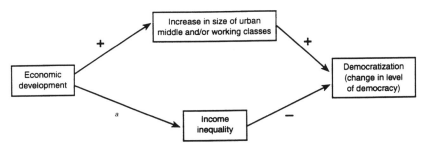

Figure 5.1 Relationship between economic development and democratization
Note: [a]Inverted U-curve relationship.

effect and a negative indirect effect on the process of democratization. A causal model of these countervailing relationships is shown in figure 5.1.

On the one hand, the process of capitalist economic development is expected to have a positive impact on democratization because it produces a shift in the labor force from agriculture to industry and services. This shift increases the size of the urban middle class (Lipset's [1959] argument; also see Huntington, 1991, figure 2.1) and the size of the urban working class (Rueschemeyer *et al.*'s [1992] argument) which fosters the *inauguration* of democracy. On the other hand, capitalist economic development also initially heightens income inequality in a country, and this is expected to have a negative impact on democratization because a high level of income inequality radicalizes the working class, enhances class polarization, and reduces the tolerance of the bourgeoisie for political participation by the lower classes. Therefore, income inequality is incompatible with the *stability* of democracy over time.

Measures

Empirical analysis of the relationships between economic development, income inequality, and change in level of democracy is constrained by the availability of data on income inequality. Before the late 1950s, these data existed for only a handful of countries. Currently, the most comprehensive set of reasonably reliable and comparable measurements of income inequality over a relatively short interval is for circa 1970, spanning the period 1965 through 1975 (Muller, 1988, table 1). A total of 55 countries with capitalist economies have information on income inequality circa 1970. Following Simpson (1990), this sample can be expanded by including income inequality data circa 1970 for three

Table 5.1 *Values of variables used in the analysis: 58 countries circa 1970*

Country	GDP per capita 1970	Income inequality (Gini coefficient) c.1970	Income share of top 20% c. 1970	Liberal democracy score[a]		
				1965	1980	Change 1965–80
High-income						
United States	9,459	0.36	42.8	92	100	+8
Canada	8,465	0.34	41.0	100	100	0
Germany, West	7,443	0.36	45.2	89	100	+11
Sweden	7,401	0.29	37.0	100	100	0
Australia	5,843	0.34	43.0	100	100	0
Norway	7,104	0.30	37.3	100	100	0
France	7,078	0.38	46.4	91	100	+9
Trinidad & Tobago	6,957	0.42	50.0	85	83	–2
Netherlands	6,915	0.30	40.0	100	100	0
Belgium	6,750	0.30	39.8	100	100	0
Venezuela	6,608	0.47	54.0	73	89	+16
New Zealand	6,595	0.31	41.4	100	100	0
United Kingdom	6,319	0.31	39.2	99	100	+1
Austria	5,843	0.37	44.0	97	100	+3
Japan	5,496	0.30	41.0	100	100	0
Italy	5,028	0.38	46.5	97	100	+3
Upper-middle-income						
Spain	4,379	0.36	45.2	10	83	+73
Argentina	4,002	0.41	50.3	53	6	–47
Chile	3,687	0.43	51.4	97	6	–91
Ireland	3,628	0.30	39.4	97	100	+3
South Africa	3,609	0.53	58.0	59	56	–3
Uruguay	3,453	0.40	47.4	100	17	–83
Barbados	3,147	0.34	44.0	100	100	0
Mexico	3,063	0.52	64.0	75	56	–19
Iran	2,816	0.52	62.7	45	33	–12
Portugal	2,575	0.40	49.1	39	94	+55
Middle-income						
Costa Rica	2,300	0.41	50.6	90	100	+10
Nicaragua	2,292	0.51	60.0	55	17	–38
Peru	2,285	0.54	61.0	87	72	–15
Panama	2,093	0.54	61.8	77	28	–49
Gabon	2,082	0.55	67.5	45	28	–17
Brazil	1,782	0.56	66.6	61	39	–22
Colombia	1,711	0.48	58.5	71	72	+1
Turkey	1,702	0.49	58.6	76	11	–65
Guatemala	1,544	0.46	58.8	40	44	+4
Malaysia	1,525	0.47	56.4	80	67	–13

Table 5.1 (*cont.*)

Country	GDP per capita 1970	Income inequality (Gini coefficient) c.1970	Income share of top 20% c. 1970	Liberal democracy score[a]		
				1965	1980	Change 1965–80
El Salvador	1,358	0.46	54.4	72	6	−66
Bolivia	1,237	0.49	61.0	36	0	−36
South Korea	1,189	0.33	42.7	53	33	−20
Philippines	1,094	0.43	54.0	93	33	−60
Tunisia	1,076	0.46	55.0	64	28	−36
Thailand	1,063	0.44	53.4	17	67	+50
Ivory Coast	1,028	0.49	57.2	46	17	−29
Sri Lanka	1,018	0.34	44.5	86	83	−3
Low-income						
Honduras	927	0.57	67.8	50	17	−33
Senegal	760	0.47	60.9	54	39	−15
Sudan	683	0.41	49.8	38	22	−16
Egypt	671	0.39	47.5	39	33	−6
India	576	0.38	49.2	91	94	+3
Ghana	568	0.39	47.8	24	83	+59
Indonesia	559	0.39	52.0	10	33	+23
Kenya	552	0.51	60.4	58	33	−25
Sierra Leone	459	0.42	52.5	75	33	−42
Malawi	301	0.34	50.6	58	17	−41
Tanzania	283	0.39	50.4	63	28	−35
Communist regimes						
Germany, East	5,863	0.20	30.7	18	11	−7
Hungary	4,379	0.25	33.4	12	17	+5
Yugoslavia	2,885	0.35	41.4	51	28	−23

Note: [a] Democracy scores are from Bollen (1969, 1993).

countries with communist regimes (East Germany, Hungary, and Yugoslavia) and for two countries with data from sources other than those used in Muller (1988, note 5) (Austria and Ghana, (Simpson, 1990, appendix).[3]

Bollen (1980, 1993) constructed measures of liberal democracy for 1960, 1965, and 1980 that meet stringent standards of reliability and validity. The measure ranges from 0 (authoritarian) to 100 (democratic). Of the 60 countries with income inequality scores circa 1970, 58 have liberal democracy scores in 1965 and in 1980.[4] This sample of 58 countries is used to estimate the effects of economic development in 1970 and income inequality circa 1970 on change in level of democracy for the period 1965–80 with economic development in 1970 and income inequality over 1965–75 as intervening variables between the initial level of democracy in 1965 and the subsequent level of democracy in 1980. Scores on these variables are listed in table 5.1. Level of economic development in 1970 is measured by real gross domestic product (GDP) per-capita (Summers and Heston, 1988). Income inequality is measured by the Gini coefficient and by the share of personal income received by the richest quintile. The measures of liberal democracy in 1965 (Bollen, 1980) and 1980 (Bollen, 1993) range from 0 to 100; the change is the difference between 1980 scores and 1965 scores. Countries are listed in descending order of GDP per-capita and are grouped as high income, upper middle income, middle income, low income, and communist regimes with centrally planned economies.

All 16 high-income countries have 1965 and 1980 democracy scores in or near the upper quarter of the range. These countries can be classified as stable democracies. Over half have a Gini coefficient indicating relatively low-income inequality (≤ 0.35); almost two-fifths have a Gini coefficient indicating an intermediate level of income inequality (0.36 to 0.45); only one (Venezuela) has a Gini coefficient indicating very high-income inequality (≥ 0.46). Thus, with the exception of Venezuela, high-income countries tended to be relatively egalitarian and have a stable high level of democracy.

Democratization among the ten upper-middle-income countries differs markedly from that in the high-income countries. There are only two stable democracies (Barbados and Ireland) in this group, and only two countries (Portugal and Spain) registered substantial increases (a gain of 20 or more points) in democracy scores between 1965 and 1980. Most of these countries registered either substantial declines in democracy scores (Argentina, Chile, Uruguay, and Mexico) or the political system remained authoritarian and scores remained low (Iran and South Africa). Thus four upper-middle-income countries moved away from democracy, and two moved toward it. This trend of decreasing democratization may reflect the influence of income inequality since all countries in the upper-middle-income group that had a low level of income inequality also were able to maintain stable democracy, whereas half of those with intermediate to high levels of income inequality experienced substantial declines in levels of democracy.

The 18 middle-income countries were also much more likely to move away from democracy than toward it during this period. Only Costa Rica and Sri Lanka maintained a stable, relatively high level of democracy. The vast majority of middle-income countries (13 of 18) registered a substantial decline in democracy scores or remained at a low level with relatively little change. Most middle-income countries also had high-income inequality and all of these extremely inegalitarian middle-income countries either declined substantially in level of democracy or remained at a relatively stable authoritarian level.

Three of the 11 low-income countries had low and stable democracy scores (Egypt, Senegal, and Sudan). Slightly less than one-half of these countries experienced substantial declines in level of democracy (Honduras, Kenya, Malawi, Sierra Leone, and Tanzania). There was only one stable democracy (India), one substantial increase from an authoritarian democracy score to a high score (Ghana), and one substantial increase that nevertheless remained in the authoritarian range (Indonesia). Most low-income countries had low to intermediate levels of income inequality.

Finally, the three countries with communist regimes and centrally planned economies had low levels of income inequality and very low or declining democracy scores. These communist countries contrast markedly with the capitalist countries where a low level of income inequality coincided with a stable high level of democracy in every instance except Malawi and South Korea.

Analysis

Among capitalist countries, the relationship between level of economic development in 1970 and *change* in democracy from 1965 to 1980 appears to be non-monotonic rather than positive and monotonic. If economic development promotes democratization, the democracy scores for most middle- and upper-middle-income countries should increase from 1965 to 1980. In fact, however, only one country in the middle-income group registered a substantial increase (Thailand), while two-thirds registered a substantial decline. And only one-fifth of the countries in the upper-middle-income group registered a substantial increase in democracy scores, while two-fifths registered a substantial decline. Indeed, as level of economic development increases, the percent of countries experiencing a substantial *decline* in democracy scores is 45 percent for low-income countries, 67 percent for middle-income countries, 40 percent for upper-middle-income countries and 0 percent for high-income countries. Table 5.2 presents the 55 countries with capitalist economies cross classified by levels of economic development and income inequality.

Why did countries at the middle levels of economic development apparently fail to promote democratization during the 1965–80 period? The model of economic determinants of democracy proposed here

Table 5.2 Change in democracy score from 1965 to 1980 by income inequality and level of economic participation (circa 1970): 55 capitalist countries

Income inequality and change in democracy score	Level of economic development			
	Low-income	Middle-income	Upper-middle income	High-income
High inequality				
Declining democracy	Honduras, Kenya	Brazil, Bolivia, El Salvador, Ivory Coast, Panama, Peru[a], Malaysia[a], Nicaragua, Tunisia, Turkey	Mexico	—
Stable democracy	—	—	—	Venezuela
Increasing democracy	—	—	—	—
Authoritarian	Senegal	Colombia, Gabon, Guatemala	Iran, South Africa	—
Intermediate inequality				
Declining democracy	Sierra Leone, Tanzania	Philippines	Argentina, Chile, Uruguay	—
Stable democracy	India	Costa Rica	—	Austria, France, Germany, Italy, Trinidad and Tobago, United States
Increasing democracy	Ghana, Indonesia	Thailand	Portugal, Spain	—
Authoritarian	Sudan, Egypt	—	—	—
Low inequality				
Declining democracy	Malawi	South Korea	—	—
Stable democracy	—	Sri Lanka	Barbados, Ireland	Australia, Belgium, Canada, Japan, Netherlands, New Zealand, Norway, Sweden, United Kingdom
Increasing democracy	—	—	—	—
Authoritarian	—	—	—	—

Note: [a]Borderline (decline from above to below the high range of liberal democracy).

(figure 5.1) postulates that the relationship between economic development and democratization is more complex than a simple positive monotonic association because of the inverted U-relationship between economic development and income inequality. If the relationship between economic development and income inequality conforms to an inverted U-curve, and if income inequality has a negative effect on democratization, then countries at intermediate levels of economic development may decline in democratization because of their high levels of income inequality. The tendency for income inequality to vary in an inverted U-curve fashion with level of economic development is strikingly apparent from table 5.2: The proportion of countries with a high level of income inequality is much higher for middle-income countries (13 of 18 countries, or 72 percent) than it is for low-income countries (3 of 11 countries, or 27 percent) or for upper-middle-income (3 of 10 countries, or 30 percent) and high-income countries (1 of 16 countries, or 6 percent). The critical question, then, is whether income inequality has a direct negative effect on change in level of democracy.

Table 5.3 presents regression coefficients estimating the effects of economic development and income inequality on change in level of democracy. The dependent variable is the 1980 democracy score; the 1965 democracy score is included among the independent variables. Thus, I explain 1980 democracy scores net of 1965 scores. The first two models focus on the relationship between economic development and change in democracy scores, controlling for the presence of a communist regime (scored 1, otherwise 0). In model 1, level of economic development is specified as having a monotonic effect (positively decelerated because the GDP per-capita variable is logged). This model also includes the rate of economic growth, defined as the average annual percent change in GDP during the 1960s. Rate of economic growth is taken into account because Huntington (1991, pp. 49–54) argued that poor macroeconomic performance, as reflected in low or negative rates of growth, undermines the legitimacy of authoritarian regimes and is thus a cause of democratization. If this argument is correct, then the rate of economic growth should have a negative effect on democratization (i.e., low or negative growth rates should be associated with increased levels of democracy). However, the results for model 1 do not support this hypothesis – the coefficient for the economic growth variable is positive and is not statistically significant. The 1970 level of economic development has the expected significant positive effect, and the communist regime variable has the expected significant negative effect on democratization.

In model 2, the economic growth variable is omitted and the 1970

Table 5.3 *Coefficients for regression of 1980 democracy score on selected independent variables: 58 countries, circa 1970*

Independent variable	Model 1	Model 2	Model 3	Model 4	Model 5	Model 6
Intercept	−100.40	433.85	102.58	7.99	147.44	45.09
Democracy score, 1965	0.37*	0.24	0.17	0.18	0.16	0.16
	(2.04)	(1.45)	(1.09)	(1.14)	(1.0)	(1.04)
ln(GDP per capita, 1970)	17.14*	−125.14*	−12.46	14.63*	−17.16	12.65*
	(3.47)	(−2.01)	(−0.18)	(3.48)	(−0.26)	(2.94)
ln(GDP per capita, 1970)^2	–	9.51*	1.82	–	2.01	–
		(2.30)	(0.39)		(0.44)	
Growth in GDP per capita, 1960–70[a]	0.47	–	–	–	–	–
	(0.35)					
Income inequality, c. 1970	–	–	−164.35*	−176.25*	–	–
			(−3.01)	(−3.90)		
Top 20 percent income share, c. 1970	–	–	–	–	−1.71*	−1.84*
					(−3.11)	(−3.99)
Communist regime	−35.92*	−40.25*	−67.42*	−69.11*	−69.69*	−71.62*
	(−1.86)	(−2.23)	(−3.53)	(−3.74)	(−3.62)	(−3.85)
Adjusted R^2	0.41	0.46	0.53	0.54	0.54	0.55
Number of countries	57	58	58	58	58	58

Notes: *$p \leq 0.05$ (one-tailed tests).
[a]Average annual percent change in GDP per capita, 1960–70; data missing for Indonesia.
Numbers in parentheses are *t*-ratios.

level of economic development is specified as having a non-monotonic effect on change in level of democracy, which should conform to a U-shaped curve. Because the coefficients for 1970 GDP and its square are significant and in the expected direction, and because the R^2 for model 2 is higher than that for model 1,[5] it appears that a U-curve function best describes the relationship between economic development and democratization. That is, countries at an intermediate level of economic development in 1970 tended to have much greater declines in level of democracy between 1965 and 1980 than countries at either low or high levels of economic development.

Model 3 addresses the question of whether income inequality explains the U-curve relationship between economic development and democratization. If income inequality is the direct cause of decreases in democracy among countries at intermediate levels of development, then the U-curve relationship between economic development and democratization should disappear when income inequality is introduced into the equation. Model 3 shows that when income inequality is taken into account it has a significant negative effect on democratization and there is no longer any significant U-curve effect of economic development on democratization. The U-curve relationship between economic development and democratization thus appears to reflect the fact that countries at intermediate levels of development tend to have inegalitarian distributions of income.

Model 4 shows that the effect of economic development on democratization is positive and monotonic when the negative effect of income inequality is controlled for, as predicted by the conventional economic development hypothesis. Models 5 and 6 demonstrate that these results are robust when an alternative measure of inequality – the size of the income share received by the richest quintile – is substituted for the Gini index.

Two important conclusions can be drawn from the evidence in table 5.3. First, income inequality hinders democratization, and this negative effect explains the paradoxical trend among countries at intermediate levels of economic development for democracy to decrease instead of increase. These countries are more likely to experience substantial declines in democracy than are countries at low or high levels of development because their high levels of income inequality make it difficult to sustain a relatively high level of democracy over time. Second, when the negative effect of income inequality on change in level of democracy is controlled, then economic development has the expected positive impact on democratization. A properly specified model of the relationship between capitalist economic development and democratization thus *requires* that income inequality be taken into account.

Robustness of the effects of economic development and income inequality

Although there is reason to postulate that economic development and income inequality are the most important economic determinants of democracy, the effects of other potentially relevant non-economic variables must be taken into account to determine the extent to which their inclusion modifies the effects estimated for economic development and income inequality. Bollen and Jackman (1985b) found that, in addition to a strong positive effect of level of economic development, three non-economic variables had significant effects on cross-national variation in levels of democracy in 1965. Two cultural variables, British colonial heritage and the percentage of the population that is Protestant, had positive effects, and an indicator of dependency in the world capitalist economy, peripheral world-system status, had a negative effect.[6]

Another potentially relevant cultural variable is the percentage of the population that is Islamic. Countries with a large percentage of Islamic citizens have been unlikely to inaugurate democratic political systems, and the few that have established democracies have been unable to maintain stable democracies (e.g., Lebanon, Malaysia, and Turkey – a secular Islamic country). Huntington (1984) argued that Islam has been inhospitable to the development of political democracy because Islamic religious culture is a "consummatory" culture in which "intermediate and ultimate ends are closely connected" and "no distinction exists between religion and politics or between the spiritual and the secular, and political participation was historically an alien concept" (p. 208). Therefore, Huntington (1984, p. 216) argued that the prospects for democratization in Islamic countries are poor. The percentage of the population that is Islamic thus should have a negative effect on change in level of democracy from 1965 to 1980. For the percentage of the population that is Islamic, I use Taylor and Hudson (1972, table 4.17).

The four non-economic variables, for the most part, correlate with the economic variables.[7] Therefore, if the non-economic variables have significant effects on change in democracy, then their inclusion in a model could reduce the magnitude of the effects of the economic variables. The non-economic variables are taken into account as possible determinants of change in level of democracy in the regression equations reported in table 5.4. Model 1 includes British colonial heritage, percentage Protestant, and percentage Islamic, as information on these variables is available for all counties with data on income inequality and level of democracy. Model 1 shows that the coefficients for the Gini index of income inequality and economic development are signed correctly and are statistically significant when these cultural variables are controlled for. The coefficient for British colonial heritage is also significant and in the expected direction; the coefficient for percentage Protestant is in the wrong direction and is not significant; and the coefficient for percentage Islamic is virtually 0 and not significant. Model

2 is estimated across the 55 countries with information on peripheral world-system status, which is included in addition to the relevant explanatory variables from model 1. The coefficient for peripheral world-system status is signed in the correct direction, but is not statistically significant. In models 3 and 4, income inequality is measured by the top 20 percent income share, and the pattern of effects is the same as those for models 1 and 2. Thus, British colonial heritage appears to have promoted democratization between 1965 and 1980; but percentage Protestant, percentage Islamic, and peripheral world-system status are unrelated to change in level of democracy.

Comparing models 1 and 2 in table 5.4 with model 4 in table 5.3, the values of the coefficients for income inequality are similar. This is also the case for the coefficients for the top 20 percent income share estimated in model 6 of table 5.3 and models 3 and 4 of Table 5.4. By contrast, the coefficients for 1970 GDP per-capita are considerably larger for the models that include non-economic variables than for the simple economic determinants models (models 4 and 6 of table 5.3). The magnitude of the positive effect of economic development on change in democracy thus appears to be underestimated if British colonial heritage – the relevant non-economic variable – is omitted. In any case, because the negative effect of income inequality and the positive effect of economic development remain significant and strong, there is no evidence that omitted-variable bias affects the substantive conclusions derived from the simple economic determinants model.

Another possible source of omitted-variable bias is a reciprocal negative effect of democracy on income inequality. This is not a problem with regard to level of democracy in 1965. In a model of simultaneous reciprocal causation, Bollen and Jackman (1985b) showed there is no significant monotonic association between level of democracy in 1965 and income inequality circa 1968 (spanning the years from 1958 to 1975). The regression equations in tables 5.3 and 5.4 show that income inequality circa 1970 has a negative monotonic effect on level of democracy in 1980, controlling for level of democracy in 1965. Thus, the effect of income inequality on level of democracy in 1980 is not a spurious reflection of effects of level of democracy in 1965 on both subsequent income inequality and level of democracy. A country's accumulated years of democratic experience, however, may have a negative effect on income inequality circa 1970 (Muller, 1988), particularly if years of democratic experience are measured by Rustow's (1967) index of years of continuous elections (Muller, 1989).[8] And if change in level of democracy from 1965 to 1980 is in part a positive function of a country's previous

Table 5.4 *Coefficients for regressions of 1980 democracy score on selected economic and non-economic independent variables: 58 countries, circa 1970*

Independent variable	Model 1	Model 2	Model 3	Model 4	Model 5	Model 6
Intercept	−57.37	−19.54	−18.97	2.83	−55.81	−29.60
Democracy score, 1965	0.07	0.05	0.05	0.05	−0.07	−0.08
	(0.44)	(0.34)	(0.35)	(0.29)	(−0.32)	(−0.37)
ln(GDP per capita, 1970)	23.90*	18.37*	21.58*	17.40*	20.44*	19.06*
	(4.07)	(3.24)	(3.59)	(3.0)	(3.82)	(3.57)
Income inequality, c. 1970 (Gini)	−165.76*	−162.11*	−	−	−112.54*	−
	(−3.64)	(−3.39)			(−1.76)	
Top 20 percent income share, c. 1970	−	−	−1.72*	−1.61*	−	−1.21*
			(−3.70)	(3.28)		(−1.91)
Communist regime	−69.20*	−73.23*	−71.38*	−73.93*	−64.12*	−66.22*
	(−3.92)	(−4.07)	(−4.01)	(−4.05)	(−3.29)	(−3.38)
Non-economic variables						
Former British colony	29.27*	27.05*	29.02	26.64*	25.53*	25.28*
	(2.78)	(2.41)	(2.76)	(2.36)	(2.49)	(2.48)
ln(percent Protestant, 1964)	−4.09	−	−4.0	−	−	−
	(−1.55)		(−1.52)			
ln(percent Islamic, 1964)	−0.52	−	−0.86	−	−	−
	(−0.20)		(−0.33)			
World-system periphery, 1965	−	−4.98	−	−4.01	−	−
		(−0.61)		(−0.48)		
ln(years of continuous elections to 1965)	−	−	−	−	3.47	3.41
					(.83)	(.85)
Adjusted R^2	0.58	0.57	0.59	0.56	0.58	0.58
Number of countries	58	55	58	55	58	55

Notes: *$p \leq 0.05$ (one-tailed tests).
*Estimated for 55 countries with information on peripheral world-system status.
Numbers in parentheses are *t*-ratios.

years of democratic experience, then the negative effect of income inequality circa 1970 on democratization could be a spurious reflection of the influence of years of democratic experience on both income inequality and change in level of democracy.

Years of continuous election to 1965[9] is negatively and relatively strongly correlated with income inequality and the top 20 percent of income share ($r = -0.58$ and -0.61, respectively). Consequently, the observed negative effects of these indicators of income inequality on democratization could be spurious when years of continuous elections are taken into account if years of continuous elections also have a positive effect on democratization. Model 5 in table 5.4 shows, however, that the negative effect of income inequality on democratization is significant when years of continuous elections is controlled, and that years of continuous elections does not have a significant positive effect on democratization independent of income inequality.[10] Similar results are obtained using the top 20 percent of income share instead of the Gini index. The results of models 5 and 6 are further evidence, then, of the robustness of the negative effect of income inequality on democratization.

The effects of economic development, and income inequality, and British colonial heritage on change in level of democracy also could be sensitive to changes in sample composition and to outliers or other influential cases. Regarding changes in sample composition, Denmark, Finland, Israel, Nepal, Switzerland, and Zambia have information on income inequality for years during the four-year period from 1976 through 1979, while our second measure of level of democracy is in 1980. Thus, the sample could be expanded by extending the measurement period for income inequality from 1965–75 to 1965–79 and including the six additional countries.[11] Model 1 in table 5.5 replicates model 1 in table 5.4 across the 64 countries that have data on income inequality using the extended measurement period. The relevant variables are the same in both tables, and the coefficients for GNP per-capita and income inequality (Gini) are virtually the same. The only appreciable difference is that the coefficient for British colonial heritage is reduced by approximately one-half. Model 2 in table 5.5 replicates model 2 in table 5.4 across those countries with information on peripheral world-system status. Again, the relevant variables are the same, the coefficients for GNP per-capita and income inequality are virtually the same, and the magnitude of the coefficient for British colonial heritage is reduced, but still significant. Model 3 in table 5.5 reports coefficients for a trimmed model explaining change in level of democracy that includes only the rel-

Table 5.5 *Coefficients for regression of 1980 democracy score on selected independent variables: expanded sample of 64 countries*

Independent variables	Model 1	Model 2	Model 3	Model 4
Intercept	−27.87	−2.87	−35.53	−54.87
Democracy score, 1965	0.06	0.05	0.04	0.05
	(0.43)	(0.32)	(0.30)	(0.34)
ln(GDP per capita, 1970)	20.50*	16.28*	19.90*	21.94*
	(3.90)	(3.07)	(4.24)	(4.37)
Income inequality, 1965–79 (Gini)	−172.03*	−160.69*	−155.69*	−
	(−4.0)	(−3.57)	(−3.76)	
Income inequality, 1965–75 (Gini)	−	−	−	−150.35*
				(−3.38)
Communist regime	−70.22*	−72.78*	−71.51*	−70.83*
	(−4.13)	(−4.20)	(−4.21)	(−4.01)
Non-economic variables				
Former British colony	20.94*	22.16*	18.84*	24.84*
	(2.30)	(2.21)	(2.10)	(2.43)
ln(percent Protestant, 1964)	−3.32	−	−	−
	(−1.41)			
ln(percent Islamic, 1964)	−1.10	−	−	−
	(−0.47)			
World-system periphery, 1965	−	−5.14	−	−
		(−0.65)		
Adjusted R^2	0.60	0.59	0.60	0.58
Number of countries	64	60	64	58

Notes: $*p \leq 0.05$ (one-tailed tests).
Numbers in parentheses are *t*-ratios.

evant economic and non-economic determinants. The model is estimated across the expanded sample of countries with information on income inequality. These results are similar to those for model 4 in table 5.4, which is a trimmed equation estimated across the 58 cases with information on income inequality for the 1965–75 period. Thus, substantive conclusions about the effects of economic development, income inequality, and British colonial heritage are not affected by increasing the size of the sample with information on income inequality.[12]

Regarding influential cases, there are no severe outliers (standardized residuals greater than ±3.0) for models 3 and 4 in table 5.5, and almost all cases are relatively well predicted, with residuals in the range of ±2.0. Moreover, examining regression diagnostics for identifying potentially influential cases such as the DFITS index (Belsley, Kuh, and Welsch,

1980), the parameter estimates are not substantively affected by influential cases.[13]

Conclusion

Since Lipset (1959) introduced his seminal theory that a country's chances of sustaining democracy depend fundamentally on its level of wealth, analyses of the structural causes of democracy have emphasized economic development. Lipset's thesis spawned a host of quantitative cross-national studies that confirmed the existence of a strong positive correlation between indicators of level of economic development and level of democracy. In recent analyses of the conditions that promote democratization, Dahl (1989, p. 251) argued that economic development along with the syndrome of factors associated monotonically with development,[14] which together produce a "modern dynamic pluralist society," are especially favorable to the development of democracy (or polyarchy); while Huntington (1991) concluded that "the two key factors affecting the future stability and expansion of democracy are economic development and political leadership" (p. 315).

The form of the relationship between level of economic development and level of democracy implies that the largest gains in democracy should occur in countries at intermediate levels of development, because rich countries already have achieved high levels of democracy and are expected to maintain stable high levels. Yet during the 1960s and 1970s, middle-income and upper-middle-income countries that fit the prediction of the economic development hypothesis (e.g., Portugal, Spain, and Thailand) were vastly outnumbered by middle-income and upper-middle-income countries that did not fit it (e.g., Argentina, Bolivia, Brazil, Chile, El Salvador, Ivory Coast, Malaysia, Mexico, Nicaragua, Panama, Peru, the Philippines, South Korea, Tunisia, Turkey, and Uruguay). What, then, went wrong? Why did economic development bring instability and authoritarianism rather than stable democracy to some modernizing countries?

Proponents of the economic development explanation of democratization assume that reduction of income inequality goes hand-in-hand with economic development and that income inequality has no significant effect on democratization independent of level of economic development. But income inequality is not a characteristic of an MDP (modern dynamic pluralist) society that is highly correlated monotonically with economic development. Instead, income inequality is an inverted-U function of level of economic development. Countries at intermediate levels of economic development thus tend to have the highest levels of income inequality. And, as the cross-national data reported here demonstrate, countries with high levels of income inequality circa 1970 were much more likely to suffer a substantial decline in level of democracy from 1965 to 1980 (65 percent) than were countries with relatively low levels of income inequality (14 percent). Moreover, multivariate analysis of structural determinants of change in level of democracy from 1965 to 1980 shows that income inequality has a robust negative impact on democratization that can counteract the positive impact of economic development. Income inequality therefore appears to be important in explaining why economic development has often failed to promote stable democracy.

Corroborating evidence of the negative impact of income inequality on democratization comes from two other studies. First, in a cross-national analysis that focused on 33 countries that could be classified as democracies in 1960 (Muller, 1988), a strong point-biserial correlation of -0.80 was observed between income inequality (measured by the size of the income share of the richest quintile of families) and a binary variable, stability versus instability of democracy from 1960 to 1980. All 17 democracies with upper quintile income shares of less than 45 percent were stable; 7 of the 10 democracies with upper quintile income shares in the range of 45 percent to 55 percent were stable; and all 6 democracies with upper quintile income shares greater than 55 percent were unstable. The conclusion that income inequality has a negative effect on the stability of democracy was disputed by Bollen and Jackman (1989, p. 619), who objected to the dichotomous measurement of the dependent variable. The relationship is not an artifact of measurement procedures, however, because when democracy is measured as a continuous variable, using indexes constructed by Bollen (1980, 1993), income inequality still has a negative impact on change in level of democracy.

Second, in a cross-national analysis of macrolevel structural and microlevel attitudinal determinants of change in average level of democracy from the 1970s to the 1980s, the single strongest influence on democratization was a negative impact of income inequality (Muller and Seligson, 1994). Thus, the negative effect of income inequality on democratization observed here for change in level of democracy from 1965 to 1980, when the global trend was one of decreasing democratization, also holds for a later time period when the global trend was in the direction of increasing democratization.

In sum, evidence from this study and others indicates that high levels of income inequality are incompatible with the development of a stable democratic political system. An inverted U-relationship between economic development and income inequality, together with a direct negative effect of income inequality on change in level of democracy, is probably the principal structural reason why countries at intermediate levels of economic development often have difficulty sustaining stable democratic systems of government. Thus, optimism about the current "third wave" of democratization must be tempered by the fact that the prospect for long-term consolidation of democracy is poor in countries where highly inegalitarian income distributions prevail.

NOTES

This chapter is virtually identical to an article published in the *American Sociological Review* subsequent to its presentation at the conference in New Brunswick, and is reprinted here with the kind permission of that journal. Any revisions in the article were prevented by Professor Muller's untimely death.

1 Diamond (1992) concluded from a comprehensive review of cross-national research on economic development and democracy, that "given the considerable variation in quantitative methods, in countries and years tested, in the measures of democracy employed, and in the vast array of different regression equations (testing more than 20 different independent variables), this must rank as one of the most powerful and robust relationships in the study of comparative national development" (p. 110).

2 The threshold argument originated with Neubauer (1967), who, after finding weak correlations between indicators of socioeconomic development and an index of level of democracy among countries with relatively high scores on the democracy index, hypothesized that democratization is a threshold phenomenon such that a certain level of socioeconomic development is necessary for countries to reach a relatively high level of democracy, but that once a country has surpassed the threshold, continued increases in socioeconomic development have little effect on level of democracy. Jackman (1973) conducted the first explicit test of the threshold hypothesis across countries at all levels of development. He found that the association between energy consumption per-capita and level of democracy in 1960 was best described by a curvilinear, positively decelerated function congruent with the threshold hypothesis.

3 Simpson used data for Denmark (1966), Switzerland (1968), and Pakistan (1970 and 1971). These countries are omitted here because the Danish and Swiss measures are derived from tax statistics that are not comparable with measures derived from population surveys (Sawyer, 1976, p. 23), while the Pakistani data seriously underestimate the income share of upper-income groups (van Ginnekan, 1976, p. 14).

4 Zimbabwe does not have a 1965 liberal democracy score; Taiwan does not have a 1980 liberal democracy score.

5 If model 1 is re-estimated for 58 countries with economic growth deleted, R^2 remains 0.41.

6 British colonial heritage is a binary variable, scored 1 if a country became

independent after World War II and was formerly a colony, self-governing dependency, protectorate, or trust territory under British control, and scored 0 otherwise (Bollen and Jackman, 1985b, p. 446). For the 58 countries analyzed in table 5.3, those classified as having British colonial heritage are Barbados, Ghana, India, Kenya, Malawi, Malaysia, Sierra Leone, Sri Lanka, Tanzania, and Trinidad and Tobago. The percentage of the population that is Protestant is from Taylor and Hudson (1972, table 4.16). Peripheral world-system status is from Snyder and Kick (1979, pp. 1110, 1114).

7 British colonial heritage is correlated moderately with logged GDP per-capita ($r = -0.47$) but is uncorrelated with the Gini index of income inequality ($r = -0.04$) and the top 20 percent income share ($r = 0.02$). The logged percentage of the population that is Protestant is correlated moderately with logged 1970 GDP per capita ($r = 0.40$), the Gini index of income inequality ($r = 0.42$), and the top 20 percent of income share ($r = -0.44$). The logged percentage of the population that is Islamic is correlated strongly with logged GDP per-capita ($r = -0.65$), but is weakly correlated with the Gini index of income inequality ($r = 0.19$) and the top 20 percent income share ($r - 0.24$). Peripheral world-system status is correlated moderately with logged 1970 GDP per-capita ($r = -0.51$), the Gini index of income inequality ($r = 0.48$), and the top 20 percent income share ($r = 0.54$).

8 Bollen and Jackman (1989) criticized measures of years of democratic experience (1) as conceptually regressive because the measures reduced democracy to a binary variable and democracy is either present or absent in a given year, and (2) invalid because level of democracy and stability of democracy are confounded. Muller (1988) argued that regarding the question of whether democracy has egalitarian consequences, there is a compelling theoretical rationale for hypothesizing that a negative effect of democracy on income inequality must be incremental and long run. If Muller's theoretical argument is accepted (also see Hewitt, 1977), then a measure of accumulated years of democracy is more appropriate (or valid) for testing this particular hypothesis than are measures of level of democracy in a single year or over a brief period (Rueschemeyer *et al.*, 1992, note 3:310; Weede, 1990, pp. 516–17).

9 The initial year of continuous popular elections for contemporary democratic political systems as of 1967, defined as "regimes based on three or more consecutive, popular, and competitive elections," is given in table 5 of Rustow (1967, pp. 290–1). The list of democracies was amended subsequently to exclude Mexico (Rustow, 1970, p. 349). Rustow omitted several small states with populations under 1,000,000, including Barbados and Trinidad and Tobago, which meet the three-elections criterion for the date used here, 1965. The initial year of continuous popular elections is 1946 for Barbados and 1950 for Trinidad and Tobago. Also, Colombia does not meet the three-elections criterion for 1965. The years of continuous elections variable is logged (base e) after adding 1.0 to all scores.

10 When income inequality is not included in the equation, years of continuous elections has a significant positive effect on democratization independent of economic development and British colonial heritage. The positive effect of

years of continuous elections on democratization thus is explained by its association with income inequality.

11 The source of the data is the World Bank (1984a, 1985). The Gini coefficients for income inequality and top 20 percent income share are, respectively, 0.29 and 37.5 for Denmark, 0.29 and 36.8 for Finland, 0.32 and 39.2 for Israel, 0.47 and 59.2 for Nepal, 0.29 and 38.0 for Switzerland, and 0.50 and 61.1 for Zambia.

12 Results are also virtually identical if the equations reported in table 5.5 are estimated using the top 20 percent income share as the indicator of income inequality.

13 If the cutoff point for considering a case to be potentially influential is set at DFITS values greater than ±1.0 (i.e., deletion of the case produces a change in fit greater than the standard error of fitted scores), then the only case that exceeds this criterion for models 3 and 4 in table 5.5 is Yugoslavia. However, deletion of Yugoslavia does not appreciably affect the magnitude of the coefficients for the explanatory variables.

14 These factors are "a high level of urbanization, a rapidly declining or relatively small agricultural population, great occupational diversity, extensive literacy, a comparatively large number of persons who have attended institutions of higher education, an economic order in which production is mainly carried on by relatively autonomous firms whose decisions are strongly oriented toward national and international markets, and relatively high levels of conventional indicators of well-being, such as physicians and hospital beds per thousand persons, life-expectancy, infant mortality, percentage of families with various consumer durables, and so on" (Dahl, 1989, p. 251).

6   Informational inequality and democracy in the new world order

Miles Simpson

In two centuries, democratic practices have spread from Northern Europe and North America to a majority of nations around the world. While this remarkable transformation appears to be inexorable, regularly, democratization suffers reversals. In the past 25 years, Algeria, Argentina, Chile, Gambia, Pakistan, Philippines, and Rwanda have experienced declines in democratic practices and institutions. The old Eastern bloc struggles to create democratic institutions while teetering on the edge of totalitarianism. Nearly half of the world's democracies are brand new having emerged between 1980 and 1990 in a third wave of democratization (Diamond and Plattner, 1993; Huntington, 1992, 1993). Of 186 nations in 1993, 107 held elections and extend a few political and individual rights (Lipset, 1994). Democracy, in its weakest form, appears in slightly more than half of the nations yet it involves less than half the world's population. In light of the explosive growth of democratic institutions, the instability of new democratic regimes, and the large segment of the world remaining under totalitarian or autocratic rule, we need to know more about the forces that advance or retard democratization.

Although no single cause can explain various nations' transition to democracy, we must continue the search for Lipset's requisites. Recently, some scholars have rejected the search for underlying structural and cultural causes of democracies' rise or decline (Huntington, 1992; Shin, 1994) and stress the political elites' maneuvers or crafting of political institutions through political will and action (Diamond and Linz, 1990; Di Palma, 1990, see this volume). Still empirical evidence strongly suggests that democracy flourishes in only certain cultural and structural conditions (Huntington, 1993; Inkeles, 1991; Lipset, 1994; Lipset, Seong, and Torres, 1993; Olsen, 1968). Power resources, economic inequality and institutional structures, have been the main focus of most studies of democracy (Bollen, 1980; Crenshaw, 1996; Lipset, 1994; Muller, see this volume; Olsen, 1968; and Vanhanen, 1984, 1990, 1992) and without denying the importance of other external or internal

156

conditions, I argue that informational equality is the critical requisite for democratization.

Democracy depends on a public who can process complex information and actively participate in politics (Gonick and Rosh, 1988; Hadenius, 1990; Putnam, 1996; and Zolo, 1992). While other structural and economic factors may play key roles in triggering a movement toward cognitive equality, where the population is well informed, democratization is more likely to occur. Democratization in turn tends to decrease income inequality (Simpson, 1990). Furthermore, increasing informational equality and not rising economic well being is critical during Huntington's third wave of democratization.

Literature

In his nineteenth-century study of a new and exotic American form of government, de Tocqueville (1945 [1835, 1840]) attributed American democracy to a confluence of factors – an absence of inherited aristocracy and institutionalized moral inequality, an infrastructure that promotes participation at the local level such as the New England township system, widespread education that produced a literate population, a religion that emphasized individual liberty, a common cultural heritage, and freedom from attack due to a lack of land routes available to powerful adversaries (de Tocqueville, 1945 [1835, 1840]). Democracies were forming elsewhere in areas that had some but not all of these characteristics. England, the lowlands, and Scandinavia had several of these characteristics and developed strong democratic institutions. Although de Tocqueville saw education and literacy as important preconditions for democracy, neither prosperity nor GDP was on his list. Rather he emphasized social equality including an absence of an aristocratic tradition, which separated the elite and the population, and the presence of common culture both of which facilitate information equality by removing class and cultural barriers to ideas and information.

Reflecting on the recent growth of new democratic regimes or the third wave of democracy, Huntington (1993) provides a somewhat different list of causes – performance legitimacy crisis of authoritarian regimes from economic and military failures, rapid global economic growth including education, and a growing urban middle class; the doctrines of the Second Vatican of 1963–5 that transformed the Catholic Church from a defender to an opponent of authoritarian regimes; policy changes of the European Community, the United States, and the old Soviet Union; and a snowballing effect of success in one regime becoming a model for later democratization of neighboring regimes

(Huntington, 1984, 1993). Failed democratic regimes encounter another constellation of problems – key elites and/or the general public not valuing democracy, severe economic setbacks, social and political polarization often resulting from too rapid social transformations, determined conservative upper and middle classes who exclude leftist and lower-class elements from participation, decline in law and order stemming from terrorist insurgency, simple conquest or intervention of a foreign power, and a reverse snowball effect (Huntington, 1993, p. 9). Huntington emphasizes external more than internal forces. International organizations such as the International Monetary Fund and World Bank, in this view, are critical for the recent surge in nations undergoing democratization. According to Huntington (1993), internal forces that influence democratization or its failure stem from changes in prosperity, education, an expanding urban middle class, a recalcitrant conservative upper class, inept left-wing parties and their failed social programs, or chaos due to insurgence whose rise may be due to any number of reasons. Although Huntington's list contains features that have appeared during changes in government, they appear as well without either subsequent democratization or a retreat from democracy as well. Thus their causal status has yet to be demonstrated.

Political inequality and informational inequality

Democracy extends power to groups other than a small political elite. Bollen (1980, 1993) defines democracy as "the extent to which the political power of the elite is minimized and that of the non-elite is maximized" (Bollen, 1980, p. 372). He further distinguishes liberal democracy from Lenin–Marxist regimes in that in liberal democracies, the system entails political liberties and democratic rule (Bollen, 1993). Critical liberties include freedom of assembly, freedom of speech, freedom of the press and electronic media, and the right to join political parties. Democratic rule occurs when government's authority flows from the people through regular elections. The crux of liberal democracy is the balance of power between the elite and non-elite sectors of society. When the balance favors the elite, they respond minimally to the non-elite demands but when the balance favors the masses having access to government, they block actions of the elites and promote their own interests.

According to group competition theory, group power flows from three sources, relative group size, group organization, and group resources (Bierstedt, 1950; Blalock, 1967; Olson, 1982). Elites offset their small size with superior organization and resources. Communication and information influences both group organization and resources. A group must view itself as separate from other groups and understand that its interests differ from other groups before it will take political action. Elites meet this basic criteria and if allowed they will then keep their activities secret, make sure that the non-elite has little understanding of the political system, and limit non-elites' awareness of successful alternatives to current conditions. Informational equality, therefore, is the equal distribution of ideas and knowledge among the members of a society. These include government's performance, the relative economic standing of the various groups in society, and the disposition of justice. Availability of ideas and information depends on both open channels of communication and the individual's willingness and skills in utilizing the information. Societies may differ widely in the amount and kind of information they generate, the means of transmitting ideas, and the means of storing ideas. As opposed to societies two hundred years ago, the volume of technical knowledge required to run a modern society is vast, although it creates economic and military power this power is shared widely over a substantial portion of the population. Technically sophisticated groups, who can skillfully employ military force, can resist coercion.

Informational inequality arises from two sources: structural blocks to the flow of information available, and group differences in capacity to input and understand complex material. Structural cleavages promote or retard informational inequality. High languages or other cultural cleavages reinforcing vertical economic levels, diminish the vertical flow of critical political information. Concentrated control of information channels, such as newspapers, book publishing and distribution, movie and electronic media, provide powerful blocks to information flow. Official secrecy slows down the flow of vital information. Once this blockage is in place, the in-groups can exploit the information until the out-group ferrets out the information. Time and effort to retrieve secret knowledge, set against its perceived worth, probably accounts for a considerable informational inequality. Knowledge is more expensive for those low in information-processing capacity and access to information. Holding ease of access constant, low information-processing-capacity individuals will be less likely to pursue the same information than those with better processing capacity.

Although individuals differ in their ability and in part these differences may have physiological basis – childhood nutrition, disease, or trauma – the major equalizer is education which increases both general knowledge and the capacity to process knowledge. Differences in knowledge of current events as well as general knowledge persists between different educational groups in the same cohort long after they have passed through the educational system (Hyman, Wright, and Reed, 1975). Trent and Medsker (1969) showed that university education, as opposed to working, influences major personality dimensions such as authoritarianism, complexity, and thinking inversion.[1]

Simple literacy, according to Goody and Watt (1968), allows individuals to compare moral standards with current performance. Written language brings together people who are socially and spatially separated. Literacy fosters a critical outlook. A written message maybe read over and over again and compared with other written material. This undermines the traditional hierarchy by separating the voice and status cues of the author from the content of the text (McLuhan, 1962; Goody and Watt, 1968). Literacy, therefore, creates a new consciousness, that allows evaluation of information in ways that are radically different from the oral traditions. Literacy in a word promotes reflectivity, the key component of modernity (Beck, 1994; Inkeles, 1974).

The early modernization literature linked literacy to economic development. Literacy increases the capacity to empathize with people outside an individual's immediate community that in turn increases media participation and interest in politics (Lerner, 1958). Traditional life and the community's hold on the individual weakens with literacy (Goody and Watt, 1968; Deutsch, 1961) thereby facilitating political mobilization (Pye, 1966). Information inequality and literacy, in particular, play a more central role in both the rise of democracy and economic development.

Democratic institutions involving a majority of the population did not appear until printing and mass education had produced substantial literacy. Prior to 1700, people relied mainly on word of mouth and handwritten material for information. Political and religious drama emphasized the power of the hierarchy in preliterate societies and literate societies before mass literacy. Although examples of direct democracy can be found in the anthropological record (Bollen and Paxton, see this volume; Ember, Ember, and Russett, see this volume), these were in the main small-scale hunting and gathering societies where generally there was little formal structure and the government was open to almost all adults. An early large-scale agricultural society with representational democracy, Hellenic Athens which rotated its leadership in fact limited political participation to non-slave elite males (Bollen and Paxton, see this volume; Midlarsky, see this volume). While larger and more complex than hunting and gathering societies, Athens cannot be compared with contemporary societies with their complex technologies, populations in the millions dispersed over hundreds and even thousands of miles.

Oral communication places an upper limit on the size of democracy. Although the elite of Athens and republican Rome had writing and many were able to communicate over long distances through letters, they were not able to communicate to large numbers of people. Preliterate democracies were confined to oral transmission of knowledge. In these early democracies, debates had to be conducted face to face within earshot of a substantial percentage of the citizens who then communicated the outcome to others. Democracy, without mass media, is therefore limited to small scale, San Marino sized populations.

Modern democracies did not appear on any scale until the 1700s. Some small-scale communities or localities evidence democratic practices at some level, even if it were only a house of lords or guild halls (Swanson, 1967). Yet, nowhere in Europe did hundreds of thousands, let alone millions, of voting citizens live under a single democratic regime until the nineteenth century. Political activity was primarily an elite matter until very recent times.

Historically, democracy appears only well after the development of the first printing press. Widespread literacy became possible after the perfecting of mass printing and production of inexpensive paper. The appearance of the printing press did not immediately produce an avalanche of democratization, but it made possible the next step, universal education and later the newspaper.

In the late eighteenth and nineteenth centuries, armed with inexpensive printed material, governments could educate their population. State expansion theorists view the modern educational system as an outgrowth of state building and not industrialization (Meyer, Ramirez, Rubinson, and Boli-Bennett 1979, 1981; Meyer, Ramirez, and Soysel, 1992; Thomas and Meyer, 1986). Mobilization depends on the reaching large segments of the population rapidly (Coulter, 1975; Cutwright, 1963; Deutsch, 1961; Lerner, 1958; Lipset, 1959; and Pye, 1966). Mass literacy, once made possible through the printing press and inexpensive paper, became quickly recognized as a powerful tool of the state that allowed the ruler to communicate with a spatially dispersed and culturally diverse population. The rulers push for universal education to create a population that identified more with the state than the local community, who could respond to a central government and who would participate in modern industry. But, they got more than they bargained for – a population with critical political resources, with information about the government's strengths and weaknesses, and therefore a broader view of the world and a sense of competence. In sum, literacy produced more contentious interest groups demanding more rights and calling for the curtailing of the elites' privileges.

Information inequality in general and literacy in particular featured prominently in several works on revolutions. The decision to allow literacy to spread was not taken lightly by traditional elites (Stone, 1969). In his study of the English civil war, Stone (1969) noted that the conservative wing of the aristocracy was aware that illiterate citizens were easier to govern and exploit than critical, literate citizens. The great revolts against traditional authority – the English, the French, and Russian revolutions – occurred when the proportion of men who were minimally literate had exceeded one-third (Stone, 1969, p. 183). These revolts were also fueled by dashed economic expectations, and in the French and Russian cases as they experienced an inverted J-curve in economic conditions (Davies, 1979). Literacy did not predict which French province would revolt while type of government – centrally controlled or locally controlled – the economic conditions, adequacy of roads, and city size could be indications of revolt (Markoff, 1985). Markoff determined a province's level of literacy as the percent of husbands who signed their marriage contract, a minimal definition at best although it probably correlated with the percent of men and women who could read. Informational equality did find support. Good roads and urbanity predict revolt. Both spread knowledge and misinformation among literate and illiterate alike. Of course neither the French nor the Russian revolution culminated in democracy. Revolts and rebellions erupted time and again throughout Europe from the year 1000 to 1800 with little change in type of government (Cohn, 1961). During this early period, only two, the British and American revolutions, had any appreciable effect on democratization.

Governments have excluded groups from politics by denying them education and even outlawing literacy. In the North American South, literacy was denied to the blacks by law and to poor whites through inferior education when it was available at all. Helper (1960 [1857]) showed that illiteracy was considerably greater among Southern Whites than their Northern counterparts. He concluded that "Slavery is hostile to general education; its strength, its very life, is in the ignorance and stolidity of the masses; it naturally and necessarily represses general literary culture" (Helper, 1960 [1857], p. 253).

In development research communications are central to economic and political development. Communication variables, including literacy, school enrollments, newspaper and magazine readership, load on a social development factor in contrast to an economic factor on which indicators of development, such as GDP and energy consumption, are loaded (Hadenius, 1992). Communications as a component of social development have been argued to precede economic and political development. Cutwright (1963) constructed a communications index that consisted of mainly printed material circulation, newsprint consumption, telephones, and domestic mail. The communication index correlated highly with his political development index revealing little about causal direction. Also, of Cutwright's (1963) communication index's indicators, all but telephones per population, are directly linked to literacy. An early model of democratization (McCrone and Cnudde, 1967) combined the correlates found by Cutwright and Lipset into a communication theory that begins with urbanization which in turn promoted education and mass communication consumption, the proximal cause of democratization. Unfortunately, McCrone and Cnudde (1967) could not study these effects over time and therefore the causal direction between communications and democracy remained debatable (Rustow, 1970).

In a cross-sectional times series study for the period 1955–65, when controlling for GNP per-capita, state centralization, world-system position, Kondratieff waves, and urbanization, Gonick and Rosh (1988) found that raw percent literate predicts democratic rights. In this study, the dependent variable was Bollen's (1980) democratic rights index constructed from Banks' (1971) cross-polity survey. Gonick and Rosh (1988), employing the quality of life approach, found that literacy was the best predictor of democratic functioning even though Gonick and Rosh (1988) did not examine the logistic relationship between literacy and democratic rights thereby potentially underestimating the relationship. Also, Bank's (1971) annual data included many extrapolated estimates which tend to reduce error variance as opposed to years with valid data and artificially increasing the strength of variables with many extrapolated points. While suggestive, Gonick and Rosh (1988) were far from definitive. Gastil's measure of political and civil rights correlated with literacy as well (Dasgupta and Weale, 1992). Literacy, Das Gupta and Weale (1992) suggested, provided critical cognitive resources that allow the citizen actively to seek and interpret information and convert into knowledge and action.

Belief systems and inequality: the impact of ideology and religion

Religion provides a belief system which may either promote innovation and active participation or reaction and passive withdrawal (de Tocqueville, 1945 [1835, 1840]; Weber, 1958). Protestantism, through worldly asceticism, individualism, and stressing economic success as an indicator of good conduct, encouraged the expansion of Northern European commerce and the birth of modern capitalism. But the emergence of the reformation needed explanation. Areas of Europe, where the government was based on the principle of "immanence," failed to follow the reformation (Swanson, 1967). Immanence is the divine authority of the ruler. Disagree with the ruler and you disagree with God. Under immanence dissent is heresy. But in other areas of Europe, where at some level of government, equals may present differing views, debate their merits, and vote binding the ruler to the decision, Protestantism arose even if later it was suppressed by external military force or exterminated as were the Huguenots and Cathars. The placing of religion at the center of government tends to polarize all political issues into believers and non-believers thereby not allowing compromise, the foundation of political democracy (Bollen and Jackman, 1985a).

Although eventually most of Europe adopted democracy and immanence disappeared from Europe, the original Protestant nations were the seedbed for the modern rise of democracy. The expansion of the reformation was accelerated by the Protestant sects employing the printed word and mass literacy to carry their message. During the counter reformation, Catholics also used the printed word as the Mass Media and abandoned immanence in the secular realm and developed democratic governments soon after democracy had swept Northern Europe.

Although immanence is not a basic tenet of fundamentalist Islamic groups, they come very close to this position through the absolute nature of the Koran and Islamic law. Islamic fundamentalists require that political leaders practice Islam and follow Islamic law. The lack of separation of state and religion plays a role in the religious struggles in Iran and North Africa. Despite its individualism, unitarianism, puritanism, and aversion to hierarchy, Islam provides little support for democracy due to its refusal to separate the secular and religious communities. Fusing the state and church stifles dissent. By secularizing the state, only Turkey, among the Islamic nations, has been able to sustain a democratic tradition. There the great leader, Ataturk, successfully formed a modern state based on a secular government. All other Islamic attempts at democracy have failed or are failing (Huntington, 1993; Wright, 1992).

Islamic education and literacy in Arabic may not provide the reflectivity needed for participation in democracy. In Nigeria, Armer (1992) found that literacy in English was associated with social psychological effects including political participation but these effects did not appear among persons who were only literate in Arabic. How reading is taught or what one reads in becoming literate may be as important for participation in a democratic society as literacy (Simpson, 1972). If this is true, Islam and Islamic education may retard democratization.

Cultures stressing unity, in particular, the spiritual unity of the group, restrict individual and group dissent. Hence, a strong collectivistic moral code emphasizing personal duty is poor soil for democracy and, when imposed from without, poor ground for sustaining it. China, that bastion of totalitarianism had ancient Taoist and Confucian ethics that places individual desire far below collective duty (Huntington, 1993). Group unity, in the face of perpetual external military threats dictates the forming of a militaristic society (Spencer, 1876) as contrasted with merchant societies, such as England and the United States, militant societies such as nineteenth-century Prussia and Russia.

In an early study, although Protestantism had an independent impact on political democracy, British colonial status and new nation status were predictors of liberal democracy (Bollen and Jackman, 1985a, 1985b). While these findings hold promise, does the imposing of a political system through colonization last? The length of the colonial period and the intensity of the contact may have an impact. The greater the difference between indigenous and colonial culture, the less likely the foreign influence would survive after the end of colonization.

Our main task will be to test the simple proposition that democracy depends not only on wealth or power resources but more on cognitive capacity and societal values. I argue that informational equality through literacy is the single most important force driving the expansion of democracy. I will pit literacy, properly specified by a logit transformation, against Vanhanen's Index of Power Resources, a composite measure, and the log of the gross domestic product in order to see which predicts political democracy best. The actual test of literacy is a residual of the difference between 1980 and 1969 Index of Power Resources. Lastly the impact of religion particularly Protestantism is sufficiently widespread to employ in a cross-national study and seems to emphasize relative individual autonomy. Islam emphasizes close adherence to its teachings and trusts religion in the center of politics.

Methods

Three measures of democracy will be employed: Vanhanen's (1984, 1990, 1992) democratic performance measure, and Gastil's Political Rights Index and Civil Rights Index. Vanhanen's measure of democratization involved political competition, size of legislative opposition, and public participation, voter turnout which follows from Dahl's

(1971) two dimensions of democracy, public contest and the right to participate. Vanhanen correctly understood that the right to participate does not insure that individuals will participate and not retreat into private pursuits. Competition without participation does not allow democratic dynamics either and may represent merely an in-house squabble among the elite. Vanhanen therefore, used two measures of democratization: degree of competition in the political system, which he calculated by subtracting the percent of votes won by the largest party, and he measured election participation by simply employing the percent of the actual population who voted in recent elections. These are multiplied together to form the Indicator of Democratization.

Vanhanen's participation and competition may have serious flaws and be poor measures of democracy (Bollen, 1993). In his multivariate indicator of democracy, Bollen (1993) excluded both voter participation and legislative competition from his analysis. Higher turnout does not mean greater legitimacy when citizens must vote by law as is the case in the old Eastern bloc socialist countries where only one party appears on the ballot. The issue of voter turnout also avoids the direct measurement of franchises and groups who are excluded from the political system. Falsification or miscounts of elections provide additional grounds for discounting voter participation. National legislature composition have similar problems (Bollen, 1993). In an earlier paper (Simpson, 1993b), I employed Bollen's 1965 and 1980 measures and literacy proved a powerful predictor but Huntington (1984) saw that, during this period, democracy retreated. This is substantiated by Muller's (see this volume) change scores for Bollen's 1965 and 1980 measures. Of the 58 nations reported there, 18 dropped 20 points or more while only five rose 20 or more points. For the entire sample 9 nations, mainly OECD countries, experienced no change in democracy, 18 rose, and 31 declined during the late 1960s and the 1970s. Given the contrasting increase in democracies during the 1980s, it is important to consider the entire 25-year period.

Bollen does not have an index for the late 1980s or early 1990s. Only Gastil's and Vanhanen's measures span the entire 25-year period. Since Bollen (1993) questions the adequacy of Vanhanen's Index, as a check I correlated Vanhanen's measures with Bollen's measures for the 1969–1975 and 1979 and 1980 periods. For Eastern bloc nations, Vanhanen's Index for 1969 and Bollen's 1965 Index correlated, $r = 0.64$, $n = 10$ while for Vanhanen's Index for 1979 and Bollen's Index for 1980, $r = 0.09$, $n = 10$. For non-Eastern bloc nations the correlations were more consistent with Bollen's (1965) and Vanhanen's (1969) measures correlating $r = 0.71$, $n = 89$ and for Bollen's (1980) and Vanhanen's (1979) measure, $r = 0.75$, $n = 89$. Despite its problems, Vanhanen's measure shares roughly half of its non-Eastern bloc variance with Bollen's Index for both time periods and is an acceptable proxy for Bollen's Index.

The Political Rights Index and Civil Rights Index for the year 1988 are taken from Gastil (1991) and for the earlier period, averaged over the years 1973–7, from Taylor and Jodice (1983). These measures were formed by coding nations on a seven-point scale, 1 (highest) to 7 (lowest). The Political Rights Index's top scores (1 and 2) are assigned to political systems that have elections where most of the citizens can vote. The election must be fair. Freedom to organize politically is assured. The middle range 3–5 describes systems that to increasing degrees involve fraud with constitutional restrictions barring participation by a few to almost all adults. These undemocratic practices have a substantial impact on the outcome of elections. The right to organize is significantly curtailed. The bottom of the scale (6 and 7) indicates either no elections or single candidate elections. Groups are forbidden to organize in opposition to the government.

The Civil Rights Index begins with the top scores (1 and 2) assigned to nations where the judiciary is structurally independent of the administration, where the courts have the power to resist the arbitrary actions of the authorities and from mob rule. The media is not censored or prevented from criticizing the government or its officials. Middle-range nations (3–5) interfere with the judiciary to varying extents. Individuals may be jailed without due process or proper evidence. Life and property are threatened. Martial laws are not uncommon. At the bottom of the scale the citizen has no rights and the state has complete dominance over the individual. Censorship is complete with no criticism of the government allowed.

The Gastil Indices have come under criticism from Bollen (1990, 1993) for what he calls method error or systematic error resulting from employing expert judges whose own political position tends to anchor their judgments. Conservative judges may be lenient on right-wing regimes, liberal judges do the same for socialist governments. Incomplete information is another problem. Often, judges will have to make decisions without all the current facts. This means that past facts will be substituted and this will produce inertia and inflate the stability of ratings.

Independent variables include percent of the adult population, 15 and over, who are literate circa 1965 from Banks (1971). On inspection, literacy formed the classic logistic S-curve with the dependent variables.

Given that literacy is a variable that involves a growth process from a set with a floor of zero literacy, the strong possibility of an S-relationship requires a test for the logit transformation. The logit is

$$y = \log (X/(100-X))$$

where X is the percent literate.

Gross National Product per Population (GDP) is for the year 1965 (Banks, 1971). Religious adherents are recorded in the United Nations Demographic Yearbook for Catholicism, Protestantism, and Islam. The index of Power Resources is from Vanhanen (1984, 1992) and is a composite measure. When we examine the effects of literacy, our general strategy will be to compare the lagged effects of literacy, GDP, and the Power Index controlling for the measure of democratic performance or rights at time 1.

In this study, British colonies differed from previous measures. Bollen and Jackman (1985a) included protectorates, self-governing dependencies, trust or mandate territories, and former colonies who became independent after World War II. The absence of the major colonies such as the United States, Canada, Australia, and New Zealand is misleading. Also, I will include Ireland that for centuries has been under tight British rule and only established an independent government just after World War I. British rule influenced these older colonies through substantial immigration as well as government.

As Eastern bloc nations are very different from the remainder of the world, we do not expect the continuous variables necessarily to have the same effect among Eastern bloc and non-Eastern bloc nations. The preferred method of analysis of data with such strong contextual variables is the nested analysis of covariance. In the nested design the main effects of the nested variables are dropped and only the interaction terms are included for the nesting variables and variables that are not influenced by the nesting variable. The nesting variables are contexts such as hospitals or wards that differ on a wide range of unknown variables. Type of regime is a classic nesting variable.

Multicollinearity poses a problem for interpreting results. Substantial interrelation between independent variables has the effect of inflating the error variance of the parameter estimates which in turn could result in missing a significant independent variable. The variance inflation factor (VIF) provides us with a guide to the severity of multicollinearity. VIF is defined $1/(1-R_i^2)$ where R_i^2 is the coefficient of determination of the ith independent variable on all other dependent variables in the equation. The conventional cutoff points for VIF are five-fold or ten-fold (Freund and Littell, 1986). As multicollinearity's negative effect

Table 6.1 *Means and standard deviation for political rights, civil rights, and Vanhanen's Indicator of Democratization by regime – Eastern bloc*

Independent variables	Eastern block			Non-Eastern block		
	Mean	S.D.	n	Mean	S.D.	n
Indicator of Democratization, 1969	0.47	0.69	10	8.86	11.47	98
Indicator of Democratization, 1979	5.25	15.59	10	8.29	12.03	98
Indicator of Democratization, 1990	16.30	16.45	10	12.39	13.58	98
Political Rights Index for mid-1970[1]	6.65	0.46	10	4.06	2.19	101
Political Rights Index for 1978	6.60	0.52	10	3.98	2.20	101
Political Rights Index for 1988	6.30	0.92	10	3.48	2.19	101
Civil Rights Index for mid-1970[1]	6.32	0.56	10	3.84	1.95	101
Civil Rights Index for 1978	5.90	0.74	10	3.82	1.99	101
Civil Rights Index for 1988	5.80	1.03	10	3.64	2.05	101

Notes: [1]Both the Political Rights Index and the Civil Rights Index are a seven-point scale ranging from 1 most rights to 7 fewest rights.
[2]These means are based on cases for which valid data were reported for all three time periods.

declines as the R^2 increases, they recommend rejecting VIF exceeding the benchmark $1/(1-R^2)$. Any VIF exceeding this benchmark could be assumed to significantly underestimate the significance of the equation's parameters (Bollen and Jackman, 1985c; Freund and Littell, 1986).

Results

The data confirm Huntington's (1993) third wave – the democracy indexes trend up and not down from 1970 to 1990. Even without Eastern bloc nations, the non-Eastern bloc nations show small gains in democracy (table 6.1). During this period, the mean value of Vanhanen's Index of Democratization increases dramatically within the Eastern bloc nations and is accompanied by a parallel increase in standard deviation. Although nations such as Cuba, China, and North Korea have remained steadfastly communist, the Eastern European nations have adopted democratic practices. Non-Eastern bloc nations also show an increase in democratization, by roughly 50 percent, with only a small increase in the standard deviation. Gastil's Political Rights Index, in contrast, shows only minor changes toward more political rights (the lower the score, the more political rights), hardly more than a quarter of the standard deviation for non-Eastern bloc nations and even less for Eastern bloc countries. The Gastil Civil Rights Index indicates even less change over the roughly 15-year period. Gastil's measures, therefore, downplay the momentous changes occurring in the old Eastern bloc while Vanhanen's crude measure of performance is very sensitive to these transformations. Gastil's measures pose a methodological problem for our panel analysis. Given the very stable Gastil measures, we must assume either little change in their underlying source of variance even over a 20-year period – democracy has not had an upswing as Huntington (1984, 1993) reported and Vanhanen's (1992) measures revealed – or that Gastil's' measures tend to average over longer periods and do not reflect the peaks and valleys in regimes' democratic performance. I lean toward the latter explanation and accept Bollen's (1990, 1993) charge of a leveling bias for Gastil's expert opinion approach to measuring democracy (see table 6.1). Expert estimates have a tendency to preserve and change slower than objective conditions and Gastil's measures are no exceptions.

When we examine the effects of literacy, Vanhanen's Democracy Index, Gastil's Political Rights Index, or the Civil Rights Index, within both the Eastern and non-Eastern blocs, the analysis of the Index of Democratization without the lagged term or Vanhanen's Power Resources Index, literacy, is significant and the regression coefficient for the Eastern bloc is over twice the coefficient for non-Eastern bloc (table 6.2). The impact of literacy on the breakup of the communist countries and the speed at which they move toward democracy is dramatic. Eastern bloc and GDP (logged) within the Eastern bloc have a negative and significant independent effect on Vanhanen's Indicator of Democracy. The addition of the Indicator of Democratization 1969 and the Index of Power Resources changes the picture slightly. Only the Indicator of Democratization 1969, and literacy are significant (table 6.2, equation 2). The relationship between literacy and Vanhanen's Indicator of Democratization 1969 remains significant in the non-Eastern bloc. Also in equation 2 of table 6.2, the slopes for the relationship between literacy and Vanhanen's Indicator of Democratization 1969, within the non-Eastern bloc and Eastern bloc nations, differ and the main effect for the Eastern bloc is not now significant. The total R^2 for the model 0.75. Economic development is only relevant for democracy if it contributes to literacy, a point we will address subsequently. When VIF coefficients were produced for the non-Eastern bloc countries, only one coefficient reached the critical level and that was for literacy.[2] As multicollinearity is inflating literacy's error variance, it underestimates literacy's significance, this means only that the statistical significance of literacy is being

Table 6.2 *Lagged analysis of covariance for Vanhanen's Indicator of Democratization, 1990 controlling for the Indicator of Democratization, 1969, and lagged analysis of covariance for Gastil's Political Rights Index and Civil Rights Index for 1988 controlling for the Political Rights Index, 1965, Civil Rights Index, 1965, with Vanhanen's Index of Power Resources, 1969, gross domestic product/capita, 1965, and literacy, 1965 nested within Eastern bloc 111 countries*

Independent variables	Democratization Index		Political Rights Index, 1988		Civil Rights Index, 1988	
	1	2	1	2	1	2
Indicator of Democratization, 1969	–	0.36@	–	–	–	–
Political Rights Index for mid-1970s[1]	–	–	–	0.63@	–	–
Civil Rights Index for mid-1970s[1]	–	–	–	–	–	0.66@
Eastern bloc	–54.39*	25.15	–12.07	–6.72	–11.30	–6.10
Index of Power Resources 1969 nested						
Non-Eastern bloc	–	–0.03	–	–0.02	–	.01
Eastern bloc	–	0.07	–	–0.02	–	–.02
GDP/capita 1965 (natural log) nested						
Non-Eastern bloc	1.25	1.43	–0.00	0.22	–0.13	0.08
Eastern bloc	–10.90*	3.29	–1.73	–0.70	0.44	1.08
Percent literate adults 15+ (logit) nested						
Non-Eastern bloc	4.16@	3.07@	–0.65@	–0.40@	–0.60@	–0.33&
Eastern bloc	10.00@	7.50@	0.23	0.12	–1.73	–0.08
Constant	58.53*	–11.14	15.90	6.40	16.02*	8.23
R^2	0.66	0.75	0.63	0.74	0.68	0.79
Number of countries	111	108	107	98	107	98

Notes: $*p < 0.05$; & $p < 0.01$; @ $p < 0.001$.
[1]Both the Political Rights Index and the Civil Rights Index are a seven-point scale ranging from 1 most right to 7 fewest right.

underestimated in this equation. Therefore, there is little loss due to multicollinearity.

For the Political and Civil Rights Index, a similar pattern emerges but there is an important difference. When the lagged variable for 1970 is left out (table 6.2, for both Political Rights and Civil Rights, the only independent variable to produce a significant effect is literacy within the non-Eastern bloc.[3] The contrast between the findings employing

Vanhanen's Index of Democratization and Gastil's measures need to be explored. Why did Gastil's measures not pick up the changes in the Eastern bloc countries? Technically the answer is simple-autocorrelation. The autocorrelations for the Political Rights Index 1970s to 1988 is $r = 0.98$, $n = 10$ for the Eastern bloc nations, and $r = 0.82$, $n = 101$ for non-Eastern bloc nations. For the Civil Rights Index 1970–88, the autocorrelations ran $r = 0.74$ for the Eastern bloc and $r = 0.86$ for non-Eastern bloc countries. The Index of Democratization's autocorrelation was dramatically lower again reflecting dramatic change. For democratization 1969–90, the autocorrelation is $r = -0.07$, $n = 10$ for Eastern bloc nations and $r = 0.75$, $n = 98$ for non-Eastern bloc nations. The high autocorrelations for the Political and Civil Rights Index means that we have less change to explain. Multicollinearity does not appear to play a major role in these findings also.[4] The challenges posed by Bollen (1990) against Gastil's expert ratings approach are partially substantiated. Experts ratings are stable in the face of changes, some dramatic, when more objective criteria are employed.

The cultural variables which indicate historical tendencies toward or away from individualism will be included in table 6.3. They are percent adherents to Islam, percent adherents to Protestantism, a dummy variable for experience with Confucianism, and dummy variable for British colony or protectorate. The inclusion of the religions that reputedly influence democracy, Confucianism, Islam, and Protestantism, revealed mixed results. Confucianism and Protestantism had no significant relationships (table 6.3). Islam predicted the Index of Democratization but neither the Political or Civil Rights Index. Experience in the British Empire and its more democratic institutions were related to the Index of Democratization as well and not to the Rights Index.

Conclusions

Although confirming Huntington's (1993) third wave of democratization from 1970 to 1990, these findings challenge Huntington's (1993) interpretation. The more literate the population in 1965, the more democratic the nation will be 15–25 years later. These findings also contradict Lipset's (1959, 1993) and Muller's (see this volume) conclusions that economic development underlies the modern expansion in democracy. Economic development as measured by gross domestic product per-capita has had little independent impact on democratization over the past 25 years. A nation's economic conditions, as measured through the standard natural log of gross domestic product per-capita, did not have an independent influence on democratic

Table 6.3 *Lagged analysis of covariance for Gastil's Political Rights Index, 1988, Civil Rights Index, 1988, Vanhanen's Index of Power Resources, 1990 controlling for Political Rights Index, 1969, Civil Rights Index, 1969, Index of Power Resources, 1969, Protestantism, Islam, gross domestic product, 1965, and Literacy, 1965 within Eastern bloc: 106 countries*

Independent variables	Indicator of Democracy, 1990	Political Rights Index, 1988	Civil Rights Index, 1988
Indicator of Democratization, 1969	0.40@	–	–
Political Rights Index for mid-1970[1]	–	0.67@	–
Civil Rights Index for mid-1970[1]	–	–	0.68@
Protestantism	−0.03	−0.01	0.01
Islam	0.06	−0.01	0.01
Confucianism	−1.08	−0.10	−0.07
Former British colony	−4.20*	0.45	0.18
Eastern bloc	39.65	−5.73	−8.39
GDP/capita 1965 (natural log) nested			
Non-Eastern bloc	2.10*	0.11	0.03
Eastern bloc	3.68	−1.25	−1.25
Percent literate adults 15+ (logit) nested			
Non-Eastern bloc	2.42@	−0.02*	−0.22*
Eastern bloc	7.37&	0.04	0.07
Constant	−25.87*	6.42	9.09
R^2	0.79	0.78	0.81
Number of countries	106	105	105

Notes: *$p < 0.05$; & $p < 0.01$; @ $p < 0.001$.
[1]Both the Political Rights Index and the Civil Rights Index are a seven-point scale ranging from 1 most rights to 7 fewest rights.

performance or rights. The relationship between economic and social variables should be carefully explored over time and not assumed to be a syndrome merely because they intercorrelate at one point in time. Additional time periods in different historical epochs would allow further test of the informational inequality hypothesis.

Since literacy predicts changes in democratic rights and performance, maybe the changes in policy during the second Vatican and evidenced by the policy shifts by the world powers are in part a response to a more literate global population. The snowballing effect noted by Huntington (1993) finds least resistance following a path laid down by literacy. Despite the totalitarian hold communism had on the old Eastern bloc nations, it eventually lost its power due to many factors including a failing economy, but the rising literacy of the populations of the Eastern bloc may have contributed to democratization. The likelihood, that a nation will adopt democracy and remain democratic, appears to be a function of the level of informational inequality. Unstable regimes such as Burma, Pakistan, Peru, and Sudan (Arat, 1988) have moderately low literacy rates and their instability may in part be due to a population that is ill equipped for democracy and competition with a literate elite class.

This chapter raises two methodological issues. The high correlation for both the Political Rights Index and Civil Rights Index supports Bollen's (1993) objections to such rating schemes on the grounds that there would be year to year autocorrelations due to area specialists failing to detect or report rapid changes in their nation's democratic practices. Area specialists have a vested interest in the countries they study and tend to take longer to report new problems, so their past performances most likely influence present ratings. Hard counts of voters and opposition members avoid this type of error.

Vanhanen's Indicator of Democratization has flaws as well. First, in Sri Lanka with a high competition score and a modest participation score a sizeable portion of the adult population cannot vote. Excluding persons from voting represents a much lower commitment to democracy then mere low eligible voter turnout. Second, high levels of competition in the legislature may represent no more than schisms among the elite. The issue then is how deep and how permanent is democratization for these new arrivals. If it is not deep, a dictator may allow a couple of parties to participate in elections. Will such nations just as quickly lose their veneer of democracy when the Huntington snowball moves in the other direction?

Our main construct, informational inequality, was measured by one variable, literacy, which by all accounts is poorly measured. It is rarely measured directly and may even represent bare minimum competence. More refined measures are needed which look at the differences in knowledge between groups. On an international level this is a major undertaking but over time, it may prove a sensitive indicator of basic changes in political power.

As a new construct, informational inequality requires a rethinking of the origins of democracy. Literacy is but one factor in the distribution of information. Future research should be directed toward other factors that might differentially increase or decrease a class or ethnic group's average cognitive capacities. Mere literacy may not be sufficient protection against a sophisticated media blitz. Modern media may shape issues. The concentration of media under the control of a few giant corporations sets the stage for the serious undermining of democracy. Their capacity to frame agendas by repetition of pseudo problems accompanied by shaky evidence that directs the public's attention away from lines of thought which threaten corporate interests poses the greatest threat (Zolo, 1992). Recent studies of the decline in American civic culture points to television as a major culprit (Putnam, 1996) which is supplanting newspaper reading and public participation. The more Americans watch television the more they overestimate the amount of crime and the less they participate in civic or political life (Putnam, 1996).

The capacity of elites to control sources of information may have an impact on democracy. When a foreign observer stands on the banks of the nearly one-thousand-year-old Grand Canal in China and views the riot of commercial traffic flowing chaotically North and South, the thought that this level of capitalism and economic growth occurs within a regime that for hundreds of years has limited the information available to its people must be jarring. Today contact with groups outside of China is forbidden, foreign reading material is carefully controlled, and even the wealthiest of Chinese may not own dish antennae. Whether such control will remain, poses the critical question not only for the 25 percent of the world's population in China but the world's population in marginal democratic regimes. Control over the media and internet may be the next hurdle for democracy.

Despite reservations about the future prospects of democracy in the electronic age, the conclusion is clear, modern mass democracy appeared in Europe only after the printing press and mass education was established and the current wave of democratizing countries is associated with increasing literacy. If snowballing and outside forces pushed regimes with illiterate populations to adopt democratic institutions, these new democracies are at great risk of relapsing back to authoritarian rule.

NOTES

1 Hagen (1962) argued that a predominately authoritarian population impeded development. Authoritarians are aggressive, rigid, and lack creativity, characteristics which do not foster economic change. Education, literacy and more important well-developed reading skills have an impact on authoritarianism. Simpson (1972) and Duckitt (1992) found that in the authoritarian educational systems, such as Mexican and Afrikaans schools, education has little impact on anti-democratic attitudes.

2 VIF scores were calculated for both the Eastern bloc and the non-Eastern bloc nations. With ID90 as the dependent variable, the VIF for ID69 was

2.14 and for GDP65, 2.97 and as suspected the VIF for IPR69 and literacy were higher, 4.23 and 4.92 respectively. GDP fell below the critical thresholds while literacy approaches the first critical threshold. But this means that the significant coefficient is being suppressed which is irrelevant here since it was significance despite the effects of multicollinearity.

3 The negative coefficient is due to Gastil's scoring that ranges from 1 high to 7 low.

4 Although the Civil and Political Rights Indexes correlate over time, multicollinearity was not a problem with either measure. With the non-Eastern bloc nations, for the Political Rights Index the regressors Political Rights Index 1970s, ID69, GDP65, and Literacy 1965, all were below with Literacy 1965 VIF being the highest at 3.89. The Civil Rights Index had the same pattern with the highest VIF being literacy 1965 at 3.88. All the VIF coefficients fall below the conservative cutoff of 5 for Freund and Littell's (1986) criteria. Multicollinearity, therefore, is not a serious problem. If anything, literacy has a stronger relationship to democracy than reported here.

7 Modernization and thresholds of democracy: evidence for a common path and process

Michael Coppedge

Prepared for the project on "Inequality and Democracy," for the Center for International Conflict Resolution and Peace Studies, Rutgers University. Valuable research assistance was provided by Ronna Montgomery. Mark Gasiorowski, Kenneth Bollen, Manus Midlarsky, the late Edward Muller, Marion Levy, Guillermo O'Donnell, Brian Crisp, and Deborah Yashar all made helpful comments and are in no way responsible for my failure to take all of their good advice.

The influential body of research born in the 1960s and known as modernization theory claimed, sometimes explicitly and sometimes implicitly, that there was a common path to democracy and a common process causing countries to move along it (Lipset, 1963, Lerner, 1958). A recurring theme in this literature was that developing countries were undergoing a process of political modernization whose end-state, stable democracy, would be achieved to the extent that they achieved socioeconomic modernization – urbanization, the spread of mass media, and rising levels of education, wealth, and equality. This thesis was soon criticized from several angles. Area studies specialists objected to the ethnocentrism implicit in the notion that developing countries would follow the path blazed by the industrialized countries, and questioned the appropriateness of Western-style democracy as a goal for the developing world. At the same time, some comparative theorists considered the thesis of modernization-driven democratization overly optimistic (Valenzuela and Valenzuela, 1978). Huntington (1968), for example, argued that modernization would lead to instability, not stable democracy, if organizational efforts did not keep pace with socioeconomic transformation. World-system and dependency theorists argued that exploitation by the industrialized core stunted or distorted the political development of the periphery (Wallerstein, 1974; Cardoso and Faletto, 1979). Guillermo O'Donnell (1979) took this critique a step farther, arguing that the most "modern" Latin American countries were likely to develop not democracy, but bureaucratic-authoritarian regimes. The wave of authoritarianism that swept South America in the 1960s

177

and 1970s seemed to confirm this pessimistic view, and modernization theory became widely discredited.

With the wave of democratization beginning in the mid-1970s, however, there has been a revival of thinking in the modernization tradition. As authoritarian regimes gave way to new democracies, the military rule of the previous decade came to be considered a temporary setback or a regional aberration (Przeworski *et al.*, 1996, p. 41). Pressures for democracy in countries where it had never taken root before, from Africa to Asia, as well as the collapse of communism in Eastern Europe, encouraged new optimism, suggesting that the critics of modernization theory had been too impatient (Pye, 1990). In the meantime, large-scale comparative research on modernization and democracy, which had never completely died out, accumulated evidence that vindicated the connection between aspects of modernization and democratization (Cutright and Wiley, 1969; Bollen and Jackman, 1985a; Muller, 1988). In particular, the robust association between wealth – usually operationalized as per-capita GNP – and democracy came to be widely recognized as a fact (Diamond, 1992; Rueschemeyer, Stephens, and Stephens, 1992).

The reasons for these empirical associations between modernization and democracy, however, remain open to interpretation. It has been maddeningly difficult to demonstrate which aspects of modernization are causes of democracy, which are effects, and which are only spurious associations. The frustration results from the fact that both democracy and socioeconomic development are complex and multifaceted phenomena. All aspects of socioeconomic development – per-capita GDP, income distribution, life expectancy, infant mortality, industrialization, occupational diversification, urbanization, literacy, school enrollments, and access to mass media – correlate with democracy, and most of these aspects of development are intercorrelated as well. There is some evidence that democracy may be as much a cause of some aspects of socioeconomic development as it is their effect.[1] The same may be true of another possible "determinant" of democracy – political culture (Putnam, 1993). Moreover, the impact of development on democratization is probably not immediate, but cumulative and delayed by lags of indeterminate and varying lengths. And the fact that democratization (and its reversal) tends to occur in waves suggests that there are some international causal relationships as well.

Although this chapter will not identify precisely what the common path and process of democratization are, it will present evidence that a common path and a common process exist, contrary to claims that the political systems of different regions of the world develop completely differently in response to socioeconomic development. This thesis should not be interpreted crudely, to mean that all countries throughout history have been driven, without interruption and at the same pace (although with varying timing), solely by socioeconomic modernization through identical institutional arrangements, eventually culminating in democracy. It should be interpreted probabilistically and in the long term, allowing for stalled progress, reversals, setbacks, and detours in the medium term, as well as for a small proportion of outlier countries that do not conform to the general trend. It is also a conditional thesis that allows for the impact of modernization to be mediated or over-whelmed by other determinants or obstacles to democracy, such as ethnic divisions, difficulties consolidating the state, elite behavior, war and other international pressures, and presidentialism and other insti-tutions. And, finally, it is flexible with regard to the institutional criteria for democracy and degrees of democracy.

The thesis being argued here makes two more modest claims. First, that most of the political systems of the world are arrayed along a single dimension corresponding to Dahl's concept of polyarchy (Dahl, 1971). Despite the tremendous diversity of their political institutions, countries all over the world tend strongly to develop and practice the same few combinations of degrees of electoral fairness, pluralism in the media, and freedom of organization and expression even though many more combinations are mathematically possible. This single dimension can be interpreted as a well-trodden path. Whether countries are becoming more democratic or less, whether they are changing rapidly or slowly or remaining stagnant, and whether they are European, American, African, or Asian, they tend to be located on this path rather than some-where off to its side.

Second, other things being equal, and with a few minor exceptions, the relationship between polyarchy and aspects of socioeconomic mod-ernization does not vary significantly in different regions of the world; it only seems to vary because the relationship is indeed different at dif-ferent thresholds of polyarchy, and each world region is skewed toward a different level of modernization. That is, some aspects of moderniz-ation are useful for understanding relatively high levels of polyarchy, while others are useless at high levels but much more useful for under-standing variation among relatively unpolyarchic countries. The relationships can be complex: some aspects of modernization are related to the middle of the polyarchy continuum, and others only to the extremes. But once these variations by threshold are controlled for, almost all of the variation in the relationship by region disappears. Thus relationship between levels of socioeconomic modernization and levels of polyarchy is the same, for the most part, in Europe, the Americas, Africa, and Asia. There is a common process driving countries along a common path.

The polyarchy scale as the common path

"Democracy" is operationalized here by the polyarchy scale (Coppedge and Reinicke, 1990). For most applications it makes little difference which measure of democracy one uses, for differences in levels of democracy are so large and obvious that most measures of political democracy turn up very similar results. For all of their technical short-comings, the Freedom House ratings seem to be perfectly adequate for large-scale comparative research and have the unique advantage of covering the entire world over a relatively long span of time. The poly-archy scale is probably more valid and reliable than the Freedom House ratings, but probably not by enough to make much of a difference for most purposes. The polyarchy scale correlates strongly with the Free-dom House ratings (0.934–0.938) and Vanhanen's Indices of Compe-tition (–0.895) and Democratization (–0.820) (Vanhanen, 1990).

The advantage of the polyarchy scale is not that it measures democ-racy much better, but that it measures democracy in a different way, in a way that is especially useful for interpreting the relationship between modernization and democracy at different thresholds. Most other meas-ures of democracy assign each country a single number, the practical meaning of which is hard to fathom. For example, what exactly does a 4 on the Freedom House political rights index tell us about a country? It gives a vague notion that the country falls into the "partly free" cate-gory, that it is not very democratic in some unspecified ways, and that it is less democratic than a "2" and more democratic than a "6"; but it is hard to be more specific than that. If one wanted to investigate the fairness of elections or censorship of the media, such a rating would be useless; information about elections and censorship was taken into account as the rating was being assigned, but it was lost when it was aggregated with all the other information that went into the rating.

The polyarchy scale is different: because it is a Guttman scale, no information is lost during aggregation. Therefore, it describes both the overall degree of polyarchy in a country and the more specific political characteristics of the country that are captured by individual compo-nents of the scale. More concretely, the scale is composed of four com-ponents – indicators of meaningful and fair elections, freedom of organ-ization, freedom of expression, and pluralism in the media. Empirically, these four indicators are so strongly associated that they can be considered to reflect the same underlying dimension – contestation, which because of expanded suffrage throughout the world, is now by default the principal component of polyarchy. Each indicator is a set of three to four ordered categories, with each category having a score from 1 to 3 or 4. The polyarchy scale is merely the sum of the scores for each indicator (less 4, to convert it to a 0–10 range); this produces a set of 11 ordered categories, ranging from full polyarchies (scale score 0) to the completely unpolyarchic countries (scale score 10). Most importantly, each score on the polyarchy scale corresponds to a distinct combination of ratings on the four components and each rating corresponds to a description of the institutions and practices found at that level. The meaning of the polyarchy scale is thus quite clear. The interpretations of each of the scale scores are presented in table 7.1.

This characteristic of the polyarchy scale makes it uniquely useful for the kind of analysis presented here: pinpointing which aspects of democracy are affected by socioeconomic development. A consistent finding of this study is that indicators of socioeconomic development have a different relationship to the polyarchy scale at different points along its length, in two ways: either (1) the relationship is not statistically significant for some range of values, or (2) the slope of the relationship changes as polyarchy increases, i.e., the relationship is curvilinear or even more complex. Other measures of democracy can identify ranges of significance and curvilinear relationships equally well, but only the polyarchy scale gives clues about which institutions and practices are associated with these socioeconomic indicators and which are not.

The claim that the polyarchy scale represents a common path of democratization rests on the Guttman scaling procedure. A Guttman scale can be formed only when the component variables are unidimensional, i.e., they measure the same underlying dimension (Gorden, 1977). In this case, unidimensionality means that countries that rate high on fair elections also tend to rate high on freedom of organization, freedom of expression, and media pluralism; and vice versa. If there were many countries that had fair and free elections but permitted no independent media or brooked no public dissent or banned all political parties, or practiced other similar incongruities, then the component variables would not be measuring the same underlying dimension and a Guttman scale could not be formed. The fact that the polyarchy scale can be formed shows that polyarchy and its component variables are unidimensional. Previous research based on all 170 independent countries as of 1985 verified the unidimensionality of polyarchy. More specifically, 90 percent of the component variable ratings were consistent with the progression of component scores listed in table 7.1, and

Table 7.1 *Interpretation of polyarchy scale scores*

Scale Score	Component Scores	Description
0	1111	Meaningful fair elections are held, there is full freedom for political organization and expression, and there is no preferential presentation of official views in the media.
1	1112	Meaningful fair elections are held and there is full freedom for political organization and expression, but there is preferential presentation of official views in the media.
2	1122	Meaningful fair elections are held and there is full freedom for political organization, but some public dissent is suppressed and there is preferential presentation of official views in the media.
3	1222/2122	Undefined due to lack of cases
4	2222	Elections are marred by fraud or coercion, some independent political organizations are banned, some public dissent is suppressed, and there is preferential presentation of official views in the media.
5	3222	No meaningful elections are held, some independent political organizations are banned, some public dissent is suppressed, and there is preferential presentation of official views in the media.
6	3322	No meaningful elections are held, only non-political organizations are allowed to be independent, some public dissent is suppressed, and there is preferential presentation of official views in the media.
7	3323	No meaningful elections are held, only non-political organizations are allowed to be independent, some public dissent is suppressed, and alternatives to the official media are very limited.
8	3423	No meaningful electons are held, all organizations are banned or controlled by the government or official party, some public dissent is suppressed, and alternatives to the official media are very limited.
9	3424	No meaningful elections are held, all organizations are banned or controlled by the government or official party, some public dissent is suppressed, and there is no public alternative to official information.
10	3434	No meaningful elections are held, all organizations are banned or controlled by the government or official party, all public dissent is suppressed, and there is no public alternative to official information.

Note: The first component score is for the fair elections variable, the second for freedom of organization, the third for freedom of expression, and the fourth for alternative sources of information. For full descriptions of the coding criteria, see Coppedge and Reinicke (1990).

137 countries (80.6 percent of the universe) fit the perfect scale types (Coppedge and Reinicke, 1990, p. 56). With three or four possible ratings on each of four component variables, there are 1,038,643,200 possible paths between the most and the least polyarchic extremes of the scale, but only 25,200 of these paths are unidimensional. Thus the chances of forming a Guttman scale from these data are only 1 in 41,216; the fact that more than 80 percent of the cases are found on one of these paths strikingly confirms the existence of a common path to polyarchy.

The nature of the path can be discerned by tracing the changes in institutions and practices from one scale score to the next. Let us start in the middle of the scale and work our way in both directions. Scale score 5 corresponds to a prototypical authoritarian regime, such as Chile under Pinochet, in which no meaningful elections are held, some political parties are banned, government critics are sometimes arrested and punished, and the government ensures that its views are presented preferentially by the media, although most of the media may well remain in private hands. A country with the next-most polyarchic score is largely the same in these respects except that it does hold elections, even though they are marred by fraud and coercion, sometimes enough to guarantee the victory of the official party or candidates, and sometimes just enough to change the margin of victory. At scale score 3, the government still gets preferential treatment in the media and represses some critics, but it holds elections that are for the most part fair, and it allows all parties to organize and compete. At the next level, critics are no longer punished but official views are still given preferential coverage. At the level of full polyarchy (score 0) the media are much more competitive and independent of official influence.

Moving down from scale score 5, all independent political parties are banned, leaving only non-political organizations (perhaps including trade unions) to exist. At scale score 7 controls on the media are tighter, making alternatives to official information available only to a small elite or for restricted issues or short periods of time. In less polyarchic countries, not even non-political alternatives to officially sponsored organizations are allowed to exist. At scale score 9, all alternatives to official information are eliminated, and at the least polyarchic extreme, enforcement of conformity with official views is so effective that citizens are wary of expressing political opinions even in private.

The ordering of institutions and practices just described was not simply postulated a priori; it was found to fit 137 countries as of 1985. This path probably should not be applied very rigidly because it is based on a cross-sectional "snapshot" taken in a single year (which was in the middle of a wave of democratization). It is possible that the path could change somewhat over time, much as rivers change their course. I doubt, however, that it changes very much or very often. Also, the existence of a path does not mean that countries ever necessarily move from their position on the path, or that when they move, they move up rather than down, or that they move one step at a time rather than leaping several scale scores at once. It means only that if a country leaves its position on the path, it is highly likely to occupy another position on the path rather than a position off it.

Independent variables

One disadvantage of the polyarchy scale is that it rates countries for one year only, and therefore cannot be used to examine the relationship between socioeconomic *change* and changes in the level of polyarchy. The conventional wisdom in quantitative research on the conditions for democracy holds that only studies of change can yield inferences about causation. Although this position is perfectly sound from the standpoint of methodological principle, there is also reason to believe that the analyses of change that are feasible today are no better than a good cross-sectional analysis, and may in fact be misleading.

The problem with studies of change is that they almost always examine change over relatively short periods of time, such as five to ten years. It is practically impossible to examine longer spans due to the lack of reliable time-series indicators of democracy. If we believed that socio-economic development influenced democratization over such short spans – if we believed, for example, that a 10 percent increase in GNP per-capita, or a five-point improvement in the literacy rate, would lead to a similar increase in the level of democracy within a few years, other things being equal – then analyses of short-term change would be justified. But some of the best research, such as Putnam's comparison of civic culture in northern and southern Italy over several hundred years, suggests that the true relationships between development and democracy are discernable only over periods of several decades (Putnam, 1993).

If this is true, then contrary trends that prevail in the short run, such as the overlapping of the debt crisis and redemocratization in Latin America, could lead to exactly the wrong conclusions.[2] This example is an obvious one that would not be hard to detect and interpret correctly, but if such short-term trends can lead to conclusions that are the opposite of the truth, then less obvious trends could easily lead the analyst to wrongly dismiss a variable as insignificant or spuriously related

Table 7.2 *Independent variables and sources**

ENR1, ENR2, ENR3 = Number of students enrolled in primary, secondary, and post-secondary education, as percentage of age group (1984). All from World Bank (1987b).
FARMS = Percentual share of family farms of the total area of holdings (various dates, 1960–80). From Vanhanen (1990).
GDPPC = Per-capita gross domestic product (1986 for most; 1985 for 16 countries). From UNIDO (1988).
GINISEC = Gini coefficient of sectoral inequality (1970). All from Vanhanen (1990).
ILLIT = Percentage of adults who were illiterate (1985). All from United Nations (1993) except Jamaica (1990 data); Barbados, Belize, Grenada, St. Christopher & Nevis, St. Lucia, St. Vincent, Dominica (1970 data); Italy (1981 data); USA and Vanuatu (1979 data); and Cyprus (1979 data); which are from World Bank (1991).
INFMORT = Infant mortality rate (1985). All from World Bank (1987b).
LABAG, LABIND, LABSVC = Percentage of work force employed in agricultural, industrial and service sectors (1980). All from World Bank (1987b).
LIFEXP = Life expectancy (1985). All from World Bank (1987b).
NAP = Non-agricultural population as percentage of total population (around 1980). All from Vanhanen (1990).
PAPER = Newspaper circulation per 1,000 population (1980–6). All from World Bank (1987a).
RADIO = Number of people owning or registered with radio receivers, per 1,000 (1975). All from Taylor and Jodice (1983).
STUD = Students per 100,000 inhabitants (around 1980). All from Vanhanen 1990.
TV = Number of people with television sets, per 1,000 (1975). All from Taylor and Jodice (1983).
URBAN = Urban populations as a percentage of total population (around 1980). All from Vanhanen (1990).

Note: *I am grateful to Ronna Montgomery for collecting these data.

to democracy, or to reverse the arrow of causation in error. There may well be greater safety in a cross-sectional analysis, because cross-national differences are relatively unaffected by short-term trends and reflect more faithfully the long-term trends that seem to matter most for the establishment of democracy. The ideal, of course, would be to have time-series measures of democracy and development spanning a century or more, but until these data become available both cross-sectional and time-series analysis should be encouraged as checks on each other.

Preliminary cross-sectional analysis for this chapter began with 18 independent variables as indicators of socioeconomic development. They are described in table 7.2, along with their sources. Dates for the data match the date of the polyarchy ratings (1985) as closely as possible, but not always very closely. The polyarchy scale rates 159 countries;[3] the number of cases for which data were available ranged from

156 (life expectancy) to 97 (newspaper circulation). Missing data from some of these independent variables reduced the number of cases that could be used in this analysis to 104. As the analysis proceeded problems with multicollinearity and the need to maximize the sample size made it necessary to select a subset of these independent variables for further analysis. Eventually six were identified as having a relatively independent association with polyarchy in ordinary least squares models and representing a variety of aspects of socioeconomic modernization. These six are: (1) life expectancy in years (LIFEXP); (2) students (primarily university) per 100,000 inhabitants (STUD); (3) non-agricultural population as a percentage of total population (NAP); (4) the Gini coefficient of sectoral inequality (GINISEC); (5) the inverse of per-capita gross domestic product (INVGDP); and (6) the degree of concentration of non-agricultural resources for countries where the concentration is at least 90 percent (CONCEN). For other countries, this variable is set to 0.[4]

The only two variables that have a relationship to polyarchy that are relatively independent of the other 16 are per-capita GDP and GINISEC. (Independence was judged by their correlations with other variables and by the robustness of their coefficients in many trial regression models.) While most scholars have used the log of per-capita GNP in their regression research, I found that the inverse of GDPPC, for which the curve is bent at a sharper angle, consistently provided a better fit with the polyarchy scale. GINISEC is a measure of inequality, but inequality of productivity across the agricultural, industrial, and service sectors. It is a highly aggregated measure, to say the least, but it does seem to capture gross socioeconomic inequalities, for it remains significant even when controlling for wealth, urbanization, and occupational structure. Using the 19–20 cases for which data are available, GINISEC correlates at 0.63 or better with the percentage of income earned by the top 10, top 20, and bottom 40 percent of households.

Fifteen of the variables appear to belong to three clusters.[5] They are clusters in the sense that they are correlated more strongly with one another than with variables in other clusters, and no two variables of any cluster can be significant simultaneously when regressed against the polyarchy scale. The combinations making up the clusters are interesting. One reflects basic education and the physical quality of life – primary and secondary school enrollments, illiteracy rates, infant mortality, and life expectancy. A second cluster reflects urbanization and occupational structure – URBAN, NAP, LABAG, LABIND, and LABSVC. These variables cluster together because urbanization and the growth of the industrial and service sectors go hand in hand, while the more rural and agricultural societies tend to lag behind.[6] The third cluster can be called higher education and mass media and is composed of university enrollment, numbers of (presumably university) students, newspaper circulation, and radio and television ownership. LIFEXP, NAP, and STUD were chosen to represent each of these clusters because they offered the best combination of significance in regressions and availability for the cases in the sample. Whenever they are used here to draw conclusions about the relationship between these larger clusters and polyarchy an appropriate disclaimer is appended because further testing would be necessary either to certify their representativeness or to develop a reliable index for each cluster.

Ordinary least squares is an appropriate technique for selecting independent variables for the purpose at hand because it indicates the sort of model other researchers who use OLS might produce if they were working with the same pool of variables. This model appears in the first column of table 7.3. However, because the polyarchy scale is a set of ordered categories rather than a truly continuous variable, logistic regression is more appropriate for evaluating the adequacy of this model, as well as for exploring the possibility that there are different models for different thresholds of polyarchy (Demaris, 1992).[7]

The apparent importance of regions

Conclusions about the relationship between polyarchy and socioeconomic indicators are highly sensitive to the mix of countries in the sample. One way to gain an appreciation of this sensitivity is to hold the model constant while varying the size and composition of the sample of countries. No statistician would recommend this procedure as a serious analytic method due to problems of comparability introduced by modifying the sample, but social scientists in effect do it constantly, because every new study is based on a slightly different sample of countries. The procedure is performed here merely to illustrate how radically the substantive conclusions may diverge. Table 7.3 presents a series of ordered logistic regression (OLR) estimates in which the sample varies by region.[8]

Clearly the selection of countries can have a decisive impact on findings about the relationship between polyarchy (or democracy) and modernization. The explanatory power of all of the models is about the same, ranging from 84.5 to 89.5 concordance, but the substantive implications could not be more different. One model confirms the assumption that the modernization variables have unvarying effects at all thresholds of polyarchy, while all the others (including seven more not

Table 7.3 *Consequences of varying the samples*

Method	OLS	OLR	OLR	OLR	OLR	OLR
Sample	FULL	FULL	WALM	WLM	WS	WM
N	104	104	73	59	53	35
GINISEC	0.054*	−0.036	−0.099***	−0.092*	0.006	−0.167*
	(0.021)	(0.019)	(0.035)	(0.044)	(0.025)	(0.085)
NAP	0.039	−0.020	−0.053*	−0.029	0.011	−0.132
	(0.022)	(0.019)	(0.027)	(0.035)	(0.030)	(0.069)
STUD	−0.035*	0.041*	0.038*	0.041	0.112*	0.020
	(0.016)	(0.017)	(0.019)	(0.022)	(0.048)	(0.034)
LIFEXP	−0.150**	0.094*	0.105	0.107	0.094	0.833***
	(0.049)	(0.044)	(0.062)	(0.082)	(0.065)	(0.262)
CONCEN	1.52*	−1.48*	−2.67*	−2.82*	−0.67	−0.62
	(0.64)	(0.58)	(1.26)	(1.38)	(0.73)	(1.98)
INVGDP	505*	−431*	−955***	−542	−384	4,587*
	(198)	(183)	(320)	(530)	(236)	(1,840)
Intercept 1	9.35***	−5.46*	−2.10	−4.13	−9.31*	−48.6***
	(2.71)					
Intercept 2		−4.78*	−1.45	−3.39	−8.08*	−47.3***
Intercept 3		−4.32	−0.84	−2.79	−7.73*	−46.6***
Intercept 4		−3.19	0.54	−1.66	−6.28	−43.1**
Intercept 5		−2.66	1.23	−1.05	−5.73	N/A
Intercept 6		−1.93	2.67	0.39	−5.33	−39.8**
Intercept 7		−0.89	3.82	2.04	−4.26	−38.8**
Intercept 8		0.36	4.70	2.81	−2.76	−37.9*
Intercept 9		1.31	5.09	3.42	−1.30	−37.0*
R-squared/% concordant	0.652	84.5	85.5	87.7	86.4	89.5

Notes: Coefficients are unstandardized. Standard errors are in parentheses, but are not reported for ordered intercepts due to lack of space.
W = Western Europe and North America.
L = Latin America and Caribbean.
M = Middle East and North Africa.
S = Sub-Saharan Africa.
A = Asia and Pacific.
*Significant at $p < 0.05$.
**Significant at $p < 0.01$.
***Significant at $p < 0.005$.

presented here) disconfirm that assumption. Every independent variable is significant in some models and non-significant in others, and the magnitudes of their coefficients, even considering only the significant ones, cover a wide range, including at least one dramatic reversal of signs.[9] There is a tendency to believe that anyone who has gone to the trouble of collecting data for the 30–40 cases required for a regression analysis is on safe ground making inferences. This belief is clearly false, at least when one fails to take into account the potential for varying relationships at different thresholds of polyarchy.

There are two ways to assess the importance of regions more directly. First, one can add a dummy-variable intercept for each region to the right-hand side of the equation, to test for some regional impact on the odds of being polyarchic even when controlling for the substantive variables. Alternatively, one can divide each of the modernization variables into separate regional modernization variables, so that the impact of modernization on polyarchy can be estimated separately for each region. To the extent that any of these regional intercepts or regional variables is significant, it suggests that there may be regional differences in the relationship. I have carried out this analysis and found consistent confirmation of the apparent importance of regions.[10] But these results will not be reported in detail for the simple reason that they are all based on ordered logistic regression, which all but one of the models so far have shown to be based on the untenable assumption that the relationship between polyarchy and modernization is invariant at different thresholds of polyarchy.[11] The only appropriate technique for further analysis is therefore the more common binary logistic regression (which will be abbreviated as BLR), which requires the estimation of a separate model for each threshold of polyarchy.

Regions and thresholds

There are three basic possible explanations for the apparent importance of regions in the OLR estimates. First, we know that countries in different regions are disproportionately clustered around different thresholds of the polyarchy scale: Western countries are found mostly at the higher end, Sub-Saharan countries tend to rank at the lower end, and Middle Eastern, Latin American, North African, Asian, and Pacific countries are mostly scattered in between. Figure 7.1 illustrates this regional clustering. If modernization variables have different effects at different thresholds, as the OLR estimates have suggested, then any model that wrongly assumed invariant effects would attribute different effects, and often a different intercept, to each region when some or all of the difference is really due to threshold effects. This possibility can be tested by running separate binary logistic regressions instead of a single ordered logistic regression.

Second, it is possible that all of the modernization variables included in the model have similar effects across regions, but other variables that would be especially useful for predicting polyarchy in a certain region

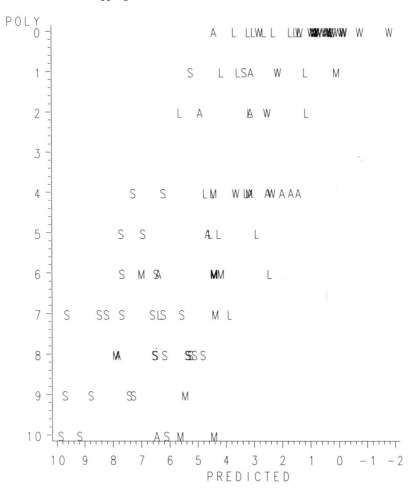

Figure 7.1 Modernization predictions of polyarchy scale by region
Notes: W = Western Europe and North America.
L = Latin America and the Caribbean.
M = Middle East and North Africa.
S = Sub-Saharan Africa.
A = Asia and Pacific.
For a list of countries in each region, see note 8.

have not been included, and therefore the model systematically over or underpredicts polyarchy levels for countries in this region. In this case, regional intercepts would pick up this variance whether the technique being used was OLS, OLR, or BLR. This possibility can be tested by including regional intercepts in the BLR models and estimating the significance of their coefficients. Third, it is possible that the modernization variables do in fact have different effects in different regions, even when taking threshold effects into account. Perhaps a culture of respect for learning gives university students a greater impact on democratization in Asia than they have in Africa, for example. Or perhaps a rising per-capita GDP has no effect on polyarchy in the Middle East because most of the wealth flows to, and through, a repressive state. These sorts of questions can be examined by adding separate, region specific variants of GINISEC, NAP, STUD, LIFEXP, and INVGDP to the BLR model.

The second and third explanations were confirmed in only two limited instances. First, it appears that levels of polyarchy in the countries of the Middle East and North Africa are not as well predicted by the modernization indicators as levels of polyarchy are in other regions of the world, because some of this region's intercepts and regional variables were significant at several thresholds. Second, social modernization seems to have a more positive impact on full polyarchy in Western countries (Europe and the Americas) than it does elsewhere. In all other instances, comprising 93.7 percent of the hypotheses tested, the first explanation was supported: the apparent regional effects are illusions created by a strong threshold effect. Therefore, the relationship between polyarchy and socioeconomic modernization is different at different thresholds of polyarchy, but in most instances this more complex model works equally well for all regions of the world (with the possible exception of the communist bloc, which is excluded from the analysis.)

Tables 7.4 and 7.5 contain the evidence to support these conclusions. Complete testing of these propositions – 174 hypotheses in all – required the estimation of 87 separate models, which obviously cannot all be presented here. Table 7.4 therefore contains only the nine benchmark models for each threshold, without regional intercepts or variables, and table 7.5 contains the eight models that indicate 11 significant regional effects. None of the other 163 hypotheses for regional effects is confirmed at the 0.05 level.[12] In table 7.4, the model designated POLY0 estimates the effects on the log odds of having scale score 0 as opposed to any score from 1 to 10; POLY1 estimates the effects on the log odds of having scale scores from 0 to 1 as opposed to any score from 2 to 10; and so on. A positive sign means that the variable increases the odds of being in the more polyarchic portion of the dichotomy. (This is true of inverse GDP per-capita also, but the sign must be reversed when thinking in terms of untransformed GDP.) A comparison of the coefficient magnitudes and significances reveals a definite threshold effect,

Table 7.4 *Binary logistic models of polyarchy without regional effects*

Threshold	POLY0	POLY1	POLY2	POLY4	POLY5	POLY6	POLY7	POLY8	POLY9	Regional average
No. top cases	30	38	44	58	64	72	83	93	98	
No. bottom cases	74	66	60	46	40	32	21	11	6	
GINISEC	-0.120*	-0.107**	-0.074*	-0.066	-0.53	-0.019	-0.003	-0.072*	-0.047	
	(0.050)	(0.040)	(0.034)	(0.035)	(0.032)	(0.027)	(0.026)	(0.036)	(0.041)	
NAP	-0.045	-0.073*	-0.066*	-0.078*	-0.049	-0.025	0.005	-0.046	-0.039	
	(0.042)	(0.035)	(0.030)	(0.034)	(0.032)	(0.030)	(0.030)	(0.040)	(0.047)	
STUD	0.024	0.028	0.045	0.057	0.049	0.054	0.111	0.068	0.041	
	(0.021)	(0.023)	(0.024)	(0.033)	(0.034)	(0.041)	(0.068)	(0.080)	(0.066)	
LIFEXP	0.129	0.119	0.161*	0.211**	0.134	0.125	0.020	-0.030	-0.022	
	(0.098)	(0.084)	(0.071)	(0.081)	(0.073)	(0.073)	(0.067)	(0.092)	(0.115)	
CONCEN	(variable omitted due to lack of cases at thresholds 0–2)			-1.51	-2.34*	-1.88*	-1.41	-1.48	-0.42	
				(1.22)	(1.18)	(0.86)	(0.72)	(0.87)	(1.13)	
INVGDP	-1,414	-2,139*	860	-649	-552	-308	-157	-886*	-732*	
	(1,103)	(1,003)	(497)	(370)	(318)	(274)	(233)	(363)	(351)	
Intercept	3.41	0.07	4.68	-6.41	-3.07	-4.57	-0.27	10.26	-8.76	
	(6.35)	(5.18)	(4.20)	(4.29)	(3.82)	(3.72)	(3.39)	(5.36)	(6.31)	
Percent concordant in:										
Full sample	94	93	92	94	93	92	89	90	83	
W. Europe and N. America	91	91	91	100	100	100	100	100	100	97
Lat. America and Caribbean	75	75	67	79	83	96	100	100	100	86
Asia and Pacific	79	71	57	93	100	93	93	93	93	86
Middle East and N. Africa	92	100	92	67	58	58	75	75	83	82
Sub-Saharan Africa	100	93	93	90	80	73	50	87	90	84

Notes: Coefficients are unstandardized. Standard errors are in parentheses. All models use the full sample of 104 countries.

*Significant at $p < 0.05$.

**Significant at $p < 0.01$.

as different variables are useful for explaining different thresholds of polyarchy. The substantive implications of these benchmark models will be discussed in the concluding section.

For now it is more important to interpret the models that show some regional effects. Models a and b in table 7.5 show a significant regional intercept for the Middle East and North Africa (the "M intercept"): these countries are less likely to be found either at polyarchy score 5 or above, or anywhere above the least polyarchic category, than are other countries at equivalent levels of socioeconomic modernization. This suggests that some different independent variable should be added to the model to keep it from overpredicting polyarchy in this region. Such a variable would not be rentier state dominance in the oil-exporting countries, because this effect is already adequately captured by the resource concentration variable. Other possible explanations are frequent war, the fusion of church and state in some Islamic societies, or some aspect of Islamic culture.

Models c, d, and e show significant regional variants of urbanization and life expectancy for this same region. It could be that these variables are simply picking up some of the variance that would be explained by the missing mystery variable and would drop out if it were included, but their substantive interpretations are worth examining. First, at threshold POLY7, which divides countries that allow some freedom of non-political organization from those that do not, urbanization is not normally a significant explanatory factor, as indicated by the non-significant coefficient for urbanization in all countries. (According to table 7.4, it has an effect at thresholds 1–4 only). The regional coefficient for urbanization should be interpreted as a regional correction to this global tendency. The net effect is therefore obtained by summing the two, and when this is done the result is that the already insignificant global tendency is almost entirely cancelled out in the Middle East and North Africa at this threshold. This "regional effect" can therefore be safely ignored.

For life expectancy, however, a non-significant global association is augmented into significance, indicating that high life expectancies are associated negatively with polyarchy at thresholds 7 and 9 in the Middle East and North Africa, but nowhere else in the world. Globally, life expectancy is positively associated with polyarchy, and only at thresholds 2–4. While it is hard to know exactly why this counterintuitive relationship exists, one plausible possibility is that life expectancy (and perhaps other physical quality of life indicators) is an effect of polyarchy levels rather than a cause. Life expectancy could be higher in less polyarchic countries because in the Middle East and North Africa the least

Table 7.5 *Binary logistic models with significant regional effects*

Threshold	a POLY5	b POLY9	c POLY7	d POLY7	e POLY9	f POLY0	g POLY0	h POLY0
GINISEC	-0.033	-0.037	0.019	0.026	-0.034	-0.134*	-0.170*	-0.178*
	(0.031)	(0.049)	(0.028)	(0.030)	(0.049)	(0.061)	(0.068)	(0.071)
NAP	-0.030	-0.025	0.064	0.024	-0.018	-0.053	-0.075	-0.113*
	(0.033)	(0.054)	(0.046)	(0.034)	(0.055)	(0.046)	(0.050)	(0.055)
In region M			-0.057*					
			(0.028)					
In region W								0.046**
								(0.017)
In region S			-0.054					
			(0.030)					
In region L								0.047**
								(0.017)
STUD	0.062	0.061	0.096	0.107	0.074	-0.044	0.022	0.024
	(0.039)	(0.086)	(0.082)	(0.078)	(0.094)	(0.040)	(0.026)	(0.026)
In region W						0.120*		
						(0.047)		
In region L						0.080*		
						(0.037)		

LIFEXP	0.103 (0.76)	-0.068 (0.144)	-0.064 (0.083)	-0.026 (0.077)	-0.065 (0.145)	0.113 (0.103)	0.059 (0.122)	0.100 (0.124)
In region M				-0.51* (0.022)	-0.054* (0.026)			
In region W							0.045* (0.018)	
In region S				-0.034 (0.021)				
In region L							0.044* (0.017)	
CONCEN	-2.38* (1.19)	0.10 (1.30)	-1.25 (0.75)	-1.17 (0.76)	0.19 (1.30)	omitted due to lack of cases		
INVGDP	-628 (330)	-994* (441)	-274 (256)	-308 (266)	-964* (430)	-1,172 (1,019)	-1,671 (1,314)	-1,722 (1,282)
Intercept	-2.41 (3.94)	11.58 (7.92)	3.05 (4.05)	2.27 (3.94)	10.85 (7.76)	-1.67 (6.17)	2.49 (7.64)	2.26 (7.66)
M intercept	-2.49* (1.01)	-2.93* (1.45)						
Percent concordant	94.1	90.1	91.0	91.3	91.3	95.7	96.5	96.6

Note: Coefficients are unstandardized. Standard errors are in parentheses. All models use the full sample of 104 countries. Significance levels and regional designations are as in table 7.3.

polyarchic countries – Saudi Arabia, Iraq, Libya, Oman, and Algeria among others – may be more stable than, say, Chad or Lebanon, and as a result better able to provide these benefits to their citizens.[13] It may also be that improvements in life expectancy do favor polyarchy, but only after a long lag that has not yet been reached in this region.

Models f, g, and h in table 7.5 show significant regional variables at the threshold of full polyarchy for Western Europe, North America, Latin America, and the Caribbean, which can be lumped together as "the West."[14] According to model f, student population has a net positive effect on full polyarchy in the West only. Model g shows a net positive association between full polyarchy and life expectancy, also in the West only. And according to model h, urbanization has a significant *negative* effect on full polyarchy globally (as it does on polyarchy at thresholds 2–4), but the net effect is about 40 percent less negative in the West than it is elsewhere. This finding is surprisingly contrary to most modernization theory, which focuses on the strongly positive bivariate relationship. My multivariate analysis consistently points to a negative partial effect of urbanization, which implies that either the positive tendency in the bivariate relationship is spurious or multicollinearity is biasing the coefficients reported here.

It is interesting to note that the three variables with significant regional effects that favor polyarchy in the West are the indicators of *social* modernization – urbanization, student population, and life expectancy. Although one can only speculate on this point, it is possible that some quality of Western culture, such as pluralist attitudes or a proclivity to form and join associations, allows social modernization to have a more positive effect on full polyarchy in the West than it does elsewhere.

Although this discussion of significant regional effects is interesting, it distracts attention from the larger and more important conclusion that, overall, there are very few regional effects: the relationships between modernization and the thresholds of polyarchy are largely the same in all regions of the world. As indicated at the bottom of table 7.4, three-quarters of the predictions for each region are at least 80 percent concordant. The tests of regional intercepts show that the standard model in table 7.4 does not systematically over- or underpredict levels of polyarchy for any region of the world except the Middle East and North Africa, and even then only at thresholds 5 and 9. There are no significant regional differences at all for the indicators of economic modernization – per-capita GDP, resource concentration, or sectoral inequality. The social modernization estimates require regional correction only at the threshold of full polyarchy for the West, and at thresholds 5, 7, and 9 for the Middle East and North Africa; no regional corrections are necessary for Asia, the Pacific, or Sub-Saharan Africa at any threshold, or at thresholds 1, 2, 4, 6, or 8 for any region. This is empirical justification for the claim that there is a common modernization process placing countries on a common path to polyarchy.

Interpretations

This analysis is certainly not the last word on the question of what causes polyarchy. It is cross-sectional, and therefore says nothing about causation; the models are certainly underspecified, so the estimates are easily questioned; and collinearity among the explanatory variables clouds their interpretations.[15] These pitfalls make one less confident about the nature of the common path and process than about the fact that there is one. They do, however, suggest that there is a progression among aspects of modernization. In this sample, the most significant difference between the least polyarchic countries and all the rest is their low per-capita GDP. In these highly repressive countries, where citizens are not allowed alternatives to official media, private organizations, or even private political opinions, to say nothing of meaningful elections, people are too poor even to try to challenge state authority. They lack the material means to do it. Poverty continues to be important at threshold 8, although for unknown reasons sectoral inequality also seems to matter.[16] At threshold 7, where some non-political organization is first allowed, resource concentration replaces per-capita GDP as the most significant variable and it remains in first place through thresholds 6 and 5 as well. This may mean that where citizens have greater material means, state resources must be highly concentrated if a high level of repression is to be maintained.

At the threshold between countries that hold meaningful (even though sometimes fraudulent) elections and those that do not (scale score 4), resource concentration loses significance and life expectancy takes over. Again, this could mean that countries that hold elections and allow the degree of freedom corresponding to that level of polyarchy tend to have healthier citizens, or even to do a better job of feeding, clothing, and schooling them, perhaps because the elections provide some accountability. Or, it could mean that citizens who are well fed, clothed, and have some basic education are better able to take an interest in politics and to demand that the state hold elections. Whatever the reason, this relationship persists at threshold 2, where there is no longer much fraud or coercion in the elections and bans on political parties have been lifted. At both thresholds, other things being equal, the more urbanized countries are, the less likely they are to be in the more polyarchic category, for reasons that are unknown. At threshold 2, sectoral inequality begins to matter: the greater the inequality, the less likely a country is to keep its elections fair and allow all parties to compete (or to allow the corresponding levels of freedom of expression and media pluralism).

At threshold 1, dividing countries that allow full freedom of expression from those that sometimes punish critics of the government, inequality matters even more. Per-capita GDP is once again associated with greater polyarchy, while urbanization continues to have a negative effect. Finally, at the threshold of full polyarchy only sectoral inequality is significant. Unfortunately, these models do not tell us whether these high levels of polyarchy promote economic growth and equality and discourage urbanization, or whether growth, equality, and a rural society push countries over these last two thresholds of polyarchy. Many interpretations are compatible with this evidence.

My interpretation of the relationships in the upper half of the scale is that economic and social modernization empowers citizens. All of the countries in the 0–4 interval have democratic institutions – elections, legislatures, several parties, and so on. But in practice, full polyarchy requires more than democratic institutions; it requires citizens who are able to make those institutions work. Some of these countries are more democratic than others because in the countries at the lower levels of socioeconomic development the citizens lack the power to force the government to provide clean elections, fair competition, freedom of speech, and diverse information, even though the electoral machinery is in place. These shortcomings order themselves into a nice Guttman scale because some of these goals are more difficult to achieve than others, and therefore require a more powerful civil society.

In an electoral regime with a weak society, the government can get away with banning entire parties from competition, even very large ones (polyarchy score 4). If society is a bit stronger, the government may have to allow all parties to compete, but can still get away with manipulating elections to some extent (score 3). Where citizens are fairly strong relative to the state, a government that has to hold fair elections may yet abuse its power to punish its critics (score 2); and where such selective repression provokes too much protest, a government may have to settle for putting its own slant on the news on its own broadcasts (score 1). This last failing is the most difficult for citizens to eliminate (partly because it is comparatively innocuous), and is therefore the last threshold to cross before reaching full polyarchy. This interpretation is presented not as the only possible set of reasons for the relationships that have been revealed in this chapter, but as an illustration of the sort of common path and process that, with very few regional variations, countries tend to follow.

NOTES

1 For the best existing evidence to the contrary, see Burkhart and Lewis-Beck (1994).
2 A temporary recession could well undermine an authoritarian government, or a new democracy could be the cause more than the consequence of poor economic performance, but in the long run no one doubts that a prolonged economic decline would be disastrous for democracy.
3 The original polyarchy scale rated 170 countries. Most of the cases completely excluded from this analysis were the "anomalies," i.e., countries that were gross departures from the perfect scale type – Andorra, Liechtenstein, Monaco, Vatican City, Syria, South Africa, and Western Samoa. Also excluded were Brunei, Nauru, San Marino, and Tuvalu, for which insufficient data were available.
4 Vanhanen (1990) compiled an index of the "concentration of non-agricultural resources" in the hands of the state, private-sector economic groups, and foreign capital as of 1980. This index correlates at −0.83 with the polyarchy scale for 1985, and its means at different levels of polyarchy plot a smooth, straight curve from top to bottom. This index is too good to be true. When it is included in regression models, it explains so much of the variance that the other independent variables either become insignificant or turn up with bizarrely counterintuitive coefficients. After examining Vanhanen's coding criteria, I concluded that this variable is too soft to be used in serious research in its entirety. The data on which its values are supposedly based are sketchy, inconsistent, and often bear no straightforward relationship to the value assigned. I strongly suspect that some unconscious fudging went on that made this variable much more strongly associated with democracy than it should be. However, for values of at least 90 percent, the coding criteria are fairly consistent in reflecting overwhelming state, rather than private or foreign, control of resources, so I feel safe in using its 90–100 range as a modified dummy variable for extensive state control of the economy.
5 The sixteenth variable, FARMS, is not very highly correlated with any of the other variables (best is 0.31 with GDPPC) and yet adds nothing significant to regression models. Factor analysis would of course be a better way of identifying clusters of variables, but will have to wait for further research.
6 This does not explain the handful of unusually rural, agricultural polyarchies, or near-polyarchies – India, Papua New Guinea, Botswana, and Honduras – which turn up as outliers in some scatterplots.
7 I owe a huge debt to Mark Gasiorowski and other authors in the "Inequality and Democracy" project for suggesting logistic regression for this analysis.
8 Countries in **Western Europe and North America** are Australia, Austria, Belgium, Canada, Cyprus, Denmark, Finland, France, West Germany,

Greece, Iceland, Ireland, Italy, Luxembourg, Malta, Netherlands, Norway, Portugal, Spain, Sweden, Turkey, United Kingdom, and the United States. Those in **Middle East and North Africa** are Algeria, Egypt, Iran, Iraq, Israel, Jordan, Kuwait, Mauritania, Morocco, Saudi Arabia, Sudan, and Tunisia. Those in **Latin America and the Caribbean** are Argentina, Barbados, Bolivia, Brazil, Chile, Colombia, Costa Rica, Dominican Republic, Ecuador, El Salvador, Guatemala, Guyana, Haiti, Honduras, Jamaica, Mexico, Nicaragua, Panama, Paraguay, Peru, Surinam, Trinidad and Tobago, Uruguay, and Venezuela. Those in **Sub-Saharan Africa** are Benin, Botswana, Burundi, Cameroon, Central African Republic, Congo, Ethiopia, Gambia, Ghana, Guinea, Ivory Coast, Kenya, Lesotho, Liberia, Madagascar, Malawi, Mali, Mauritius, Niger, Nigeria, Rwanda, Senegal, Sierra Leone, Swaziland, Tanzania, Togo, Uganda, Zaire, Zambia, and Zimbabwe. Those in **Asia and the Pacific** are Burma, Fiji, India, Indonesia, Japan, Malaysia, Nepal, Papua New Guinea, Pakistan, Philippines, Singapore, South Korea, Sri Lanka, and Thailand. The only country included in the full sample that is not in these regions is Yugoslavia. The signs are reversed in the OLR estimates in table 7.3 because in OLS the dependent variable takes on higher values at the least polyarchic extreme, while in OLR the dependent variable is the log odds of being in the more polyarchic categories.

9 One OLR model not reported in the text was estimated without GINISEC on the right-hand side because the missing values for this variable were largely responsible for the exclusion of all but one of the communist bloc countries from the analysis. Omitting GINISEC increases the sample size to 132 through the addition of Afghanistan, Albania, the Bahamas, Bangladesh, Bhutan, Bulgaria, Cape Verde, Comoros, Cuba, Czechoslovakia, Equatorial Guinea, Guinea-Bissau, Hungary, New Zealand, North Korea, Laos, Mongolia, Mozambique, Oman, Poland, Qatar, Romania, Somalia, the Solomon Islands, Switzerland, United Arab Emirates, the USSR, and Vietnam. This model produces 84.8 percent concordant pairs, and estimates coefficients for NAP and STUD that are in the ballpark defined by most of the other OLR models. Life expectancy and per-capita GDP become less significant, as should be expected given Eastern Europe's high statistics in this respect relative to its level of polyarchy in 1985. The most significant variable in the estimate by far is resource concentration. Only the first of the ordinal intercepts is statistically significant.

10 Regional intercepts and regionally disaggregated modernization variables (with the exception of CONCEN) were included singly in a series of 11 models. The regional intercepts for Western Europe and North America and for the Middle East and North Africa were found to be significant in OLR. All of the regional variables were significant for Western Europe and North America, Latin America and the Caribbean, and Asia and the Pacific. In addition, the Sub-Saharan regional versions of GINISEC, INVGDP, and LIFEXP were significant, as was the Middle East—North African version of INVGDP.

11 The "proportional odds assumption," which is used to test the null hypothesis that the modernization variable effects are independent of polyarchy

thresholds, is rejected at $p > 0.0001$ for all of the estimates except the one based on the Western Europe–North America and Middle East–North Africa sample, for which it is accepted at $p = 0.446$.

12 Aside from the 174 hypotheses tested with these 87 models, there were eleven other hypotheses involving regional intercepts and 85 involving regional variables that could not be tested due to insufficient representation of certain regions above or below various thresholds of the scale.

13 Per-capita GDP would seem to be the more obvious difference, but it cannot account for this significant regional effect because it is already taken into account by the model.

14 Although many outside observers consider Latin America non-Western, most Latin Americans adamantly identify themselves as Western on the basis on their Iberian languages and culture, Catholic religion, and, of course, their location in the Western Hemisphere.

15 We also should not assume that the significant independent variables at a given threshold are related only to the component of the polyarchy scale – fair elections, media pluralism, or freedom of organization or expression – that changes at that threshold. The validity of any such relationship rests on the assumption that the component of polyarchy whose threshold is being crossed is the only component that is changing in response to socioeconomic development, which is not necessarily the case. Other components of polyarchy could be changing as well even though they do not happen to cross any of their own thresholds defined by the coding criteria of the polyarchy scale. The precision of the interpretation depends on whether one assumes that the thresholds represent sharp, discontinuous changes that are manifested in a sequence, affecting one component of the scale at a time, or that all four components vary continuously and in parallel, with thresholds amounting to arbitrary demarcations. Precise claims about connections between certain levels of development and specific institutions and practices in one component variable are justified under either assumption. But if the second assumption is correct (which seems more likely), then there may also be connections between certain levels of development and variation within the corresponding categories of the other three component variables of the scale.

16 It is interesting to see what happens when the sample is enlarged to include many communist-bloc countries. Because average wealth is higher in the Soviet-dominated countries, per-capita GDP becomes only marginally significant ($p = 0.081$) and resource concentration in state hands becomes highly significant ($p = 0.0001$). These estimates are from the regression reported in note 9, which omits GINISEC. The greater significance of CONCEN at threshold 9 may owe more to the omission of GINISEC than to the inclusion of Soviet-dominated countries, because without GINISEC, CONCEN becomes the only significant variable at thresholds 4–7 as well even though there are few such countries above scale score 8.

8   Markets and inequality in the transition from state socialism

Victor Nee and Raymond V. Liedka

It is a widely held belief that in a market economy the conditions of exchange benefit the strong and rich, but undermine the economic position of the weak and poor. From dependency theory (Amin, 1974, 1976; Evans, 1979) to Merton's (1973 [1942]; 1968) cumulative advantage hypothesis that "the rich get richer at a rate that makes the poor become relatively poorer," markets have been linked to the production of inequality. The sociological literature is suffused with this view, reflecting the influence of Marx, who argued that the bargaining power of direct producers is limited in a market economy where the means of production are concentrated in the hands of capitalists. In Marx's view, because capitalists maximize their profits by driving down the cost of labor and by driving out competitors, the dynamics of capitalist economic development give rise to a growth in income inequality insofar as smaller capitalists fall to the wayside and producers are reduced to impoverished and dispossessed proletarians. In the sociological literature, whether capital is concentrated in core metropolitan countries or, in the case of scientists, in elite research universities, markets are seen inexorably to result in increasing inequalities.

Although Polanyi (1957) took issue with many of Marx's claims about modern capitalism, like Marx he viewed market economies as driven by profit and greed, a "satanic mill" that treated labor power as a commodity to be bought and sold, and ultimately discarded. He maintained that the institutional logic of the market economy was destructive of the social institutions that embed man in a natural community, rendering him unprotected from the "ravages of the satanic mill." Rather than the class struggle, what Polanyi emphasized was the ruinous impact of markets on the fabric of society. Society needed to protect itself from the self-regulating market, lest it be destroyed by it.

The legacy of Marx's view of markets is evident in recent work on the transitions from state socialism. For example, Szelenyi and Manchin maintained that for those at the "bottom of the income hierarchy" in Hungary a "real pauperization took place" (1987, p. 122). The shift to markets sparked price inflation which led to the erosion of welfare programs and subsidies. Cadres in the core redistributive sectors and entrepreneurs were able to fend off the worst effects of inflation, but the weak and poor lacked the political and economic resources to weather the twin threats of inflation and erosion of welfare subsidies. They hypothesized that the shift to markets has an initial equalizing effect, but this is followed by growing inequality. More recent social science scholarship on the emergence of a market economy in Eastern Europe endorses the view of markets as a cause of inequality, imposing greater hardships on the poor and weak, while benefiting a privileged few (Hankiss, 1990; Staniszkis, 1991; Rona-Tas, 1994).

The economic literature concurs that economic growth in market economies exacerbates inequality, especially in the early stages of modern economic development. Lewis (1954) attributed rising inequality in developing market economies to two factors. First, the newly acquired wealth of entrepreneurs can be expected to result in increased inequality between the rich and poor. Second, the movement of a small number of agricultural workers to industrial employment at the initial stage results in increasing income inequality between these households and those remaining in subsistence agriculture. There is thus a trade-off between economic growth and income equality. Indeed, according to Lewis, inequality is a necessary cost of growth because it provides the needed incentives for the rich to save and invest in economic development. Kuznets (1955) suggested that the relationship between economic development and inequality in the distribution of income takes the shape of an inverted-U. As a country's per-capita GNP rises, income inequality can be expected to increase through the intermediate stage of development; but when GNP reaches a level characteristic of industrial economies, the distribution of income may then become more equal. Fei and Ranis (1964) extended Lewis's surplus-labor model to demonstrate that as the supply of cheap labor moving out of agriculture is exhausted, this induces corresponding increases in industrial wages, producing the eventual decline in income inequality predicted by Kuznets. The sequence of rise and decline in income inequality posited in the economics literature contradicts what Marx forecast for capitalist development and neo-Marxists predict for reforming state socialist economies.

Overall Kuznets' inverted-U hypothesis has held up well in light of subsequent studies of income inequality (Gillis *et al.* 1987). However, confirmation of Kuznets' hypothesis has been based on cross-section data of countries at various stages of development. There have been few time-series analyses of the dynamics of income inequality for particular countries. Moreover, Ahluwalia (1974) demonstrated in a study of 58 countries that the hypothesized curvilinear relationship accounted for only one-quarter of the variation in Gini coefficients. Many individual countries (i.e., Taiwan and South Korea) depart from the predicted pattern. In part for this reason, Fields (1980) concluded that the curvilinear relationship between growth and inequality may not be inevitable. Instead he maintained that it is possible, depending on the institutional context and specific government policies, to achieve growth with equity. His is the optimistic view of the relationship between markets and the distribution of income.

Discrepancy in the sociological and economic literatures on the impact of markets on the structure of inequality can be traced to the differing legacies of Karl Marx and Adam Smith. In the Marxist tradition, widening inequality is viewed as accompanying capitalist economic development. Its basic proposition is that as capital becomes more concentrated, poverty becomes more widespread. By contrast, the Smithian tradition has emphasized the gains from trade, and maintains that wealth is distributed more equitably after nations become industrialized. Its underlying proposition is that as wealth is accumulated through expanding trade and the supply of cheap labor shifting from agriculture to industry is spent, non-farm wages will increase as employers compete for a limited supply of workers and will be more evenly distributed, resulting in a reduction in the extent of inequality generated in the early stages of industrialization. In sum, the Marxist tradition focuses attention on class differentiation in the course of economic development, while the Smithian tradition emphasizes inequality caused by the higher productivity of industry relative to agriculture, which in the course of economic development will decline.

An institutional analysis of inequality

Although the classical tradition continues to influence contemporary scholarship on inequality, the institutional framework of economic development has received insufficient attention. The neoclassical model in economics emphasized the role of human capital in explaining income inequality in developing economies, virtually ignoring the institutional framework (Chiswick, 1971). Ahluwalia (1976 a and b) specified alternative causal mechanisms giving rise to inequality by examining the relative importance of the agricultural sector, the size of the urban population, expansion of educational attainment, and population growth. Although his model expanded the standard neoclassical model, he acknowledged that a "limitation of our exercise is the lack of explicit recognition of the role of the institutional framework in which development takes place" (p. 328).

In sociology, dependency theory hypothesized that the concentration of capital and technology in core countries worked to the disadvantage of poor countries. The empirical literature it spawned focused on testing the proposition that dependence on foreign investment and trade caused distorted economic development in poor countries, manifested in economic stagnation, income inequality, and persistent poverty (Chase-Dunn, 1975; Bornschier and Chase-Dunn, 1985; Boswell and Dixon, 1990; Evans and Timberlake, 1980). Recently Firebaugh and Beck (1994), employing a difference model to retest the core proposition of dependency theory, confirmed the Smithian proposition that economic growth benefits the masses, leading them to reject the claims of dependency theory. Yet, like Ahluwalia (1976 a and b), their model did not focus attention on the institutional framework of development. If, however, as they contend, international trade and investment do not cause harmful effects, and instead only economic development matters, then much of the variation in income dispersion and life chances in developing economies cannot be explained.

Our main argument is that institutions matter in the determination of income growth and inequality. Defined as the rules of the game, institutions specify the costs and rewards of a limited set of alternative courses of action. In doing so, they shape the structure of incentives through differential access to opportunities (Merton, 1968). Change in this structure has distinct distributional consequences. As individuals and organizations seek marginal gains by exploiting change in the institutional environment, the structure of inequality is also transformed concomitantly as some groups benefit while others lose. An example is the reform of tax laws, a rules change that not only alters the structure of incentives for political and economic factors, but also has distributive consequences. Examining the effect of institutional change on the distribution of rewards and structure of inequality change in the Chinese transition from state socialism provides, we believe, a rare opportunity to shed new light on this role of the institutional framework.

A distinguishing feature of the Chinese market reform, compared with that of Eastern Europe and the former Soviet Union, is that the shift to a market economy has been accompanied by rapid economic growth. When markets stimulate improved economic performance, the adage that all boats rise with a rising tide may describe the increase in living standards experienced by households (Danziger and Gottschalk, 1986). This is a crucial difference because the increasing inequalities reported in Eastern Europe and Russia may be the result of the sharp economic downturn experienced in those regions following regime change, rather than of market transition per se. By contrast in China, markets coupled with economic growth have provided conditions that favor a more equitable distribution of income. Indeed recent analyses of income inequality have confirmed the growth-with-equity trend reported in earlier studies based on smaller provincial samples. Khan, Griffin, Riskin, and Zhao (1993) report that the Gini coefficient of rural income inequality in 1988 was 0.315. The World Bank study finds it virtually the same, having dropped from 0.32 in 1978 to 0.31 in 1986, showing a slight decline in income inequality. Thus, contrary to widely held cultural beliefs equating marketization with widening income inequalities, the social science literature conveys evidence of growth with equity characterized by increases in household income and relatively stable income distribution among rural households (Zhu and Wen, 1990; Zhu, 1990; Nee, 1991; Griffin and Zhao, 1993). Studies of urban income trends also have reported declining income inequality in the 1980s (Walder, 1990; Bian and Logan, 1996). Not until the 1990s did income inequality increase sharply in cities.

Despite such evidence of stable or declining income inequality in the 1980s in rural China, trends in income inequality are inadequately understood. This can be attributed to multiple mechanisms at work in the determination of income, all responding to broader parameter shifts in the institutional environment during the transition to a market-based economy. Our aim in this chapter is to examine the impact of institutional change on the structure of inequality in the transition from state socialism. We analyze longitudinal data on rural household income conducted in China in 1989/90. Regional variation in institutional contexts and extent of marketization allows us to identify emerging patterns in the structure of inequality after 12 years of market reform. We analyze regional variation in institutional structures to map the effect of the institutional environment on inequality.

Institutional change and market expansion

In the transitions from state socialism, only when markets replace socialist redistribution as the dominant institutional arrangement is a market economy established. Institutional changes giving rise to the emergence of a market economy do not occur overnight, in a "big bang" market-creation explosion of formal rule changes. The experiences of Eastern Europe and Russia demonstrate that even after the collapse of communist political power, the new regimes must struggle to dismantle the economic institutions of state socialism even while they strive to con-

struct market institutions (Murrell, 1992). The timing of the transition
to a market-based economy need not coincide with regime change.
Despite major efforts at pursuing radical reforms, a hybrid redistributive
economy has persisted in Russia as the dominant institutional form well
beyond the collapse of the socialist state (Burawoy and Krotov, 1992).
In Eastern Europe, the trajectories of transitions from state socialism
have been strikingly path dependent and incremental (Stark, 1996).

The critical institutional transformations in the emergence of a market
economy center on changes that restructure the role of the state, expand
the mix of property rights, and sustain the shift to reliance on markets.
Following market reform, the timing and extent to which the central
state apparatus makes the transition from a redistributive state to a regu-
latory state is critical to its capacity to institute the framework of a
market-based economy (Shirk, 1993; Naughton, 1995). It is the state
that plays the key role in defining the constitutional framework specifying the structure of property rights and their enforcement mechanisms
(North, 1981). In turn the mix of property forms in an economy reflects
the extent of diversity in organizational forms. The greater this, the more
broadly based are the institutionalized avenues for profit and gain, and
the greater the scope for socioeconomic mobility. When private property
forms are suppressed, and barriers to entry for non-state property forms
are kept high, clearly the structure of opportunity is controlled by the
state. Increasing representation of non-state property forms hence
increases access to opportunities for profit and gain for economic actors.
And, finally, Smith's (1776) proposition that the extent of the market
limits the division of labor can be reformulated to state that the size
of market structures determines the range of opportunities outside of
subsistence agriculture. As markets grow and differentiate, the gains
from trade and specialization improve the livelihood of producers,
whether through commercial agriculture, non-farm employment, or private entrepreneurship. The greatest gains are experienced under conditions of rapid expansion of market institutions, as demand for labor
and factor resources increases the bargaining power of direct producers
and hence their gains. In the transitions from state socialism, these institutional transformations entail far-reaching changes in the underlying
rules of the game for both political and economic actors.

In China, the role of the state in instituting a market-based mixed
economy has entailed implementing new policies and rules that have
redrawn the boundaries between the state and firm. Institutional change
has involved not only policy changes and new rules, but the lax enforcement of old regulations that no longer accommodate the interests of
political and economic actors. For example, the lax enforcement of

restrictions on the mobility of labor – for rural migrants and state employees – has been critical to the emergence of labor markets.

Fiscal decentralization by the central state improved incentives for political actors to create conditions favorable to local economic growth (Byrd and Lin, 1990; Oi, 1992). Also, rather than extensive reliance on privatization of public assets as in Eastern Europe and the former Soviet Union, the institutional innovation of profit-sharing has limited the government's take of the economic surplus and partitioned rights in a way that improves incentives for managers and workers. Retained profits improve wages and bonuses to the extent the firm succeeds in competitive markets (Jefferson and Xu, 1991). The resulting productivity gains also contribute to increasing revenues for local government. Further, the creation of a dual-pricing system of state and market prices has reduced the state's direct control over the economy previously maintained by fiat power in setting prices of goods and services. It opened the way for a gradual shift to competitive market prices and reliance on indirect macroeconomic controls by the state (Naughton, 1995). Further still, new regulations restricting direct microinterventions by economic bureaucrats in state-owned enterprises have contributed to increasing enterprise autonomy for factory directors (Jefferson and Rawski, 1994). Enterprise autonomy has been crucial to the emergence of competitive production markets in the industrial economy. Lastly, barriers to entry and expansion have been lowered for private entrepreneurs and non-state firms through market-supporting interventions. Differences in the timing of reform and geographical specifications of state policies have given rise to regional variation in the institutional environment. These have favored rapid economic growth in the more developed maritime provinces (Lyons, 1994).

Institutional effects hypotheses

The cumulative effect of far-reaching institutional changes has been to create a market-preserving federalism in which local governments, striving to build thriving industrial districts, compete for investments and market share by providing conditions favorable to economic growth (Weingast, 1993; Qian and Xu, 1993; Nee and Su, 1996). Local corporatist arrangements have defined a positive role for institutions in the emerging market-based economy. They are societal institutions rather than state organizations because they incorporate political and economic actors in a community-owned multidivisional firm. The emergence of corporatist institutional arrangements has provided non-state firms with the backing they needed to compete with larger and better capitalized state-owned enterprises and to make the leap into the global market economy by establishing joint ventures with foreign partners. Much of the explosive economic growth in the coastal provinces of China has been due to the success of local corporatism as a hybrid governance structure. Growth rates of industrial output of township enterprises averaging 30 percent per annum through the 1980s and 1990s has greatly augmented the revenue base of local corporatist governments (Oi, 1992).

In corporatist communities, local governments operate like the board of directors of a multidivisional firm (Oi, 1990; Qian and Xu, 1993). Control rights over collective enterprises enable corporatist local governments to redistribute resources through the allocation of high-paying non-farm jobs, local infrastructure projects, welfare spending, or by imposing discriminatory taxes and levies on private businesses. Because the beneficiaries of corporatist development are residents of the community, Che and Qian (1994) argue that the community constitutes the boundary of the corporatist firm. For this reason, local corporatist economic development increases social solidarity in the community. This is manifested in more sharply demarcated social boundaries and a more intense moral order in which the economic dependence of actors on the conjoint production of goods and services increases social solidarity.

The distributional consequence of corporatist institutional arrangements is evident in the close link between increasing per-capita income in a community and what is considered socially acceptable income for local cadres (Byrd and Gelb, 1990). Local cadres have an incentive to improve the general standard of living in the community because their salaries are tied to increasing per-capita income. Formal and informal monitoring impose limitations on local officials using positional power to secure exceptional private advantages (Nee and Lian, 1994). Corporatist communities provide subsistence guarantees to the poor and limit the profits of entrepreneurs through distributional norms characteristic of the moral economy widely observed in small communities (Thompson, 1966; Scott, 1976; Wilson, 1994). We hypothesize that local corporatist governance structures, by promoting economic growth, increase the odds of income mobility, even while the moral economy of the community limits the extent of inequality.

The explosive entry of private enterprises coupled with the rapid growth of collective firms significantly altered the structure of property rights and the mix of organizational forms in the industrial economy. These non-state enterprises rapidly expanded their share of industrial production from 23 percent in 1978 to over 50 percent by 1993 as market transition gathered momentum. The effect of a massive shift to market-oriented production in the industrial economy has been particularly evident in rural townships and villages where virtually all industrial firms are market oriented (Byrd and Lin, 1990). Productivity gains stimulated by the shift to markets had led to higher income from participation in off-farm work. Thus, we hypothesize that change in the structure of ownership toward a greater representation of non-state firms has a net positive effect on household income mobility.

Both collective and private ownership forms rely principally on markets for factor resources and for the distribution of their products. They comprise local production markets in which firms compete for factor resources (i.e., investment capital and skilled workers) and market share. Because the extent of the local production market determines the size of the labor market for off-farm employment, it is probably the most important indicator of marketization in a locality. In general, the larger the size of the production market, the thicker the market environment in a locality. Although the growth of commodity markets also indicates the extent of marketization, it does not have the same effect on the structure of income inequality as production markets in rural areas. It follows, as the size of market structures determining the extent of opportunities for non-farm employment grows, so does the odds of income mobility for households increase.

The main cause of increasing income inequality is regional variation in the growth of rural industry and unequal access to non-farm jobs (Rozelle, 1994). It follows therefore that the size of the labor market corresponds with increasing income inequality. It is this mechanism that matches surplus agricultural labor to higher paying non-farm jobs. Rural commodity markets serve the marketing needs of farmers, while the extent of the production market determines the number and diversity of non-farm jobs available to absorb surplus labor from agriculture. As the size of the off-farm labor markets grow, inequality concomitantly increases, but when many households have non-farm income earners, income inequality begins to level off, giving rise to an inverted-U-shaped pattern.

Data and measures

To test our institutional effects hypotheses, we analyze data from the China–Cornell–Oxford national survey of rural communities and households to examine empirically the impact of institutional change on household income mobility and the structure of inequality. Institutional changes leading to a rapid shift to markets began first in the rural economy. By focusing on one sector, our analysis is not confounded by inequality caused by rural–urban differences in earnings, which in China is considerable (Zhao, 1993). Moreover, rural China provides an excellent site for research on the causes of increase in income inequality because decollectivization left households in a community with equal per-capita distributions of productive assets: land and equipment. We examine changes in household income over a 12-year period, from the start of market reform in 1978 to 1989, as well as cross-sectional household income inequality in 1989.

The data come from a multistage nationwide social and medical survey of 138 administrative townships (*xiang*), 138 villages (*cun*), and 7,950 households in rural China carried out in the fall and winter of 1989–90. The data were collected by the Chinese Academy of Preventive Medicine (CAPM), using trained teams of public health field interviewers. The initial survey was conducted in 1983. Sixty-five counties were selected non-randomly; within each of these counties, two townships and then two villages were selected randomly, as were the households interviewed within the villages (see Chen, Campbell, Li, and Peto, 1989; Parpia, 1994 for further details). The 1989 resurvey added four additional counties and incorporated multilevel socioeconomic questionnaires. These data have been supplemented with official reports of provincial level production output for the years 1987, 1988, and 1989. Numerous sources of household income were included to calculate total household income in 1989. These sources are net income from the sale of agricultural products, the cost of food produced by the household, and the contribution of non-agricultural income – private business, cadre salary, factory jobs, service, sidelines, and an unspecified "other" category. Income for 1978 is retrospective; though prone to error, subjects' memories were aided by noting that year as the start of post-Mao reform.

Institutional environment is measured at both a regional and a local level. The regional measure is developed in a cluster analysis reported below. Each province is classified according to the institutional structure shaped by the mix of property forms in the industrial economy: *Laissez-faire, corporatist,* and *redistributive* coastal provinces are contrasted with the inland provinces as a set of dummy variables.

Local market institutional structure is captured by three variables. *Production market* is the natural logarithm of the number of private and collective firms in the township. The concept of production market stems from White's (1981) theory of markets, which views the market as a social structure rather than as a mere medium of exchange. The neoclassical preoccupation with exchange markets, according to White, led economists to overlook the central feature of market institutions – that they are social structures reproduced through signaling and communication among participants. A production market, then, is a group of firms that view themselves as constituting a market and that are perceived as such by buyers. In White's definition, "markets are tangible cliques of producers watching each other" (1981, p. 543). The production market can be viewed as a local business group in which producers communicate with each other, both to compete and to cooperate in gaining access to resources and securing larger market shares. The higher the number of private and collective firms, the thicker the local market environment. A second indicator of the extent of marketization comes from considering the emergence of markets for non-farm labor. *Labor market* is the proportion of the village population engaged in non-farm work outside the village in construction, factories and workshops, self-employed in private business, or as travelling craftsmen and peddlers. The higher the proportion, the greater the extent of the local labor market.

We also measure whether or not most village people find non-farm jobs through the government (Government finds non-farm jobs = 1) or through kin, friendship, advertisement, or private agencies (Government finds non-farm jobs = 0). When most people find such positions through network ties or private agencies and ads, the local government controls neither the agricultural economy nor the allocation of non-farm jobs. Although local corporatism is a dominant institutional form in two central coastal provinces – Jiangsu and Zhejiang – it is also present elsewhere in the coastal region, and to a more limited extent in inland provinces.

The level of industrialization in a locality and economic growth are measured by two variables. Industrial output is per-capita industrial output for the township. This measures the extent of rural industrialization. The greater the level of output per-capita, the more industrialized the township. Economic growth is a dummy variable indicating whether the village economy has grown over the six years prior to the data collection (economic growth = 1), or whether the economy has declined or remained stagnant over the period (economic growth = 0). These variables control for causal mechanisms stemming from economic development that give rise to income inequality.

Regional differences

Attention to regional differences in the extent of marketization casts light on the correspondence between market penetration and changes in the structure of inequality. We determine the institutional environment at the provincial level with a cluster analysis of provincial data on the value of industrial production in the private, collective, and state sectors (Nee, 1996). Private and collective enterprises are overwhelmingly located in rural townships and villages, growing respectively by 60 and 30 percent per annum during the 1980s. The growth of private industrial production mainly generates income through self-employment, since the size of private firms has remained small due to the lack of institutional safeguards for private property rights. However, by the late 1980s in the southeastern coastal provinces of China, some private firms grew into medium-sized industrial enterprises. There private firms gained the critical mass needed to compete directly with larger collective and state-owned enterprises. Although state-owned industrial firms are few in number in rural townships, their presence in county towns and cities provide opportunity for non-farm work for surplus agricultural labor. Collective enterprises, however, are the main source of rural non-farm employment. This is a community ownership form, but, as noted above, control rights over collective assets are in the hands of officials in local government. Examining the relative contribution of these ownership forms measures the changing structure of property rights and mix of organizational forms in the rapidly growing industrial sector of the economy.

Since 1978 the coastal provinces of China have benefited the most from the economic reform policies which targeted these provinces as the experimental grounds of their new development strategy. Post-Mao reformers established special economic zones and "open" cities, accelerated the implementation of profit-sharing arrangements and promoted decentralized market institutions in this region. In the coastal provinces marketization involved not only expansion of domestic markets, but also rapid incorporation into the global economy.

However, even in the coastal provinces, there is considerable variation in institutional environment. The southeastern coastal provinces (Guangdong and Fujian) have already made the transition to hybrid market economies. In 1989, these provinces were characterized by over 55.2 percent of production output in firms in market settings. In these provinces the marketized sectors of the economy have grown rapidly – in 1987 the proportion was barely greater than 36.6 percent – and have replaced the non-marketized state sector as the dominant sectors of the economy. Their geographical proximity to Hong Kong, Macao, Taiwan, and overseas Chinese communities in Southeast Asia have favored them as sites of foreign investments and trade agreement (Johnson, 1994). Market-oriented policies favoring the coastal provinces, in combination with a higher level of prior economic development, have led to explosive rates of economic growth in the southeastern coastal provinces.

On the other hand, the central coastal provinces (Zhejiang and Jiangsu) have relied more extensively on corporatist strategies in which local governments play a decisive role in economic development, thereby perpetuating local socialist power. Although these areas have experienced a transition to greater reliance on markets, what characterizes corporatist areas is the dominance of collective ownership forms in the mixed economy (Nee, 1992). Production output in these areas is heavily concentrated in collective firms – 60.8 and 59.1 percent in 1988 and 1989 respectively. Yet many collectively owned firms are in fact privately owned or operate as semi-private entities (Liu, 1992; Peng, 1992). Coastal corporatist provinces hence represent an intermediate mixed economy midway in the continuum between redistributive and market institutional environments.

Finally, the remaining coastal provinces (Hebei, Shandong, and Shanghai) have maintained a predominantly redistributive institutional environment. These provinces are still dominated by state ownership of productive capacity. In 1989, over 53.8 percent of output came from the state-owned sector. However, in contrast to the inland provinces, the redistributive coastal provinces have seen a growth of market-oriented industrial production – in 1989 46.2 percent of output, one-third larger than the inland provinces. The label coastal redistributive is somewhat misleading if it diverts attention from the increasing scope of market-oriented economic activity in these provinces. The rural location of most private and collective enterprises implies that the growth of these market-dependent organizational forms has a disproportionate impact on the opportunity structure facing rural households in the coastal redistribution provinces.

These four regions – inland, coastal redistributive, coastal corporatist, and coastal laissez-faire – partition China in 1989 into clusters of provinces with similar structures of property rights and extent of emergence of a market economy. In order to control for differences in institutional environment in the next analyses, we use dummy variables to distinguish the three kinds of coastal provinces. Their respective institutional environments are shaped by differing mixes of property forms in the industrial economy, and are clearly differentiated from the inland provinces.

Income mobility

Table 8.1 presents a cross-classification of households according to income quintile in 1978 and 1989. What is most notable in the mobility

Table 8.1 *Income mobility of rural Chinese household from 1978 to 1989*[a]

	Top quintile 1989	2nd quintile 1989	3rd quintile 1989	4th quintile 1989	Bottom quintile 1989	Total
Top quintile 1978	581	357	223	143	134	1,438
	40.40	24.83	15.51	9.94	9.32	
2nd quintile 1978	346	369	313	248	162	1,438
	24.06	25.66	21.77	17.25	11.27	
3rd quintile 1978	279	318	300	294	245	1,436
	19.43	22.14	20.89	20.47	17.06	
4th quintile 1978	178	245	312	377	327	1,439
	12.37	17.03	21.68	26.20	22.72	
Bottom quintile 1978	113	187	287	349	501	1,437
	7.86	13.01	19.97	24.29	34.86	
Total	1,497	1,476	1,435	1,411	1,369	7,188

Note: [a]Cell counts are provided, as are the outflow percentages. The row and column marginals are not evenly distributed, as quintiles are defined for all households in 1978 and all households in 1989 separately; not all such households were in existence at both time points.

table is the generally high level of income mobility. While approximately 40 percent of the top income quintile in 1978 remained in the top income quintile over the 12-year period, 19.26 percent fell to the fourth or fifth quintile. That is a lot of downward income mobility. In the other direction, a similar 20.87 percent moved from the fifth quintile in 1978 to the top two quintiles in 1989.[1]

Model and method

What is the relative role of institutional and economic factors in the movement of households along the income distribution? Our models control for human capital, household composition, and alternative explanations of location along the income distribution. Such alternative explanations include the presence in the household of cadres who hold redistributive power in the community, and private entrepreneurs who are likely to benefit the most from market exchange. These households are likely to be disproportionately represented in the top income brackets in rural China and less likely to be among the poorest households. We also control for the education of the household head as specified in human capital models of income inequality. We focus on the distribution of households across income quintiles. One might question why we do not utilize the actual data on income rather than the grouped format. First, using quintiles reduces the potential impact of any measurement error, especially that found in the retrospective reports of income for 1978. Second, and more importantly, utilizing quintiles places the emphasis of the analysis on the relative position of a household in the income distribution, rather than on the specific amount – we can explicitly model the mobility along the income distribution in this way.

We employ cumulative logit models (McCullagh and Nelder, 1989; Agresti, 1984) to model the association between origin quintile in 1978 and destination quintile in 1989.[2] This may be intuitively understood as follows, in relation to the standard binary logit model. Take a multicategory response and binarize it at some cutpoint between any two categories. For example, suppose we have a five-category response variable, and we binarize it so that we collapse the first two categories into a single category, and the last three categories into a second category. We have now, through the collapsing, a binary variable and we could readily fit a standard logistic regression model. But we could have binarized the response between category 4 and 5 rather than between categories 2 and 3. We could then fit a standard logistic model to this binarization of the original five-category response. There are a total of $k-1$ possible ways of binarizing a k-category response while maintaining the ordering of the response categories. We could then fit a standard logistic model to each of these $k-1$ binarizations and determine the effect of covariates for each one. The cumulative logistic model does precisely this, with the further constraint that the regression parameters are identical across the $k-1$ ways of binarizing the response. Thus the antilogs of estimated regression parameters give the effect of the independent variable on the odds of falling into the top versus the bottom set of categories for any way one cuts the multiple responses into a binary response. An advantage the cumulative logit model has over more common loglinear models for mobility tables is that individual level covariates can be included in the model. The primary reason this model has not been exploited in social mobility research has more to do with the requirement that the response categories must be given an a priori ordering than any lack of appropriateness. Thus, we shall be able to examine the effect of covariates for institutional structure on income mobility and not be limited to the study of the association of origin and destination.

Results

Model 1 in table 8.2 includes only measures of the institutional environment and the origin effects. In this model, we see that the substantively interesting variables for institutional structure are all positive and significant. The positive coefficients indicate that the distribution across the income quintiles is shifted toward the top quintiles. The set of intercepts are the cut-points separating the five categories, and are not of any substantive interest. The ordering seen in the intercepts is a consequence of the ordering of the response – the ordering implicit in the income quintiles.

Thus, if the set of quintiles in 1989 is cut between any two categories, and a household is located in the laissez-faire provinces, then the odds of being above the cut is 2.45 times (= exp(.8969)) that of a household located in an inland province. For example, the odds of being in the top quintile versus the lower quintiles is 2.45 times greater for laissez-faire located households than for inland households. The odds are the same for other cuts, such as the top three quintiles versus the bottom two quintiles. For the quantitative factors, such as the production market, a unit increase will increase the odds of the higher response by a factor of 1.07 – in this case each unit is an additional private or collective firm. An increase of ten firms in a township leads to an increase in the odds of being above the cut-point of 1.36 (= exp(10 × .0312)). The effects of origin are as precisely as we would expect. Households that originate in the top quintiles are more likely to remain in the upper quintiles and those originally in the lower quintiles are more likely to have destinations in the lower quintiles.

The core idea of the development economics literature is that the level of industrialization and economic growth will improve the economic outcomes for households. We expect this proposition to hold true in Chinese rural society. Our aim is to highlight the independent effects of institutional environment and economic development. The role of institutions needs to be examined net of the effects of economic development. Toward this goal, in model 2 of table 8.2 we add a set of covariates for economic growth and development.

Two of the economic factors – village economic growth and industrial per-capita output – have positive and significant effects on the odds of a household falling above a cut-point (for example, top two quintiles rather than the bottom three). These effects are just as predicted by economic theory and the adage of a rising tide. The negative coefficient for agricultural output likely has more to do with the poorer financial rewards of farming relative to industrial production. Note also that the estimate is only very slightly significant.

Our contention that institutional structure has independent effects on household income is seen in the significant positive effects of the various measures of the institutional environment. The role of institutional fac-

Table 8.2 *Cumulative logistic regression model of income mobility*

Variable	Model 1	Model 2	Model 3
Intercept 1	−2.2006***	−2.3964***	−5.9933***
	(0.0731)	(0.0903)	(0.4913)
Intercept 2	−1.0448***	−1.2394***	−4.6953***
	(0.0686)	(0.0864)	(0.4894)
Intercept 3	−0.0950	−0.2879***	−3.6334***
	(0.0675)	(0.0853)	(0.4882)
Intercept 4	1.0146***	0.8244***	−2.4215***
	(0.0697)	(0.0866)	(0.4872)
Institutional environment			
Coastal redistributive	0.5279***	0.4968***	0.0830
	(0.0833)	(0.0837)	(0.0892)
Coastal corporatist	0.5389***	0.5285***	0.4149***
	(0.0712)	(0.0714)	(0.0744)
Coastal laissez-faire	0.8969***	0.8716***	0.8530***
	(0.0764)	(0.0766)	(0.0793)
Production market	0.0312**	0.0265*	0.0244*
	(0.0135)	(0.0135)	(0.0140)
Labor market	1.5501***	1.4528***	0.3414
	(0.2926)	(0.2934)	(0.3056)
Government finds			
non-farm jobs	0.3833***	0.3653***	0.4372***
	(0.0477)	(0.0480)	(0.0495)
Economic environment			
Agricultural output per			
capita		−0.1441*	−0.1514*
		(0.0791)	(0.0832)
Industrial output per			
capita		0.1698**	0.1692*
		(0.0825)	(0.0869)
Village economic growth		0.2610***	0.2369***
		(0.0690)	(0.0705)
Control variables			
Age			0.1306***
			(0.0202)
Age squared			−0.0015***
			(0.0002)
Primary school			0.1602***
			(0.0548)
Junior middle school			0.1673**
			(0.0717)
Advanced schooling			0.1179
			(0.1125)
Farm labor			0.0892***
			(0.0148)

Table 8.2 (*cont.*)

Variable	Model 1	Model 2	Model 3
Non-farm labor			0.9109***
			(0.0350)
Entrepreneur			0.7382***
			(0.0893)
Cadre			0.5139***
			(0.0658)
Top quintile 1978	0.8824***	0.8858***	0.7916***
	(0.0705)	(0.0705)	(0.0734)
Second quintile 1978	0.3205***	0.3133***	0.2493***
	(0.0687)	(0.0687)	(0.0706)
Fourth quintile 1978	−0.4135***	−0.4184***	−0.3672***
	(0.0692)	(0.0692)	(0.0708)
Bottom quintile 1978	−0.8976***	−0.8908***	−0.8187***
	(0.0702)	(0.0702)	(0.0717)
−2*Log likelihood	20462.262	20443.414	18972.260
N	6,758	6,758	6,613

Notes: $*p < 0.10$.
$**p < 0.05$.
$***p < 0.01$.

tors remains even after controlling for economic growth. The net effect of changing institutional environment is clearly demonstrated. In particular, the diffusion of private property forms and market institutions in the laissez-faire provinces boosts the odds of a household falling into higher-income quintiles more than other regions, followed by the coastal corporatist region. Local market structures such as production markets and labor markets also improve the odds of a household falling into higher-income quintiles.

The third column of table 8.2 contains model 3 which adds a set of individual level covariates as controls for heterogeneity across households. These control effects are essentially what one would expect: human capital increases the odds of falling in the higher quintiles, increased levels of household farm and non-farm workers also have a positive effect on destination quintile, as does the presence of a cadre in the household or the establishment of a household business enterprise.

In this final model the effects of the economic variables pertaining to industrial and agricultural output are very mildly significant. The effect of economic growth remains strong and highly significant. This contrast would suggest that the rising tide needs to be greater economic growth rather than merely higher levels of industrial output. Households in villages sustaining growth over the six-year period between 1983 and 1989 have odds of falling above a cut point 1.26 times those households in no growth or declining villages.

As to the effect of institutional environment, even after controlling for individual factors and economic growth, it still matters. Local market structure nearly fades away as local labor markets are no longer statistically significant, and production markets very mildly so. Local corporatist institutional arrangements remain strong and significant – in townships where most non-farm jobs are obtained through the local government, the odds of a household falling above a cut point is 1.55 times that of a household in townships where the local government does not control the distribution of non-farm jobs. The effect of institutional structure at the provincial level is positive and statistically significant for corporatist and laissez-faire institutional environments. In contrast to the strength of local redistribution, provincial level redistributive power is not significantly different from the inland provinces. Households in corporatist and laissez-faire regions are more likely to end up in the upper quintiles than those households in the inland or redistributive coastal areas.

There are two main conclusions to be drawn from this analysis of income mobility. First, institutional structure in the form of corporatist and laissez-faire arrangements improves the income mobility chances of households. This effect holds up even when controlling for household level factors, and economic growth and development. A second conclusion to draw is that economic growth increases the mobility chances of households, and industrial development only mildly so.

Table 8.3 presents the proportion of total income for each of five income quintiles, along with the coefficient of variation and the Gini coefficient. The most striking finding here is that across all 12 years and four regions, the top quintile in China held nearly half the income. Also notable is that for the nation as a whole, and within each of the four regions, inequality initially declined from 1978 to 1983. This time period corresponds to the early stages of economic reform, and resembles the finding reported by Zhu (1990) for an inland province. Following the initial stages, inequality took off to the point where in 1989 inequality is higher than at the end of the Maoist period.

This pattern of declining inequality, followed by a rapid increase is sharpest in the most laissez-faire provinces. The initial decline was transitory; with subsequently higher inequality. This is consistent with the pattern of inequality based on the analysis of rural households in a southeastern coastal province (Nee, 1991). Of additional interest is that for the two regions which stand at somewhat opposite extremes – the

Table 8.3 *Percentage of aggregate rural household income earned by income quintile and institutional structure, with coefficient of variation and Gini coefficient.*

Inland	Bottom quintile	4th quintile	3rd quintile	2cd quintile	Top quintile	Coefficient of variation (CV)	Gini coefficient
1978	2.37	7.81	14.50	23.65	51.68	1.079	0.477
1983	4.66	9.75	15.47	22.74	47.38	0.873	0.421
1989	2.27	8.18	14.46	22.83	52.26	1.207	0.497
Coastal redistributive							
1978	3.27	7.64	13.11	20.40	55.59	1.177	0.506
1983	4.28	9.01	14.46	22.35	49.90	0.930	0.445
1989	2.30	6.82	14.43	26.03	50.41	0.954	0.492
Coastal corporatist							
1978	3.68	7.91	14.58	24.53	49.30	1.012	0.465
1983	4.49	9.57	15.05	24.46	46.43	0.850	0.422
1989	4.44	10.98	16.58	24.82	43.18	0.729	0.388
Coastal laissez-faire							
1978	4.15	8.92	14.85	21.32	50.77	1.001	0.455
1983	5.81	10.57	16.31	23.55	43.77	0.760	0.381
1989	2.52	8.23	14.82	22.78	51.66	1.135	0.489
Nation							
1978	2.75	7.55	13.99	23.20	52.50	1.124	0.490
1983	4.56	9.50	14.96	23.48	47.50	0.883	0.428
1989	2.31	8.04	14.09	23.14	52.42	1.172	0.497

still redistributive inland provinces and the highly market-oriented laissez-faire provinces – the level of inequality in 1989 is the highest in the nation.

Looking at the corporatist provinces, we see that the level of inequality follows the same pattern as the other regions. However, comparing the level of inequality with the other coastal institutional environments suggests that institutional context can be decisive. The level of inequality is substantially lower for corporatist provinces. While market forces have led to rather high levels of inequality in Guangdong and Fujian, these pressures have been partially checked in Zhejiang and Jiangsu, where local corporatist governments led the shift to markets without abandoning redistributive policies aimed at providing a safety net for the poor.

Conclusion

The empirical findings reported here indicate that variation in the institutional environment matters in the determination of household income mobility and the structure of inequality. Moreover, institutional effects held up after controlling for economic development and household attributes. Although we examined a special case of market-driven economic development, our results shed light on the more general case of income determination and well-being. First, it adds further confirmation to sociological studies (Firebaugh and Beck, 1994; Barrett and Whyte, 1982; and Nee, 1991) that point to the beneficial effect of market-driven economic development on the well-being of the masses. Far from impoverization, households located in institutional environments undergoing rapid marketization were more likely to move into higher-income brackets and improve their standard of living. To be sure, relative inequality also increased; nonetheless material well-being improved for the rural masses.

Second, our findings reinforce the argument first articulated by revisionist scholarship in development economics (Ahluwalia, 1976a and b; Fields, 1980), that the Kuznets' U-shape pattern ought not be viewed as an iron law of economic development. Instead, the institutional structure within which development occurs matters in shaping the dynamics of income growth and pattern of inequality. Specifically we argued that political and social institutions play a significant role both in promoting income growth and in limiting the extent of inequality. We found that at both the regional and local level, corporatist institutional arrangements increased the odds of a household's falling into a higher-income quintile, yet they also limited the extent of relative inequality. Both government policy and community norms of fairness and justice were at work in producing growth with equity in corporatist communities.

In making the case that institutions matter, we also sought to specify the economic institutions and organizational forms that encompass the causal mechanisms giving rise to increased odds of income mobility, improvements in living standards, and patterns of inequality. We argued that the structure of property rights matters because increasing representation of market-oriented non-state firms promotes income growth. First, the entry of private firms increases opportunities for non-farm work through self-employment and entrepreneurship. Second, the growth of market-oriented collective firms increases the odds of moving out of subsistence agriculture into high-paying industrial jobs. Combined, private and collective firms make up the population of non-state firms that constitute the local production market. The extent of the production market corresponds to increased odds of falling into a higher-income quintile net of economic development and household attributes.

In the latter half of the 1980s rural households adjusted to the worsening terms of exchange through a variety of mechanisms. The primary means was high-paying non-farm jobs in rural industry. Another means was private entrepreneurship. Overall, households with redistributive and market power were more successful in adjusting to the market environment. Households in the bottom income quintile typically rely on quota-grain sale to the state as their main source of cash income, making them more vulnerable to price inflation in factor and consumer products. These households however did not participate in the emerging market economy; instead they hung on to the declining state-socialist redistributive economy, and were adversely affected by market-driven economic growth as soaring inflation in the late 1980s eroded their real income set by a redistributive exchange with the socialist state. As a result, households in the bottom quintile experienced a slight decline in real income in 1989 below the income obtained at the start of reform in 1978 (Nee, 1994). This decline, however, should be viewed as a special case of adverse price scissors affecting farmers still locked in the redistributive economics of grain production for the state. The exceptions were households in the corporatist provinces, where the bottom quintile experienced a modest gain in real income.

Insofar as growth with equity gives rise to a stable middle class and a more moderate level of inequality, this provides conditions favorable to democratization. The experience of Taiwan is consistent with this view. Taiwan in the 1950s was an authoritarian single party regime. The economic policies pursued by its leaders, however, produced equitable growth, which produced a growing middle class and contributed to the evolution of stable democratic reforms. Whether or not mainland China's political and social institutions will follow a similar evolution as Taiwan is not clear, and there are reasons why this is not likely (Wan, 1994). Regime change along the lines of Eastern Europe and the Soviet Union cannot be ruled out. Yet, sustained market-induced economic growth and extremes of inequality moderated by corporatist institutional arrangements may well produce a stable development strategy. If so, corporatist regions may negotiate the shift to a market society without the same extent of widening inequality reported by observers of Eastern Europe and the former Soviet Union, and in the laissez-faire regions of China.

NOTES

The research for this chapter was funded by a grant from the National Science Foundation (SES-9309651). Victor Nee wishes to express appreciation of the Russell Sage Foundation, which supported work on this chapter during his year in residence as a visiting scholar, 1994–5.

1 This is not to say that there was not any semblance of stability – for nearly all origin (1978) income quintiles a plurality of cases do not exhibit any mobility, and for all origins over 60 percent of households were within a single quintile of their origin.

2 Agresti's presentation is strictly tied to the cross-classification table to emphasize its similarity to various loglinear models for tables. The model is also known as the proportional odds model, and McCullagh and Nelder (1989) present an extensive discussion.

Part III

Responses to democratization

9   Democracy and inequality: tracking welfare spending in Singapore, Taiwan, and South Korea

Steve Chan

In another chapter of this volume, Ned Muller studied the impact of income distribution on changes in democracy. His results show that while economic development contributes directly to democratization, it also indirectly undermines the latter process among the upper-middle- and middle-income countries. This indirect negative effect is due to the tendency for economic development to increase the distributive gap between the rich and poor in these countries, a tendency that exacerbates social and political tension which in turn often augurs a reversal in the democratization process.

In this chapter, I reverse the causal inquiry presented in Muller's chapter. Instead of examining the effects of inequality on democracy, I search for any evidence of democracy affecting inequality. More accurately, this chapter inquires whether the initiation of the democratization process matters for tangible policy conduct, operationalized below as actual resource commitments to welfare programs whose purpose is to redistribute the economic product and to extend a social safety net to the society's less fortunate.

As explained in more detail below, I study the public expenditure data for three newly industrializing economies (NIEs) in East Asia: Singapore, Taiwan, and South Korea. The average per-capita income of these upwardly mobile countries is rapidly approaching or has already reached levels characteristic of the advanced industrial countries. During much of the past quarter century, however, they fell into the World Bank's classification of the upper-middle-income category – a group that seems to be most vulnerable to the democratic reversals analyzed by Muller.

Although hardly representative of the other countries in this category, an examination of the historical performance of these East Asian NIEs seems especially apposite precisely because they have featured *concurrently* rapid and sustained economic growth, impressive income equality, and substantial recent progress in democratization. Indeed, this concurrence in itself presents an important empirical puzzle and a theoretical challenge because, as will be discussed further below, the stylized facts emerging from the relevant literature (including Muller's chapter just mentioned) question the existence of a simple synergism among these phenomena and suggest instead that powerful negative feedback processes are often at work.

The remainder of this essay is organized into five sections. First, I present the broad theoretical rationale motivating this study. Second, I explain the selection of countries and indicators. Third, I sketch the logic of inquiry behind the quasi-experimental design. Fourth, the regression model is specified and the results are discussed. Fifth and, finally, the conclusion summarizes the substantive and theoretical implications.

Theoretical rationale

Why should one care about the relationship between democracy and inequality? One cares because political scientists are concerned about *regime performance*. They are deeply interested in matters of "who get what, when, how?" (Lasswell, 1936), and one of the basic tenets of the profession is that the character of the governing authority makes a systematic difference to policy conduct and its social outcome. Inquiries about the relationship between democracy and inequality therefore address a central and enduring concern of the discipline's research agenda.

Of course, there already exist a substantial number of studies on the question of whether democratic polities have more egalitarian income distribution (e.g., Bollen and Grandjean, 1981; Bollen and Jackman, 1985b; Chan, 1989; Cutright, 1967; Hewitt, 1977; Jackman, 1975, 1974; Muller, 1988, 1985; Rubinson and Quinlan, 1977; Simpson, 1990; Weede, 1982, 1980). These studies, however, are based mostly on *comparative statics*. That is, they seek to establish cross-sectional correlations between the level of democracy and the level of inequality among a particular set of countries. Put differently, we lack longitudinal analyses that try to determine whether a *change* in the independent variable (democracy) has had any effect on *changing* the dependent variable (inequality). Our ability to make *causal inference* suffers accordingly, because any sound attempt at such inference requires minimally (1) the specification of a clear temporal sequence whereby the alleged cause precedes the ostensible effect, and (2) the demonstration of a non-trivial change in the state of the dependent variable between the introduction of the hypothesized cause and some subsequent point in time. The fact that we lack finely grained time series data on income distribution, or that changes in this distribution tend to evolve slowly over time, does not absolve us from these requirements.

The following analysis seeks to understand how the *initiation* of a democratic opening is likely to affect policy choices (in this case, various categories of expenditures devoted to public welfare). Attention therefore goes not so much to the cross-national differences in the attainment of democratic level by specific countries. Rather, we are interested in the policy effects of democratic opening in specific countries. Instead of focusing on the possible differences between the income distributions of established democracies and those of non-democracies, we ask whether *major regime changes* in the direction of greater democracy matters for public policy.

But why a focus on public policy or, more exactly, on budgetary allocations for various welfare categories? As already mentioned, the general analytic inclination has heretofore been to determine some historical association (or the lack thereof) between the presence (or level) of democracy for some set of countries and the degree of income equality characterizing these countries. The *policy medium* through which democratic politics is likely to affect a country's performance on distributive justice is usually left unspecified and unexplored. Budgetary priorities accorded to public welfare point to one such policy medium, whereby the nature of a regime can significantly influence social equity.

Note that fiscal allocations merely reveal a regime's political priorities and indicate its *policy effort*. We can expect relatively quick changes in this policy effort after a regime change, whereas the effects of this effort on income inequality may take many years to realize. Muller (1988) pointed to the importance of this temporal consideration, arguing that one should not expect recent democracies to alter immediately their income distribution. One should indeed be surprised to find a high correlation between democratic and income changes for countries that have just recently begun a democratic transformation.

Democratization is generally expected to alter the distribution of political power to the relative benefit of the poorer people. Mass suffrage, for example, is often seen to facilitate the election of candidates from the workers' or social democratic parties. There has not been, however, much effort to establish whether these officials actually implement legislative or executive programs that help to reduce inequality. Only a few analysts interested in the relationship between democracy and inequality have actually examined public policy, such as the relative size of a government's social service expenditures or its distribution of the tax burden (e.g., Cutright, 1967; Hewitt, 1977; Jackman, 1974; Parkin, 1971). In short, then, this chapter seeks to move beyond a search for static correlations between regime characteristics and income sizes to an inquiry that actually asks what do democratic (or democratizing) governments actually do that can potentially reduce income inequality in the long term.

Although policy effort in the form of greater welfare spending may not be able to achieve this long-term goal, it seems even less likely that this goal will be met in its absence. In any case, distinguishing policy effort from policy outcome has the virtue of disentangling the empirical inquiry. The analyst is invited to tackle two separate and distinct questions: (1) Do democracies and non-democracies pursue systematically different spending policies? and (2) Do these policy differences produce systematic differences in inequality?

As already suggested, one major advantage of this distinction is that we no longer have to settle for cross-sectional analysis, and need no longer be immobilized while waiting for history to unfold and present us with more data points on income equality. We search instead for any tangible evidence of policy *shifts* shortly after regime changes. The *effects* of such policy shifts in promoting greater equality may, however, take years and perhaps even decades to materialize.

Selection of cases and indicators

Prior cross-national research on the relationship between democracy and inequality tends to show that, when properly specified and controlling for the effects of economic development, the impact of the former on the latter tends to be quite slight (Bollen and Grandjean, 1981; Bollen and Jackman, 1985b; Chan, 1989; Cutright, 1967; Hewitt, 1977; Jackman, 1974; Muller, 1988; Weede, 1982). Moreover, this literature shows that income inequality tends to be related curvilinearly with economic development (Ahluwalia, 1976; Kuznets, 1963, 1955; Lenski, 1966; Weede, 1980).

Nevertheless, the results of these cross-national studies are quite unstable because, as pointed out by Bollen and Jackman (1985b), they are often based on different empirical measures and samples. Moreover, depending on which control variables are introduced and how these control variables are operationalized, the empirical patterns can differ quite substantially from study to study. Among the various control variables that have been considered are population growth, regime ideology, state strength, foreign economic dependency, world-system position, colonial heritage, and Protestant culture (e.g., Bollen and Jackman, 1985b; Bornschier and Ballmer-Cao, 1979; Bornschier *et al.*, 1978; Chan, 1989; Chase-Dunn, 1975; Cutright, 1967; Dixon and Moon,

1986; Evans and Timberlake, 1980; Hewitt, 1977; Moon and Dixon, 1985; Muller, 1988; Rubinson, 1976; Rubinson and Quinlan, 1977). Questions regarding proper specification and measurement have produced various replications, summaries, and exchanges in the pages of leading journals (in addition to those articles already cited, see Bornschier, 1981; Kohli, 1986; Kohli *et al.*, 1984; Ravenhill, 1986a, 1986b; Weede and Tiefenbach, 1981b, 1981c)

As already suggested, this chapter shares a common interest with those past studies (e.g., Ames, 1987, 1977; Bunce, 1986, 1981, 1980; Huang, 1992; Dixon and Moon, 1986; Roeder, 1986, 1985) that seek to determine the effects, if any, of regime transition or leadership succession on a government's resource allocations. These allocations refer to expenditure categories such as education, health, housing, and social security. These expenditures all have a short-term effect in redistributing income to the relative benefit of the poorer segments of society and, if successful, constitute long-term social investments that help the disadvantaged groups to enhance their socioeconomic status. At the very least, these expenditures serve as an important safety net that prevents the gap between the rich and poor from becoming too wide such as when severe economic recessions cause massive unemployment.

But why a focus on East Asia? As already mentioned, Singapore, Taiwan, and South Korea present "anomalies" because their performance to date contradicts the prevailing conventional wisdom suggesting various trade-offs among economic growth, political stability, income equality, and democratization. More specifically, we know from the relevant literature that, while a high *level* of economic development promotes political stability and liberal democracy (e.g., Lipset, 1994, 1963; Neubauer, 1967), a rapid *rate* of economic growth tends to hinder the achievement of these desiderata as well as income equality (e.g., Huntington, 1968; Jackman, 1975; Olson, 1963; Strouse and Claude, 1976; Ward, 1978). Moreover, this literature shows that economic development bears a curvilinear relationship to income inequality (e.g., Kuznets, 1963, 1955; Lenski, 1966), which tends to be exacerbated among the middle-income countries. This inequality, in turn, undermines political stability and democratic progress (e.g., Muller's chapter in this volume; Muller, 1988, 1985). To compound the paradoxes, long-term political stability and democratic pluralism are sometimes seen to cause institutional sclerosis and policy cycling to the detriment of economic growth (e.g., Miller, 1983; Olson, 1982). This particular contention, however, has been challenged by other more recent studies arguing that liberal democracy, capitalist institutions, and economic development tend to reinforce each other (Burkhart and Lewis-Beck, 1994; Olson, 1993).

While hardly paragons of virtue, the three East Asian NIEs – Singapore, Taiwan, and South Korea – have compiled a very impressive economic record of "rising from rags to riches." In addition to this economic achievement that sets them apart from the rest of the developing world, they have succeeded in defying the cross-national norm suggesting that rapid economic growth is incompatible with either political stability or income equality. They have arguably established much more stable and egalitarian societies than their counterparts among the middle-income and upper-middle-income countries. Whereas many of these countries – predominantly from Latin America – have suffered democratic setback as shown in Muller's chapter, the three East Asian NIEs have made steady and remarkable strides in democratization (especially since the late 1980s). In all these respects, the latter countries are "outliers" whose *combined* national performance on growth, stability, equity, and democratization has been unusually successful (recent surveys of these countries' political economies can be found in Borthwick, 1992; Friedman, 1994).

In addition to these substantive and theoretical reasons, there is another methodological reason for selecting the three East Asian countries. As will be explained in greater detail below, this study adopts a research design based on the logic of investigating "most similar systems" and conducting quasi-experimentation. Taiwan and South Korea are quite similar in many respects of their polity and society. Both have also experienced a relatively abrupt turn toward democratization in the 1980s. This turn presents a "stimulus" in the quasi-experiment that seeks to identify any interruption caused by this "stimulus" in the time series for welfare expenditures. In contrast to Taiwan and South Korea where a major democratic opening occurred, politics in Singapore did not change significantly during the period being examined. Therefore, the latter country serves as a "control case" which did not experience a sharp break in regime continuity.

Logic of inquiry

How do we propose to determine any non-random change in welfare expenditures in response to democratization? As just mentioned, this analysis combines the logic of quasi-experimental design with the logic for comparing "most similar systems" in order to infer cause–effect relationships and to guard against spurious interpretation (Campbell and Stanley, 1963; Przeworski and Teune, 1970).

Although political liberalization in Taiwan is still an ongoing process, the critical turning point occurred in mid 1987 when the then president, Chiang Ching-Kuo, lifted martial law and abolished the Emergency Decree on the basis of which the Kuomintang had ruled the island since 1949. This action subsequently led to the legalization of opposition parties and the introduction of popular elections. In March 1996, this island was scheduled to have its first direct popular election of the president.

We treat the cancellation of martial law and the abolition of the Emergency Decree as the key "test intervention" in the quasi-experimental design. The object of the inquiry is to determine whether and, if so, how much effect this democratic opening has had in altering the level and trend of the island's welfare expenditures in the post-test period.

Comparing the "before" and "after" states of affairs in the manner just described offers a basis for making causal inference, but does not remove the possibility of misattribution. To guard against the latter possibility, the case of South Korea is introduced. It so happens that this latter country also underwent a democratic transition in late 1987. In that year mass demonstrations and student riots finally forced the regime to accept the popular election of the president. Roh Tae Woo, with 35.9 percent of the popular votes, won this election over a badly split opposition (Kim Young Sam with 27.5 percent of the votes and Kim Dae Jung with 26.5 percent). The quasi-experimental results for South Korea can be compared with those obtained for Taiwan. Although the democratic openings in these countries are not identical, our confidence in the quasi-experiment would be enhanced to the extent that the results for these countries are convergent. This convergence would be especially helpful for alleviating concerns about "idiosyncrasy" – namely, the charge that we cannot trust the analysis results because similar quasi-experimental stimuli can produce different response patterns.

There is, however, the additional possibility that the observed post-test changes in the Taiwan and South Korean time series can be an artifact of some other event that just happened to coincide with their democratic openings. To check against the danger of "irrelevance" (that is, different experimental treatments producing similar response patterns), Singapore – which has not experienced a comparable political transition – is introduced as a control case. Did Singapore's time series show post-1987 patterns that are similar to those of Taiwan and South Korea? If so, we should be justifiably skeptical about interpreting these patterns as the effects of the latter two countries' democratic openings.

Thus, causal inference is attempted not only on the basis of comparing the pre- and post-test observations for the same country, but also on the basis of comparing this country's time series with its most similar counterparts (one of which received a comparable quasi-experimental stimulus, and the other did not).

Quasi-experimental model

Box and Tiao (1975) offer one popular approach to studying interrupted time series (for other examples, see Campbell, 1969; Campbell and Ross, 1968; Caporaso and Pelowski, 1971). This approach requires the analyst to identify and estimate a noise model for the pre-test period so that it can be used as a basis for determining the effect, if any, of the test intervention. Because, however, of the relatively small number of pre-test observations (17 for South Korea and 22 for Taiwan) in this study, this approach seems inappropriate.

Instead, I follow Lewis-Beck's (1986, 1979; see also, Lewis-Beck and Alford, 1980) suggestions which seek to take advantage of the information contained in the entire data series. This alternative approach was most recently exemplified by Huang (1992). It treats the analysis of interrupted time series as a variation of the classic multiple regression model. In this approach, various independent variables – intended to capture the effects of trends, events, and intervening factors – are introduced in the regression to explain the overtime variation in the dependent variable. The test event is represented by (1) a dichotomous dummy variable designed to indicate any intercept change, and (2) a post-test time counter intended to reflect any slope change. Any significant change in intercept could be interpreted to indicate the test event's immediate and short-term effect in affecting the level of the dependent variable, while that in slope suggests a longer-term effect in altering the dependent variable's pre-test trend.

Some of the control variables in this study are explicitly included in the regression model, while others are implicitly recognized by using the most-similar-systems design. Several prior studies have suggested the importance of protestant culture, state strength, regime ideology, world-system position, recency of democratic experience, and dependence on foreign trade or capital as determinants of a country's performance on inequality (e.g., Bollen and Jackman, 1985b; Bornschier *et al.*, 1978; Chan, 1989; Chase-Dunn, 1975; Hewitt, 1977; Kohli *et al.*, 1984; Muller, 1988; Rubinson and Quinlan, 1977). Although hardly identical (Clark and Chan, 1995), the three cases being examined here are quite similar on these dimensions (e.g., sharing a Confucian culture, pursuing an export-oriented industrial policy, and featuring strong developmental states with a conservative ideology). Moreover, two of these cases – Taiwan and South Korea – also have a common Japanese colonial legacy, which continues to influence their developmental paths (Cumings, 1984). These factors are not explicitly included in the regression model, because the countries being studied are relatively alike in these respects and because these factors have not changed significantly for them during the period being examined.

However, the rate of economic growth is explicitly introduced in the regression model. Economic growth, of course, provides the wherewithal for financing welfare expenditures. It also perhaps indicates the need for such expenditures during periods of economic hardship (e.g., recessions). Indeed, this need can be high even when – and some (e.g., Kuznets, 1963, 1955; Olson, 1963) may argue, precisely when – the economy is expanding rapidly, because this expansion often produces severe social dislocations. The rate of population growth has been suggested as another relevant control variable in investigating income inequality (e.g., Ahluwalia, 1976; Bollen and Jackman, 1988; Fiala, 1987). Poor people have higher birth rates, which in turn lead to lower average income and thus further exacerbation of inequality. Higher population growth also implies higher demand for public social services. Finally, as can be seen below, per-capita income is used as a control variable; presumably, with rising per-capita income, the aggregate demand for welfare support may decline. This variable, reflecting in part the average *level* of socioeconomic development, is conceptually and empirically distinct from the *rate of change* of the macroeconomy.

Public welfare expenditures, the dependent variable, are examined both in terms of absolute per-capita value and as a relative share of the government's general budget. It is, of course, possible for a government to raise (or lower) the absolute per-capita level of welfare support without changing the welfare spending's proportion of a larger (or smaller) overall budget for public expenditures. Conversely, changes in the welfare spending's relative share of the overall budget may be compatible with increases, decreases, or a constant level of public assistance measured in per-capita value. Accordingly, different categories of welfare spending are studied both in terms of their percentage of the general budget and in terms of their per-capita value.

The regression model is specified with the following terms:

$$Y_t = b_0 + b_1 T_t + b_2 D_t + b_3 C_t + b_4 \text{GNP}pc_t + b_5 \text{GNPrate}_t + b_6 \text{POPrate}_t + e_t$$

where
  Y_t = various categories of welfare expenditures, either as a share of the overall budget or in per-capita value;
  b_0 = regression intercept;

T_t = trend variable, a time counter that assigns 1, 2, 3 . . . from the first to the last year in the entire series;

D_t = dichotomous dummy variable indicating the test event, scoring 0 for the pre-test years and 1 for the post-test years;

C_t = post-test time counter, scoring 0 for the pre-test years and 1, 2, 3 . . . for the post-test years;

GNPpc_t = per-capita income;

GNPrate$_t$ = rate of change in gross national product;

POPrate$_t$ = rate of change in population size;

e_t = error term.

Ordinary least-squares regression was used by Lewis-Beck (1986) to demonstrate its general usefulness in pursuing this approach for analyzing interrupted time series. The ordinary least-squares method assumes that the regression errors are not autocorrelated. I account explicitly for the first-order autoregressive process in the following analysis.

The data for Singapore and South Korea are derived from the World Bank (1994). Because Taiwan has not been a member of the United Nations, it has been excluded from various UN-related publications (including the World Bank) reporting national statistics. The Council of Economic Planning and Development (1995) is our data source for Taiwan. The time series for this island extends from 1965 to 1994, whereas the temporal coverage for Singapore (1970–91) and South Korea (1970–92) from the World Bank data source is shorter. The latter source, however, gives us more disaggregated readings of welfare expenditures. For Singapore and South Korea, these expenditures are broken down into the following categories: education, health, social security and welfare, and housing. Conversely, Taiwan's budgetary categories for these expenditures are broader; we have only two relevant spending categories labelled "education, science, and culture" and "social security."

Analysis results

The regression results are presented in table 9.1. This table consists of three parts, reporting respectively the results for Taiwan, South Korea, and Singapore. In examining these results, the following discussion will stress seeking common patterns rather than dwelling on isolated findings. Several questions seem especially pertinent. Is there concordance or discordance in the behavior of different categories of welfare spending? Do measures of absolute and relative gains (or losses) of such spending, as indicated respectively by per-capita expenditure and percentage share of the overall budget, tend to converge or diverge? Are the effects of democratic initiation apt to involve an immediate and short-term change in the level of welfare spending (as indicated by the "dummy" variable) or are they apt to take the form of a long-term adjustment in the slope of this spending (as indicated by the "counter" variable)? And, as already mentioned, are the results for Taiwan and South Korea (the two "experimental" cases) similar, and are these results different from those for Singapore (the "control" case)?

Table 9.1 *Autoregression results*

	Education p.c. $	Education % budget	Social security p.c. $	Social security % budget
Part A Taiwan				
Trend	100.18	0.24	166.02	0.67
	(0.48)	(0.41)	(0.16)	(0.04)★
Dummy	−1053.16	−0.80	−347.54	0.44
	(0.11)	(0.62)	(0.45)	(0.82)
Counter	1236.94	−0.12	1377.32	0.24
	(0.00)★★	(0.80)	(0.00)★★	(0.62)
GNPpc	0.04	0.00	0.01	−0.00
	(0.10)	(0.90)	(0.43)	(0.39)
GNPrate	−7.27	0.04	−15.24	0.08
	(0.82)	(0.66)	(0.52)	(0.48)
POPrate	−17.94	0.36	17.11	0.01
	(0.91)	(0.42)	(0.88)	(0.98)
Constant	−1954.42	12.66	−1093.90	6.97
	(0.04)★	(0.00)★★	(0.16)	(0.01)★★
Adjusted R^2	0.95	0.37	0.95	0.76
Durbin–Watson	1.76	2.00	2.04	2.01
Part B South Korea				
Trend	53612.57	0.69	16425.52	0.38
	(0.01)★★	(0.09)	(0.06)	(0.05)★
Dummy	−29695.83	1.42	−75855.70	0.37
	(0.69)	(0.47)	(0.17)	(0.78)
Counter	72730.89	−0.86	111368.48	0.20
	(0.05)★	(0.31)	(0.00)★★	(0.65)
GNPpc	0.02	−0.00	0.01	0.00
	(0.32)	(0.65)	(0.42)	(0.91)
GNPrate	752.73	0.11	−334.93	−0.01
	(0.80)	(0.20)	(0.88)	(0.88)
POPrate	322770.72	4.69	112332.06	4.49
	(0.02)★★	(0.16)	(0.18)	(0.04)★
Constant	−949176.48	5.68	−347703.43	−5.06
	(0.01)★★	(0.51)	(0.14)	(0.37)
Adjusted R^2	0.96	0.16	0.98	0.81
Durbin–Watson	1.85	1.66	1.95	2.26

Table 9.1 (*cont*).

	Health p.c. $	Health % budget	Housing p.c. $	Housing % budget
Trend	−656.26	−0.06	2040.68	0.04
	(0.74)	(0.24)	(0.55)	(0.67)
Dummy	601.24	0.26	−30438.85	0.10
	(0.97)	(0.47)	(0.15)	(0.83)
Counter	−11687.72	−0.41	50631.53	0.56
	(0.03)*	(0.00)**	(0.00)**	(0.01)**
GNP*pc*	0.01	0.00	−0.00	−0.00
	(0.00)**	(0.05)*	(0.42)	(0.30)
GNPrate	258.28	0.02	−341.80	0.01
	(0.66)	(0.27)	(0.68)	(0.80)
POPrate	66184.01	0.50	−45544.70	−0.71
	(0.01)**	(0.35)	(0.17)	(0.37)
Constant	−233948.91	−1.13	120295.15	3.27
	(0.00)**	(0.45)	(0.17)	(0.13)
Adjusted R^2	0.98	0.73	0.95	0.48
Durbin–Watson	2.38	2.10	1.55	1.70

	Education p.c. $	Education % budget	Social security p.c. $	Social security % budget
Part C Singapore				
Trend	−34.98	−1.39	7.68	0.00
	(0.19)	(0.27)	(0.01)**	(0.99)
Dummy	−253.26	3.38	26.24	1.12
	(0.00)**	(0.29)	(0.00)**	(0.13)
Counter	33.57	−0.35	12.78	0.04
	(0.41)	(0.84)	(0.01)**	(0.91)
GNP*pc*	0.01	0.00	−0.00	−0.00
	(0.00)**	(0.29)	(0.11)	(0.89)
GNPrate	−7.83	−0.37	−1.26	−0.07
	(0.14)	(0.10)	(0.03)*	(0.14)
POPrate	−138.41	−2.69	−19.00	−0.07
	(0.01)**	(0.28)	(0.00)**	(0.88)
Constant	−574.35	12.96	93.50	2.69
	(0.08)	(0.34)	(0.01)**	(0.35)
Adjusted R^2	0.98	0.09	0.98	0.18
Durbin–Watson	1.97	1.80	1.97	1.90

	Health p.c. $	Health % budget	Housing p.c. $	Housing % budget
Trend	−17.11	−0.65	152.74	3.09
	(0.22)	(0.25)	(0.00)**	(0.00)**
Dummy	−93.75	−0.45	227.78	6.56
	(0.03)*	(0.77)	(0.05)*	(0.01)**

Table 9.1 (*cont*).

Counter	−10.10	−0.23	52.15	0.65
	(0.64)	(0.78)	(0.38)	(0.55)
GNP*pc*	0.00	0.00	−0.02	−0.00
	(0.04)*	(0.41)	(0.00)**	(0.00)**
GNPrate	−1.14	−0.07	4.98	−0.04
	(0.67)	(0.49)	(0.50)	(0.75)
POPrate	32.60	1.65	−276.16	−2.98
	(0.22)	(0.13)	(0.00)**	(0.03)*
Constant	−328.26	1.72	1719.23	40.67
	(0.06)	(0.79)	(0.00)**	(0.00)**
Adjusted R^2	0.91	0.48	0.86	0.76
Durbin–Watson	2.21	1.64	1.99	2.03

Note: Figures above the parentheses are the B coefficients, and those within the parentheses are the T significance levels (with ** indicating significance at the 0.01 level and * indicating significance at the 0.05 level). Per-capita expenditures are stated in local currencies (new Taiwan dollars, Korean won, and Singapore dollars)

A quick glance at the adjusted R^2s reported in table 9.1 suggests that the regression analyses are able to explain much better the per-capita expenditures of welfare spending than the share of this spending as a percentage of the overall government budget. Moreover, the B coefficients are very different for equations intended to explain absolute changes in dollar expenditures versus relative changes in budget shares. In particular, in the aftermath of the democratic opening in both Taiwan and South Korea, the per-capita amount spent on education and social security expenditures rose but the share size of these expenditures in the overall budget did not. Therefore, democratic initiation had a positive effect in raising the absolute level of these expenditures, without significantly improving their relative importance in the government's aggregate spending.

As mentioned above, the "dummy" and "counter" variables are intended to capture two different effects of the experimental intervention. The former should reveal any immediate post-intervention change in the regression intercept, thus pointing to a short-term (and thus one-time) adjustment in level. The latter is supposed to indicate any longer-term change in the regression slope for the post-intervention time series, and thus helps to determine whether a more permanent shift in trend has occurred.

For the two spending items (education and social security) for which data are available for both of our experimental cases (Taiwan and South Korea), we find congruent patterns. The initiation of the democratization process in 1987 did not result in an immediate major increase in per-capita expenditures (indeed, the signs of the B coefficients for the "dummy" variable are all negative, although their T-values are below conventional thresholds of significance). At the same time, the results for both countries and for both spending categories show a consistent pattern that points to a more basic impact of democratization in accelerating the trend for these expenditures. Among the independent variables included in the regression equations, the "counter" variable emerges as the most significant determinant of per-capita welfare spending. This convergence of findings between two different spending categories from two different countries (and data sources) offers an important source of validation, as stressed by the logic of inquiry presented earlier. Just as important, one finds a consistent pattern of null results regarding the impact of democratization when the spending categories are measured as a percentage of the government's overall budget. Therefore, one gains more reassurance that the threat of idiosyncrasy has been contained.

But what about the threat of irrelevance? To respond to this concern, we need to look at the results for Singapore (in part C of table 9.1). The logic of our analysis argues that we should not observe the same pattern of results for this country, because it did not experience a comparable democratic opening. Attending for the moment to the results for Singapore's spending on education and social security, it is apparent that (as in the cases of Taiwan and South Korea) the regression equations are much better in accounting for per-capita expenditures than relative budget shares. For the former measure, two different patterns characterize education and social security spending. There was a significant and abrupt decline in the level of government support for education in 1988 but, in contrast to Taiwan and South Korea, no major longer-term change in the post-1987 trend. Thus, Singapore's pattern of per-capita expenditure for education differs in a striking manner from Taiwan and South Korea whose patterns, in turn, are almost identical as discussed above. Accordingly, there seems to be a strong base for dismissing the threat of irrelevance in this case.

The same, however, cannot be said about the results for social security. Singapore's post-1987 time series shows a statistically significant rise in the level as well as in the slope of per-capita expenditure for this purpose (as reflected by the readings for the "dummy" and "counter" variables). Because Singapore (which did not experience a democratic opening) also has experienced a rising slope for this spending, it becomes difficult to attribute comparable shifts in Taiwan and South Korea to the influence of their respective democratic opening.

We have available for South Korea and Singapore, though not for

Taiwan, time-series data for two other items of welfare spending: health and housing. Do they show those before–after effects that should be present in South Korea but absent in Singapore? The post-test slope for South Korea's housing expenditures rose significantly in a pattern similar to those noted earlier for this country's spending on education and social security. In contrast, this slope change was absent for Singapore, whether changes in these expenditures were measured absolutely or relatively. However, conforming again to the patterns for its education and social security expenditures, there was a significant though one-time boost in the level of Singapore's housing spending in the year 1988 (in terms of both per-capita dollars and budget share).

There is therefore a general concordance for education, social security, and housing expenditures in the sense that the time series for these expenditures moved in similar ways for each country. Health expenditures (for South Korea and Singapore), however, tend to contradict this concordance. In South Korea, there was a significant decline in the slope for these expenditures (both absolutely and relatively) after the democratic opening. Thus, unlike the other three kinds of welfare expenditures, the trajectory for spending on public health has not improved in the wake of democratization. It has in fact suffered. The results for health spending are thus discordant with the other welfare expenditures for which the post-1987 trend has been upward. The figures for Singapore also indicate declining health spending at about the same time, although only one coefficient turns out to be statistically significant (the "dummy" variable for per-capita expenditures). This finding, however, is less discordant with the other results, because per-capita spending on education in Singapore also suffered a major drop in 1988 (a drop that was offset by rises in the spending for social security and housing).

While not the focus of this analysis, a few brief comments about the coefficients associated with the four control variables are still in order. The welfare expenditures for the three countries have been generally rising over time (with all significant coefficients for the "trend" variable being positive), although the specific spending category that has benefited most from this increase has varied among the three countries. The share of overall budget going to social security has shown the most significant rise over time in Taiwan and South Korea, whereas public spending on housing has received this favorable treatment in Singapore. About 90 percent of Singaporeans live in public housing projects.

Rising per-capita income (labeled in table 9.1 as "GNP*pc*"), however, tends to lower the Singapore government's support for public housing. Per-capita income has had the opposite effect of raising public expenditures on education and health. The positive relationship between GNP per-capita and health expenditures also applies to South Korea. The rate of GNP change bears a statistically significant coefficient in only one instance: a slower economy has historically raised per-capita social security and welfare spending in Singapore. The government has thus acted in a countercyclical manner, offering welfare funding as a "shock absorber" to economic slowdowns. The relevant coefficients indicate similar negative associations between the GNP rate and this funding for Taiwan and South Korea, although these associations are not statistically significant.

Finally, one of the more intriguing results for this analysis pertains to the effects of population growth on public spending. This variable (labeled POPrate in table 9.1) bears no relationship to these expenditures in Taiwan, a positive relationship to them in South Korea (except for housing), and a negative relationship to them in Singapore (except for health). These configurations seem to be due to these countries' relative position in the demographic transition. Singapore has made the furthest advance in this transition whereby its society is now characterized by low rates in both deaths and births. South Korea is behind Singapore in making this transition, and Taiwan is somewhere between these two countries (compared with other countries in the developing world, however, the demographic profiles of these countries are quite similar). It would be interesting for future research to explore how welfare expenditures adjust to a country's changing demographic structure.

Conclusion

This analysis has sought to determine whether democratic initiation in two East Asian countries has produced any changes in the government's allocation of tangible resources that should contribute to social equality. The results for Taiwan and South Korea suggest that public spending on education and social security has improved after their respective democratic openings. These improvements apply to an absolute dollar increase in the per-capita expenditure for these purposes, and not to the relative shares of these categories in the government's overall budget. Moreover, these improvements assume the form of a gradual longer-term gain: the relevant change raises the slope for such spending over time, as opposed to a one-time boost in its level. The consistency shown by these quasi-experimental results for Taiwan and South Korea helps to alleviate concerns about "idiosyncrasy." Moreover, the results for South Korea's expenditures on public housing offer further convergent validation for the proposition that democratization increases government efforts to reduce the gap between the rich and poor.

This proposition, however, requires greater specification and further qualification. It is important to distinguish among different types of public expenditures that are subsumed under the general heading of social welfare. For instance, government support for primary and secondary education tends to benefit the poor much more than subsidies for colleges (which cater disproportionately to the well-to-do). This need for differentiation is underscored by the results which show that health expenditures actually fell in the wake of South Korea's democratic initiation. Thus, greater democracy does not necessarily raise all kinds of expenditures that can be loosely construed to improve public well-being. Moreover, even when such expenditures do rise, it does not necessarily mean that other kinds of government spending (such as for national defense) will fall (absolutely or relatively). That is, welfare funding does not necessarily come at the expense of other kinds of expenditures (as the results of this analysis show).

It is, of course, also possible for a government to alter its budgetary decisions in the absence of any major political change. The results for Singapore illustrate this situation; table 9.1 shows quite a few significant level changes in this country's fiscal policies even though it has enjoyed remarkable political continuity. Singapore has been included in this analysis in order to respond to the possible charge of "irrelevance" and, as already noted, its results do suggest that one needs to be cautious in this regard. Even though Singapore did not experience any political changes comparable with those of Taiwan and South Korea, its social security spending displayed a positive shift in slope similar to those of the other two countries. Thus, for this spending category at least, the results for Taiwan and South Korea may be due to some broader process unrelated to their respective democratization.

The search for any association between democracy and equality faces a formidable obstacle due to the long (and usually unspecified) lag that is likely to separate the initial changes in political condition (the imputed cause) from the subsequent changes in social distribution (the ostensible effect). The relevant changes for both sets of variables are often slow and incremental, and longitudinal data for the latter are usually unavailable. Moreover, the actual policy medium through which one attribute (democracy) is supposed to influence another attribute (equality) is often unspecified. This analysis has sought to add such policy content to the discussion on democracy and equality, and to move the research on their relationship beyond the analysis of comparative statics.

10 Political regimes and industrial wages: a cross-national analysis

Mark J. Gasiorowski

It is widely believed that authoritarian regimes are less egalitarian than democratic regimes because they are less responsive to popular demands for the redistribution of society's resources and freer to use repression to suppress these demands. States under authoritarian regimes therefore face fewer obstacles in pursuing their own priorities, which may include self-enrichment, draconian economic development programs, or expansionist foreign policies that have little or no redistributive effect. The popular classes in society – especially the industrial working class, which is generally powerful enough to achieve some of its goals under a democratic regime – are therefore likely to realize slower improvements in living standards under authoritarian regimes than under democratic regimes according to this view.

An important corollary to this argument holds that newly established authoritarian regimes often severely repress the industrial working class in order to drive down wages and limit working class demands. This is especially likely to occur in Third World countries that are relatively industrialized or experiencing economic crises – conditions under which technocrats and other powerful actors often view industrial wage increases as an obstacle to economic growth. These actors may conspire with military officers to overthrow democratic or semidemocratic regimes and establish authoritarian regimes that can use repression to drive down wages and suppress workers' demands in order to stimulate the economy. The prototype for this argument was the authoritarian regime established as a result of the April 1964 coup in Brazil, which drove down industrial wages and brought about the "Brazilian miracle" of the late 1960s.

In this chapter I evaluate these arguments. My analysis is based on a dataset containing yearly time-series measures of political regime type, industrial wage levels, and several control variables for a (cross-sectional) sample of 60 third world countries. I use statistical methods to test whether industrial wages grow more slowly after transitions away from democracy, controlling for certain other factors that affect wages and examining whether this is more likely to occur in third world countries that are relatively industrialized or experiencing economic crises. I also examine the more general issue of whether industrial wages increase more slowly under authoritarian regimes than under democratic regimes. Although I find no real evidence that wage growth is slower under authoritarian regimes, some interesting results nevertheless emerge about the relationship between wages and regime change.

Political regimes and industrial wage levels

The argument that authoritarian regimes are generally less egalitarian than democratic regimes stems from the idea that the opportunities for political participation made possible by a democratic regime enable lower-class groups to make effective demands for the redistribution of society's resources, reducing inequality (Sirowy and Inkeles, 1991). Redistributional demands are most likely to be met when they are made by lower-class groups that are relatively powerful, such as the industrial working class, which is usually better organized and more vital to the economy and therefore wields more influence than other lower-class groups. The ability of the industrial working class and other groups to make effective redistributional demands also depends, of course, on how democratic the prevailing regime actually is and on whether its institutional design and other characteristics facilitate participation by the group in question. Many cross-national empirical studies have appeared on the relationship between political regime type and inequality, yielding mixed results (Sirowy and Inkeles, 1991). The most sophisticated of these studies have also been mixed, with two indicating that democratic regimes are more egalitarian (Muller, 1988; Moon, 1991, pp. 142, 253) and a third finding no significant relationship (Bollen and Jackman, 1985b).

While it is easy enough to draw a connection between the type of political regime prevailing in a society and the general level of inequality, the relationship between regime type and industrial wage levels is more problematic, primarily because states have only indirect influence over private-sector wages. States can undertake a wide variety of redistributional measures, including social welfare projects, price subsidies, progressive taxation, minimum wage laws, regulations governing the work environment, the provision of public-sector employment, and regulations dealing with labor organization and popular political participation.[1] While all of these measures affect inequality in a general sense, most of them have little bearing on private-sector wages and therefore on aggregate wage levels. Moreover, wages are strongly affected by the economic growth rate, typically rising when the economy is growing and falling when it stagnates or contracts, and by high inflation, which often erodes real wages. Consequently, while it is reasonable to expect that industrial wages increase more rapidly under democratic regimes than under authoritarian regimes because workers' demands *in general* are more likely to be met, the connection is not very direct, and prevailing economic conditions probably have a greater impact on wages.[2]

Scholars have long argued that authoritarian regimes often deliberately suppress wages to promote economic growth or for related reasons. The most eloquent statement of this position was made by Barrington Moore (1966), who argued that "labor-repressive" political systems have been used in a variety of countries to depress peasants' incomes, either to maintain landlords' profit levels or to generate surpluses that could be used to finance transitions to modern, capitalist economies. Labor repression was accomplished in these countries primarily by using coercive force to control peasant unrest and thus maintain slavery, serfdom, or other exploitative social arrangements.

Similar arguments have been made by a variety of authors about contemporary third world countries – especially about Brazil and other relatively industrialized Latin American countries. The most well-known is O'Donnell's (1979) bureaucratic-authoritarianism (BA) model, which holds that a "coup coalition" of technocrats, military officers, and members of the bourgeoisie overthrew "inclusionary" regimes in Brazil and Argentina in the mid 1960s in order to resolve economic crises by "deepening" the economies in these countries to facilitate transitions from the "easy" stage of import substitution industrialization to the "hard" stage. Labor repression was critical to these BA projects because the coup coalitions viewed high industrial wages and labor activism as fundamental causes of the prevailing economic crises and impediments to deepening. Wage cuts and labor repression in general were accomplished under these BA regimes principally by curtailing free elections, coopting and/or emasculating labor unions and parties that represented working-class interests, and imposing wage controls that depressed real wages. O'Donnell (1978) later modified this framework, arguing that labor repression was also necessary to attract transnational corporations, whose participation in deepening was regarded as essential by the BA coup coalitions.

Although O'Donnell's BA model has been soundly criticized (Collier, 1979; Wallerstein, 1980; Remmer and Merckx, 1982), several authors have proposed similar models in which authoritarian regimes – usually newly installed authoritarian regimes – engage in extensive, systematic labor repression to restructure economies in ways that will resolve economic crises. Kaufman (1979) modifies O'Donnell's basic model, arguing that deepening was merely one of several development strategies Brazil, Argentina, and other Latin American NICs could have pursued to resolve the economic crises prevailing at the time of their BA coups. Most of the alternative strategies also required labor repression and hence the installation of authoritarian regimes similar to those described by O'Donnell. Skidmore (1977) argues that the stabilization policies needed to control high inflation have such a draconian impact on the popular classes – including sharp declines in real wages – that in Brazil, Argentina, and Mexico (and presumably elsewhere as well) they could only be carried out successfully under authoritarian regimes. Schamis (1991) argues that the authoritarian coups that occurred in Chile, Uruguay, and Argentina in the early and mid 1970s were motivated not by the need to undertake deepening but rather to resolve economic crises through very different kinds of economic restructuring programs, which he describes simply as "neoconservative." These programs also required the installation of authoritarian regimes that could undertake labor repressive measures.

The foregoing discussion suggests three main hypotheses about the relationship between political regimes and industrial wages:

(1) Industrial wages are likely to fall or grow more slowly under authoritarian regimes than under democratic regimes, *ceteris paribus*.
(2) Industrial wages are likely to fall or grow more slowly after transitions to authoritarian regimes than before these transitions, *ceteris paribus*.
(3) The effects embodied in hypotheses 1 and 2 are especially likely to occur in relatively industrialized third world countries and in those experiencing economic crises.

These hypotheses have been evaluated in a number of single-country or small-sample studies, which have generally upheld them (Fishlow, 1973; Lagos and Rufatt, 1975; Crowther, 1986; Im, 1987; O'Donnell, 1988; Schamis, 1991).[3] However, industrial wages are strongly affected by the economic growth rate, the inflation rate, and other systematic factors, which cannot easily be controlled for in small-sample studies. Moreover, most of these small-sample studies focus only on a few relatively industrialized Latin American countries. Idiosyncratic factors peculiar to these particular countries, to Latin America in general, or to industrialized third world countries in general may therefore have affected these findings. The analyses presented below attempt to minimize these difficulties by evaluating these hypotheses in a relatively large sample of countries and by using control variables and statistical techniques to isolate the effects of political regime from those of certain systematic and idiosyncratic factors that affect wage levels.

Empirical measures and sample

The dependent variable used in the analyses below is the annual percent change in an index of real manufacturing wages. Assuming that wages are affected by recent (rather than current) economic growth rates, I control for this effect by including the annual percent change in real gross domestic product (GDP) during the previous year as an independent variable in multivariate regression models. Similarly, I control for the effect of inflation on real wages by including the annual percent change in the GDP deflator during the current year in these models. To examine whether wages fall or grow more slowly under authoritarian regimes during economic crises, I also use the two latter measures as indicators of the severity of recessionary crises and inflationary crises, respectively. I obtained data on all three of these measures from a tape version of World Bank (1990), which I updated where possible with data from World Bank (1992).[4] To examine whether wages fall or grow more slowly under authoritarian regimes in relatively industrialized third world countries, I use data on the percent of GDP associated with industrial activity as a measure of the extent of industrialization. These data are from a tape version of Banks (1979), which I updated with projections based on linear trends estimated from the data available for each country.[5]

To evaluate hypothesis 2, above, we need a measure of political regime type that (i) clearly distinguishes between democratic and authoritarian regimes, (ii) identifies the dates at which changes between these types of regime occurred, and (iii) is available for a fairly large, diverse sample of countries. I have recently developed a dataset that largely meets these requirements. This dataset contains yearly time-series data on the political regimes of the 97 third world countries that had populations of at least one million in 1980. Each country's time series begins with its year of independence or the date at which it first established a modern state and runs through 1992 or the date at which the country ceased to exist. Because it is evident that political regimes in many third world countries are neither fully democratic nor truly authoritarian, I decided to use three categories rather than two, classifying regimes as either democratic, semidemocratic, or authoritarian.[6] Using a variety of historical sources, I then made careful judgments about which of these three categories each country fell into at any given time and when they made transitions from one category to another.

This process yielded a dataset containing yearly time series classifying each of the 97 countries as either democratic, semidemocratic, or authoritarian and identifying the years at which changes among these three types of regime occurred. For narrative profiles of each country giving the main historical details that guided my classifications, as well as a more detailed description of the data collection procedure, see Gasiorowski (1993).

Of the 3,023 country-year observations in the post-World War II era for which data on regime type were available, only 970 had valid data on percent change in real manufacturing wages. Regime changes of one type or another occurred in 52 of these 970 country-year observations, implying that more than one type of regime existed in the country during the given year in these cases. Because I wanted to analyze only wage data for which the current regime type was unambiguously known, I dropped these 52 observations from the sample and used the remaining 918 observations in my analyses. These 918 observations produced time series for 60 of the 97 countries which varied in length from one to 25 years; wage data were not given in World Bank (1990) or World Bank (1992) for the remaining 37 countries. Among these 60 countries, three changes from democracy to semidemocracy occurred; 20 changes from democracy to authoritarianism occurred; and 21 changes from semidemocracy to authoritarianism occurred. Wage data for at least one year during the five-year period immediately after a regime change were available for only 31 of these 44 regime changes, including 17 transitions from democracy to authoritarianism and 13 transitions from semidemocracy to authoritarianism. These 31 *"transitions away from democracy"* took place in 23 of the 60 countries, with six countries experiencing two such transitions and one experiencing three.[7] In the analyses below I first examine the 31 transitions away from democracy aggregated together; then I examine separately the 17 transitions from democracy to authoritarianism and the 13 transitions from semidemocracy to authoritarianism.

Statistical methodology and research design

A dataset like the one used here that pools together time-series observations for a cross-sectional sample of units (i.e., countries) can violate the basic assumptions underlying ordinary least squares (OLS) regression analysis in two main ways. First, autocorrelation may exist in the error terms, violating the assumption that error terms are independent of one another. Second, the stochastic distributions of the error terms may differ from one unit to another, implying that unmeasured idiosyncratic factors peculiar to certain units are affecting the dependent variable; this violates the OLS assumption that error terms are homoscedastic. If either autocorrelation or heteroscedasticity is present, OLS coefficient estimates will be unbiased but inefficient and OLS variance estimates will be biased. OLS is thought to be fairly robust regarding violations of these assumptions, meaning that its coefficient estimates and hypothesis tests are fairly accurate if the violations are not too severe (Stimson, 1985).

The problem of autocorrelated error terms is probably very small in this study, for two main reasons. First, although real wages generally increase over time and therefore usually exhibit first-order autocorrelation, there is no a priori reason to think that *annual percent changes* in real wages vary systematically over time. Consequently, the dependent variable used here is almost certainly not autocorrelated and therefore probably does not impart autocorrelation to the error term. Second, while the dataset includes observations on 60 countries, the time series in the dataset on average have only 15 observations each. Even if autocorrelation does exist within some of the cross-sectional country units, it is unlikely to have the same structure across countries and therefore most likely will be washed out in the dataset as a whole because of this cross-sectional dominance (Stimson, 1985).

Between-unit differences in the distribution of the error term are more problematic here, especially in light of the dataset's cross-sectional dominance and the concern expressed above that idiosyncracies peculiar to certain types of countries may have affected the small-sample case studies of the relationship between authoritarianism and industrial wages. Two common statistical techniques can be used to address this problem. First, the least squares with dummy variables (LSDV) technique controls for between-unit differences by including dummy variables identifying each of the units in an OLS model. However, if combinations of these dummy variables are highly correlated with the explanatory variables of interest, they will produce multicollinearity that reduces the efficiency of the coefficient estimates. Second, the random effects technique controls for between-unit differences by accounting for them in a heteroscedastic error term that can be incorporated into a generalized least squares (GLS) estimator (Greene, 1993, pp. 469–80). Random effects-GLS (RE-GLS) is more efficient than LSDV and less biased than OLS when between-unit heteroscedasticity exists (Stimson, 1985). When this heteroscedasticity does not exist, it may be impossible to calculate the RE-GLS estimator. We can test for between-unit heteroscedasticity with *f*-tests that examine whether the dummy variables in an LSDV model add significantly to its explanatory power

(Greene, 1993, p. 468). Fortunately, the LIMDEP software package calculates OLS, LSDV, and RE-GLS estimators, together with this f-test, with a single subroutine (Greene, 1989). In the analyses below I use RE-GLS estimates when f-tests for between-unit heteroscedasticity are significant at 0.05 or better and OLS estimates when these f-tests are not significant at 0.05. I use LIMDEP's CRMODEL subroutine for all of these calculations.

Hypothesis 1, above, can be evaluated by regressing the wage data on dummy variables identifying whether the regime in each country during each year is semidemocratic or authoritarian. To evaluate hypothesis 2, we can consider regime change to be an "intervention" and use multiple interrupted time-series analysis techniques to examine its effect on wages. This involves regressing the wage data on dummy variables and linear trend variables that identify suitably defined pre- and post-transition periods to determine whether the level and trend of the dependent variable differ significantly from one period to another (McDowall *et al.*, 1980; Lewis-Beck 1986). This methodology is discussed in more detail below. In all of these regressions I control for the effect of economic growth and inflation on real wages by including the lagged GDP growth rate and the current inflation rate as additional independent variables where necessary.

Hypothesis 3 postulates that wages are especially likely to fall or grow slowly when authoritarianism occurs *in conjunction with* economic crises or relatively high levels of industrialization. Conjunctional relationships of this sort between pairs of variables can be examined by multiplying the two variables together and including the product term and its two component variables in a multivariate regression. If the coefficient estimate of the product term is statistically significant, the two variables affect the dependent variable in conjunction with one another. If the coefficient of the product term is not significant but the coefficients of the two component variables are, these variables affect the dependent variable independently of one another. To reduce multicollinearity the two component variables must be centered by subtracting out their means before the product term is calculated. This does not affect the coefficient estimates or standard errors of any of the variables (Aiken and West, 1991, pp. 9–47).

Empirical analysis

In evaluating hypothesis 1, I began by examining the simple trends appearing in the data. Of the 918 observations for which valid data on regime type and wages were available, 196 corresponded to democratic regimes, 97 corresponded to semidemocratic regimes, and 625 corresponded to authoritarian regimes. The mean annual percent change in real manufacturing wages for democratic, semidemocratic, and authoritarian regimes was 1.83, 2.12, and 1.18, respectively. These figures indicate that wage growth was slowest under the authoritarian regimes in the sample and fastest under the semidemocratic regimes.

To control for the effects of economic growth and inflation and to make valid inferences from this large but finite sample, we must carry out multivariate statistical analyses. Tables 10.1 and 10.2 report multivariate regression analyses that use the measures and methods discussed above. The variables listed on the left in each table correspond to the intercept term in the regression model (INTERCEPT), dummy variables indicating whether the prevailing regime is authoritarian (AUTH), or semidemocratic (SEMI), the one-year lag of the annual percent change in real GDP (LGDP), the current annual percent change in the GDP deflator (INFLATION), the percent of GDP associated with industrial activity (INDUSTRY), and the products of AUTH and SEMI with INDUSTRY, LGDP, and INFLATION.[8] The four rows at the bottom of each table give the number of observations used to estimate each regression model, the probability value for an f-test of between-unit heteroscedasticity associated with the model, the type of regression used to estimate the model in light of this f-test (i.e., OLS or RE-GLS), and the R^2s associated with OLS estimates of each model.

Table 10.1 reports a series of regression models of the impact of authoritarian regimes on manufacturing wages. Model 1 shows that the coefficient of the dummy variable AUTH is negative but not statistically significant at even the 0.10 level when it is included in a simple bivariate RE-GLS regression.[9] This finding indicates that, while wages grew more slowly under the authoritarian regimes in the sample, the effect is not large enough to infer a general trend. Model 2 adds LGDP and INFLATION as control variables to the model. The coefficients of these variables are both significant at better than 0.01 and have the expected signs, indicating that rapid economic growth has a positive effect on real wages and inflation has a negative effect. The coefficient of AUTH increases considerably in magnitude but remains insignificant in model 2, again implying that we cannot infer a general trend in the effect of authoritarianism on wages.

Model 3 adds INDUSTRY and the product term AUTH*INDUSTRY to model 2. This product term is not statistically significant, indicating that authoritarianism does not have a significantly more negative effect on wages in relatively industrialized third world countries than in less-industrialized countries. The coefficient of INDUSTRY is signifi-

Table 10.1 *Authoritarianism and changes in manufacturing wages*

Explanatory variable	Model 1	Model 2	Model 3	Model 4	Model 5	Model 6
INTERCEPT	1.338***	1.359***	1.545****	1.488****	1.488****	1.298***
AUTH	−0.628	−1.029	−0.637	−0.527	−0.524	−0.780
LGDP		0.213***	0.251****	0.253****	0.256****	0.242****
INFLATION		−0.004****	−0.004****	−0.004****	−0.004****	−0.014
INDUSTRY			0.081**	0.084***	0.085***	0.089***
AUTH*INDUSTRY			0.051			
AUTH*LGDP					−0.028	
AUTH*INFLATION						−0.014
N	909	909	857	857	857	857
f-test	0.004	0.005	0.254	0.254	0.255	0.213
Estimator	RE-GLS	RE-GLS	OLS	OLS	OLS	OLS
R^2	0.001	.033	.041	0.041	0.041	0.043

Note: Significance levels: * = 0.10, ** = 0.05, *** = 0.01, **** = 0.001.

cantly positive in model 3 and remains so when the product term is dropped in model 4, indicating that manufacturing wages increase more rapidly in relatively industrialized third world countries. The inclusion of INDUSTRY also brought the probability level of the *f*-test well above 0.05 in models 3 and 4, indicating that this variable accounted for enough of the between-unit heteroscedasticity in the error terms that RE-GLS was not warranted. The positive effect of INDUSTRY on wages is certainly plausible, suggesting that demand for skilled and sem-iskilled labor is higher in relatively industrialized countries, putting upward pressure on manufacturing wages. Because this effect is plausible and the coefficient of INDUSTRY is highly significant in model 4, I decided to keep this variable in the model.

Models 5 and 6 add the product terms AUTH*LGDP and AUTH*INFLATION to model 4. Neither of these product terms is significant, indicating that authoritarianism does not have a more negative effect on wages in countries experiencing slow economic growth or high inflation. The probability levels of the *f*-tests associated with these models remained well above 0.05, again making RE-GLS unwarranted.

Table 10.2 reports similar regression models that examine the impact of semidemocracy on manufacturing wages. The coefficients of SEMI in models 1, 2, and 4 are positive but not significant, indicating that wages grew faster under the semidemocratic regimes in the sample, but that this effect again is not large enough to infer a general trend. The remaining single-term coefficients of SEMI and all of its product-term coefficients are also insignificant, indicating that wage growth is not significantly different under semidemocratic regimes in third world countries that are relatively industrialized or experiencing slow growth or high inflation. In general the findings reported in tables 10.1 and 10.2 indicate that we cannot infer significant differences in the rates of manufacturing wage growth under democratic, semidemocratic, and authoritarian regimes, as implied by hypothesis 1.

In evaluating hypothesis 2 I again began by examining the simple trends appearing in the data. The solid line in figure 10.1 shows the mean yearly change in manufacturing wages during the ten-year periods before and after the 31 transitions away from democracy for which some data in the five-year post-transition period were available. Wage growth was evidently very slow during the five-year post-transition period, though it increased noticeably in the subsequent "post-post" period. However, while wages grew fairly rapidly in the third and fourth years before these 31 transitions, they grew very slowly in the second year before them and declined in the year immediately before them. These observations suggest that while wage growth generally may have been

Table 10.2 Semidemocracy and changes in manufacturing wages

Explanatory variable	Model 1	Model 2	Model 3	Model 4	Model 5	Model 6
INTERCEPT	1.332***	1.352***	1.495****	1.488****	1.476****	1.491***
SEMI	0.663	0.426	0.097	0.033	−0.079	0.065
LGDP		0.211***	0.255****	0.254****	0.257****	0.254****
INFLATION		−0.004****	−0.004****	−0.004****	−0.004****	−0.004
INDUSTRY			0.088***	0.088***	0.088***	0.088***
SEMI*INDUSTRY			−0.017			
SEMI*LGDP					0.088	
SEMI*INFLATION						0.001
N	909	909	857	857	857	857
f-test	0.004	0.005	0.111	0.293	0.298	0.293
Estimator	RE-GLS	RE-GLS	OLS	OLS	OLS	OLS
R^2	0.000	0.032	0.040	0.040	0.040	0.040

Note: Significance levels: * = 0.10, ** = 0.05, *** = 0.01, **** = 0.001.

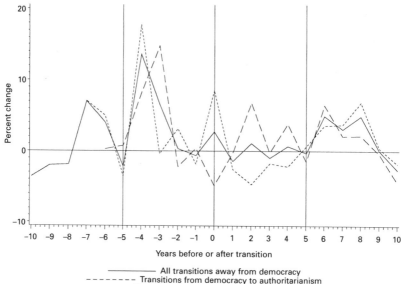

Figure 10.1 Change in manufacturing wages before and after transitions away from democracy

slower in the five-year period after these transitions than in the five-year period before them, this post-transition wage stagnation merely continued a trend that had already begun.

The tightly spaced broken line in figure 10.1 shows comparable data for the 17 transitions from democracy to authoritarianism for which some five-year post-transition data were available; the loosely spaced broken line shows similar data for the 13 transitions from semidemocracy to authoritarianism. Wage growth was considerably slower – and generally negative – after the 17 transitions from democracy to authoritarianism than before these transitions, and a downward trend in the pre-transition period and higher post-post-transition wage growth are also apparent in these cases. Wage growth appears to have been *higher* after the 13 transitions from semidemocracy to authoritarianism than in the two years before these transitions. A downward trend in wage growth is apparent in the period prior to these transitions, but post-post-transition wage growth does not seem substantially higher.

Table 10.3 reports a series of regression models of wage growth before and after the 31 transitions away from democracy. The explanatory variables INTERCEPT, LGDP, INFLATION, and INDUSTRY have the same meaning as in tables 10.1 and 10.2, as do N, f-test, estimator, and

R^2. The explanatory variables of form $D_{x,y}$ are dummy variables whose values are 1 in the years x through y depicted in figure 10.1, and 0 otherwise. These dummy variables are all *cumulative* in the sense that they denote time periods ending in year 10. Their coefficients therefore give the difference between the heights of the horizontal lines corresponding to the *non-overlapping part* of the period they denote and *the preceding non-overlapping period*, estimated from the data whose means are depicted by the solid line in figure 10.1. If these coefficients are statistically significant, the corresponding horizontal lines are significantly different in height (Lewis-Beck, 1986, pp. 213–20).[10] For example, in model 2 of table 10.3 the coefficient of $D_{1,10}$ gives the difference between the heights of horizontal lines estimated from the data for years −4 through −1 and years 1 through 5, which are the four-year pre-transition period and five-year post-transition period, respectively. (Since observations corresponding to the year of transition have been dropped from the dataset, the preceding non-overlapping period in this case does not include year 0.) This coefficient is negative and significant at the 0.07 level, indicating that the horizontal line estimated for years 1 through 5 is lower than the one estimated for years −4 through −1, but only by a marginally significant amount.

The explanatory variables of form $T_{x,y}$ in table 10.3 are cumulative linear trend variables whose values are 1, 2, ..., $y-x+1$ in years x through y of figure 10.1, and 0 otherwise. The coefficient of the first $T_{x,y}$ variable in each model gives the slope of the trend line estimated from the data for the non-overlapping part of the period it denotes. The coefficients of the subsequent $T_{x,y}$ variables give the difference between the slopes of the trend lines estimated for the non-overlapping parts of the periods they denote and the preceding non-overlapping periods.[11] For example, the coefficient of $T_{-4,10}$ in model 4 indicates that the trend line estimated for years −4 through −1 has a slope of −4.765, which is significantly different from zero. The coefficient of $T_{1,10}$ in model 4 is significantly positive, indicating that the trend line estimated for years 1 through 5, which has a slope of −4.765 + 4.870 = 0.105, is significantly more positive than the trend line for years −4 through −1. Note that the $D_{x,y}$ variables give the vertical intercepts of these trend lines rather than the difference between the heights of horizontal lines when included in a model with the corresponding $T_{x,y}$ variables.

Model 1 of table 10.3 regresses wage growth on LGDP, INFLATION, and INDUSTRY, which were statistically significant when used as control variables in tables 1 and 2. None of these variables are significant here, and none became significant when I included them alone in bivariate regressions with the dependent variable. The wage

Table 10.3 Changes in manufacturing wages before and after transitions away from democracy

Explanatory variable	Model 1	Model 2	Model 3	Model 4	Model 5	Model 6	Model 7
INTERCEPT	1.034	1.280	6.292***	1.823	1.073	1.214	1.429**
LGDP	0.157						
INFLATION	-0.011						
INDUSTRY	0.133						
$D_{-4,10}$		1.917		15.309***			
$D_{-2,10}$			-6.367**		-6.592**	-5.936**	-8.559****
$D_{1,10}$		-3.391*	-0.185	6.125	-0.086	0.304	0.795
$D_{6,10}$		2.956	2.985	0.261	2.104	2.554	2.403
$D_{9,10}$		-3.775	-3.752	-3.264	-4.249	-3.805	-3.597
$T_{-4,10}$				-4.765****			
$T_{1,10}$				4.870***			
$T_{6,10}$				1.203***			
$T_{9,10}$				-2.685			
COMPONENT					0.150	-0.033	0.040****
COMPONENT*$D_{-2,10}$					-0.129	1.096	-0.229****
COMPONENT*$D_{1,10}$					0.100	-0.090	0.050*
COMPONENT*$D_{6,10}$					0.060	-1.180*	0.023
COMPONENT*$D_{9,10}$					-0.066	0.737	-0.044
N	249	261	261	261	253	244	244
f-test	0.032	0.006	0.005	0.005	0.014	0.001	0.002
Estimator	RE-GLS	RE-GLS	RE-GLS	RE-GLS	RE-GLS	RE-GLS	RE-GLS
R^2	0.019	0.015	0.033	0.054	0.045	0.049	0.181

Note: Significance levels: * = 0.10, ** = 0.05, *** = 0.01, **** = 0.001.

data corresponding to the 31 transitions away from democracy therefore differed from the wage data in the entire sample in that they did not correlate with changes in GDP growth or inflation or with the extent of industrialization. This suggests that wages are influenced by very different sorts of factors in countries that experience transitions away from democracy than in countries that do not experience such transitions. Unfortunately, it is beyond the scope of this paper to explore this intriguing finding any further.

Model 2 of table 10.3 drops these insignificant control variables and adds dummy variables denoting the four-year pre-transition period (years −4 through −1), the five-year post-transition period (years 1 through 5), and a three-year post-post-transition period (years 6 through 8). As discussed above, the coefficient of $D_{1,\,10}$ indicates that wage growth in the five-year post-transition period was marginally slower than it was in the four-year pre-transition period. In model 3 the dummy variable $D_{-2,\,10}$ is substituted for $D_{-4,\,10}$ in order to compare wage growth in the five-year post-transition period with wage growth in the two-year pre-transition period. The coefficient of $D_{1,\,10}$ is not significant in model 3, indicating that while wage growth in the post-transition period was marginally slower than in the four-year pre-transition period, it was not significantly slower than in the two-year pre-transition period. The coefficients of $D_{6,\,10}$ are not significant in models 2 and 3, indicating that wage growth in the three-year post-post-transition period was not significantly higher than in the five-year post-transition period.

Model 4 adds linear trend variables denoting the four-year pre-transition period, five-year post-transition period, and three-year post-post-transition period. As discussed above, the coefficient of $T_{-4,\,10}$ is significantly negative and that of $T_{1,\,10}$ is significantly positive, indicating that a significant downward trend in the rate of wage growth occurred in the pre-transition period and that this trend changed abruptly in the post-transition period, becoming almost flat. The coefficient of $T_{6,\,10}$ is also significantly positive, indicating that a significant upward trend occurred in wage growth in the three-year post-post-transition period.

Models 5 through 7 of table 10.3 add interaction terms to model 3. In model 5 COMPONENT stands for the variable INDUSTRY. In models 6 and 7 COMPONENT stands for the country's real GDP growth rate and inflation rate, respectively, averaged over the year in which the transition occurred and the preceding year (i.e., years 0 and −1 of figure 10.1). The last four explanatory variables shown in table 10.3 are interaction terms containing the products of COMPONENT and $D_{-2,\,10}$, $D_{1,\,10}$, $D_{6,\,10}$, and $D_{9,\,10}$.[12] These interaction terms test whether the difference between the heights of horizontal lines estimated for the corresponding adjacent time periods differ for countries that are relatively industrialized (model 5) or for those that experienced slow or negative economic growth (model 6) or high inflation (model 7) just before and at the time of their transitions away from democracy.

The coefficient of COMPONENT*$D_{1, 10}$ in model 5 is not significant, indicating that wage growth in relatively industrialized third world countries is not significantly slower (or faster) in the five-year period after transitions away from democracy than in the two-year period before these transitions. Similarly, the non-significant coefficient of COMPONENT*$D_{1, 10}$ in model 6 indicates that wage growth was not significantly slower in the five-year post-transition period than in the two-year pre-transition period in countries that experienced slow or negative economic growth just before and at the time of their transitions away from democracy. The highly significant, negative coefficient of COMPONENT*$D_{-2, 10}$ in model 7 indicates that wage growth was much slower in the two-year pre-transition period than in the prior period in countries that experienced high inflation just before and at the time of their transitions away from democracy. Since "just before and at the time of transition" overlaps considerably with the two-year pre-transition period, this finding essentially reflects the inverse relationship between wage growth and current inflation shown in tables 10.1 and 10.2. The coefficient of COMPONENT*$D_{1, 10}$ in model 7 is positive and significant at the 0.07 level, indicating that wage growth in the four-year post-transition period was marginally *higher* than in the two-year pre-transition period in countries that experienced high inflation just before and at the time of their transitions away from democracy.

Table 10.4 reports similar regressions for the 17 transitions from democracy to authoritarianism whose means are depicted by the tightly spaced broken line plotted in figure 10.1 In model 1, wage growth is regressed on the three control variables used in tables 10.1 and 10.2. The variable INFLATION is not significant in model 1 and therefore is dropped from the subsequent analyses. Model 2 adds dummy variables denoting the four-year pre-transition period, the four-year post-transition period, and the four-year post-post-transition period, which seemed to have different trends in wage growth in figure 10.1. The coefficient of $D_{1,10}$ is negative and highly significant in model 2, indicating that wage growth was significantly slower in the four years after transitions from democracy to authoritarianism than in the four years preceding these transitions. In model 3 the dummy variable $D_{-3, 10}$ is substituted for $D_{-4, 10}$ to identify the three-year pre-transition period, which clearly had a much lower average rate of wage growth than the four-year pre-transition period in figure 10.1. The coefficient of $D_{1, 10}$

Table 10.4 *Changes in manufacturing wages before and after transitions from democracy to authoritarianism*

Explanatory variable	Model 1	Model 2	Model 3	Model 4	Model 5	Model 6	Model 7
INTERCEPT	0.289	4.847	8.802***	3.779	0.512	0.667	0.063
LGDP	0.288**	0.309*	0.304*	0.288*			
INFLATION	-.007						
INDUSTRY	0.415**	0.710****	.744****	0.647****		0.994****	0.936***
$D_{-4,10}$		1.607		13.524**			
$D_{-3,10}$			-4.388	2.040	-5.095	-5.038	-4.822
$D_{1,10}$		-9.387****	-7.392***	2.073	-10.307**	-10.348****	-9.310**
$D_{5,10}$		3.191	3.116	-6.895	2.634	2.803	2.602
$D_{9,10}$		-6.622**	-6.699***	-4.332**	-4.933	-7.815**	-6.328**
$T_{-4,10}$				4.267*			
$T_{1,10}$				0.719			
$T_{5,10}$				-0.933			
$T_{9,10}$							
COMPONENT					0.964***	0.853	-0.021
COMPONENT*$D_{-3,10}$					-0.061	0.011	0.017
COMPONENT*$D_{1,10}$					-0.181	0.460	0.035
COMPONENT*$D_{5,10}$					0.328	-0.823	0.045
COMPONENT*$D_{9,10}$					-0.624	1.383*	-0.086**
N	139	139	139	139	139	134	134
f-test	0.046	0.011	0.008	0.004	0.007	0.011	0.009
Estimator	RE-GLS	RE-GLS	RE-GLS	RE-GLS	RE-GLS	RE-GLS	RE-GLS
R^2	0.108	0.180	0.187	0.210	0.184	0.207	0.217

Note: Significance levels: * = 0.10, ** = 0.05, *** = 0.01, **** = 0.001.

is smaller in absolute value but remains significantly negative in model 3, indicating that wage growth in the four-year post-transition period was significantly slower than wage growth in this three-year pre-transition period, even when LGDP, INDUSTRY, and country-specific idiosyncracies were controlled for.

Model 4 adds linear trend variables denoting the four-year pre-transition period, four-year post-transition period, and four-year post-post-transition period. The coefficient of $T_{-4,\,10}$ is significantly negative in model 4, indicating that a significant downward trend in the rate of wage growth occurred in the pre-transition period. The coefficient of $T_{1,\,10}$ is positive and nearly equal in absolute value to the coefficient of $T_{-4,\,10}$, indicating that the rate of wage growth was almost flat in the four-year post-transition period. The coefficient of $T_{1,\,10}$ is significant at the 0.07 level, indicating that the slope of the estimated trend line in the four-year post-transition period was only marginally different from that in the pre-transition period.

Models 5 through 7 add interaction terms to model 3. As in table 10.3, COMPONENT is INDUSTRY in model 5 and the country's real GDP growth rate and inflation rate averaged over the year of transition and the preceding year in models 6 and 7, respectively. When I first ran these three interaction models, LGDP was not significant at the 0.10 level in any of them. I therefore dropped LGDP, producing the models shown here. None of the interaction terms featuring $D_{1,\,10}$ is significant, indicating that wage growth in the four-year post-transition period was not affected by the country's level of industrialization or its economic growth rate or inflation rate just before and at the time of these transitions from democracy to authoritarianism.

Table 10.5 reports a similar series of regressions for the 13 transitions from semidemocracy to authoritarianism whose means are depicted by the loosely spaced broken line in figure 10.1. The control variables LGDP, INFLATION, and INDUSTRY are not significant in model 1 of table 10.5 and therefore are dropped from the subsequent analyses. The coefficients of $D_{1,\,10}$ and $D_{6,\,10}$ are not significant in models 2 and 3, indicating that wage growth was not significantly slower (or faster) in the five-year post-transition period than in the four-year and two-year pre-transition periods and not significantly different in the three-year post-post-transition period than in the post-transition period. The coefficient of $T_{-4,\,10}$ is significantly negative in model 4, indicating that a downward trend in wage growth occurred in the four-year pre-transition period. The coefficient of $T_{1,\,10}$ is positive and barely significant at the 0.10 level, indicating that the trend in post-transition wage growth may perhaps have had a more positive slope than the trend in pre-transition

Table 10.5 *Changes in manufacturing wages before and after transitions from semidemocracy to authoritarianism*

Explanatory variable	Model 1	Model 2	Model 3	Model 4	Model 5	Model 6	Model 7
INTERCEPT	1.838	0.591	9.588***	0.591	1.485	1.489	2.382*
LGDP	-0.068						
INFLATION	-0.006						
INDUSTRY	-0.039						
$D_{-4,10}$		2.895		16.215*			
$D_{-2,10}$		-1.730	-10.413**	8.785	-11.136**	-9.988**	-11.266***
$D_{-1,10}$		-1.504	2.581	-1.492	2.318	2.949	2.399
$D_{-6,10}$		-0.373	-1.504	-4.323	-1.127	-1.557	-1.922
$D_{-9,10}$			-0.373	-4.548**	-1.005	0.064	9.967
$T_{-4,10}$				4.162*			
$T_{-1,10}$				0.836			
$T_{-6,10}$				2.405			
$T_{-9,10}$							
COMPONENT					-0.100	-0.422	0.033
COMPONENT*$D_{-2,10}$					0.185	7.039***	-0.251****
COMPONENT*$D_{-1,10}$					-0.188	1.566	0.025
COMPONENT*$D_{-6,10}$					-0.097	0.843	-0.035
COMPONENT*$D_{-9,10}$					0.288	-1.144	0.350
N	104	108	108	108	108	104	104
f-test	0.147	0.613	0.584	0.664	0.173	0.192	0.500
Estimator	OLS	OLS	OLS	OLS	OLS	OLS	OLS
R^2	0.003	0.010	0.061	0.050	0.075	0.184	0.387

Note: Significance levels: * = 0.10, ** = 0.05, *** = 0.01, **** = 0.001.

wage growth. None of the interaction terms involving $D_{1, 10}$ are significant in models 5 through 7, indicating that the post-transition wage growth rate was not affected by the country's level of industrialization or its economic growth rate or inflation rate just before and at the time of these transitions from semidemocracy to authoritarianism.

The findings reported in tables 10.3 through 10.5 provide no real support for the idea embodied in hypothesis 2 that industrial wages fall or grow more slowly after transitions to authoritarianism. Wage growth was significantly slower after the 17 transitions from democracy to authoritarianism than before these transitions, but not after the 13 transitions from semidemocracy to authoritarianism or in the sample as a whole. In both subsamples and in the whole sample wage growth declined significantly *before* transitions occurred, suggesting that the slower wage growth that occurred after transitions from democracy to authoritarianism merely continued a trend that began earlier. Moreover, the post-transition trend in wage growth was significantly more *positive* in the whole sample and marginally more positive in the two subsamples, suggesting that transitions away from democracy actually may have *stopped* the downward trends in wage growth that began earlier, a finding that directly contradicts hypothesis 2. There is little evidence that post-transition wage growth was affected by the extent of industrialization or by slow economic growth or high inflation at the time of transition. The only significant finding of this sort appeared in model 7 of table 10.3, which indicated that post-transition wage growth was marginally *higher* when transitions away from democracy occurred in conjunction with high inflation in the sample as a whole. Finally, it should be noted that the R^2s in all of the models with relevant findings were quite low, indicating that important factors affecting wage growth were not included in these models.[13]

Conclusion

In this study I have examined the widely held view that authoritarian regimes often use labor repressive measures to drive down industrial wages to stimulate economic growth. Using data on 60 third world countries and advanced statistical techniques, I first examined whether wage growth is slower under authoritarian and semidemocratic regimes. Although average annual wage growth was slower under the authoritarian regimes and faster under the semidemocratic regimes than under the democratic regimes in the sample, these differences were not large enough to infer a general trend. I then examined whether wage growth declines after transitions away from democracy. Although wage growth was significantly slower after one such type of transition (transitions from democracy to authoritarianism), it was not significantly slower overall. In fact, wage growth declined significantly in the period before the transitions away from democracy, and this downward trend stopped and flattened out after these transitions. The same general pattern occurred in the smaller sample of transitions from democracy to authoritarianism. I also examined the contention that wage growth is significantly slower under authoritarian and semidemocratic regimes and after transitions away from democracy in relatively industrialized Third World countries or in those experiencing slow economic growth or high inflation. No support for this contention emerged.

The most interesting of these results is the finding that real wage growth fell sharply two to four years before transitions away from democracy but flattened out immediately before these transitions and in the post-transition periods. The most plausible explanation of this finding is that the decline in wage growth and transitions away from democracy were *both* caused by high inflation or slow economic growth (or both) in the pre-transition period – a contention that is bolstered by my finding in a previous study that high inflation and slow or negative growth significantly increase the probability of transitions away from democracy (Gasiorowski, 1995). With wage growth already flat and poor economic conditions prevailing, newly installed authoritarian leaders in the post-transition period may generally feel that wage cuts would depress demand and hence create or exacerbate a recession. Thus while labor repression may well be a desirable goal for these leaders, their willingness to implement it may be tempered by the fragile economic circumstances that prevail in the post-transition period, leading them instead to permit the nearly zero wage growth that is apparent in figure 10.1.

This scenario may also account for the small but significant increase in wage growth that occurred in the post-post-transition period following the 31 transitions away from democracy (years 6 through 8 of figure 10.1). After eight years of nearly zero wage growth (year –2 through 5), the poor economic conditions that generally prevailed immediately before and at the time of these transitions may well have eased, reducing the urgency of wage cuts and even permitting small wage increases to occur. Together with declining wage growth in the pre-transition period, these trends suggest that wage levels and transitions away from democracy may both generally be caught up in the dynamics of business cycles: when an economy is in recession, wage growth falls and the probability of transition away from democracy increases; during a recovery wage growth remains stagnant; and wages begin to increase after a full recovery has occurred. While the findings reported here are consistent with this scenario, they obviously do not evaluate it directly. Further research on this issue is clearly warranted.[14]

These intriguing possibilities notwithstanding, the main conclusions of this study are that industrial wage growth is not significantly slower or faster under authoritarian or semidemocratic regimes than under democratic regimes and it is not significantly slower after transitions away from democracy than before these transitions. This latter finding suggests that the single-country and small-sample studies cited above that observed declining industrial wages under newly established authoritarian regimes have inadvertently misrepresented the general pattern. Since the control variables used in table 10.3 were not statistically significant, it appears that the small group of countries examined in these studies was simply atypical. The more general pattern observed here is that the type of political regime prevailing in a society does not significantly affect industrial wage levels.

NOTES

I would like to thank Hong Doan, Paul Geroski, Kit Kenney, Lynn La Motte, Tim Power, and Manus Midlarsky and the other participants in the conference on Inequality and Democracy for their valuable comments and other assistance on this chapter.

1 For a good overview of redistributional measures in a related context, see the articles in Dornbusch and Edwards (1991).

2 Similarly, income inequality – the measure used in most empirical studies of the relationship between democracy and inequality – is not directly affected by most types of redistributional measures and is strongly affected by economic trends.

3 For a broader study that found no significant relationship between regime type and wage growth, see Remmer (1990).

4 Where longer time series were available in World Bank (1992), I coded the additional data as well as values for the last three years of data available in World Bank (1992) to allow for revisions in the World Bank (1990) data. In each case I spliced the two series together by using the ratio of the first of the three sets of overlapping values to obtain uniform constant-value data.

5 Although I obtained this tape in late 1990, the industrialization data exist only through 1981 for most countries. To obtain longer time series I used ordinary least-squares regression to estimate linear time trends for countries with at least ten years of data. I then used the trend coefficient estimates and the last available data point to project additional values, yielding series of the same length as those available for the other variables. Since the industrialization data change slowly and fairly smoothly, these linear projections probably give fairly accurate predictions of the actual values.

6 *Democratic regimes* here are those in which (i) meaningful and extensive com-

petition exists among individuals and organized groups for all effective positions of government power, at regular intervals and excluding the use of force; (ii) a highly inclusive level of political participation exists in the selection of leaders and policies, such that no major (adult) social group is excluded; and (iii) a sufficient level of civil and political liberties exists to ensure the integrity of political competition and participation. *Semidemocratic regimes* are those in which a substantial degree of political competition and freedom exist, but where the effective power of elected official is so limited, or political party competition is so restricted, or the freedom and fairness of elections are so compromised that electoral outcomes, while competitive, still deviate significantly from popular preferences; and/or civil and political liberties are so limited that some political orientations and interests are unable to organize and express themselves. *Authoritarian regimes* are those in which little or no meaningful political competition or freedom exists. These definitions are based largely on Diamond, Linz, and Lipset (1990, vol. IV, xvi–xvii). The dataset also classifies a regime as *transitional* when the country is clearly moving from one regime type to another but the transition is not yet complete. In this study I recode these transitional periods to the previous regime type value, implying that regime changes occur at the end of these transitional periods.

7 Ecuador, Burkina Faso, Nigeria, Kenya, Turkey, and Bangladesh each had two transitions. Ghana had three.

8 As discussed above, I centered AUTH, SEMI, LGDP, INFLATION, and INDUSTRY before estimating each regression to reduce multicollinearity associated with the product terms.

9 To facilitate comparisons with model 2, I estimated model 1 with only the 909 observations for which data on LGDP and INFLATION were available rather than with the entire 918 observations.

10 Identical tests for the difference in heights of the horizontal lines can be carried out by replacing these cumulative dummy variables with non-cumulative dummy variables that denote only the time periods of interest (e.g., only the pre- and post-transition periods). The coefficients of these non-cumulative dummy variables give the heights of the corresponding horizontal lines, and f-tests can be used to test whether one is significantly different from the other. The advantage in using cumulative dummy variables is that these tests are made with the t-tests associated with the appropriate coefficients, which are easier to obtain than f-tests. To check my analyses I made both types of test on all of the regressions reported here.

11 Non-cumulative linear trend variables could also be used to make these comparisons. See note 10, above.

12 As in tables 10.1 and 10.2, I centered each of the variables appearing in the interaction terms before calculating these terms to reduce multicollinearity.

13 Since R^2 statistics are not strictly valid for RE-GLS regression, the R^2s reported with the RE-GLS models appearing in the tables are derived from the corresponding OLS regressions. Although these R^2s do not provide an accurate measure of the model's overall "goodness of fit," they do give a good indication of how much variance in the dependent variable is accounted for by the explanatory variables.

14 This business cycle scenario suggests two research questions that are of particular importance to our understanding of the relationship between economic conditions and regime change. First, are recoveries stronger following transitions away from democracy than in the absence of regime change, either because wage growth has been stagnant or for some other reason? Second, if transitions away from democracy are likely to occur during downswings in the business cycle, are transitions toward democracy likely to occur during upswings?

11 Social responses to neoliberal reforms in Eastern Europe in the 1990s

Béla Greskovits

Introduction

It is an often told story, how democratic political stability may be threatened by economic crises. The same has repeatedly been said about neoliberal economic transformation strategies while reference has been made to the contradiction between the exclusionary logic of rapid marketization, and the participatory logic of democratic politics.

Using these theoretical perspectives as rules of thumb led many social scientists to gloomy prophecies on post-communist transformation scenarios. After all, East Europe in the 1990s had a crisis originating in the exhaustion of its state-socialist economic system, along with radical neoliberal strategies introducing the market, which initially, aggravated the crisis. As a combined result, the region underwent a transformational recession longer and deeper than the Great Depression (Kornai, 1993).

Struck by this economic trend a number of social scientists began to worry about anti-democratic mobilization of various social groups resulting in political destabilization, and possibly the emergence of populism or authoritarianism in East Europe (Przeworski, 1991; Jowitt, 1992a; Ost, 1992; Hausner, 1992; Elster, 1993). Central to the pessimism has been the assumption, that economic hardships would provoke large-scale anti-reform and anti-system collective action: radical collective protest, the outburst of anomic movements, massive strikes, political violence.

As to the empirical foundation of the negative outlook, social scientists sometimes referred to one aspect of Southern experience in the 1980s. Some analysts – most explicitly Walton and Seddon (1994) – expected that the manifestation of East Europeans' economic grievances would be similar to the IMF-riots that swept over Latin America from the late 1970s to the mid 1980s.

However, nothing of the magnitude or intensity of IMF-riots has happened in East Central Europe, the region on which my essay focuses.

In Hungary, Poland, the Czech Republic, Slovakia, Slovenia, Romania, and Bulgaria, no threatening political destabilization or authoritarian turnabout is in sight.

Why? Why is it that in spite of the economic hardships, political life during the transformation has exhibited less instability and violence in East Central Europe than the politics of adjustment in many Southern reforming countries?

This is the question that motivated my essay.

Apparently, East European political trends question generalizations on the link between crises or neoliberal strategies, on one hand, and the intensity and typical forms of social response, on the other. It is mainly the conceptualization of this challenge that I want to contribute to. The perspective underlying my argument in general is that the relationship between economic hardship, and the intensity and ways in which people make their interests heard, is *historically conditional*. Different historical settings characterized by distinctive socioeconomic structural, institutional, and cultural features put different constraints on, and open up different opportunities for, social response to crises and reforms. It is primarily the *structural* factor to which I shall pay attention, for I think this analytic dimension is neglected or misconceptualized in interpretations of post-communism.

More specifically, I argue below that at the start of transformation it was certain structural, institutional, and cultural legacies of communism, coupled with the demobilizing effect of the crisis and reforms, that paved the way for relative political stability in the East. In order to correctly explain the differences in the political dynamics of transformation, we have to better understand the differences between socioeconomic structures, political institutional systems and mechanisms, and their implications for collective action in Latin America and East Europe.

The East has not become the South

Economic hardship and social grievances in the South in the 1980s and the East in the 1990s have, to some extent, common origins. In the 1970s and 1980s many of both the Latin American, and East European countries accumulated huge foreign debts at a time when repayment was becoming increasingly difficult due to adversely changing world market conditions. For failed interpretation of the situation, and fears of the political consequences, adjustment in most Latin American countries was postponed till problems turned out to be acute. Delays were also facilitated by the easy access to unconditional new financing until the early 1980s.

Adjustment came even more belatedly in the late 1980s and early 1990s in East Europe, where debt-induced adjustment steps happened to coincide with stabilization efforts and the much broader economic policies of systemic transformation, putting even more stress on society in the debtor countries.

Essentially similar stabilization and structural adjustment programs have been implemented in the East in the 1990s as in the South in the 1980s, although in a different historical and institutional environment and in a much broader scope. As to the socioeconomic consequences, just like the debt-induced adjustment in Latin America, systemic transformation in East Europe has been accompanied by large social losses: drops in the standard of living, rapid polarization of income and wealth, the erosion of the social safety net, skyrocketing unemployment, and new impoverishment.

In the case of the South, early fears of political risks inherent in adjustment proved to be fully justified by the events of the late 1970s and the first part of the 1980s, when Latin America was shaken by an eruption of severe protests called the IMF riots. "Riots, political demonstrations, and general strikes presented the alternatives as a choice between a new and desperate form of working-class poverty, self-imposed in the interests of foreign creditors, or the right to a living wage for shantytown residents, labor, and the middle classes" (Walton, 1989, p. 299). Masses participated in the 50 best-known and serious protests in 13 countries. Recurrent protests occurred with much violence continent wide: lootings, clashes with the armed forces, many hundreds of casualties and injuries, many thousands of arrests. The unrest was not without serious political consequences: governments' responses varied from no concessions and containment of disorder by martial law and state of emergency, to withdrawal of economic reform measures, compensation, replacement of key ministers, or return to civilian government (ibid., pp. 310 ff.).

Fears of "Latin Americanization" from similarily disruptive social responses to uncertain and deteriorating living conditions have frequently been expressed in the Eastern context as well, by politicians, political analysts, and social scientists alike. In this respect, however, paraphrasing Przeworski, the East does not seem to be becoming the South (Przeworski, 1991, p. 191). Belying scholarly expectations, East Europeans have remained remarkably patient. Contentious collective action stabilized at unexpectedly low levels. Economic reforms in the

East have thus far advanced simultaneously with democratic consolidation.

Why have East Europeans not protested more? In the following part I briefly outline the logic and the analytic background on which my answer rests.

The logic of argument and the analytic background

My aim is to explain the variation of the political dynamics of transformations under economic stress between Latin American and East European cases.

Political dynamics are shaped by the variation in characteristic *patterns of social response* to economic stress. (Undoubtedly, social response is neither the single, nor the ultimate determining factor. Instead, politics is an interactive process, where social action may provoke – or be provoked by – action by others.)

Patterns of response originate in varying social choices from a routine or newly emerging set of possible responses, referred to in various conceptual contexts: the repertoire of contention (Tilly, 1978), repertoire of collective action (Tarrow, 1994), exit and voice (Hirschman, 1970), or threats to reforms (Waterbury, 1989).

Social actors' choices to respond or not, and how to do it, is influenced – both constrained and oriented – by *their situation or location in society*, by various economic, social, political, and cultural structures and institutions. If social response is structurally and institutionally conditional, then a comparison of the orienting and constraining factors would take us a major step closer to understanding variations in political dynamics.

This is the step I will take.

I will explore how variations in socioeconomic conditions structure politics in Southern and Eastern cases. While I stress the importance of structures, and to a lesser extent institutions, I do not think that socioeconomic structures matter more than, for example, culture or ideology, nor do I claim to have a full explanation of post-communist political dynamics. Obviously, neither economic conditions, nor the geographic, occupational, organizational, property or age structures on which my comparison will focus can in themselves determine social responses to economic stress. Apparently, it is a complexity of factors and contingency at work in each concrete case.

I did not find any general theory of social response to economic grievances. Alternative views prevail as to which major types of politically relevant social action have to be included in a historically based, analytically fruitful typology. It is the various research agendas to which most classifications are adapted, and their application in other contexts can be highly problematic. Therefore, while setting up my classification, I could not build on the available theories directly and exclusively. Rather, I found several perspectives and research results relevant to my topic. I could not avoid the task of conceptual criticism and adaptation, nor could I avoid the risk of being eclectic.

For my purpose, the major analytical attraction of the mainstream of social movement research as represented, among others, by Tilly (1978), Eckstein (1989), and Tarrow (1994), is that it allows for the role of structural, institutional, and cultural factors influencing the choice of actors among various forms of collective response. Tilly's repertoire of contention, "at once a structural and a cultural concept" (Tarrow, 1994, p. 31) defined as "the whole set of means (a group) has for making claims of different kinds on different individuals or groups" (Tilly, 1986, p. 2) or Tarrow's concept of collective action is a useful starting point for developing the framework for East European cases. Corresponding to specific historical conditions the typology implied would include a wide range of protest forms, such as riots, street blockades, hunger strikes, rallies, demonstrations, strike threats, local and general strikes.

However, if our ambition is to assess the totality of politically significant societal responses to economic hardship, a repertoire of collective action tailored to the requirements of social movement research may turn out to be too narrow a concept.

First, reflecting Tilly's and Tarrow's preoccupation with social movements, their framework has contentious collective action as its focus, with an equal stress on both attributes. People or other actors, however, do not always respond either contentiously or collectively while expressing dissatisfaction with their reality. This distinction is especially significant in post-communist societies often characterized by the lack of a strong civil society, and consequently of organizational vehicles for collective action.

In this respect it is the Hirschmanian theory on social response that appears to open up a promising perspective. As Hirschman stressed, social actors usually have an alternative to *voice*, to collectively and politically express their dissatisfaction. Individuals or firms may *exit*, leave behind their unfavourable circumstances for something supposedly better (Hirschman, 1970). The magnitude of the exit response, its frequency relative to voice, and its specific forms may be no less significant in explaining variations in political dynamics than the repertoire of contention. The intensity of contentious collective action is affected by the possibility and forms of exit, and vice versa. Exit and voice may tend to either undermine or reinforce each other. Hirschman recently demonstrated how well his framework may apply to the interpretation of Eastern political dynamics. He explained the long stability and sudden collapse of the GDR by evaluating the changing impact of a specific exit option – emigration to West Germany – on political stability and the intensity of political protest (Hirschman, 1993).

In line with the Hirschmanian argument, it is possible to expand the repertoire of contention to a more encompassing typology of social responses. Substantial enrichment may follow both at the actors' level – attention can be paid not just to collective political, but collective and individual, political and economic actors – and at the level of their actions by adding non-contentious exit options.

Specifically, my typology expanded in accordance with the above considerations will include *capital flight*, and a few other exit options, which I call *going informal* in this essay.

Thus my classification is similar to the typology of *threats to reforms*, elaborated by Waterbury in order to understand social responses to neoliberal reforms in third world countries (Waterbury, 1989). Threats to reforms include riots, strikes, and capital flight, as well as other social responses to economic hardship like *hoarding, unsecured borrowing, or other preemptive, monopolist practices* by firms, or *remittance withholding* by migrant labor. The latter types cannot be classified as voice or exit. They may, however, bear an indirect relevance to political stability under economic stress.

The social movement perspective and the repertoire of collective action appears to have one more limitation: various forms of *using democratic procedures for protest purposes* remain systematically excluded from the repertoire.

If the missing attention to the *exit* option stems from the theoretical concentration on collectivities and social movements, the exclusion of the most important democratic form of voice – *protest vote* – may be a result of partly the same orientation, and partly the preoccupation of both social movement theory and democratic theory with consolidated Western democracies. The latter context makes it easy to understand why all other forms of political participation, including democratic voting, are usually strictly separated from contentious collective action. Sometimes this analytic separation manifests itself in the contrast between *conventional* and *unconventional political involvement* (Barnes and Kaase, 1979, p. 137).

I argue, however, that in this respect transforming societies might constitute a special case for the simple reason that they lack democratic political conventions. On the contrary, it is no exaggeration to think about their entire realm of politics as something that is unconventional almost by definition. After all, this is one of the core assumptions underlying the theory of non-institutionalized or non-consolidated democracies: that politics – from strikes to rallies, and from partisan activity to voting – is still uncommon and unusual for the emerging actors.

While positing a strict border between conventional and unconventional, political participation may be analytically legitimate in consolidated democracies; understanding protest in new, transitional systems might justify a less conventional scholarly approach.

Consequently, I include protest vote and other democratic procedural actions, like absenteeism, abstention, or mobilization for referenda into my typology of social responses. This is in conformity with both what we know about social movement traditions under communism, and the assumption that political participation has been in evolution from the unconventional to the conventional in new post-communist democracies.

Mobilizing abstention, negative votes, or support for non-communist candidates when it became possible, were widely used forms of protest by anti-communist social movements such as Solidarity in Poland or the Democratic Opposition in Hungary. Moreover, plebiscites had an important role in several Eastern transformation cases. Why should one assume that free elections from one day to the other entirely wiped out the protest traditions initially inherent in democratic procedures? I think that the opposite is true: the dramatic reshuffling of democratic political support among various poles of the political spectrum in new Eastern democracies, or the recurrent attempts to oppose unpopular policies through direct democratic means like referenda, may be a reflection of a prevailing continuum between unconventional and conventional features of the polity. As I hope to demonstrate later, paying attention to protest voting may substantially contribute to our proper understanding of Eastern social response to the hardships of the 1990s.

Before concretely exploring how social conditions in the East, as contrasted to the South, might have oriented and constrained social actors' choices, I have a few more suggestions about specifying the typology.

One aspect of analytical relevance is to point at the varying extent to which social response is organized and coordinated rather than spontaneous and individual. Actors in the economy and polity may pose threats to political stability and economic stabilization either by organized, common, mostly political actions, or by the multitude of individual, unorganized, mostly economic responses.

While strikes, rallies, demonstrations, and – to a much lesser extent, and only under specific conditions – riots more or less denote the first group, remittance withholding, hoarding, unsecured borrowing, capital flight, and certain forms of going informal represent the second.

The two groups of responses consist of actions which differ both in their preconditions and in their political or economic aims. Organized and coordinated response evidently needs organizers, while actions of the second type do not. Events of the first type mean mostly political action for economic or economic and political results combined. Responses of the latter type – without an explicit and direct intention to stop reforms, or to overthrow democratic and reformist governments – present economic adaptation or passive resistance, with only a contingent political impact.

From the point of view of short- and medium-term political stability, it has different implications if either organized political action – voice – dominates the arena, or, if the opposite is true, unorganized, economic response – exit – is dominant, whether due to the scarcity, disarray, or paralysis of the organizational vehicles of collective action, or other reasons.

A second analytic possibility is to differentiate among forms of protest, constituting just an important subset of social responses.

Clearly, there are types of expressions of discontent strictly bound to specific social or economic structures and groups, unavailable to others. Conversely, there are socioeconomic groups with limited freedom of choice as far as the forms of protest available to them are concerned. As an example, a strike is strictly anchored in labor organization, while elderly people, or specifically pensioners, do not have much alternative to voting against the crisis or the economic transformation strategy if deterioration of their living conditions poses everyday threats to them.

Undoubtedly, the political dynamics of transformation under economic stress are crucially affected by the availability of diverse and effective contentious responses to the major losers and opponents, or in line with my earlier point, by the characteristic pattern of social protest.

Structures, institutions, and the pattern of social responses

In conformity to the ideas presented above, my typology of social responses to economic stress under transformation lies under five categories: *riots* (including violent demonstrations, street blockades and hunger strikes); *strikes* (including strike threats and lockouts, but also general political strikes); *hoarding, unsecured borrowing, and capital flight* (but also other monopolistic practices, like lobbying for subsidies, cartels, investment restraint, or disinvestment); *going informal* (tax evasion, black employment, illegal street trading, mafia, and public firm cleptocracy); and *protest voting* (but also absenteeism, abstention, and mobilizing for referenda).

I turn now to the more detailed description of the individual types of social responses along with the characterization of what we might call their *structural and institutional embeddedness* under post-communism, in a comparative perspective.

Riots, and their socioeconomic conditions

Riots (and violent demonstrations, street blockades, and hunger strikes) may not only adversely affect or stop economic reforms by forcing the targeted policies to be withdrawn, but, especially when associated with anti-reform actions of other types, may shake or oust reformist governments, democratic and non-democratic alike, or even force regime change by questioning authority as such. Riots are often triggered by policy attempts to "slaughter the holy cows" of the preceding economic or social system, mainly by decreasing subsidies and raising prices for basic consumer items, or by radically devaluating the domestic currency with drastic inflationary consequences. Riots are protest forms characteristic of urban, unorganized, and low-income groups, the unemployed, and the poor (Waterbury, 1989; p. 47). Indeed, unorganized and poor groups rarely have an alternative to these most unarticulated and dramatic protest forms. Therefore, a comparative hypothesis on the sociopolitical risk of riots and related manifestations of political instability may be based on comparing indicators like the level and growth of per-capita GDP, income distribution, size of social groups below or near to poverty line, level of urbanization, share of metropolitan population, education standards, and traditions of political instability in the South and in the East.

Data on levels and growth of per-capital GDP indicate that East Central Europe has not yet managed to escape from the poverty and stagnation zone which is associated with a high risk of political instability in the LDCs in general (Londregan and Poole, 1990). Both low per-capita incomes and poor recent growth performance make the region comparable to Latin America as far as the risk of riots is concerned (World Bank, 1991, pp. 262–3).

However, inherited egalitarian income distribution patterns and the still limited extent of poverty in East Central European societies, relative to extremes in Latin-America, certainly might have contributed to defending Eastern transformation from violent forms of political destabilization. Moreover, considering that many of the Southern riots, violent demonstrations, and political murders have been rooted in the grievances of marginalized shanty-town dwellers of megapolises, it is a stabilizing factor that East Europe is urbanized to a much lesser extent than Latin America. The concentration of impoverished masses in metropolitan shanty-towns has not happened in the East so far (ibid., pp. 264–5). The higher overall level of education in the East may further reduce the chance for unarticulated outbursts becoming a major protest form (ibid., pp. 260–1).

In addition, historical legacy may in principle be a factor protecting the East from another type of political extremity: frequent military coups, associated with the above-mentioned violent forms of political destabilization. According to Londregan and Poole, past country-specific traditions of the violent seizure of executive power may increase the chance for future coups to occur (Londregan and Poole, 1990). Coups soon breed other coups, and to some extent this may be true for riots and other forms of political instability as well. With regard to violent political traditions Eastern Europe has been performing to some extent better than much of Latin America.

Strikes and their socioeconomic conditions

Strikes may adversely affect economic transformation either by paralyzing the economy (rail and port transport, or strategic industries) or by threatening stabilization via the wage–price spiral. Not infrequently, strikes have led to government or regime collapse.

It is organized labor, blue- and white-collar unions, and professional associations that may initiate strikes which – especially if the actors concentrate on key sectors of the economy – may pose an effective threat. A tentative statement on the socioeconomic risk of strikes may be advanced through a comparison of indicators like the level of unionization of the work force; its concentration in strategic branches; the country-specific institutional bases and traditions of union activity; and the credibility and organizational capacity of labor unions.

Data show that East Central Europe has in general been more unionized than Latin America (Haggard and Kaufman, 1992; OECD-ILO; 1993). There is no doubt that Eastern unions cover – even more than their Latin American counterparts – branches of strategic relevance for the entire economy: the iron and steel sectors, mining, transportation, and industries of military significance.

However, while there are important country-specific differences, most Eastern labor movements suffered initially from lacking or declining credibility, rooted in their close links with the outgoing communist power. Due to their handicapped situation, many unions in the region lost much of their organizing capacity and influence during the early transition years. Later, due to rapidly growing unemployment, competition among unions, and in some countries a government strategy of "divide et impera," unions and the strike-weapon seem to have lost significance as important risk factors for economic adjustment (Bruszt, 1994).

Hoarding, unsecured borrowing, capital flight, and their social conditions

The hoarding of imported raw materials while facing devaluation, unsecured borrowing from banks, and forced credits from suppliers, monopolistic output cutbacks and inflationary price rises to cover efficiency gaps, and lobbying to sidestep stabilization policies are specifically attributed to public enterprises in literature (Waterbury, 1989, p. 48). Responses like these may threaten economic, and, indirectly, political transformations by disrupting stabilization plans, the financial system, and foreign balances, as well as by causing disruptive bottlenecks in producers' markets and shortages in consumers' markets.

Capital flight (or investment restraint or disinvestment) associated mainly with the private sector (private importers, financial services firms, foreign exchange brokers) may cause the sudden collapse of the exchange rate and of the entire financial system by exhausting the currency reserves. Capital flight has been considered by many analysts to be one of the main threats to sustainable economic and political stabilization in plenty of reforming LDCs (Waterbury, 1989, p. 48; Commisso et al., 1992).

On the one hand, a tentative statement on the socioeconomic risks of hoarding, unsecured borrowing, and other monopolistic practices may be advanced by comparing indicators like the share of public sector in GDP, employment, and investment; traditions of public firm behavior; and of state-owned enterprises' reactions to economic reform measures as reflected by the stock of bad debt, forced interfirm credits, and reactions to price liberalization.

This comparison would find that state ownership in the East expanded far beyond the scope that any populist and statist government in Latin America ever dreamt of. This legacy has been clearly reflected by the long traditions of firm behavior under soft budget constraints, as explored in the paradigmatic analysis by Kornai. Public firms' behavior in communist shortage economies involved hoarding, unsecured borrowing, different forms of pressure for subsidies, and assertion of monopoly power against buyers and consumers via monopolistic price increases and poor quality (Kornai, 1980). This behavioral tradition partly translated into more serious threats to economic stabilization than the public firms' preemptive reactions to adjustment measures in Latin America. Unlike "textbook" firms, state owned enterprises (SOEs) in the East reacted to radical, initial reform steps – price liberalization and elimination of subsidies – by unexpectedly high price increases, and output and real wage contraction. Moreover, both the SOEs' ability to escape from credit cuts even in case of insolvency, and their option to enforce "credits" from suppliers and from social security funds, put a heavy constraint on the rapid success of economic stabilization attempts. As a consequence, a complicated web of forced credit relations and insolvent firms has emerged all over East Europe, posing a formidable burden to the budget, the entire financial system, and successful economic transformation in the medium run.

On the other hand, the fact that the rapidly growing private sector has had a subordinate role in the East for the time being does not imply that reformers have not worried about capital flight when initiating and implementing policy reforms.

The threat of capital flight in the East may be related not only to private (mostly foreign) firms or institutional owners of (sometimes "hot" money) deposits, but also to better off local individuals and households holding significant currency reserves in foreign exchange accounts at home or – illegally – abroad. Estimations of these accounts reflect the significant potential losses, threatening national financial balances in cases where policies are suspected to be disadvantageous or non-credible by the owners. Worries about currency flight have shaped policy makers' views wherever they have attempted to target the "correct" exchange rate (as it was in the case of the Polish and Jugoslavian stabilization), or planned risky steps toward convertibility or a unified taxation.

However, in order to correctly apply categories of threatening social responses related to the public and the private sector for comparative purposes, a distinction between economies in the South and the East has to be made. One certainly has to take into account that the emerging private sector in East Europe has not yet detached itself from the public sector's umbilical cord. Rather, for the time being privatization in the East implies the emergence of a *hybrid* sector regarding ownership, resources, and regulation, as opposed to a withdrawal of the state from the commanding heights of the property structure and a clear separation of public and private sectors (Abromeit, 1986; Greskovits, 1993; Stark, 1996).

What is public, and what is private in the East?

While traditionally the private has emerged in the shadow of the public in the East, close interrelationships between the two sectors have often been maintained during the transformation.

As a consequence of privatization, many of the transformed SOEs represent mixed property rights (Voszka, 1992). Many new private or hybrid (public and private) entrepreneurs originate in the public sector as regards their skills, habits, attitudes, and – what is most important – their networks of acquaintances and connections. Many emerging entrepreneurs initially have maintained their jobs in the state sector. Using public resources for private aims has deep roots in the Eastern European tradition, and this attitude has partly prevailed at least at the beginning (Laki, 1993). Private or hybrid firms often assert monopoly power in economic transactions – again a legacy of the shortage economy. Furthermore, the lack of a clear separation of the private and the public is further reflected by both the heterogeneity of membership and the overencompassing strategy of new and old business associations (Tóth, 1992). The private sector just like parts of the public one, has been subsidized and supported in other forms by the state during the initial years of transformation. (The main forms of support have been: profit tax holidays, exemptions from wage policies, subsidized credits for privatization, and job creation.) Eligibility for various subsidies has been extended to the hybrid sector, being logically considered a dynamic area of ownership transformation. Through this policy approach, hybridization not only helped the private to penetrate the public (forcing the SOEs to become more efficient), but had the opposite effect as well. Subsidies may have contributed to prevailing firm strategies, reflecting typically public firm attitudes: dependency on state paternalism, competition for subsidies and exemptions, and economy-wide risk aversion (Laki, 1993; Major, 1993). Multinational corporations, "the heavy artillery of capitalism" joined indigenous, hybrid, public and private entrepreneurship in benefitting from the Eastern governments' involvement in supporting privatization. Competing host governments in the region have lured the MNCs with a wide variety of privileges, and there is also some evidence of their own requirements often exceeding the generosity of the hosts.

The implication is that hybridization of the economy hybridizes the public and private economic agents' attitudes as well as their politico-economic weapons. In the East, it is the inventive combination of typically "public" or "private" responses by actors of the hybrid economy which reformers have to fear probably much more than their fellow reformers in Latin America.

Voting against crisis and reforms and their social conditions

Voting against economic transformation, or reformist parties and governments, does not pose a threat in authoritarian regimes that restrict democractic rights. Evidently voting cannot play a decisive role in most of the interelection period either, when reformers may act relatively free of electoral concerns. However, market-oriented transformation strategies obviously may be stopped or adversely affected by democratic procedures, through elections. Voting may therefore pose a crucial threat to economic adjustment in democracies and democratizing systems. Voting against reform *per se* does not pose a danger to democracy, unless it helps to empower authoritarian regimes.

All citizens eligible to vote may threaten reforms aimed at radical economic transformation by voting against them. However, while many groups or individuals may pose other threats as well, or do not vote at all, others, like pensioners for instance, basically have no other defence. Elderly people in general, and pensioners in particular, cannot strike or riot, even if they feel aggrieved. Often the same is the case with members of the rural society, who only rarely strike because they lack organization, and cannot "efficiently" riot as they live dispersed in the countryside.

An assessment of the sociopolitical risks of voting becoming a major and significant form of expression of discontent in the South and the East implies a comparison of the share of pensioners, or elderly in general, and the share of unorganized, rural sectors in the entire population and in the electorate. In addition one has to comparatively assess the above groups' chances to vote freely, as they may be supported or constrained by the electoral system, and other institutional, educational, or cultural factors. Comparisons of data of the type above suggest that the structural importance of socioeconomic groups without any alternative threat to reforms except for voting against them – like the old, retired, and rural population – tends to be much larger in East Central Europe than in much of Latin America (Nelson; 1994). Also, it should be considered that due to generally higher educational standards, old and rural people in the East may be less constrained in effectively using their only weapon of protest – voting – than is the case in the South.

Going informal, and its social conditions

Tax evasion, black employment, and illegal street trading enrich the empirical context of this type as much as mafia, public firm cleptocracy, or the drug economy.[1] While certain forms of going informal can be interpreted as specific coping strategies for economic hardships rather than weapons against the reforms, others have different implications in this respect. The threat potential inherent in going informal may be assessed on the basis that both economic and political reforms are conditional on a certain degree of formality and acceptance of the rule of law, in order to be considered effective at all. Going informal, therefore, may threaten reforms from the point of view of ruining the required level of legality and formality.

Economic, and in the medium run political, transformations may be eroded by various actors among both the popular sectors and better-off groups, or even among parts of elites, going informal on different, often group-specific paths. The significance of the groups, and the characteristic paths in the South and the East, may be assessed by comparing factors such as: growth rate of unemployment; drops in GDP and the number of subsequent recession years; the resulting drop in earnings and living standards – regional and country-specific traditions with formality and legality; volume of tax-burdens, social security, and unemployment benefit contributions; traditions and experience with the borders between private and public economy; freedom of travel, including tourist trade; regional political and military instability, waves of refugees – geographical proximity to international routes for illegal trade (of drugs, cars, fur, arms, etc.).

Needless to say, it is difficult to go beyond anecdotal evidence by collecting reliable data on the informalization processes of economic activity, not to mention the problems with comparing the intensity of Southern and Eastern developments in this respect. Nevertheless, while it is not easy to interpret the threat potential associated with the latter risks, even in a qualitative way, most estimates available on recent Eastern trends suggest the *increasing risks of going informal*. Without a doubt, complex and contradictory effects have to be considered.

The final part of my essay consists of my tentative conclusions about how the typology outlined above might be useful for comparative interpretations of the political dynamics of post-communist politico-economic transformations.

On the political economy of protest and patience in the South, and the East[2]

My aim clearly is limited to stressing some probable, important differences in the politics of Eastern transformation as compared with Southern cases, rather than providing a credible political assessment and forecast. If my comparison and my arguments will succeed in challenging Przeworski's and other pessimist theorists' early generalizations of "the East becoming the South," I shall not be bothered by the multitude of problems left unsolved for the time being.

Explanations of the non-violent nature of the Eastern transformation process tended to focus on the *historical moments of 1989–90*, the peaceful takeover of power, on the one hand, and have tried to find *elite-centered explanations* in elite attitudes and behavior, on the other. According to Urbán it was "the special role played by the so called reformers within the Communist Party," on the one hand, and, on the other, "spontaneous privatization" providing ways for "major beneficiary groups of the old regime to join the new system as net gainers," that were "responsible for the exceptionally peaceful Hungarian transition" (Urbán 1991: 309).

The comparison with Latin America, in turn, may help to explain why changes have *continued to advance in a non-violent way* from 1991 until 1996. Moreover, it provides us with the chance to enrich the general picture with a couple of *society-centered* arguments.

Society-centered explanations can start with the observation that communism left behind societies characterized by the relative lack of the structural, institutional, and cultural risks associated with violent collective action. Those include the lack of extreme income inequality, the lower size of the marginalized poor strata, the relatively lower level of both the urbanization of the population and its concentration in metropoles, and the absence of recent, violent tradition for coups and riots. It is also important to mention in this context that reformers in the East have not been in a hurry to eliminate the "premature communist welfare states" (Kornai, 1995). In sum, in contrast to the South, large popular sectors in the post-communist region disposed of relatively substantial *reserves to survive* hard times.

This might have weakened the risk of violent social response to economic stress in the East. Violent political mass actions, like riots or aggressive demonstrations with looting and casualties, have been less likely to substantially shape the political process of the Eastern transformation than used to be the case in the South.

Still, poverty exists in the East as well. There are groups under desperate living conditions who lack the above resources. However they live *geographically more dispersed,* and their numbers are smaller than is the case in Latin America or elsewhere in the South. But it is not just for this reason that organizing political action has mostly turned out too difficult a task for them; their potential *organizers and allies* seem to have been missing as well. We do not see much solidarity across social groups in the newly democratizing post-communist states. Instead, there is some evidence that in close association with the transitional situation, it is mostly rivalry, struggle for legitimacy, exclusivity, and attempts to monopolize constituencies, rather than the solidarity and cooperation essential for successful political action that is characteristic of relations among political parties, labor unions, social movements, and other civil actors (Greskovits, 1995). Though any further deterioration of their livelihood might be fatal for them, while left alone by the vocal social organizations the poor have not many alternatives to political "patience."

Given that East Europe's workforce has been far more unionized than that of many LDCs, and that unionization has included many strategic branches, it is remarkable how relatively few strikes have occurred. As a consequence, labor protest did not significantly shape transformation politics, either. Initially, this might have happened because much of the region's labor movement suffered from the lack, or at least from the decline, of credibility. It is also true that the few credible unions occupied a pro-reform position initially. Later, however, it was the transformation crisis, the living standard drops combined with the rapidly growing unemployment and government tactics, that might have put a brake on labor's collective action. The tradition of collusion between labor unions and management, and of common lobbying, originating in overwhelming state ownership, also might add to our understanding of the cooperative rather than confrontational stance adopted by most unions. The implication is that not just the poor, but also the more numerous, and in principle more vocal, labor groups had to remain patient while facing hardships associated with the crisis and the reforms.

In different forms and to different extents all population groups, including the workers and the poor, have had an important alternative to voice: massive exit from the formal economy, or legality in general, during the entire transformation period. Non-criminal exit forms as alternatives to disruptive, collective protest might have had a stabilizing effect, at least over the short run (Sík, 1994). More short-term relief might have stemmed from the gradual adaptation of public, private, and hybrid firms to the harsh conditions of the post-communist economy. While the typical response of economic agents – hoarding, unsecured borrowing, monopolistic practices, tax evasion, enforcing paternalistic intervention – definitely might have put stress on successful economic transformation, their negative effect has taken a longer period to unfold. In the short run, however, firms' defensive responses may have facilitated political stability. By keeping their staff overmanned initially, firms may have decreased the risks both for strikes from organized labor and for the disruptive potential of other types of threats just at the crucial starting points.

Attracted by the blurred boundaries between formal and informal, legal and illegal, as well as oriented by their traditionally ambivalent attitude toward the rule of law, Easterners have gone informal, or exploited their employers' capacities to enforce protective state intervention instead of protesting violently and collectively under the pressure of need. *Rather than voice, it has been exit* that has dominated the pattern of social responses to economic stress in the East, and it is partly this that political stability is due to.

This does not mean, however, that there was no massive protest, only that its form was specific.

All, in all, it is not just the poor and labor groups who were sentenced to political patience. They have been joined by those major social groups whose only defence has been voting: elderly people in general, and pensioners in particular, and the rural society. Both groups basically had no alternative protest to the economic reforms other than voting against them. This is the context within which we have to consider the importance of the fact that because of the structural, institutional, and cultural legacies of the previous system, the societal weight and significance of those who had no alternative to the protest vote as a weapon against economic hardship has been relatively large under post-communism.

Consequently, the characteristic post-communist pattern of *voice has been biased in favor of using democratic procedures for protest purposes* rather than the rest of the repertoire of contention. This, in turn has had important implications regarding the political dynamics of transformation. Unlike all other contentious groups, like rioters, strikers, hunger strikers, or violent demonstrators who pose direct threats to politicians, protest voters cannot disregard the institutional-chronological rhythm of democratic procedures. Even if electorates want to stop or reshape economic or political strategies by voting immediately against them, they have to postpone action until the next democratic calendar date of election periods, referendums, votes of non-confidence, voting on the budget, and the like.

Therefore, the pattern of social protest biased in favor of democratic procedures provides economic reformers and democratic politicians both with *more chances for political calculation*, and a *longer grace period* to implement and consolidate economic and political reforms, than if the opposite were the case.

While it is impossible to tell whether "longer" will mean "long enough" ultimately, the implication of the above argument is that there has been more possibility than frequently assumed for both economic reforms to be implemented and democracy to be consolidated in the East.

This allows me to make a case against the widespread argument that democratization threatens economic stabilization by releasing participatory claims on popular control over policy making associated with excessive pent-up economic demands of previously excluded social groups. As I argue, it is just the opposite that occurred in the post-communist East: the new political institutions have played the role of a *safety valve* in chaneling social discontent into the delaying and balancing paths of democratic procedures. Instead of causing harm to economic stabilization and transformation, democratization turned out to be their political vehicle.

This latter statement, however, requires specification.

If voting as a weapon is considered to be significant in the East, it also implies that any (planned or unplanned) multiplication of the chances for voting may increase the risk of the grace period granted to parallel economic and political reforms to shrink, and for unwanted individual reform measures or entire reforms to be postponed, adversely reshaped, or even stopped as a consequence of protest votes. Any time when the electorate is provided with the chance to protest through voting, economic transformation may become a major and sensitive campaign issue. The chronological rhythm of democracy can speed up, the institutional calendar as a whole can be rewritten by referendums, presidential elections, and no-confidence votes resulting in governments' resignation between regular election terms. This is a point where country-specific variables of the democratic institutional system have to be considered when explaining why Polish reforms had to face more frequent and risky electoral challenges than Hungarian ones. Therefore, country-specific differences of the institutional calendar of democracy are relevant regarding country-specific political patterns of economic transformation. So are factors explaining country-specific differences of the democratic calendar: characteristics of the party system, the political institutions, and political power.

Keeping in mind all of the above arguments, we can conclude with a few statements on the political structures characteristic of the new Eastern democracies. The bias toward expressing even contentious political involvement through democratic procedures implies the dominance of political parties over labor unions and business associations, along with their superiority over other social organizational forms, like grassroots organizations, non-governmental organizations, or social movements. It is the political parties, rather than other organizations of the civil and the civic society, that play overdominant roles in the political arena, and shape the political future of East Europe.

If the statement on the dominant role of parties is valid, it may be relevant to ask about the parties' economic and political visions and practice in order to predict future political and economic chances for the East.

In this respect, due to the grave macroeconomic situation and a varying degree of external influence, a sort of *uniform subordination of the politics of policy choice to emergency economic conditions* can be observed in the East Central European transition. Neither the country-specific characteristics and developments of the political institutional system, nor the ideological preferences of the incumbents seem to be much reflected in the economic policy choices of the subsequent governments: the policies implemented tend to be fairly uniform in East Central Europe. It seems much more to be the case that tough stabilization and transformation policies "preselect" their reliable executors in the political arena, rather than that the various political parties select economic policies reflecting their ideological preferences, be they rightist, leftist, or populist by nature.

First, this implies that there has not been much reason to associate the leftist comeback with economic populist dangers, with unrealistic economic adventures. On the contrary: politicians – be they leftist or populist – will have to wait for some period of recovery in order to gain essential influence over economic policy choices again.

The other implication is that the most characteristic threat to reform in the East, the democratic *protest vote, may be only apparently effective.* Citizens vote out economic policies injurious to their immediate interests, only to witness their stubborn recurrence under new and different party banners.

NOTES

1 I'm indebted to Mihály Laki, who drew my attention to the potential significance of this category with regard to both the polity, and economy of the transition in Central and Eastern Europe. On various forms of informal economic activity, its political effect, and the difference between the informal economy and the communist "second" economy, see Sík (1994).

2 Clearly, my phrase bases on the terms developed by Offe (1991), and Hirschman (1981a).

12 Market, state, and citizenship in new democracies

Giuseppe Di Palma

The recent global wave of democratizations, and especially the fall of communism and the difficulties of post-communist democracies, have given new impetus to a neoliberal perspective that makes markets and capitalism a nearly sufficient key to democratic development and success. This chapter argues that the emphasis is making us overlook the role of the national constitutional state: a role of absolute preeminence especially in the difficult democracies commonly found in the post-communist world and in Latin America.

I submit the following:

1 There is no democracy without a national constitutional state, because the constitutional state is the essential agent in the development and operation of a democratic civil society. Thus the antinomy between state and civil society (less state, more civil society; and vice versa) is a false one: a mere slogan without connotations.
2 The market may be necessary for civil society, but it is not sufficient, and it is not, at any rate, a direct agent. Its sustaining role must be buttressed and possibly corrected by the constitutional state.
3 In fact, the market is not in the position to operate in a socially and contractually congenial environment without the legal buttressing and the socio-political mediations of the state. Therefore the antinomy between state and market (less state, more market) is similarly misplaced, precisely from the perspective of the market.
4 The most successful democratic states, both politically and economically, have been based on what Gabriel Almond (1991) calls a welfare compromise, reconciling the reproduction of capital with the reproduction of popular consent.

Next I submit that the present rise of a neoliberal paradigm, by cumulating with pressures toward marketization and globalization and with other state-debilitating developments mostly related to recent regime changes, creates serious problems of performance for the more difficult among new democracies. For one thing, a well-rooted constitutional state is essential in order to rationalize the economies of the new democracies, and yet such a state may not be available. And, paradoxically, one of the factors that may undermine this economic role of the state in the new democracies may be precisely the drive to create healthy competitive economies. For another thing, the debility of the state may hamper the fruition of citizenship. It may do so, in particular, by hampering the state's essential role in securing the rule of law throughout its territory and in bridging the political consequences of socioeconomic inequalities.

In short, what seems in question, presently and for the foreseeable future, is not democracy but the democratic state; i.e., not the diffusion of Schumpeterian democracy to new countries but its constitutional rooting in an enabling state. The real issue is not so much whether the new democracies will endure, but how: the issue is one of governance.

While it is the performance of new democracies that interests me in this contribution, I will suggest in the conclusions that old democracies, despite a long-standing national-constitutional record, are by no means unaffected by neoliberal trends. The issue of democratic performance is, to different degrees, a global one.

A historical overview

I shall begin with a historical overview of the role of the constitutional state in the fostering of an open competitive system. The general thesis is the continuity of that role, as we move from nineteenth-century liberal oligarchies to twentieth-century mass democracies (Holmes, 1991). It is, in other words, historically imprecise to see constitutionalism, given its liberal nineteenth-century origins, as no more than an individualizing constraint on the collective purposes of democracy. Historically, the constitutional state has been essential in empowering a fully competitive, fully participatory, society – in three ways:

1 The constitutional state has legally guaranteed the exercise of universalistic political and civil rights. Since we tend to equate constitutionalism with liberalism and liberalism with individual freedoms, this is its best-known effect. Taken alone, the achievement would still be quite compatible with the conventional view of liberalism and constitutionalism as somehow at loggerheads with democracy.

2 More important, the constitutional state, *qua* state, has offered more than declaratory and individualizing bills of right. It has offered the ways and means – the legally constituted institutional backing – for channeling individual freedoms into the joint and competitive exercise

of citizenship. In sum, it has offered the institutional empowerment of civil society. And within civil society, it has facilitated the political bridging of inequalities: the mediation of ancestral as well as arbitrary social hierarchies – for instance, the hierarchies of market-oriented possessive individualism. The constitutional state has offered what the market alone cannot offer. These achievements coincide with the passing of *régimes censitaires et capicitaires*. Under those regimes, the question of how to enable citizenship was relatively secondary, since citizenship was extended only to those who, presumably, could practice it effectively and with forethought – that is, males of education and property to begin with. But as suffrage expanded, the constitutional state was progressively called to compensate for social inequalities. Extension of the suffrage rested not only on the pressure of excluded majorities, but also on the logic of liberal citizenship itself, which supplied new claimants with the most compelling argument for casting their claims: the universalism of liberalism made resisting the extension of citizenship on any but prudent and contingent grounds ultimately indefensible. In turn, once citizenship expanded, the issue of ensuring its concrete fruition became central.

3 The constitutional state has done all the above because and to the extent that it has protected its citizens and its territory from the extralegal claims of subnational, parochial, and privatized forces. This institutional achievement, another dimension of universalism, is an additional factor allowing civil society to flourish, expand, redefine its ambit, under the aegis of and in exchange for a comfortably rooted lawful state.

As a consequence of these developments, society and the state, while preserving reciprocal autonomies, reveal themselves interdependent: in particular, the constitutional state is embedded in liberal society. Liberal embeddedness manifests itself in two ways, both of significance in building up, rather than restricting, the liberal state *qua* state. The first is the increasing trust in the authority of the state; the second, in turn, is the increasing range of state capabilities and activities. When a state as the repository of positive law embeds itself in a society that looks at the state not as something to curb but something to steer on its own behalf, something unstoppable is born. The essential premises now exist for everexpanding collective pursuits, at the center of which is the state.

Here is a fundamental difference between liberal governance and governance before liberalism – not only under feudal and *ständestaat* rule, but also under the relatively more dynamic absolutist state. Before liberalism, the process and business of government were defined and inscribed within the traditional and fixed prerogatives of ascriptive and exclusive groups – be they the privileged estate orders or annointed kings and their ennobled officialdom. With liberalism, the business of government passes into the hands of secular and potentially open entities: the state, as the repository of ever-changing positive law, and an inclusive civil society. As Gianfranco Poggi (1978, p. 104) describes it: "Such a political system must of necessity always be generating new themes for public concern and for authoritative action." It must always orient itself to general, ever-receding targets; and must at any time be ready to upset the balance of winners and losers (ibid., p. 111).

To be sure, the dynamism of the liberal state mirrors the dynamism of liberal society – of bourgeoisies, of markets, of capitalism. But I am suggesting that it also mirrors the special division of labor, based on trust and empowerment, that assigns the new contrivance – the modern state – extraordinary capacities.

It is therefore no surprise that the liberal and then democratic state often turned out to be a more powerful tool than autocracy – both past (absolutism) and contemporary. One fundamental reason is liberal embeddedness. Hence, liberal polities were already in a better position than autocratic ones to invite cooperation from their citizens, and address it toward collective endeavors and the provision of public goods (Holmes, 1991, p. 84).

As the liberal and democratic states become progressively embedded in society, the fact that social inequalities continue to exist is less important to my argument than how they combine with political inequalities: the real issue is the ability of those who find themselves disadvantaged (within any arbitrary or ancestral hierarchy) to give their plight legal-legitimate expression in the public arena. Democracy does not guarantee the lessening of social inequalities as such, nor is it supposed to. Further, other systems do occasionally better, either by *de facto* lessening inequalities or by making them part of the natural and just order of things. In fact, a degree of social equality or welfare may be a relatively conscious trade-off for a more cramped competitive system (Germany before World War I) or for none at all (some Gulf emirates). But no democracy can comfortably claim authenticity that cannot point to a politically empowered and therefore trusting society. This is part and parcel of the democratic ideal that Gabriel Almond and Sidney Verba pointed to when they set themselves to test empirically the virtues of the "civic culture" (Almond and Verba, 1963). It is no coincidence that, perhaps with the partial historical exception of the United States, the democracies most democratic theorists have come to mention as paradigmatic are not so much those where social inequalities are objectively less severe or opportunities for social mobility greater, but those where a civic culture gives people confidence in the fairness of the political game.

They are democracies where conflict was tamed precisely by its full articulation, and where such articulation was embodied in a full spectrum of associabilities (parties, movements, labor and industrial organizations, interest groups, peak associations, cultural religious and regional constituencies). They are also democracies where associationism, whatever its first causes, was sustained in the last analysis by political facilitation and indeed by its continuous exchange with the state. Finally, these are democracies where, at least until the seventies, there was still a can-do confidence that the defects of associationism – factionalism, particularism, localism, the prevalence of privileged policy networks – could be cured. The range of countries that fall in this group – in terms of policy and constitutional styles, legal traditions, perceptions of salient social inequalities, structures of associationism, institutions for conflict resolution – is fairly ample. It includes Scandinavian social democracies, where the state was central in fostering and indeed shaping associationism, especially in the labor and economic sphere. But it may also include, at least in its New Deal and post-war era, the United States, where the role of the federal state seems more difficult to pin down, less central, less continuous and, possibly, less concerned with the associability of inequalities.

To conclude, let me reiterate that, within my state-centered perspective, universalistic civil and political rights, though necessary, are plainly insufficient to enable citizenship. Even less sufficient is the presence of a market – the commodification of land, labor, goods, and services. For the market does not give freedoms legal tender, and freedoms, as we just saw, are not enough anyway. To paraphrase Christopher Hill (1967, p. 128), universalism of rights and a market can only set up a Ritz Hotel version of citizenship. The doors of the Ritz were open to all, but the impecunious took up lodging under the stars. To be sure, universal rights, contractualism, the individuation of human relations, the very lack of moral justification of the new market inequalities, are all modern premises to the art of competitive associationism, in the economic and hence other spheres. But fulfilling these premises assumes something obvious, yet something which, historically, the market by itself has not delivered. It assumes that the state is not repressive: if it is (the case of capitalist authoritarian states) the enforcement of civil and political rights, let alone the facilitation of civil associationism, lose as a minimum their legal certainty. And it also demands that where the state is instead constitutional and bound to legality, the state does not limit itself to being the impartial doorman of the Ritz Hotel. It must also be, as it has been historically, an enabling state: it must help correct in practice the cramping effects that market and other inequalities have on the exercise of citizenship.

This demand strikes some as less than obvious or indeed quite questionable. For one thing, it may not appear necessary that the state step in. For another, it may appear that where the state has stepped in, worse damage has been done. Still, concerning market inequalities, Adam Smith himself was not insensitive to the danger that capitalist self-interest would conspire against the public, and not opposed to the corrective role of the legislator. More to my point, a corrective role with respect to the market is precisely what the constitutional state has historically assumed. Public choice theory about the market inefficiencies of democracy notwithstanding, the record of "real-existing" capitalist democracies indicates that they achieved what Gabriel Almond (1991), and similarly Robert Dahl (1992), call a welfare accommodation: market capitalism prospered without recourse to a repressive apparatus (the apparatus of capitalist authoritarian states) precisely when capitalism went along with a state that took upon itself the task of closing the civic deficit of market-induced inequalities. In other words, the welfare accommodation has allowed the state to act as a political facilitator: to tame class conflict, while buttressing the reproduction of capital. Indeed, each task has benefitted from the fulfillment of the other.

Almond (1991, p. 473) remarks that the welfare accommodation is not static, but also suggests that the amplitude of the swings may be reduced by "a learning process over time." I have submitted in the opening sentences that one such swing in the pendulum, away from the welfare accommodation, is presently and globally underway. I have also submitted that this development occurs in the context of a larger neoliberal swing. As a consequence of it, presently at issue is not only the role of the state in fostering citizenship, but also the role of the state in fostering, and not just correcting, the market. This raises three questions, of particular relevance in new democracies. First, why the swing? Second, what precisely is the swing doing to the double role of the new democratic states, in regard to citizenship and in regard to creating sustainable competitive economies? Third, can the swing be contained by Almond's learning process over time? Or, less pretentiously, is the swing a temporary reflection of special and unavoidable contingencies? The rest of the chapter is mainly devoted to the first two questions. Answers to the third question will be more tentative and elliptical.

Why the present swing?

I have no simple answers to the question. They would be premature. Let me suggest, rather, a shopping list of converging global changes. I use global in two opposite meanings: to combine changes that are common to all with changes that are geographically scattered and diverse, and possibly temporary in their effects. Thus convergence is partially accidental, yet synergetic, at least for the time being.

1 I top the list of changes with a subjective factor. It has to do with the way political actors and political analysts have tended to interpret the last wave of democratizations.

In some cases (Chile, Spain, some NICs) democratization followed the successful expansion of market economies; in others (most of Latin America) it came in on private economies variously decimated by patrimonialized or parasitic states, inflationary populism, and huge domestic and foreign debts; in yet others (communist dictatorships), the new democracies inherited state economies which had miserably and unequivocally failed to provide a material and moral alternative to capitalism.

In all cases, the same undifferentiated lesson has been drawn by many policy influentials: markets and dictatorships are in the long run incompatible. If dictatorships do not destroy the market, the market eventually destroys them; if dictatorships destroy the market, it is the lack of the market that eventually undoes them. Where market economies expand, dictatorships become progressively obsolete and democracies sooner or later follow. But dictatorships may also fall because their economies, distorted or plainly appropriated by party-states or state camarillas and clienteles, turn out to be non-competitive.

The step from the diagnostic to the prescriptive part of the analysis is short (but treacherous in my view): the market, unhampered by the state, is all that is needed, not only for growth but for democracy. The reconstitution of a comprehensive civil society has little to fear and much to hope from the generous performance of the market, for the market evens out any starting material and civic deficit. Therefore, where the market is in disarray or non-existent, and much else is not available, the prescription, to borrow from Jon Elster (1990), is a gigantic and daring "bootstrapping act." In other words, the diffusion of the market in new democracies is being driven not just by the weight of its own economic and political achievements as it expands – achievements which are still to be demonstrated – or by the pressure of international operators, but also by a faintly unscientific act of faith, by a precommitment to a model with still vague empirical and normative connotations. Ideas have political consequences. And at times they may reflect a new orthodoxy.[1]

My point is that Elster's bootstrapping act may be unavoidable, but it is not without political costs.

2 There is another, objective, reason why the wave of democratizations of the last 20 years has extolled the role of the market. The wave occurred at the same time as processes of globalization of national economies accelerated. These processes have at least two aspects of relevance to our analysis. First, by giving primacy to market liberalization, globalization shrinks the role of the national state not just as economic policy maker but also as functional and territorial mediator between relevant social formations. For instance, the increasing mobility of private capital (hence the opportunity literally to "exit," if threatened) makes it more difficult for the state to redistribute resources and life opportunities among national social formations. Second, by giving primacy to programs of economic stabilization, where these are needed because of inflationary debt-ridden economies, globalization similarly constrains the options of both the state and the social constituencies affected by stabilization. For instance, it deprives popular constituencies of the safety net traditionally provided by a public-spending state. Both aspects of globalization are found in new as well as old democracies; but they sit more heavily on new democracies, as well as those old democracies where economic performance is shakier.

In the case of new democracies, the dilemma is as follows. Despite its political costs, the reconstruction of the market remains necessary and urgent – especially in the post-communist democracies, where the plain alternative is material and social disorganization. And yet a task that is urgent and taxing at the same time detracts the state from other collective tasks, which are just as compelling: the establishment of the rule of law, the reconstruction of civil society. Furthermore, unless the latter two tasks are also attended too, the stabilization of the market itself will also suffer.

3 The two developments I just presented have come on the heels of a fiscal crisis of the democratic welfare state (the state described by Almond as a successful compromise). Juxtaposing this crisis of old democracies, a crisis of overextension, to the crisis of those dictatorships whose economies were clogged by state-invasive parasitism (Latin America) or by routinized nomenklaturas (real-existing socialisms), adds ammunition to a simplified analysis that affects old as well as new

democracies. In all cases, old and new, the performance of the state *qua* state is held at fault: the state encourages rent seeking, which undermines economic growth and spells the dominance of special vested interests. In all cases, the analysis denounces a singular convergence between East and West, North and South. It is not the convergence postulated by theories of modernization but, in a sort of deflection of history that only a return to the market will correct, a convergence on public corruption.

4 In a number of regions, we are witnessing ongoing processes of deconcentration, fragmentation, or reshuffling of territorial sovereignty. These processes are effects, rather than first causes, of a decline in the institutional cement of the nation-state. The causes are to be found, directly or indirectly, in the processes of economic globalization and regionalization, but also in the institutional tensions and incoherence that accompany the most difficult among the democratic transitions. The most conspicuous manifestation of the territorial issue is the revival of putatively ancestral mininationalisms, whose aggressiveness undermines civic coexistence and mutual respect for liberties, as well as the construction of modern competitive economies. But even where there are no mininationalisms to contest the legitimacy of the state, the slippage of the national state may have similarly negative effects. The effects may be especially detrimental where the presence of the national state is most needed: in the areas of social and territorial marginality, in the constitutional "peripheries."

In sum, taken together, this list of four global changes seems to amount to one thing: the market is in but the state is out. I will nuance such a blanket assertion by restating that, especially in some cases (South Eastern Europe, Russia, Central America with the exception of Costa Rica, part of South America), the constitutional debility of the state has specific causes, some conjunctural and some historical, that go beyond the common pressures of marketization and stabilization. Around the world, then, the market is in but the state is out for converging objective reasons: because processes of economic globalization by-pass the national state and rely on policy circuits that cut across the state functionally and territorially; because transitions to democracy have at times affected the territorial integrity of the state; because (especially in the cases I just mentioned) the transitions, in part still unfinished, have inherited *and* produced states that are variously discredited, in disarray, or still infiltrated by rent-seeking interests; because the fiscal resources of the democratic welfare state have proven self-depleting. But the discredit of the state, and the attraction of the market, have subjective reasons as well: this is the way in which policy analysts have been reading the changes, and an intellectual bandwagon effect seems presently at work.

And there lies my concern. To recapitulate: neither citizenship and civil society nor the market itself can prosper in a democracy without the aid of an embedded constitutional state. Yet that role is placed in jeopardy today, especially where the constitutional state is most needed – in the new democracies.

Since this general analysis assumes different colorations and emphases in different regions, I will deal first with former communist countries and then move to Latin America. I am aware that the expository separation entails at times sacrificing commonalities, at times indulging instead in repetition.

Post-communist democracies: markets, nations, and citizenship

As I have presented them, the present problems with civil society and citizenship are mainly lodged in contemporary global developments, and are therefore shared by new and old democracies. To be sure, new democracies, especially post-communist ones, start with weak civil societies (no market, no civil society; no traditions of constitutionalism, no civil society). But forceful introduction of marketization that sacrifices political interplay compounds the weakness. The present, not just the past, is the problem. The matter is better approached if we start from the bottom: by looking at how, in post-communist societies, people react, as citizens but also as consumers and family members, to marketization.

One official motive behind forceful post-communist marketization is to foster a more prosperous (and freer) society by fostering a free productive economy. In most cases, the motive is genuine. Thus, as Claus Offe (1991) remarks, the present processes of marketization differ in telling ways from the emergence of commercial capitalism in early modern Europe. At the time, the process was driven by a class of self-interested proprietors seeking *their own* Lockean rights and *their own* personal gain. The process went hand in hand with, and indeed justified, new social and political inequalities, based on merit and achievement, even as old ascriptive ones were condemned. How and when private property would eventually foster greater prosperity and freedom for all was not an issue demanding urgent public attention. There was time. Post-communist marketization, instead, is driven by government reformers that seek material results (everything else will accordingly follow) and expect popular support for their action. At stake are public performance and collective benefits. And the crucial point is that the costs in emerging inequalities, although inescapable, are meant to be temporary.

If we cast these remarks in the broader perspective of modern democratic history, we have here an interesting, and troubling, contemporary paradox, the significance of which goes in fact beyond post-communist countries. I will call it the paradox of prosperity through parsimony – where parsimony seems nowadays necessary but prosperity nevertheless is more than ever the central promised and expected goal. In a nutshell, the paradox is as follows: ever since liberal democracy acquired the features of mass welfare democracy, economic performance, growth, and prosperity have become central goals to democratic governance, propelled by organized participation (Sartori, 1995). They remain central even as the welfare state has turned unaffordable (i.e., into a threat to prosperity), as neoliberal retrenching and sacrifices are invoked, and as popular forms of organized participation dwindle. The democratic promise is still one of fair, indeed better, opportunities for all, through retrenching if need be.

But, to revert back to post-communist countries, since its citizens have now the right to complain and to vote, and since prosperity is what they have been promised, the question of how long they are willing to wait before prosperity materializes is not inconsequential. This much has been remarked by many analysts: the introduction of competitive markets creates inequalities, indeed considerable deprivations, and deferred promises. Therefore, some analysts offer extremely bleak prognoses: persons who suffer the adverse consequences of the market will nonetheless lend their immediate approbation "only if," as Robert Dahl (1992, p. 84) puts it, "they act not from rational self-interest but rather from a commitment to the general good." But such commitment does not come natural to ordinary people anywhere – especially if they do not enjoy the protection of a stable system of associations.

There are reasons to believe that the social costs of marketization, in either Eastern Europe or Latin America, may not stop democracy in its tracks. Among the reasons is the fact that people abandoned communism and turned toward democracy not because of material considerations alone, since those of Eastern Europe were revolutions of citizenship (Garton Ash, 1990); the fact noted by many analysts that, in Latin America, many intransigent leftists had lowered their expectations with regard to the social and material benefits of political democracy; and the fact that lack of economic reforms may be just as painful and therefore as resented (Geddes, 1994a). Nonetheless, the problem of popular compliance cannot be dismissed out of hand.

For one thing, expectations concerning the material performance of the new democracies, especially post-communist democracies, have risen again. One reason, stemming from the paradox above, is the very emphasis placed by the new regimes on the task of marketization, which demands sacrifices but also promises to deliver. Another is the fact that memories of the mostly abysmal material performance of past regimes, which made democracies more attractive by comparison, have become less compelling over time. The more those memories fade – the more, for that matter, the number of dictatorships decreases and the number of democracies increases – the more democracies ask to be judged in their own terms: in terms of the quality and the style of life they can deliver. And another thing: people do not know how long they will have to endure sacrifices, but they observe two disturbing facts. First, the sacrifices are unequally distributed. Second, this is not entirely the inevitable result of reforms doing their job, but often of individual dodging, luck, and corporate resistance by nomenklaturas and the like. In addition, there are no clearly formed organizations yet to represent the people when the time to compensate them for their sacrifices should come. What the people mainly have is a ballot to cast.

In sum, the social inequalities emerging in post-communist democracies have one drawback with respect to the historical inequalities found in established democracies. The latter were socially engendered, and also tamed in their political effects. The organized struggle for political equality has been a fixed and legitimate feature of established democracies. The former are the product of a highly constrained political choice, a daring act still without a sufficiently sturdy safety net, and *above all* with a paucity of means with which to weave the net.

The last paragraphs suggest that popular disenchantment with marketization and its costs is dictated by plain and simple self-interest, and nothing more. Even under normal and fair circumstances, it is difficult for most people to discount present sacrifices against future gains. Other analysts, however, prefer to go deeper. Much has been written about the true and tragic legacy of Leninism, with its false and leveling conformity. The legacy is apathy, suspicion, reciprocal envy, particularism, egotism, indifference, materialism, consumerism – all traits of post-communist mass culture. True enough, perhaps. What seems less convincing is the argument that the main reason why the market is resented by East Europeans resides in the "uncivic" cultural pathologies inherited from real-existing socialism, not just in a calculus of interests, reasonable under the circumstances. It resides in post-communist electorates who are habitually materialistic, who wish immediate personal benefits, but are at the same time distrustful, by the force of past experience, of politics and official promises.[2] Thus Kenneth Jowitt (1992b, chapters. 7, 8, and 9) argues that the uncivic amalgam of apathy, suspicion, envy, populism, particularism, and occasional extraparliamentary action that runs through post-communist democracies is nothing new and unexpected: it is the debased cultural legacy of communism. Similarly, Václav Havel (1993, p. 8) reminds us that, as a system of domination, communism brought history to a halt, enforced sameness and feigned compliance, leaving behind nothing to go by but selfishness, a desire for self-affirmation, consumerism, and a carpetbagging morality. In addition, as Robert Dahl (1992, p. 87) remarks, some proponents of the free market tell us that the old amalgam is kept alive by present democratic processes, which allow the unenlightened to turn their short-run self-interest against the cure-all market. Thus, in the perspective of these proponents, democracy, far from being a cure, is actually a nuisance. And, since democracy cannot reshape Leninist political culture, one paradoxical implication is that economic reforms may better be driven by yet another iron hand.[3]

But why point the finger at "uncivic" voters? Voters respond to what post-communist officials and organized politics present them with, and whether they are willing to accept collective sacrifices may well be a function of whether they are, in fact, collectively heard. Reciprocally, the sustainability of painful reforms rests on the ability of democratic reformers to build stable coalitions of political support.[4] To be sure, the scenario, in this regard, is not reassuring. It points to flux and uncertainty in organized politics, and that is where presently the problem lies.[5]

On one side, there is no escaping the special, almost unique, difficulties post-communist democracies face in reconstructing aggregative systems of political representation. Owing to their collectivist economies and to efforts to uproot civil society, "eastern social systems seem very 'amorphous' in their structures and it is difficult to imagine how the parties and interest associations that are characteristic of all types of 'western' democracy could emerge, stabilize their respective publics and contribute to the general consolidation of the regimes" (Schmitter and Karl, 1994, pp. 179–80). Under these conditions, parties and representation become fragmented and government action may fall prey to indecision, internal divisions, and drift (Körösényi, 1994). None of this encourages popular confidence in the steadiness of policy action.

On the other side, there is also evidence that, for a host of subjective and objective reasons – including the lack of reconstituted and reliable institutional routines in state and society, but also the pressure of international agencies and impatience with self-regarding citizens – harried post-communist policy makers choose to work from above, on matters of economic reform, by adopting decisions that depend on technical know-how and by-pass the search for consultative and representative channels. In fact, the very fact that organized interests and representative institutions are originally weak and fragmented may offer opportunities for executive action. But none of this improves the prospects of popular support. If voters are confronted with a distant and technocratic style of politics – one that does without democratic accountability precisely at a moment when civil society and the structures of representation need reconstruction – the consequence may be a self-fulfilling prophecy: a depletion of that trust and civic-mindedness the effects of which concern reformers. Popular demobilization, or populist resentment, may ensue. It may not happen immediately. One reason is that public opinion may temporarily put up with emergency executive measures, the more so if the economic crisis is particularly serious. But it may happen in the medium term. In the medium term, popular demobilization debases democratic institutions, and so does populist resentment.

As Przeworski (1995, p. 85) put it: "It is precisely the strength of democratic institutions, not exhortations by technocrats, that reduces the political space for the pursuit of immediate particularistic interests, for 'populism.' 'Populism' is to a large extent an endogenous product of technocratic policy styles." Thus, if the cultural legacy of Leninism is hard to remove, this is not because democracy naturally favors self-regarding behavior. On the contrary, it is democracy's present institutional limits and defects that, in a negative synergy, give new reason to the civically unsuitable habits of the past. I am reminded of John Hall (1995, p. 93): without public voice – without, that is, effective citizenship and a state that facilitates it – trust in government, and similarly trust in each other and a sense of community, wilt.

In fairness to liberal reformers, I must stress again that reformers – often dissidents catapulted to precarious political office – may have little to go by in the way of established routines, binding institutions, and supportive officialdom. Even where the unity of the national state is not threatened, uncertainty and flux hamper the capacities and priorities of the state. The defects of the post-communist states may be magnified by the processes of economic globalization. But they also have older roots: as Miles Kahler (1990) remarks, market reform paradoxically requires a capable state; such was not the communist state.

Communist institutions long accustomed to central guidance, sameness and uniformity, feigned compliance or philistine avoidance, are not easy to resocialize, especially under the pressure of compounded emergencies. They are not made to deal with crises. Behind the *étatiste* traditions of collectivist economies there is, in effect, a very primitive and poorly articulated administrative state, highly fragmented into a series of mutually indifferent corporate bailiwicks (Murrell and Olson, 1991) and substantially weak. A state that does everything by itself, that monopolizes the entire economic cycle, from the recruitment of human and material resources to production and distribution, turns ironically into an undifferentiated entity, without internal (let alone external) checks, balances, and feedbacks. Its internal coordination, although presumably essential to a collectivist economy, can be more easily faked. Precisely because it is primitive, it can run undisturbed much more easily than a state that is called to implement, through complex processes of mediation and legal articulation, an open market. For one thing, if a collectivist state does poorly, nobody is there to control and redress its performance, except by occasional summary banishment of the culprits: hardly a tool of policy innovation. After all, the collectivist test of performance is not qualitative innovation but quantitative delivery, meeting assigned quotas.

It is not difficult then to imagine what may happen when a state apparatus, used to doing everything alone, poorly, and by faking, is called to act in concert with others. Since this state lacks the appropriate know-how and institutional norms, since this happens while the state apparatus suffers from material and status deprivation, its likely responses are mounting incompetence, or indifference, or downright resistance, or some combination thereof.

Given all of this, the new governing class, poorly served by the inherited state and itself of recent extraction, may be induced to adopt, as Valerie Bunce and Maria Csanadi note (1993), a technocratic style of government propelled by improvisation, reactivism, and a self-generating agenda of priorities. In this climate of emergency, there seems to be precious little time for building organizational linkages between government and the people. Hence a vicious circle.

The predicament can be particularly serious when it comes to the consolidation of the initial shock-therapy reforms.[6] When it comes instead to the initial reforms, post-communist democracies may have some advantages. The argument is that painful economic reforms are less likely to find resistance among constituencies of the old regime if the break with the past has been, factually and morally, particularly sharp, if the old economic model has lost all credibility, if the economic crisis inherited from the old regime has been particularly serious and systemic, if people and constituencies are convinced that its seriousness warrants sacrifices, if further the market recipe is generally seen not just as an emergency measure, an interlude, but as an integral part of the democratic blueprint. On all these grounds, most post-communist democracies may do better than Latin American democracies, where the cultural, economic, and political break with the past has been generally less sharp and extensive, where old parties have survived, and where the economic crisis has at times appeared to be the less worrisome effect of politico-economic contingencies. In comparison, widespread institutional confusion and disarray may provide post-communist reformers with a higher degree of beneficial insulation for the initial and more painful reforms (Nelson, 1994). On the other hand, the more total disarray and obsolescence of the post-communist state could be of no help, but on the contrary may turn into an added serious impediment when it comes to the final task of institutionalizing economic reforms, and inscribing them within the democratic blueprint. To modernize economies which, despite the break, are still largely statist and primitive, to build sustainable national economies, to integrate them in a new global economy, to go in sum past the initial shock therapy, are tasks that government reformers may not be able to carry out without the aid of an already and swiftly reformed state.[7]

To summarize, the predicament of post-communist democracies is as follows. The market is not self-generated and cannot be improvised because it is a legal-political construction. Such a construction requires first of all a state that possesses the legal culture and the experience of interaction with civil society within which the market can emerge. This is where the post-communist state (and in different ways the Latin American state) is defective. Unquestionably, a democratic state will in the long run tend to gain from a healthy competitive economy. It will gain in fiscal and financial resources, in public expenditures, in debt management, in the ability to select investment priorities, in the very pursuit of collective civic tasks that are not within the competence of the market. But that liberalized economy is not yet in place. Meanwhile, precisely because the push to create the market inevitably taxes the limited or indeed distorted capabilities of the unreformed post-communist state, it strains the wider triangulation, state–market–citizen. Market and globalization processes are running ahead of the post-communist state's capacity to reconstitute that triangulation: to recruit its citizens to the transparency of the market by equipping them politically against its injustices.

But there is more. Where the triangulation is defective, mininationalisms may step in and try to exit from the predicament by redrawing national identities and political maps. They may find space especially if a vacuum is created by the absence of an early constitutional founding moment (Ackerman, 1992, chapter 4). Mininationalisms further erode the prospective authority of a new democratic state, by factually preventing its performance in the peripheries and by claiming to define who is a citizen of what. In other words, although mininationalisms may not be the first cause of the faltering of state capacities, they have a reinforcing, potentially ravaging, effect. Their rise is aided by the objective difficulties which the state meets in reconstituting a devastated associational life, difficulties also fed by the unavoidable disarray-cum-obsolescence of state routines and by the emergencies created by forced marketization and economic globalization. In this context of constitutional debility, compounded with material scarcity and emerging inequalities, mininationalisms (somewhat similarly to the naked marketization recipe) offer a metademocratic quick fix to the classical democratic issue of "who gets what, when, and how." Winners shall take all. Thus mininationalisms expel other sources of legitimate conflict, provide a non-competitive solution to the problem of unequal access to scarce goods, and legitimize an exclusionary and "cleansed" social order in place of an inclusionary civil society. They propose an exit from modernity.

I close with two closely connected paradoxes. Although markets are often friendly to civil society, the process of establishing them is at present threatening to undermine it. Although markets are supposedly ontological enemies of mininationalisms, the same process is at present unwittingly nurturing them. But all paradoxes have a resolution: they are incomplete analyses that leave something out. In our case, they leave out the state, a key player which is also undergoing a transition.

Latin American democracies: markets, states, and citizenship

Is Latin America different? In some ways it is not; save for mininationalisms, much of what I have just said, about markets and citizenship in post-communist states, applies. In some ways it is, so that both the objective issues and the political discourse that publicize them show regional specificities. In Latin America, conflict and social inequalities are inherited. And unlike communist regimes in their Leninist phase, Latin American dictatorships did not so much aim at removing the causes of inequalities as at repressing their "subversive" effects by repressing the less-equals – bloodily, but also with scarce results.

Because of this, because Latin American dictatorships, especially in their more recent bureaucratic-authoritarian incarnation, relied upon privileged social and institutional coalitions and upon political economies with often unpopular redistributive effects, because at the same time they tolerated some opposition from selected groups, it follows that in that region open conflict, even under repressive regimes, shows an endemic quality. By comparison, conflict in communist countries was sporadic. Therefore the new Latin American democracies (and similarly the old ones) combine inherited historical inequalities with inequalities induced by the coalition policies of the dictatorships. In this sense, Latin American transitions have been socially conservative transitions, where electoral democracy – the right of the people to choose their governors and hold them accountable – goes together with the survival of politically depleting injustices and inequalities rooted in both the old societies and the old regimes. It goes together with the survival of a Latin American state whose viability as a facilitator of citizenship has always been in question.

With few exceptions, in South and especially Central America we range from cases where the state as a lawful institution, providing personal safety and a minimum of services, has been only intermittently present in its territorial and social peripheries, to cases where the state has practiced lawlessness in more or less competitive cohabitation with privatized extralegal powers. Also, an intermittent state has tended to coexist with an internally fragmented national economy emphasizing disequalities and marginalization. This is not to say that state and economy have never offered protection to the dispossessed. It is to say that they have offered the conditional protection of patronage and political dependency within localized markets, not the universal protection of constitutional empowerment within national economies.

True, advocates of stabilization and liberalization look at them as correctives of this predicament: when competitive markets operate, the state shall no longer nurture rent seeking among the "haves" and political dependency among the "have-nots." The implication is that Latin American societies should then move in a more promising constitutional direction, where citizenship is sustained and expanded. However, crucial as the market may be to the formation of democratic state institutions, such matters as the exact shape and functioning of these institutions, the relations they will entertain with society, the policies of relevance to citizenship they will foster, the accountability of democratic institutions, their viability, do not depend on the market alone. The market is insufficiently determinative in regard to these matters. And, in matters of citizenship, its initial effects may be deleterious. Thus to announce a beneficial spillover from market to citizenship is premature. Getting "there" remains the problem.

Even when needed stabilization reforms are being implemented, the spillover requires a parallel transformation: a state that is already reformed or oriented toward reforming itself – both in its administrative capacities and in its democratic accountability. Otherwise, economic reforms may aggravate, instead of relieve, the inherited defects of the state, further eroding public arenas and public trust.[8] In turn, all of this may have the paradoxical effect of rendering market reforms themselves less sustainable: they too need a capable state to stabilize them.

Unless a demanding intellectual and material investment in rethinking state tasks and reforming state and state-relevant institutions (political parties in particular) accompanies it, economic liberalization is likely to encourage and perpetuate, in the territorial and social peripheries of Latin American societies, what Kiren Chaudhry (1993) calls fragmented jurisdictions. They are fragmented because the authority of the state arrives there with different, often muffled, intensity; or because the dominion exercised upon those peripheries is not that of the state but that of alternative enclaves of power. These enclaves may be constituted by fractions of the state and/or coalitions of extralegal local interests, possibly allied with international networks. The alliances may be engaged in the international economy, in mass international tourism, but also in organized crime, drug trafficking, the sale of arms, the export of terrorism, or the gainful dilapidation of tropical forests and other precious patrimonies.

Guillermo O'Donnell (1993) has also focused attention on the phenomenon of fragmented jurisdictions in Latin America. He reminds us that not all democratic states enjoy the same degree of homogeneous lawful presence in the territory and hierarchies of society, and that, when the state is absent, alternative power seekers, often fragments of the state, take over. It is not coincidental, he remarks, that the Latin American countries with a more solid democratic tradition are also those where the presence of the state has been more homogeneous.

Here, then, is an instructive contrast with the post-war democratic reconstructions of Western Europe. In the first place, homogeneous states with at least a modicum of constitutional traditions had existed there before the dictatorships. To quote myself (Di Palma, 1990, pp. 94–5), these "constitutional traditions construed the state as the impersonal carrier of specified public functions, indeed duties, in the continuous determination, allocation, and delivery of collective goods . . . [T]hey [were] . . . traditions anchored to notions of professionalism, legalism, impartiality, continuity of service, and institutional autonomy from partisan politics – that is, to notions that, myth or substance, are central to democracy as well." This legacy facilitated the reconstitution of homogeneous constitutional states after the war. A partial and instructive exception is Italy, where precisely the relative weakness of the national state in the Italian South, before and after the war, is partially responsible for the spreading of political corruption and eventually the political colonization of much of the region by organized crime. It is also one of the factors in the present crisis of the country's post-war democratic model.

In the second place, the immediate economic agendas of post-war democracies were rather straightforward and comfortably predictable. Mostly, they were agendas of national economic reconstruction after defeat and demobilization. They were formulated within already existing and collectively guaranteed international economic and financial regimes, rather than in defensive – and defenseless – reaction to shifting economic regimes. They were politically and materially sponsored by the United States in a promising context of international solidarity and emerging regional integration. And they were agendas driven by the national states; indeed, agendas that gave the reconstituted democratic states a new leeway and new opportunities eventually to reconfigure their national economic policies and their societal coalitions. All of this assisted comfortable economic growth and also encouraged the reconstitution of collective actors (a civil society) with a stake in democracy, which finally puts in greater relief the reasons why the reconstitution of collective actors in Latin American democracies turns out to be, given the special domestic and international circumstances, a much more demanding endeavor.

Yet, to return to Latin America, more troubling than politically and socially costly neoliberalism (neoliberalism unaccompanied by civic and constitutional reform) is the prospect of neoliberalism failing or faltering. As dissatisfied as people may be about socially costly economic reforms, dissatisfaction may be even greater if reforms are slowed down, for it is not social concerns but most likely narrow particularisms that will slow them down. And citizenship does not stand to gain.

The prospect of neoliberalism failing or faltering is not at all inconceivable in the Latin American state. One reason is resistance by adversely affected constituencies; the same constituencies that may also resist constitutional reform. What I have in mind is not the resistance of popular strata. Although these may suffer in the short run from policies of economic retrenchment, they may also have insufficiently focused resources and alternatives, or insufficient reasons, to organize significant opposition (Geddes, 1994b). I have in mind the more significant resistance of dominant rent-seeking constituencies and their patrons in the state. It is this resistance that goes to the core of the problem. Without elaborating,[9] it stands to reason that state institutions and government cadres that can best afford to act independently of dominant rent-seeking groups, and with a longer time perspective, can better implement painful economic reforms. Therefore, it is not surprising that, for instance, the developmental states of Asia are in a better position to pursue neoliberal policies that redefine their very role than the patrimonialized, or downright predatory (Evans, 1989) states of Latin America. Thus we are back to the state.

Although not insurmountable,[10] resistance to reform coming from the institutional core is an obstacle whose effect on the economy, but also on democracy and its constitutional peripheries, can be quite deleterious. This should be true irrespective of whether resistance is against emergency stabilization measures or against the long-range reforms designed to institutionalize the neoliberal model. In the first case, resistance may be less likely or less successful, because stabilization may appear necessary, its costs may be dispersed, and the administrative enactment of stabilization policies does not demand the mobilization of political support (Maravall, 1994). Still, were resistance to occur, its immediate consequences would be intuitively devastating. And, in the second case, the failure to institutionalize reforms would make the effects of stabilization ephemeral: economic reforms would become less sustainable. In both cases, a faltering liberalization sets in the following scenario: (1) the economy stagnates even more (or again), while inflation and public debt mount; (2) social reforms are still absent, because the state is still intermittent and the economic crisis subtracts resources; (3) rent-seeking continues to be protected by fractions of the state that resist liberalization.

In this social and economic scenario, a perverse cycle takes hold, whereby everyone, expecting the worse possible behavior from everyone else, i.e., behavior that discounts others, behaves perversely. Those who can, scramble for particularistic short-term gains, mostly by taking advantage of a state apparatus that remains porous and clientelized. This heightens the sense of injustice and powerlessness among those whom the clientelistic scramble leaves unprotected. Overall, society is progressively disarticulated and atomized. As de Tocqueville (1955, p. 107) remarked about French society under absolutism, its members are taken to meet on their "sore spots." Trust in government and in each other declines. Collective, long-range, strategies to address the crisis are squeezed out, and coming out of the crisis becomes even more difficult.

When this point is reached, where the economic crisis appears more and more to be embedded in the nature of the unreformed state, curbing the crisis is no longer a problem of finding technically correct economic reforms. Well-designed as economic reforms may be, their success, being finally a matter of implementation and reception, always implies an underlying social contract. But that contract may be fading in the presence of a spiraling economic crisis. A similar point is made, in reference to inflation, by Albert Hirschman. Fighting contemporary inflation requires altering a collective attitude which is ultimately responsible for the embeddedness of inflation. It is an attitude that, while aware of the collective damages of inflation, is not ready to make sacrifices for its removal. As Hirschman (1981b, pp. 301–2) describes the attitude: "inflation reflects increasing combativeness or . . . 'bloody-mindedness' on the part of various social groups that have heretofore been viewed . . . as 'cooperating' in the generation and distribution of the social product." To remove this attitude, a "new social contract" is needed. I call it trust, for it would require mutual sacrifices in exchange for future equitable returns. Joan Nelson (1994, p. 19) speaks of the need for a "positive consensus."

But a social contract needs recognizable *collective* contractors to begin with. These contractors are more likely to exist in the old democracies, but even there they have not agreed so easily on the issue of inflation. It does not take much to understand how a new social contract is much more difficult to fashion and monitor in much of Latin America. The task of fashioning it falls on civil society as well as on the new democratic state. The prospective contractors are indeed located in civil society, but they are presently fragmented, have unequal resources, and are unequally represented. Indeed, it is the very fact that market-oriented reforms are stymied which is in part responsible for the present predicament of civil society: the failure of new collective forces (parties, organized interests) to emerge fully in an open competitive economy and the survival of traditional protected interests. That leaves the state, but the state exhibits those incapacities which, I just suggested, are likely to stymie necessary economic reforms to begin with. Under such conditions, chances are that Hirschman's "bloody-mindedness" will remain a popular response.

Yet, without institutional innovation, there is no way out. The prospects of successful economic reforms, especially long-range reforms capable of engaging and benefitting society and politics, do not rest on economic know-how and technical expertise.[11] Those prospects rest on a social contract. And the reconstitution of that contract rests on the reconstitution of political institutions lodged in civil society and the state. I have just indicated the great obstacles that exist, in the state itself and in state-dependent sectors of civil and political society, to institutional innovation. There are other obstacles as well. Most important is the fact that institutional innovation does not always produce the policy innovations it promises and that policy innovations take time to produce stable material and civil results. One faint ray of hope is offered by the following consideration. Despite the obstacles, the manipulation of political institutions and institutional incentives – in sum, constitutional engineering – is not only more immediately consequential for democracy than the alteration of market institutions, it also happens to be, in terms of know-how about its behavioural consequences and incentives, comparatively easier (Sartori, 1994).

I close with two comments that tie the Latin American case to that of the post-communist countries.

First, it is sanctimonious to chastise the voters for lack of civic spirit – especially those voters who, unprotected by the state, remain at the margins. If the state is not able or willing to forge a social contract, it is not the voters's fault if there is no exit from the perverse cycle that atomizes society.

Second, it follows from this that government impulses to respond to the emergencies of the situation, including those produced by the old and new incapacities of the state, by adopting technocratic forms of *decisionismo*, or what Guillermo O'Donnell (1994) refers to as delegative democracy, do not offer a solution. By ignoring the long-range need for a stable social contract among recognizable collective actors, *decisionismo* feeds the fever it wishes to bring down, in society and in the state. Nor, in addition, should we ignore the very distinctive possibility that, in Latin America, *decisionismo*, with its corollary of *personalismo* and plebiscitarianism, more than being a necessary but possibly temporary shocktherapy response to the lack of a stable social contract, may be its well-rooted historical antecedent: a style of politics both reflecting and feeding the poverty and volatility of institutions, and thus finally undermining, rather than sustaining, needed government autonomy. This is one of the reasons behind the recent debate on the failures of presidentialism in Latin America (Linz and Valenzuela, 1994).

Although Sparta cries, Athens does not laugh

It could be argued, not without very good reasons, that the difficulties which many of the new democracies are facing with regard to the reconstitution of a working relation between citizenship, the state, and the market are contingent, as well as specific. They result from the necessarily strenuous process of democratic transition and consolidation, as well as from the new democracies' particularly unfortunate legacies. In so concluding, however, we would overlook the fact that, as I suggested, some of the factors that account for the difficulties faced by those democracies are presumably global, "deeper," and most likely enduring. The crisis of the welfare accommodation, to which I referred at the beginning of this chapter, manifested itself first in the old democracies of the West. Already in the late sixties and seventies, social scientists were speaking of a crisis of democratic governability or a crisis of over-extension (Crozier *et al.*, 1975). Such crisis, and the resulting discredit of the democratic state, have only been compounded by more recent developments.

It follows that the best evidence on the effective role of global factors should be garnered precisely from the study of old democracies. Unlike new democracies, they possess institutional and constitutional routines that have proved enduring and are not easy to dislodge. Yet let me point out in these conclusions that it is these routines as much as substantive performance – processes as much as outcomes – which are nowadays at issue. There exists an institutional problem, in the old democracies as well as in the new ones. I can hardly think of another period in history during which political actors and social scientists have paid more atten-tion to institutional engineering.[12] The fact is suggestive and invites us to look for commonalities in causes and manifestations.

As to manifestations, there seems to be a shift toward some similar institutional patterns among old and new democracies. If new democ-racies seem to resort to a delegative style of government (O'Donnell, 1994) Western democracies show some signs of convergence toward an "American" style of government that uneasily combines delegative with plebiscitarian aspects. The convergence has been commented upon by Jack Citrin (1994).

The convergence presents a number of features that are admittedly puzzling but not necessarily contrasting. Two of them intend to take power away from national representative and state institutions and return it to the voters. One is what we may call *poll democracy*: the spreading use, likely to reinforce divisions, of popular referenda and initiatives to decide divisive issues. The other, to borrow from Hanna Pitkin's concept of descriptive representation (1967, p. 60), is *descriptive democracy*: increasingly, voters do not vote for parties but for persons, preferably close to them and their community because of residence or professional and social background. Conversely, elected officials do not respond to distant national electorates and agendas but to electorates identified by local residence or other common background. Thus representation is demographic and local: one gets elected to represent one's own. A third feature is, to borrow from O'Donnell (1994), *delegative democracy*: a trend toward greater and more personalized executive rule (line-item veto, direct election of more powerful presidents or prime ministers). Although seemingly intended to concentrate power at the top, this feature is not necessarily at loggerheads with the first two. It is itself a way of circumventing representative and bureaucratic institutions which are perceived as distant, slow, and befogging. It is a way of placing democracy in the hands of people who are recognizably "like us." Similarly, a fourth feature of institutional convergence removes a series of crucial distributive issues from the competitive arena, as well as from the agenda of mediating institutions, on the principle that one cannot trust delivery from politicians whom one has not personally elected. Thus I refer to this feature as *preempted democracy*: the adoption of decisional rules and other devices designed to freeze or precommit the initiative of the government and the governed alike (special majorities, balanced budgets, mandated expenditures, earmarked revenues, quotas, group entitlements). Popular initiatives and referenda may also belong in this category. True, some of these devices (special majorities, balanced budgets) seem anti-statist, the others seem statist and redistributive. But the real point of all these devices is their shared discomfort with the uncertain outcomes of an open democratic game and a continuous give and take. That the rules of the game are certain, and that the state is called to sustain them, no longer seems to be quite as reassuring.

These shared institutional trends allow, as a conclusion, three tentative suggestions that embrace Western democracies as well. They concern the nature of the common malaise, its common causes, and the role of institutions in addressing (or compounding) the malaise.

1 As to the nature of the malaise, I have already suggested that Western democracies lend themselves better than new democracies to the argument that the malaise may not be contingent. In the West, the malaise seems to reflect a contentious redefinition of the boundaries of citizenship and civil society – what they include and what they keep out. To put it bluntly, we may be witnessing an escalation of Hirschman's "bloody-mindedness," the coming apart of confidence in mutually decent behavior – a confidence which, under the aegis of a well-bounded and trusted state, often managed to keep together the haves and the have-nots, the main-streamers and the marginals. In the new democracies, the malaise and the contentiousness are natural when at issue is

the construction of civil societies where they were hardly present. But here too some of the reasons are not contingent but global.

2 As to the deeper global springs of the malaise, they may be located in the fact that, in the old as well as the new democracies, the territorial and functional jurisdictions of the state are presently in flux. Often propelled by diffusion, the causes are the same for all democracies: the end of communism, the stretching of democracy beyond its old borders, unprecedented demographic movements, processes of globalization of markets, but also of politics and culture. Where conditions are not favorable, all of these changes may converge to crowd people backward into a global village: borderless, cacophonous, without narratives. A global overcrowded village encourages exclusion and separation. It encourages defensive reaffirmation of territorial, cultural, and functional identities – mine against yours. It encourages self-naming and name-calling. One problematic manifestation in Western democracies is the emergence of a new class of marginalized people: migrants, political and economic refugees, ethnics, the dwellers of inner cities or other constitutional peripheries, and other apparently redundant and parasitic groups. These new marginal classes are often seen as the carriers of cultural stigmata that invite exclusion on one side and, in reaction, a new politics of group entitlements on the other. These developments may manifest themselves in Western and non-Western democracies with importantly different intensities. But at issue is always citizenship, identity, and the state.

3 As to the role of state institutions in addressing (or compounding) the malaise, I submit that, although institutions are not prime causes, they are in turn consequential. Recognizing that the malaise is somehow present across old and new democracies, despite institutional (and other) differences, is insufficient to dismiss institutions. With regard to new democracies, I have indicated that neither civil society nor the market are self-generated. I have placed the task of reconstituting both of them on the state and argued, therefore, for the priority of a virtuous constitutional moment (Ackerman, 1992). But I have also pointed out the strenuousness of the task. Such is the institutional deficit in the new democracies. In the case of the old democracies, the institutional deficit is of a different kind. There, rules and institutions have been in place for a long time. But I have suggested a converging trend toward a relatively new style of politics that is both plebiscitarian and delegative, and also suggested that its effects are less than beneficial. Far from being

an inventive response to the malaise, the trend may be seen as a symptom and indeed a compounding reflection of the malaise. Among Western democracies, the subject of the malaise is most clearly civil society, its boundaries and identities. The reason is the comparatively greater ability of advanced industrial democracies to adjust to, in fact to drive, globalization. Hence, however, the disruptive effects on civil society. At issue, more than markets, is civil society. And the weight of the issue is reflected in the fact that the reported institutional trends are no cure. Under the thin guise of strengthening democratic resolve, so as presumably better to face the added complexities of the new global moment, the trends reflect a defensive democratic distemper. They reflect the weakening and discredit of (at least) two essential mediating institutions designed, under the old welfare accommodation, to make the competitive game an inclusive one as well: the political parties and the national state. In the worst scenarios, those institutions are now at greater risk of being short circuited, of being replaced by mechanisms of representation and decision making that may help make the arena of civil society more fragmented and less competitive, more precommitted and less deliberative, more feudalized as well as less equal and inclusive, more demanding of politicians and yet more distant and distrustful.

In view of what I suggested in these tentative conclusions, founding or refounding democratic institutions appears a very hard priority. But a priority nonetheless.

NOTES

1 On the role of ideas in the creation of new policy paradigms, see Peter Hall (1989).
2 On this point see the closing remarks in Victor Zaslavsky (1994). However, Zaslavsky also argues that resistance to economic reform programs has been tamed by acceptance of the irreversibility of reforms, the growing depoliticization of society, and everyday adaptation to crisis.
3 But arguments in favor of economic reforms before democratization have been shown to be overgeneralized and untenable. An exhaustive review of the critical literature is in Larry Diamond (1995).
4 Although their work is not devoted to post-communist democracies, the most exhaustive analysis of this point is found in Haggard and Kaufman (1995).
5 But it is still a scenario open to operational solutions, the way a scenario built on cultural debasement is not.
6 For the distinction between shock therapy reforms aiming at economic stabilization and reforms aimed at institutionalizing a new market economy see Naím (1994).
7 I am therefore suggesting that the same period of "extraordinary politics"

(Balcerowicz 1994) that may favor early on single-handed technocratic shock therapy of the economy also opens a window of opportunity for the wider organizational and political reform of the state before nomenklaturas regroup and the new political forces start counting and differentiating each other.

8 In one extreme scenario, the pressures of economic reform, by inducing reformers to short-circuit democratic accountability, may cause populist resistance by already weak and fragmented representative institutions, triggering in turn a defensive slide into illiberal politics. The case of Peru under Alberto Fujimori comes to mind.

9 The elaborations are in Barbara Geddes (1994c, pp. 12–13).

10 On the institutional incentives to surmount resistance, see Geddes (1994c, chapters 5, 6).

11 To be sure, emergency stabilization measures have been successfully implemented in Latin America when economic crises have hit rock bottom. In the case of Argentina, when Menem replaced Alfonsín as president, and in other cases, *personalismo* and plebiscitarian appeals proved sufficient to build a mandate that presidents, once elected, relied upon to introduce unannounced and painful emergency measures (Geddes 1994b). But *personalismo* is not sufficient to consolidate reforms.

12 In addition to the already cited Sartori (1994) and Linz and Valenzuela (1994), see Lijphart (1992, 1995), Grofman and Lijphart (1986), Shugart and Carey (1992), Taagepera and Shugart (1989), Diamond and Plattner (1993, part II), Cain and Noll (1995).

13 Conclusion: Paradoxes of democracy

Manus I. Midlarsky

To conclude this wide-ranging interdisciplinary exploration of democracy and its important correlates, I will concentrate now on the nexus between inequality and democracy, the analytical base of the original conference. What have we learned? Clearly, this relationship was found to be complex with both positive and negative associations developed between various forms of inequality and measures of democracy. While Crenshaw and I found positive associations between land inequality and measures of democracy, Ember, Ember, and Russett as well as Muller, found negative associations, albeit using different forms of inequality, respectively, a social stratification measure and income inequality. Both Greskovits and Di Palma imply that the more sanguine prognosis for newly emergent democracies in Eastern Europe in comparison with those of Latin America stems from the much more egalitarian condition of the former societies as they emerged from communism in comparison with the still remaining strong inequalities of the latter.

Other chapters present mixed implications, if not direct findings, that reflect on this relationship. In confirming the greater equality in political participation found in hunter-gatherer societies when compared with ancient Athens, Bollen and Paxton indirectly confirm the importance of inequality in the structure of Athenian democracy, a prototype for later Western democracies. Nee's finding of a positive association between the reliance on markets and increased inequality suggests a contemporary variant of an embedded and endemic inequality within democracy; democracies almost always have market economies.

On the other hand, the importance of literacy to democratic development emphasized by Simpson, has opposite implications, for literacy is a great leveler of inequalities, even as it enhances democracy. Similarly, the association between a decline in real wage growth and transitions away from democracy found by Gasiorowski suggests a transition away from an equality that almost always is stimulated by wage increases, as democracy decreases. Reversing the causal direction, Chan's analysis implies the increased equality for new democracies that would come after increased spending on education, the great leveler of inequalities. Coppedge's discovery of a common path to democracy suggests that whatever the outcomes of these differing findings and implications concerning inequality and democracy, they will very likely be relevant to virtually all instances of democratic development.

How do we reconcile these divergent if not contradictory views? Perhaps stating the paradox and finding some resolution will be helpful. A paradox of democracy is that a certain degree of inequality may be required for the initiation and maintenance of democracy, yet if the inequality is extreme it can result in the failure of democracy, once initiated, or even the prevention of its introduction altogether.

At the outset, it must be emphasized that the robust finding of a positive relationship between land inequality and political rights probably signifies an element of state strength or at least elite security that in older, more mature conquest civilizations (e.g., England, Argentina), there existed the opportunity to establish a secure class of landed elites who, without serious challenge to their authority could later yield small political rights that eventually would mushroom into more encompassing ones. Thus elite security as measured by land inequality may be the operative variable.[1] Nevertheless, this response still begs the question, for to maintain a secure elite, by definition, some inequalities must exist between the elite and the mass of the population and so the paradox persists.

If, on the other hand, we take the view that there may be more complex relationships between inequality and democracy than simply positive or negative monotonic variants, then the paradox may lend itself to resolution. Consider the possibility of an inverted U-function for the relationship between inequality and democracy, shown in figure 1. To generalize the variable across time beyond land inequality and to avoid conflating with income inequality that likely has different correlates (Midlarsky, 1992a), let this variable be inequality in wealth. Large differentials in wealth generally result from ownership of the principal modes of production, as was land in the preindustrial era, and so this is an appropriate, albeit approximate generalization. Although only the portion to the left of the curve, denoted by a solid line, received empirical confirmation, it is more than likely that the dotted portion to the right, not confirmed empirically here, held sway during much of historical time prior to the contemporary period. Centralized monarchies, feudal monarchies, and other strongly hierarchical political schema clearly limited the political rights of their citizenry. Thus on the right-hand portion of the curve, the greater the inequality the smaller the extent of democracy.

Still, even in the face of the passing of absolutist monarchies, there

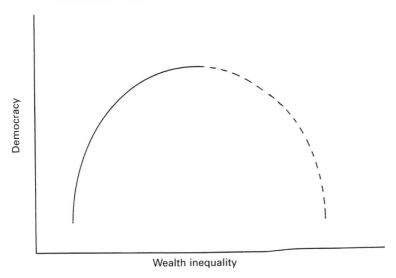

Figure 13.1 Relationship between inequality and democracy

should be some evidence of the negative impact of inequality on democracy implied by the right-hand portion of the curve, if only in the residues of inordinately larger landholdings by the *ancien* elite. Until the dawn of the modern period, this certainly would have been true, except for the prevalence of some form of land reform in many of the world's countries since the end of World War II, the time period of systematic empirical analysis for most of the preceding chapters. Even England, that did not undergo an explicit land reform, effectively experienced one as the result of the post-war Labour government's redistributive policies and the impoverishment of the old nobility. However, these land reforms either were incomplete (witness Iran's under the Shah) or have been vitiated by a later burgeoning population growth that effectively undermined the earlier efforts as the result of land impoverishment and an emergent tenancy on larger holdings (Egypt, for example). Thus, contemporary holdings in many of the world's countries are far from egalitarian, but still not at the pre-twentieth-century levels of extraordinary inequality. Only communist countries, not examined in the empirics of chapter 3, had thoroughgoing land reforms (excepting Poland) that effectively were maintained until communism's collapse.

The paradox of cooperation

Equality of circumstance fosters cooperation (Deutsch, 1985). As Putnam (1993, p. 170) concluded in his comparison between the civic regions of Italy that functioned best democratically and those that functioned least well such as Naples, in the civic regions: "Cooperation is often required – between legislature and executive, between workers and managers, among political parties, between the government and private groups, among small firms, and so on." At the same time, a certain degree of inequality appears to be necessary for a functioning democracy. Although related to the first paradox of inequality, it is not easily resolvable by the positing of a relationship as in figure 1. The difficulty here is that the choice of a point on the curve that maximizes democracy, somewhere around the maximum (curving point of inflection) would not guarantee the cooperation needed to maintain a functioning democracy. Hence, the cooperation necessary for the maintenance of democracy may be undermined by the existence of inequality necessary for its initiation. This may be one reason, among many, for the small number of democracies historically, at least outside of the contemporary period.

In a multicultural society, even small economic differences between groups can minimize cooperation. The recent disclosures of deep discontent among the African-American middle class (Cose, 1993) even when confronted with only small economic and social differences is a case in point. Such discontent can appear in the deeply divergent views on the guilt of an alleged murderer such as O.J. Simpson and be manifested overtly in an unwillingness to cooperate politically with whites to the same extent as with blacks. Of course, the more massive sorts of inequalities between the ghetto underclass and the remainder of society have given rise to a willingness to engage in social deviance of various types. That, in the long run can be equally corrosive to societal cooperation and hence to democracy.

The paradox of corruption

This third paradox of democracy may not easily present an analytic resolution. This issue concerns the tendency of contemporary democracies to have leaders who, if not corrupt, then do engage in practices that can be considered ethically dubious. The recent peccadillos of President Clinton, especially the Whitewater matter, Newt Gingrich and the House Committee on Ethics, the financial dealings of former Vice-President Spiro Agnew, and especially the nefarious activities of former President Nixon in the Watergate affair, suggest a pattern. Clearly one can condemn the moral climate of modern American life as a source of the corruption, but that is too facile an explanation. More to the point is an implication of the present analysis that modern leaders lack the influence that comes with large landholdings or other accoutrements of wealth. Without the large-scale material bases of influence, modern democratic leaders or indeed modern leaders generally, must resort to other methods of influence. Charisma, identified earlier by Max Weber, of course is one such method of influence, and organizational skill another. Interestingly, Leon Trotsky and Joseph Stalin, respectively employed these methods of influence. Stalin, as we know, was extraordinarily successful in his efforts, while for Trotsky, had he exerted his charisma more judiciously, for example, at Lenin's funeral at which he did not appear, the outcome of his conflict with Stalin might have been very different.

Soviet history provides a model *in extremis* of the basic argument, for here we have virtually no land inequality or other manifest distinguishing features among citizens of the polity and at the same time, no democracy. Failing the extraordinary oratorical skills of a Trotsky or the organizational abilities of a Stalin, the ordinary *apparatchik* had to resort to other, often more nefarious methods to ensure continued influence. Hence, corruption was a continued fact of life in communist bureaucratic systems, beyond the first blush of utopian visions in the 1920s.

Must modern democratic (and other) systems turn a blind eye to corrupt practices as the price of an increased egalitarianism in the modern age? This question has more than ethical significance although that, of course, is supremely important in itself. It touches on two areas of performance in democracies. First, there is the matter of corruption and the decline of the state, as exemplified by the history of the later Roman Empire prior to its fall (MacMullen, 1988). To be sure, in contrast to Rome, corrupt leaders in a democracy can be cast out of office, but if the culture of corruption is widespread, then the incumbent corrupt leader will simply be replaced by another of equally corrupt tendencies. Here corruption can imperil the very existence of the state for, in the extreme instance, major portions of the economy and society can simply be sold off to the highest or most threatening bidder. It is unlikely that barbarian armies will lay siege to the American polity, ultimately bringing it down as happened in the case of Rome. Instead, various officials responsible for the health of the polity (including immigration policy) could simply be bought off and no longer effectively guard the best interests of the people of the United States. Aldrich Ames, the Soviet spy in the CIA may be a case in point, for with large amounts of money as inducement, he was perfectly willing to sell the most closely guarded secrets to the Soviet Union, thus leading to the deaths of many American agents.

Second is the likely diminution of cooperation under conditions of even moderately widespread corruption. Only the corrupted would cooperate with each other, and then only as long as mutual benefits persist. "In-groups" and "out-groups" would be targeted by the criterion of who benefits from the corruption, with cooperation extending only to those defined within the in-group. And as we have seen, fairly widespread cooperation is essential for effective democratic functioning.

The paradox of environmental influence

It is indeed paradoxical that the practice of democracy which appears to be the quintessential volitional mode of governance is subject ofttimes to unyielding environmental constraints. Democracy is action oriented; it involves repeated choices and an ongoing participation by the electorate. Without the continual aggregation of individual choices, by whatever means (representative or participatory), democracy will simply cease to exist. It is no accident that the Greek *polis* was conceptualized essentially as a political community involving extreme cooperation, at least in political matters, and the continuing capacity to make public choices. As Farrar (1988, p. 155) puts it, "One reason why the *polis* is so important is that it can foster this capacity for interpretation and self-control, thereby increasing the likelihood of its own survival, and thus the survival and continued well-being of its citizens. . . ." Yet, the analysis of chapter 2 tells us that the threat of war can minimize democracy and, as we know, Athens, the originator of the type of thinking reflected in the previous quotation, succumbed to the threat and actuality of war, never to regain her former power and independence. The most volitional democratic polities, are circumscribed by environmental conditions of various sorts. Perhaps the most dangerous of these is the threat and actuality of war that can destroy the democratic polity.

The paradox of ideology

Democratic thinking is one of the oldest of political ideologies, reliant on basic political philosophies as old as the Sumerians and ancient Greeks, yet in its genesis is perhaps independent of any particular ideation. In the absence of any singular environmental constraints such as the threat of war, it may be perfectly natural for small communities to engage in collective decision making approximating a rudimentary participatory democracy. The ideology or philosophy of democracy may not be at all necessary for such a process to begin. Liberal democracy, on the other hand, may require a culture of democracy that is indeed reliant on an analytically developed justification for democratic rule. Thus, the origins of democracy are not to be found in any sort of democratic thinking or ideation, but in the absence of environmental constraints in unique cases that allowed the more primitive forms of democracy, common in many societies, to continue in several of them. Later of course, many writings emerged arguing for and justifying democracy, but as part of the culture of liberal democracy, a more recent development.

One can possibly interpret this sequence of ideation built upon an earlier material base as akin to the Marxian ideological superstructure built upon the economic base. Despite a superficial similarity, there is a fundamental difference. The Marxian view assumes that modification of the economic base (e.g., achieving a more equitable distribution of goods and services) will yield a more just and harmonious society, even to the point of approximating the infinite perfectibility of human beings. Hence, we witnessed the Soviet reluctance to release crime statistics. Here, on the other hand, the environment itself, in contrast to the economic base of Marx, admits to no facile tinkering or even major restructuring. Land borders, aridity, or a technoecological heritage can be accommodated by various political schemes, often authoritarian, but cannot be readily changed, even by draconian revolutionary methods. In this form, it is a far more pessimistic view and has a paradoxical core. A political ideology of public choice such as democracy may, in the final analysis, be conditional, at least in its origins, on constraints admitting little choice.

Although the paradox of ideology is analytically distinct from the paradox of the environment, there are certain areas of overlap. The paradox of ideology asserts the independence of early democracy from any ideological source, whereas that of the environment emphasizes the particular material influences on early democracy. Nevertheless, they are effectively two sides of the same coin. Given an absence of ideology in the development of early democracy, democratic practices must have emerged from some source or at least in the absence of constraint, here specified as environmental.

As a concluding and summary comment, it is probably sustainable democracy that is the issue of greatest importance now confronting both domestic and international politics. In emphasizing the etiologies of democracy as well as its contemporary sources and correlates, and especially the often complex relationships with inequality and economic development, it is hoped that we may have made some contribution to understanding the dimensions of this issue. How inequality in its various guises and manifestations feeds into the sustainability of democracy may be a key component of future analyses and investigations.

NOTES

1 Another process leading from land inequality to democracy may have occurred and in fact may be complementary to the first discussed in the text. The enlargement of estates in populated settings generally proceeds by means of the absorption of peasant holdings that, as a result of population increase and subdivision, are too small to be economically viable. The displaced peasant often moves to the city where large concentrations of such peasants then either organize politically or more frequently engage in protests or civil disorders that lead to concessions by the political authorities in the form of greater political rights. Thus, an increase in land inequality may have the second consequence of increasing urbanization which then leads to increased political participation and democracy. Alternatively, economic development may result from urbanization which, as we have seen, is strongly related to democracy.

References

Abromeit, Heidrun. 1986. "Privatisation in Great Britain." *Annales de l'Economie Publique, Sociale et Cooperative* 74: 153–80.

Ackerman, Bruce. 1992. *The Future of Liberal Revolution*. New Haven: Yale University Press.

Adams, David. 1983. "Why There Are So Few Women Warriors." *Behavior Science Research* 18: 196–212.

Adams, Richard E. W. 1991. *Prehistoric Mesoamerica*, rev. edn. Norman: University of Oklahoma Press.

Adams, Robert McC. 1966. *The Evolution of Urban Society: Early Mesopotamia and Prehispanic Mexico*. Chicago: Aldine.

Agh, Attila. 1991. "Transition to Democracy in East-Central Europe: A Comparative View." In *Democracy and Political Transformation: Theories and East-Central European Realities*, ed. György Szoboszlai. Budapest: Hungarian Political Science Association, pp. 103–22.

Agresti, Alan. 1984. *Analysis of Ordinal Categorical Data*. New York: Wiley.

Ahluwalia, Montek. 1974. "Dimensions of the Problem." In *Redistribution and Growth*, eds. Hollis B. Chenery *et al.* New York: Oxford University Press.

—— 1976a. "Income Distribution and Development: Some Stylized Facts." *American Economic Review* 66: 128–35.

—— 1976b. "Inequality, Poverty, and Development." *Journal of Development Economics* 3: 307–42.

Aiken, Leona S. and Stephen G. West. 1991. *Multiple Regression: Testing and Interpreting Interactions*. Newbury Park: Sage Publications.

Allison, Paul D. 1978. "Measures of Inequality." *American Sociological Review* 43: 865–80.

Almond, Gabriel. 1991. "Capitalism and Democracy." *PS: Political Science and Politics* 24: 467–74.

Almond, Gabriel and Sidney Verba. 1963. *The Civic Culture*. Princeton: Princeton University Press.

Ames, Barry. 1977. "The Politics of Public Spending in Latin America." *American Journal of Political Science* 21: 149–76.

—— 1987. *Political Survival: Politicians and Public Policy in Latin America*. Berkeley: University of California Press.

Amin, Samir. 1974. *Accumulation on a World Scale: A Critique of the Theory of Underdevelopment*. 2 vols. New York: Monthly Review Press.

—— 1976. *Unequal Development: An Essay on the Social Formations of Peripheral Capitalism*. New York: Monthly Review.

327

Arat, Zehra F. 1988. "Democracy and Economic Development: Modernization Theory Revisited." *Comparative Politics* 21: 21–36.

—— 1991. *Democracy and Human Rights in Developing Countries.* Boulder, CO: Lynne Rienner Publishers.

Armer, J. M. 1992. "Social Psychological Effects of Literacy by Language Combination in an African Society." *Sociological Inquiry* 62: 308–26.

Asian Development Center. 1992. *Key Indicators of Developing Asian and Pacific Countries.* Oxford: Oxford University Press.

Baechler, Jean. 1988. "The Origins of Modernity: Caste and Feudality (India, Europe and Japan)." In *Europe and the Rise of Capitalism*, eds. Jean Baechler, John A. Hall, and Michael Mann. Oxford: Basil Blackwell.

Bair, Frank E. 1992. *The Weather Almanac*, 6th edn. Detroit: Gale Research.

Bairoch, Paul. 1988. *Cities and Economic Development from the Dawn of History to the Present.* Chicago: University of Chicago Press.

Balcerowicz, Leszek. 1994. "Understanding Postcommunist Transitions." *Journal of Democracy* 5: 75–89.

Ballmer-Cao, Thanh-Huyen, and Juerg Scheidegger. 1979. *Compendium of Data for World System Analysis.* Bulletin of the Sociological Institute of the University of Zurich. March.

Banks, Arthur S. 1971. *A Cross-Polity Times Series.* Cambridge, MA: MIT Press.

—— 1979. *Cross-National Time-Series Data Archive: User's Manual*, rev. edn. Binghamton, NY: Center for Social Analysis, State University of New York at Binghamton.

Baran, Paul. 1957. *The Political Economy of Growth.* New York: Monthly Review Press.

Barbosa, Artemio. 1985. "The Ethnography of the Agta of Lamika, Penablanca, Cagayan." In *The Agta of Northeastern Luzon: Recent Studies*, eds. P. B. Griffin and Agnes Estioko-Griffin. Cebu City: San Carlos Publications.

Barnes, Samuel, Max Kaase *et al.* 1979. *Political Action: Mass Participation in Five Western Democracies.* Beverly Hills: Sage.

Barraclough, Geoffrey. 1984. *The Origins of Modern Germany.* New York: Norton.

Barrett, Richard E. and Martin K. Whyte. 1982. "Dependency Theory and Taiwan: Analysis of a Deviant Case." *American Journal of Sociology* 87: 1064–89.

Barry, Herbert III, Lili Josephson, Edith Lauer, and Catherine Marshall. 1980. "Traits Inculcated in Childhood: Cross-Cultural Codes." In *Cross Cultural Samples and Codes*, eds. Herbert Barry III and Alice Schlegel. Pittsburgh: University of Pittsburgh Press.

Bates, Robert H. 1981. *Markets and States in Tropical Africa: The Political Basis of Agricultural Policies.* Berkeley: University of California Press.

Beck, Ulrich. 1994. "The Reinvention of Politics: Towards a Theory of Reflexive Modernization." In *Reflexive Modernization: Politics, Traditions and Aesthetics in the Modern Social Order*, eds. Ulrich Beck, Anthony Giddens, and Scott Lash. Stanford: Stanford University Press, pp. 1–56.

Begler, E. 1978. "Sex, Status and Authority in an Egalitarian Society." *American Anthropology* 80: 571–88.

Bell, Diane. 1993. *Daughters of the Dreaming*, 2nd edn. Minneapolis: University of Minnesota Press.

Belsley, David A., Edwin Kuh, and Roy E. Welsch. 1980. *Regression Diagnostics: Identifying Influential Data and Sources of Collinearity.* New York: Wiley.

Berry, R. Albert and William R. Cline. 1979. *Agrarian Structure and Productivity in Developing Countries.* Baltimore: Johns Hopkins University Press.

Bian, Yanjie and John Logan. 1996. "Income Inequality in Tianjin: 1978 to 1993." *American Sociological Review* 61: 739–58.

Bierstedt, R. 1950. "An Analysis of Social Power." *American Sociological Review* 15: 730–8.

Blalock, Hubert M. 1967. *Toward a Theory of Minority-Group Relations.* New York: Wiley.

Blanton, Richard E., Stephen A. Kowalewski, Gary Feinman, and Jill Appel. 1981. *Ancient Mesoamerica: A Comparison of Change in Three Regions.* New York: Cambridge University Press.

Bollen, Kenneth A. 1980. "Issues in the Comparative Measurement of Political Democracy." *American Sociological Review* 45: 370–90.

—— 1983. "World System Position, Dependency, and Democracy: The Cross-National Evidence." *American Sociological Review* 48: 468–79.

—— 1990. "Political Democracy: Conceptual and Measurement Traps." *Studies in Comparative International Studies* 25: 7–24.

—— 1993. "Liberal Democracy: Validity and Method Factors in Cross-National Measures." *American Journal of Political Science* 37: 1207–30.

Bollen, Kenneth A. and Burke D. Grandjean. 1981. "The Dimension(s) of Democracy: Further Issues in the Measurement and Effects of Political Democracy." *American Sociological Review* 46: 651–9.

Bollen, Kenneth A. and Robert W. Jackman. 1985a. "Economic and Noneconomic Determinants of Political Democracy in the 1960s." *Research in Political Sociology* 1: 27–48.

—— 1985b. "Political Democracy and the Size Distribution of Income." *American Sociological Review* 50: 438–57.

—— 1985c. "Regression Diagnostics: An Expository Treatment of Outliers and Influential Cases." *Sociological Methods and Research* 13: 510–42.

—— 1989. "Democracy, Stability, and Dichotomies." *American Sociological Review* 54: 612–21.

—— 1995. "Income Inequality and Democratization Revisited: Comment on Muller." *American Sociological Review* 60: 983–9.

Bollen, Kenneth A. and S. Jones. 1982. "Political Instability and Foreign Direct Investment: The Motor Vehicle Industry, 1948–65." *Social Forces* 60: 1070–88.

Bornschier, Volker. 1981. "Comment." *International Studies Quarterly* 25: 283–8.

Bornschier, Volker and T. H. Ballmer-Cao. 1979. "Income Inequality: A Cross-National Study of the Relationships Between MNC-Penetration, Dimensions of the Power Structure and Income Distribution." *American Sociological Review* 44: 487–506.

Bornschier, Volker and Christopher Chase-Dunn. 1985. *Transnational Corporations and Underdevelopment.* New York: Praeger.

Bornschier, Volker, Christopher Chase-Dunn, and Richard Rubinson. 1978. "Cross-National Evidence of the Effects of Foreign Investment and Aid on Economic Growth and Inequality: A Survey of Findings and a Reanalysis." *American Journal of Sociology* 84: 651–83.

Borthwick, Mark. 1992. *Pacific Century: The Emergence of Modern Pacific Asia.* Boulder, CO: Westview.

Boserup, Ester. 1965. *The Conditions of Agricultural Growth: The Economics of Agrarian Change Under Population Pressure.* Chicago: Aldine.

—— 1990. *Economic and Demographic Relationships in Development.* Baltimore: Johns Hopkins University Press.

Boswell, Terry and William J. Dixon. 1990. "Dependency and Rebellion: A Cross-National Analysis." *American Sociological Review* 55: 540–59.

Box, George E. P. and George C. Tiao. 1975. "Intervention Analysis with Applications to Economic and Environmental Problems." *Journal of the American Statistical Association* 70: 70–9.

Branigan, Keith. 1970. *The Foundations of Palatial Crete: A Survey of Crete in the Early Bronze Age.* London: Routledge.

Bruszt, László. 1994. "Az Antall-kormány és a gazdasági érdekképviseletek." In *Kormány a mérlegen*, eds. Gombár Csaba, Hankiss Elemér, Lengyel László, and Várnai Györgyi. Budapest: Politikai Kutatások Központja, pp. 208–30.

Bunce, Valerie. 1980. "Changing Leaders and Changing Policies: The Impact of Elite Succession on Budgetary Priorities in Democratic Countries." *American Journal of Political Science* 24: 373–95.

—— 1981. *Do Leaders Make a Difference? Executive Succession and Public Policy under Capitalism and Socialism.* Princeton: Princeton University Press.

—— 1986. "The Effects of Leadership Succession in the Soviet Union." *American Political Science Review* 80: 215–19.

Bunce, Valerie and Maria Csanadi. 1993. "Uncertainty in the Transition: Post-Communism in Hungary." *East European Politics and Society* 7: 240–75.

Burawoy, Michael and Pavel Krotov. 1992. "The Soviet Transition from Socialism to Capitalism: Worker Control and Economic Bargaining in the Wood Industry." *American Sociological Review* 57: 16–38.

Burkhart, Ross E. and Michael Lewis-Beck. 1994. "Comparative Democracy: The Economic Development Thesis." *American Political Science Review* 88: 903–10.

Byrd, William A. and Alan Gelb. 1990. "Why Industrialize? The Incentives for Rural Community Governments." In *China's Rural Industry: Structure, Development and Reform*, eds. William A. Byrd and Lin Qingsong. New York: Oxford University Press.

Byrd, William A. and Qingsong Lin, eds. 1990. *China's Rural Industry: Structure, Development and Reform.* New York: Oxford University Press.

Cadogan, Gerald. 1976. *Palaces of Minoan Crete.* London: Barrie and Jenkins.

Cain, Bruce and Roger Noll, eds. 1995. *Constitutional Reform in California.* Berkeley: Institute of Governmental Studies Press.

Campbell, Donald T. 1969. "Reforms as Experiments." *American Psychologist* 24: 409–29.

Campbell, Donald T. and H. Laurence Ross. 1968. "The Connecticut Crackdown on Speeding: Time Series Data in Quasi-Experimental Analysis." *Law and Society Review* 3: 33–53.

Campbell, Donald T. and Julian C. Stanley. 1963. *Experimental and Quasi-Experimental Designs for Research*. Chicago: Rand McNally.

Caporaso, James A. and Alan L. Pelowski. 1971. "Economic and Political Integration in Europe: A Time Series Quasi-Experimental Analysis." *American Political Science Review* 65: 418–33.

Cardoso, Fernando H. and Enzo Faletto. 1979. *Dependency and Development in Latin America*. Berkeley: University of California Press.

Carneiro, Robert L. 1970. "A Theory of the Origins of the State." *Science* 169: 733–8.

—— 1987. "Cross Currents in the Theory of State Formation." *American Ethnologist* 14: 756–70.

Chan, Steve. 1984. "Mirror, Mirror on the Wall . . . Are the Freer Countries More Pacific?" *Journal of Conflict Resolution* 28: 617–48.

—— 1989. "Income Inequality Among LDCs: A Comparative Analysis of Alternative Perspectives." *International Studies Quarterly* 33: 45–65.

Chang, Kwang-chih. 1980. *Shang Civilization*. New Haven: Yale University Press.

—— 1986. *The Archaeology of Ancient China*, 4th edn. New Haven: Yale University Press.

Chase-Dunn, Christopher. 1975. "The Effects of International Economic Dependence on Development and Inequality: A Cross-National Study." *American Sociological Review* 40: 720–38.

Chaudhry, Kiren. 1993. "From the Global to the Local: Liberal Economics, Illiberal Politics." Unpublished manuscript, University of California, Berkeley.

Che, Jiahua and Yingyi Qian. 1994. "Boundaries of the Firm and Governance: Understanding China's Township-Village Enterprises." Unpublished manuscript, Department of Economics, Stanford University.

Chen, Junshi, T. Colin Campbell, Li Junyao, and Richard Peto. 1989. *Diet, Life-style and Mortality in China: A Study of the Characteristics of 65 Chinese Counties*. Oxford: Oxford University Press.

Cherry, John F. 1986. "Polities and Palaces: Some Problems in Minoan State Formation." In *Peer Polity Interaction and Socio-Political Change*, eds. Colin Renfrew and John F. Cherry. Cambridge: Cambridge University Press.

Chirot, Daniel. 1986. *Social Change in the Modern Era*. New York: Harcourt Brace Jovanovich.

Chiswick, Barry. 1971. "Earnings Inequality and Economic Development." *Quarterly Journal of Economics* 85: 21–39.

Citrin, Jack. 1994. "Why Can't American Government Do the Right Thing?" In *The New American Political (Dis)order*, eds. Robert A. Dahl *et al.* Berkeley: Institute of Governmental Studies Press, pp. 87–97.

Clark, Cal and Steve Chan. 1995. "MNCs and Developmentalism: Domestic Structures as an Explanation for East Asian Dynamism." In *Transnational Relations*, ed. Thomas Risse-Kappen. London: Cambridge University Press, pp. 112–45.

Clark, Grahame and Stuart Piggot. 1965. *Prehistoric Societies*. New York: Knopf.

Cohen, Ronald. 1978. "State Foundations: A Controlled Comparison." In *Origins of the State*, eds. Ronald Cohen and Elman R. Service. Philadelphia: Institute for the Study of Human Issues.

Cohn, Norman. 1961. *Pursuit of the Millennium: Revolutionary Messianism in Medieval and Reformation Europe and Its Bearing on Modern Totalitarian Movements*. Second Edition. New York: Harper & Row.

Collier, David, ed. 1979. *The New Authoritarianism in Latin America*. Princeton: Princeton University Press.

Commisso, Ellen, Steven Dubb, and Judy McTigue. 1992. "The Illusion of Populism in Latin-America and East-Central Europe." In *Flying Blind: Emerging Democracies in East-Central Europe*, ed. György Szoboszlai. Budapest: Hungarian Political Science Association, pp. 27–58.

Coppedge, Michael and Wolfgang Reinicke. 1990. "Measuring Polyarchy." *Studies in Comparative International Development* 25: 51–72.

Cose, Ellis. 1993. *The Rage of a Privileged Class*. New York: HarperCollins.

Coulter, Philip B. 1975. *Social Mobilization and Liberal Democracy*. Lexington, MA: Lexington Books.

Council for Economic Planning and Development. 1995. *Taiwan Statistical Data Book: 1995*. Taipei: Council for Economic Planning and Development.

Cowgill, George L. 1983. "Rulership and the Ciudadela: Political Inferences from Teotihuacan Architecture." In *Civilization in the Ancient Americas*, eds. Richard M. Leventhal and Alan L. Kolata. Albuquerque and Cambridge: University of New Mexico Press and Peabody Museum of Archaeology and Ethnology, Harvard University.

Crawford, Harriet. 1991. *Sumer and the Sumerians*. Cambridge: Cambridge University Press.

Crenshaw, Edward. 1992. "Cross-National Determinants of Income Inequality: A Replication and Extension Using Ecological-Evolutionary Theory." *Social Forces* 71: 339–63.

—— 1994. "Democracy and Proto-Modernity: Technoecological Influences on the Growth of Political and Civil Rights." Paper presented at the conference entitled "Inequality and Democracy." New Brunswick, NJ. February 4–6, 1994.

—— 1995. "Democracy and Demographic Inheritance: The Influence of Modernity and Proto-Modernity on Political and Civil Rights, 1965 to 1980." *American Sociological Review* 60: 702–18.

Crowther, William. 1986. "Philippine Authoritarianism and the International Economy." *Comparative Politics* 18: 339–56.

Crozier, Michel, Samuel P. Huntington and Jodi Watanuki. 1975. *The Crisis of Democracy: Report on the Governability of Democracies to the Trilateral Commission*. New York: New York University Press.

Culbert, T. Patrick. 1973. "The Maya Downfall at Tikal." In *The Classic Maya Collapse*, ed. T. Patrick Culbert. Albuquerque: University of New Mexico Press.

Cumings, Bruce. 1984. "The Origins and Development of the Northeast Asian Political Economy: Industrial Sectors, Product Cycle, and Political Consequences." *International Organization* 38: 1–40.

Cutright, Phillips. 1963. "National Political Development: Measurement and Analysis." *American Sociological Review* 28: 253–64.

—— 1967. "Inequality: A Cross-National Analysis." *American Sociological Review* 32: 562–78.

Cutright, Phillips and James A. Wiley. 1969. "Modernization and Political Representation: 1927–1966." *Studies in Comparative International Development* 5: 23–41.

Dahl, Robert. 1971. *Polyarchy: Participation and Opposition.* New Haven: Yale University Press.

—— 1989. *Democracy and its Critics.* New Haven: Yale University Press.

—— 1992. "Why Free Markets Are Not Enough." *Journal of Democracy* 3: 82–9.

Dahl, Robert A. and Edward R. Tufte. 1973. *Size and Democracy.* Stanford: Stanford University Press.

Daly, Martin and Margo Wilson. 1988. *Homicide.* New York: Aldine De Gruyter.

Danziger, Sheldon and Peter Gottschalk. 1986. "Do Rising Tides Lift all Boats? The Impact of Secular and Cyclical changes on Poverty." *American Economic Review* 76: 405–10.

Dasgupta, P. A. and M. Weale. 1992. "On Measuring the Quality of Life." *World Development* 20: 119–31.

Davies, J. C. 1979. "The J-Curve of Rising and Declining Satisfactions as a Cause of Revolutions." In *Violence in America: Historical and Comparative Perspectives*, eds. Hugh D. Graham and Ted R. Gurr. Beverly Hills, CA: Sage.

Davis, D. L. 1974. "Ikki in Late Medieval Japan." In *Essays in Institutional History*, eds. J. W. Hall and J. P. Mass. New Haven: Yale University Press.

Demaris, Alfred. 1992. *Logit Modeling: Practical Applications.* Newbury Park, CA: Sage.

De Palma, Anthony. 1996. "Income Gap in Mexico Grows, and So Do Protests." *New York Times*, July 20, 3 (A).

Deutsch, K. W. 1961. "Social Mobilization and Political Development." *American Political Science Review* 55: 493–514.

Deutsch, Morton. 1985. *Distributive Justice.* New Haven: Yale University Press.

Diamond, Larry. 1992. "Economic Development and Democracy Reconsidered." In *Reexamining Democracy: Essays in Honor of Seymour Martin Lipset*, eds. Gary Marks and Larry Diamond. Newbury Park, CA: Sage, pp. 93–139.

—— 1995. "Democracy and Economic Reform: Tensions, Compatibilities, and Strategies for Reconciliation." In *Economic Transition in Eastern Europe and Russia: Realities of Reform*, ed. Edward P. Lazear. Palo Alto, CA: Hoover Institution Press.

Diamond, Larry, Juan J. Linz, and Seymour M. Lipset, eds. 1990. *Democracy in Developing Countries*, 4 vols. Boulder: Lynne Rienner.

Diamond, Larry and Marc Plattner, eds. 1993. *The Global Resurgence of Democracy.* Baltimore: Johns Hopkins University Press.

Di Palma, Giuseppe. 1990. *To Craft Democracies.* Berkeley: University of California Press.

Dixon, William J. and Bruce E. Moon. 1986. "The Military Burden and Basic Human Needs." *Journal of Conflict Resolution* 30: 660–84.

Dornbusch, Rudiger and Sebastian Edwards, eds. 1991. *The Macroeconomics of Populism in Latin America*. Chicago: University of Chicago Press.

Downing, Brian M. 1992. *The Military Revolution and Political Change: Origins of Democracy and Autocracy in Early Modern Europe*. Princeton: Princeton University Press.

Doyle, Michael W. 1983. "Kant, Liberal Legacies, and Foreign Affairs." Part 1. *Philosophy and Public Affairs* 12: 205–35.

Drucker, Philip. 1965. *Cultures of the North Pacific Coast*. San Francisco: Chandler Publishing.

Duby, Georges. 1968. *Rural Economy and Country Life in the Medieval West*, trans. Cynthia Postan. Columbia: University of South Carolina Press.

Duckitt, J. 1992. "Education and Authoritarianism Among English and Afrikaans-Speaking White South Africans." *Journal of Social Psychology* 132: 701–8.

Duncan, Otis D. 1984. "Rasch Measurement in Survey Research: Further Examples and Discussion." In *Survey Subjective Phenomena*, ed. C. F. Turner and E. Martin. New York: Russell Sage Foundation.

Durkheim, Emile. 1893 [1964]. *The Division of Labor in Society*. New York: Free Press.

Eckstein, Susan. 1989. "Power and Popular Protest in Latin America." In *Power and Popular Protest: Latin American Social Movements*, ed. Susan Eckstein, Berkeley: University of California Press, pp. 1–60.

The Economist 331, June 25, 1994: 110.

Eisenstadt, Shmuel N. 1963. *The Political Systems of Empires*. New York: Free Press.

Eisenstadt, Shmuel N., ed. 1986. *The Origins and Diversity of Axial Age Civilizations*. Albany: State University of New York Press.

Elster, Jon. 1990. "When Communism Dissolves." *London Review of Books* January 24.

—— 1993. "The Necessity and Impossibility of Simultaneous Economic and Political Reform." In *Constitutionalism and Democracy: Transitions in the Contemporary World*, eds. Douglas Greenberg, Stanley N. Katz, Melanie B. Oliviero, and Steven C. Wheatley. New York: Oxford University Press, pp. 267–74.

Ember, Carol R. 1981. "A Cross-Cultural Perspective on Sex Differences." In *Handbook of Cross-Cultural Human Development*, eds. Ruth H. Munroe, Robert L. Munroe, and Beatrice B. Whiting. New York: Garland STPM Press.

—— 1983. "The Relative Decline in Women's Contribution to Agriculture with Intensification." *American Anthropologist* 85: 285–304.

Ember, Carol R. and Melvin Ember. 1992a. "Resource Unpredictability, Mistrust, and War: A Cross-Cultural Study." *Journal of Conflict Resolution* 36: 242–62.

—— 1992b. "Warfare, Aggression, and Resource Problems: Cross-Cultural Codes." *Behavior Science Research* 26: 169–226.

—— 1993. "Issues in Cross-Cultural Studies of Interpersonal Violence." *Violence and Victims* 8: 217–33.

—— 1994. "War, Socialization, and Interpersonal Violence: A Cross-Cultural Study." *Journal of Conflict Resolution* 38: 620–46.

Ember, Carol R., Melvin Ember, and Bruce Russett. 1992. "Peace Between Participatory Polities: A Cross-Cultural Test of the 'Democracies Rarely Fight Each Other' Hypothesis." *World Politics* 44: 573–99.

Ember, Carol R., Marc H. Ross, Michael Burton, and Candice Bradley. 1991. "Problems of Measurement in Cross-Cultural Research Using Secondary Data." *Behavior Science Research* 25: 187–216.

Ember, Carol R., Bruce Russett, and Melvin Ember. 1993. "Political Participation and Peace: Cross-Cultural Codes." *Cross-Cultural Research* 27: 97–145.

Ember, Melvin. 1991. "The Logic of Comparative Research." *Behavior Science Research* 25: 143–54.

—— 1997. "Evolution of the Human Relations Area Files." *Cross-Cultural Research* 31: 3–15.

Ember, Melvin and Carol R. Ember. 1994. "Cross-Cultural Studies of War and Peace: Recent Achievements and Future Possibilities." In *Studying War: Anthropological Perspectives*, eds. S. P. Reyna and R. E. Downs. Langhorne, PA: Gordon and Breach.

Ember, Melvin and Keith F. Otterbein. 1991. "Sampling in Cross-Cultural Research." *Behavior Science Research* 25: 217–34.

Epstein, S. 1971. "Customary Systems of Reward in Rural South India." In *Economic Development and Social Change: The Modernization of Village Communities*, ed. George Dalton. Garden City, NY: Natural History Press.

Estioko-Griffin, Agnes. 1985. "Women as Hunters: The Case of an Eastern Cagayan Agta Group." In *The Agta of Northeastern Luzon: Recent Studies*, eds. P. B. Griffin and Agnes Estioko-Griffin. Cebu City: San Carlos Publications.

Evans, Peter B. 1979. *Dependent Development*. Princeton: Princeton University Press.

—— 1989. "Predatory, Developmental and Other Apparatuses: A Comparative Political Economy Perspective on the Third World State." *Sociological Forum* 4: 561–87.

Evans, Peter B. and Michael Timberlake. 1980. "Dependence, Inequality, and the Growth of the Tertiary: A Comparative Analysis of Less Developed Countries." *American Sociological Review* 45: 531–52.

Farrar, Cynthia. 1988. *The Origins of Democratic Thinking: The Invention of Politics in Classical Athens*. Cambridge: Cambridge University Press.

Fei, J. C. and Gustav Ranis. 1964. *Development of the Labor Surplus Economy*. Homewood, IL: Richmond and Irwin.

Fiala, Robert. 1987. "Labor Force Structure and the Size Distribution of Income within Countries, 1960–80." *International Studies Quarterly* 31: 403–22.

Fields, Gary S. 1980. *Poverty, Inequality, and Development*. Cambridge: Cambridge University Press.

Finley, M. I. 1973. *The Ancient Economy*. Berkeley: University of California Press.

—— 1981. *Early Greece: The Bronze and Archaic Ages*, rev. edn. London: Chatto and Windus.

—— 1982. *Economy and Society in Ancient Greece*, eds. Brent D. Shaw and Richard P. Saller. New York: Viking.

—— 1985. *Democracy Ancient and Modern*. London: Hogarth Press.

Firebaugh, Glenn. 1979. "Structural Determinants of Urbanization in Asia and Latin America, 1950–1970." *American Sociological Review* 44: 199–215.

Firebaugh, Glenn and Frank D. Beck. 1994. "Does Economic Growth Benefit the Masses? Growth, Dependence, and Welfare in the Third World." *American Sociological Review* 59: 631–53.

Fishlow, Albert. 1973. "Some Reflections on Post-1964 Brazilian Economic Policy." In *Authoritarian Brazil: Origins, Policies, and Future*, ed. Alfred Stepan. New Haven: Yale University Press.

Fogg, C. D. 1971. "Smallholder Agriculture in Eastern Nigeria." In *Economic Development and Social Change: The Modernization of Village Communities*, ed. George Dalton. Garden City, NY: Natural History Press.

Fox, John. 1991. *Regression Diagnostics*. Newbury Park, CA: Sage.

Frank, Andre G. 1967. *Capitalism and Underdevelopment in Latin America*. New York: Monthly Review Press.

Freund, R. J. and R. C. Littell. 1986. *Regression in SAS*. Cary, NC: SAS Institute.

Fried, Morton H. 1967. *The Evolution of Political Society*. New York: Random House.

Friedman, Edward, ed. 1994. *The Politics of Democratization: Generalizing East Asian Experiences*. Boulder, CO: Westview.

Fromm, Erich and Michael Maccoby. 1968. *Social Characteristics in a Mexican Village*. Englewood, NJ: Prentice-Hall.

Furtado, Celso. 1970. *Economic Development of Latin America: Historical Background and Contemporary Problems*. London: Cambridge University Press.

Galtung, Johan. 1971. "A Structural Theory of Imperialism." *Journal of Peace Research* 8: 81–117.

Garton Ash, Timothy. 1990. "Eastern Europe: The Year of the Truth." *New York Review of Books* February 15.

Gasiorowski, Mark J. 1993. *The Political Regime Change Dataset*. Baton Rouge: Louisiana Population Data Center, Louisiana State University.

—— 1995. "Economic Crisis and Political Regime Change: An Event History Analysis." *American Political Science Review* 89: 882–97.

Gastil, Raymond D. 1985. "The Past, Present and Future of Democracy." *Journal of International Affairs* 38: 161–79.

—— 1986. *Freedom in the World: Political Rights and Civil Liberties 1985–1986*. Westport, CT: Greenwood Press.

—— 1988. *Freedom in the World: Political Rights and Civil Liberties 1987–1988*. New York: Freedom House.

—— 1991. *Freedom in the World: Political Rights and Civil Liberties 1989–1990*. Westport, CT: Greenwood Press.

Geddes, Barbara. 1994a. "Challenging the Conventional Wisdom." *Journal of Democracy* 5: 49–63.

—— 1994b. "Economic Liberalization and Democracy." Paper presented at the Conference on Regime Change and Democratization in Comparative Perspective, University of California, Los Angeles, May 19–21.

—— 1994c. *Politician's Dilemma: Building State Capacity in Latin America.* Berkeley: University of California Press.

Geertz, Clifford. 1963. *Agricultural Involution: The Process of Ecological Change in Indonesia.* Berkeley: University of California Press.

Gillis, Malcolm, Dwight H. Perkins, Michael Roemer, and Donald R. Snodgrass. 1987. *Economics of Development.* New York: Norton.

Gomme, Arnold W. 1967. *The Population of Athens in the Fifth and Fourth Centuries BC.* Chicago: Argonaut.

Gonick, L. S. and R. M. Rosh. 1988. "The Structural Constraints of the World-Economy on National Political Development." *Comparative Political Studies* 21: 171–99.

Goody, Jack A. and Ian Watt. 1968. "The Consequences of Literacy." In *Literacy in Traditional Society*, ed. Jack Goody. London: Cambridge University Press, pp. 27–68.

Gorden, Raymond L. 1977. *Unidimensional Scaling of Social Variables: Concepts and Procedures.* New York: Free Press.

Graham, J. Walter. 1987. *The Palaces of Crete*, rev. edn. Princeton: Princeton University Press.

Grant, Michael. 1987. *The Rise of the Greeks.* New York: Collier Books.

Gratton, N. E. 1992. "Pintupi." In *Encyclopedia of World Cultures: Oceania*, ed. T. E. Hays. Boston, MA: G.K. Hall.

Greene, William H. 1989. *LIMDEP, Version 5.1.* Unpublished manuscript.

—— 1993. *Econometric Analysis*, 2nd edn. New York: Macmillan.

Greskovits, Béla. 1993. "Is the East Becoming the South? Where Threats to Reforms May Come From?" Unpublished manuscript, Central European University, Budapest.

—— 1995. "Hungerstrikers, the Unions, the Government and the Parties. A Case-study of Hungarian Transformation: Conflict, the Social Pact and Democratic Development." Essex: Essex University, Centre for European Studies.

Griffin, Keith and Renwei Zhao. 1993. *The Distribution of Income in China.* New York: St. Martin's Press.

Grofman, Bernard and Arend Lijphart, eds. 1986. *Electoral Laws and their Political Consequences.* New York: Agathon Press.

Gurr, Ted R. 1968. "A Causal Model of Civil Strife: A Comparative Analysis Using New Indices." *American Political Science Review* 62: 1104–24.

Haas, Jonathan. 1982. *The Evolution of the Prehistoric State.* New York: Columbia University Press.

Hadenius, Axel. 1992. *Democracy and Development.* Cambridge: Cambridge University Press.

Hagen Everett. 1962. *On the Theory of Social Change: How Economic Growth Begins.* Homewood, IL: Dorsey Press.

Haggard, Stephan and Robert R. Kaufman. 1992. "The Political Economy of

Inflation and Stabilization in Middle-Income Countries." In *The Politics of Adjustment: International Constraints, Distributive Conflicts, and the State*, eds. Stephan Haggard and Robert R. Kaufman. Princeton: Princeton University Press.

—— 1995. *The Political Economy of Democratic Transitions*. Princeton: Princeton University Press.

Hall, John. 1995. "After the Vacuum: Post-Communism in the Light of Tocqueville." In *Markets, States, and Democracy*, ed. Beverly Crawford. Boulder, CO: Westview Press, pp. 82–100.

Hall, Peter, ed. 1989. *The Political Power of Economic Ideas*. Princeton: Princeton University Press.

Hammond, Norman. 1988. *Ancient Maya Civilization*. New Brunswick: Rutgers University Press.

Hankiss, Elemer. 1990. *East European Alternatives*. Oxford: Clarendon Press.

Hansen, Mogens H. 1991. *The Athenian Democracy in the Age of Demosthenes*. Oxford: Basil Blackwell.

Hausner, Jerzy. 1992. *Populist Threat in Transformation of Socialist Society*. Warsaw, Poland: Friedrich Ebert Foundation.

Havel, Václav. 1993. "The Post-Communist Nightmare." *New York Review of Books* May 27.

Hayami, Yujiro and Masao Kikuchi. 1981. *Asian Village Economy at the Crossroads: An Economic Approach to Institutional Change*. Baltimore: Johns Hopkins University Press.

Headland, Thomas N. 1993. "Agta." In *Encyclopedia of World Cultures: Volume 5: East and Southeast Asia*, ed. Paul Hockings. Boston: G. K. Hall.

Helliwell, John F. 1994. "Empirical Linkages Between Democracy and Economic Growth." *British Journal of Political Science* 24: 175–98.

Helper, H. 1960. "The Impending Crisis." In *Ante-Bellum*, ed. Harvey Walsh. New York: Capricorn Books.

Herr, Richard. 1989. *Rural Change and Royal Finances in Spain at the End of the Old Regime*. Berkeley: University of California Press.

Hewitt, Christopher. 1977. "The Effect of Political Democracy and Social Democracy on Equality in Industrial Societies: A Cross-National Comparison." *American Sociological Review* 42: 450–64.

Hill, Christopher. 1967. *Reformation to Industrial Revolution: A Social and Economic History of Britain, 1530–1780*. London: Weidenfeld & Nicholson.

Hilton, R. H. 1978. "Agrarian Class Structure and Economic Development in Pre-Industrial Europe." *Past and Present* 80 (August).

Hirschman, Albert. 1970. *Exit, Voice, and Loyalty: Responses to Decline in Firms, Organizations, and States*. Cambridge, MA: Harvard University Press.

—— 1981a "The Changing Tolerance for Income Inequality in the Course of Economic Development." In *Essays in Trespassing: Economics to Politics and Beyond*, ed. Albert Hirschman. Cambridge: Cambridge University Press, pp. 39–58.

—— 1981b. "Morality and the Social Sciences: A Durable Tension." In *Essays in Trespassing: Economics to Politics and Beyond*, ed. Albert Hirschman. Cambridge: Cambridge University Press.

—— 1993. "Exit, Voice, and the Fate of the German Democratic Republic: An Essay in Conceptual History." *World Politics* 45: 173–202.

Holmes, Stephen. 1991. "The Liberal Idea." *The American Prospect* 7: 81–96.

Holmes, Steven A. 1996. "Income Disparity Between Poorest and Richest Rises." *New York Times*, June 20, 1(A) and 18(A).

Homer-Dixon, Thomas F., Jeffrey H. Boutwell, and George W. Rathjens. 1993. "Environmental Change and Violent Conflict." *Scientific American* 268(2): 38–45.

Hoover, Greg A. 1989. "Intranational Inequality: A Cross-National Dataset." *Social Forces* 67: 1008–26.

Huang, Chi. 1992. "Leadership Change and Government Size in East Asian Authoritarian Regimes." In *The Evolving Pacific Basin in the Global Political Economy: Domestic and International Linkages*, eds. Cal Clark and Steve Chan. Boulder, CO: Rienner.

Hucker, Charles O. 1975. *China's Imperial Past*. Stanford: Stanford University Press.

Hunt, Richard N. 1984. *The Political Ideas of Marx and Engels*, vol. II. Pittsburgh: University of Pittsburgh Press.

Huntington, Samuel P. 1968. *Political Order in Changing Societies*. New Haven: Yale University Press.

—— 1984. "Will More Countries Become Democratic?" *Political Science Quarterly* 99: 193–218.

—— 1991. *The Third Wave: Democratization in the Late Twentieth Century*. Norman: University of Oklahoma Press.

—— 1993. "Democracy's Third Wave." In *The Global Resurgence of Democracy*, eds. Larry Diamond and Marc F. Plattner. Baltimore: Johns Hopkins University Press.

Hyman, Herbert, Charles Wright, and John Reed. 1975. *The Enduring Effects of Education*. Chicago: University of Chicago Press.

Im, Hyug Baeg. 1987. "The Rise of Bureaucratic-Authoritarianism in South Korea." *World Politics* 39: 231–57.

Inkeles, Alex. 1974. *Becoming Modern: Individual Change in Six Developing Countries*. Cambridge, MA: Harvard University Press.

—— 1991. *On Measuring Democracy*. New Brunswick, NJ: Transaction Publishers.

Inkeles, Alex and Larry Sirowy. 1983. "Convergent and Divergent Trends in National Educational Systems." *Social Forces* 62: 303–33.

Inkeles, Alex and David H. Smith. 1974. *Becoming Modern: Individual Change in Six Developing Countries*. Cambridge, MA: Harvard University Press.

Issar, Arie S. 1995. "Climatic Change and the History of the Middle East." *American Scientist* 83: 350–5.

Jackman, Robert W. 1973. "On the Relation of Economic Development to Democratic Performance." *American Journal of Political Science* 17: 611–21.

—— 1974. "Political Democracy and Social Equality: A Comparative Analysis." *American Sociological Review* 39: 29–45.

—— 1975. *Politics and Social Equality: A Comparative Analysis*. New York: Wiley.

Jacobsen, Thorkild. 1943. "Primitive Democracy in Ancient Mesopotamia." *Journal of Near Eastern Studies* 2: 159–72.

Jefferson, Gary H. and Thomas G. Rawski. 1994. "Enterprise Reform in Chinese Industry." *Journal of Economic Perspective* 8: 47–70.

Jefferson, Gary H. and W. Xu. 1991. "The Impact of Reform on Socialist Enterprises in Transition: Structure, Conduct, and Performance in Chinese Industry." *Journal of Comparative Economics* 15: 45–64.

Johnson, Aaron C., Marvin B. Johnson, and Rueben C. Buse. 1987. *Econometrics: Basic and Applied.* New York: Macmillan.

Johnson, Graham E. 1994. "Open for Business, Open to the World: Consequences of Global Incorporation in Guangdong and the Pearl River Delta." In *The Economic Transformation of South China: Reform and Development in the Post-Mao Era.* eds. Thomas P. Lyons and Victor Nee. Cornell East Asia Series, no. 70. Ithaca: East Asia Program.

Jones, Arnold H. M. 1957. *Athenian Democracy.* Oxford: Basil Blackwell.

Jowitt, Kenneth. 1992a. "The Leninist Legacy." In *Eastern Europe in Revolution,* ed. Ivo Banac. Ithaca: Cornell University Press, pp. 207–25.

—— 1992b. *The New World Disorder: The Leninist Extinction.* Berkeley: University of California Press.

Kahler, Miles. 1990. "Orthodoxy and Its Alternatives: Explaining Alternatives to Stabilization and Adjustment." In *Economic Crisis and Policy Choice: The Politics of Adjustment in the Third World,* ed. Joan Nelson. Princeton: Princeton University Press, pp. 33–61.

Kaufman, Robert R. 1979. "Industrial Change and Authoritarian Rule in Latin America: A Concrete Review of the Bureaucratic-Authoritarian Model." In *The New Authoritarianism in Latin America,* ed. David Collier. Princeton: Princeton University Press.

Keightley, David N., ed. 1983. *The Origins of Chinese Civilization.* Berkeley: University of California Press.

Kelly, Gail P. 1984. "Colonialism, Indigenous Society and School Practices: French West Africa and Indochina, 1918–1938." In *Education and the Colonial Experience,* 2nd edn, eds. Phillip G. Altbach and Gail P. Kelly. New Brunswick, NJ: Transaction Books.

Kent, Susan. 1992. "The Current Forager Controversy: Real versus Ideal Views of Hunter-Gatherers." *Man* 27: 45–70.

Kerr, Clark, John T. Dunlop, Frederick H. Harbison, and Charles A. Myers. 1960. *Industrialism and Industrial Man: The Problems of Labor and Management in Economic Growth.* New York: Oxford University Press.

Khan, Azizur Rahman, Keith Griffin, Carl Riskin, and Renwei Zhao. 1993. "Household Income and its Distribution." In *The Distribution of Income in China,* eds. Keith Griffin and Renwei Zhao. New York: St. Martin's Press.

Kleinbaum, David G., Lawrence L. Kupper, and Keith E. Muller. 1988. *Applied Regression Analysis and Other Multivariable Methods,* 2nd edn. Boston: PWS-Kent.

Kohli, Atul. 1986. "Examining the 'Reexamination' of 'Inequality in the Third World.'" *Comparative Political Studies* 19: 269–74.

Kohli, Atul, Michael F. Altfeld, Saideh Loftian, and Russell Mardon. 1984.

"Inequality in the Third World: An Assessment of Competing Explanations." *Comparative Political Studies* 17: 283–318.

Kornai, János. 1980. *Economics of Shortage*. Amsterdam: North-Holland.

—— 1993. "Transzformációs visszaesés: Egy általános jelenség vizsgálata a magyar fejlődés példáján." *Közgazdasági Szemle* 78: 569–99.

—— 1995. "Négy jellegzetesség: A magyar fejlődés politikai gazdaságtani megközelítésben." Discussion papers 19. Budapest: Collegium Budapest/Institute for Advanced Study.

Körösényi, András. 1994. "Demobilization and Gradualism: The Political Economy of the Hungarian Transition, 1987–92." In *A Precarious Balance: Democracy and Economic Reforms in Eastern Europe*, ed. Joan Nelson. San Francisco, CA: ICS Press.

Kramer, Samuel N. 1963. *The Sumerians: Their History, Culture, and Character*. Chicago: University of Chicago Press.

—— 1981. *History Begins at Sumer*, 3rd edn. Philadelphia: University of Pennsylvania Press.

Kuznets, Simon. 1955. "Economic Growth and Income Inequality." *American Economic Review* 45: 1–28.

—— 1963. "Quantitative Aspects of the Economic Growth of Nations VIII: The Distribution of Income by Size." *Economic Development and Cultural Change* 11: 1–80.

—— 1976a. "Demographic Aspects of the Size Distribution of Income: An Exploratory Essay." *Economic Development and Cultural Change* 25: 1–14.

—— 1976b. *Growth, Population and Income Distribution: Selected Essays*. New York: Norton.

Lagos, Ricardo and Oscar A. Rufatt. 1975. "Military Government and Real Wages in Chile: A Note." *Latin American Research Review* 10: 139–46.

Laki, Mikhály. 1993. "The Chances of Acceleration of Transition: The Case of Hungarian Privatization." *East European Politics and Societies* 7: 440–52.

Lasswell, Harold D. 1936. *Who Gets What, When, How?* New York: McGraw-Hill.

Layne, Christopher. 1994. "Kant or Cant: The Myth of the Democratic Peace." *International Security* 19: 5–49.

Leacock, E. 1978. "Women's Status in Egalitarian Society: Implications for Social Evolution." *Current Anthropology* 19: 247–75.

Lee, Richard. 1979. *The !Kung San: Men, Women and Work in a Foraging Society*. Cambridge: Cambridge University Press.

—— 1982. "Politics, Sexual and Non-Sexual, in an Egalitarian Society." In *Politics and History in Band Societies*, eds. Eleanor Leacock and Richard Lee. Cambridge: Cambridge University Press.

Leinbach, T. R. 1984. "Rural Service Delivery in Indonesia." In *Rural Public Services: International Comparisons*, eds. Richard E. Lonsdale and Gyorgy Enyedi. Boulder, CO: Westview Press.

Lenski, Gerhard E. 1966. *Power and Privilege: A Theory of Social Stratification*. New York: McGraw-Hill.

Lenski, Gerhard E. and Jean Lenski. 1987. *Human Societies: An Introduction to Macrosociology*. New York: McGraw-Hill.

Lenski, Gerhard E. and Patrick Nolan. 1984. "Trajectories of Development: A Test of Ecological-Evolutionary Theory." *Social Forces* 63: 1–23.

Lerner, Daniel. 1958. *The Passing of Traditional Society: Modernizing the Middle East*. New York: Free Press.

Levi, Margaret. 1988. *Of Rule and Revenue*. Berkeley: University of California Press.

Lewis, W. Arthur. 1954. "Economic Development with Unlimited Supplies of Labor." *The Manchester School* 22: 139–91.

Lewis-Beck, Michael S. 1979. "Some Economic Effects of Revolution: Models, Measurement, and the Cuban Evidence." *American Journal of Sociology* 84: 1127–49.

—— 1986. "Interrupted Time Series." In *New Tools for Social Scientists: Advances and Applications in Research Methods*, eds. William D. Berry and Michael S. Lewis-Beck. Beverly Hills, CA: Sage, pp. 209–40.

Lewis-Beck, Michael S. and John R. Alford. 1980. "Can Government Regulate Safety? The Coal Mine Example." *American Political Science Review* 74: 745–56.

Lijphart, Arend. 1984. *Democracies: Patterns of Majoritarian and Consensus Government in Twenty-One Countries*. New Haven: Yale University Press.

—— 1995. *Electoral Systems and Party Systems*. Oxford: Oxford University Press.

Lijphart, Arend, ed. 1992. *Parliamentary Versus Presidential Governments*. Oxford: Oxford University Press.

Lin, Nan. 1995. "Local Market Socialism: Local Corporatism in Action in Rural China." *Theory and Society* 24: 301–54.

Lindblom, Charles E. 1977. *Politics and Markets: The World's Political – Economic Systems*. New York: Basic Books.

Linz, Juan and Arturo Valenzuela, eds. 1994. *The Failure of Presidentialism*. Baltimore: Johns Hopkins University Press.

Lipset, Seymour M. 1959. "Some Social Requisites of Democracy: Economic Development and Political Legitimacy." *American Political Science Review* 53: 69–105.

—— 1963. *Political Man: The Social Bases of Politics*. Garden City, NY: Doubleday.

—— 1993. "Reflections on Capitalism, Socialism and Democracy." *Journal of Democracy* 4: 43–53

—— 1994. "The Social Requisites of Democracy Revisited." *American Sociological Review* 59: 1–22.

Lipset, Seymour M., Kyoung-Ryung Seong, and John C. Torres. 1993. "A Comparative Analysis of the Social Requisites of Democracy." *International Social Science Journal* 136: 155–75.

Liu, Yia-ling. 1992. "Reform from Below: The Private Economy and Local Politics in the Rural Industrialization of Wenzhou." *China Quarterly* 130: 293–316.

London, Bruce. 1987. "Structural Determinants of Third World Urban Change: An Ecological and Political Economic Analysis." *American Sociological Review* 52: 28–43.

London, Bruce and Thomas Robinson. 1989. "The Effect of International

Dependence on Income Inequality and Political Violence." *American Sociological Review* 54: 305–8.

Londregan, John and Kenneth Poole. 1990. "Poverty, the Coup Trap, and the Seizure of Executive Power." *World Politics* 42: 151–83.

Luria, Aleksandr. 1976. *Cognitive Development: Its Cultural and Social Foundations*, ed. Michael Cole, trans. Martin Lopez-Morillas and Lynn Solotaroff. Cambridge, MA: Harvard University Press.

Lydall, Harold. 1979. *A Theory of Income Distribution*. New York: Oxford University Press.

Lye, Keith and Shirley Carpenter. 1987. *Encyclopedia of World Geography*. New York: Dorset.

Lyons, Thomas P. 1994. "Economic Reform in Fujian: Another View from the Villages." In *The Economic Transformation of South China: Reform and Development in the Post-Mao Era*, eds. Thomas P. Lyons and Victor Nee. Cornell East Asia Series, no. 70. Ithaca: East Asia Program.

MacMullen, Ramsey. 1988. *Corruption and the Decline of Rome*. New Haven: Yale University Press.

MacPherson, Crawford B. 1962. *The Political Theory of Possessive Individualism*. Oxford: Oxford University Press.

Major, Iván. 1993. *Privatization in Eastern Europe: A Critical Approach*. Brookfield, VT: Edward Elgar.

Malefakis, Edward E. 1970. *Agrarian Reform and Peasant Revolution in Spain: Origins of the Civil War*. New Haven: Yale University Press.

Mansfield, Edward D. and Jack Snyder. 1995. "Democratization and the Danger of War." *International Security* 20: 5–38.

Maoz, Zeev and Nasrin Abdolali. 1989. "Regime Types and International Conflict, 1816–1976." *Journal of Conflict Resolution* 33: 3–35.

Maoz, Zeev and Bruce Russett. 1993. "Normative and Structural Causes of Democratic Peace, 1946–1986." *American Political Science Review* 87: 624–38.

Maravall, José María. 1994. "The Myth of the Authoritarian Advantage." *Journal of Democracy* 5: 17–31.

Markoff, J. 1985. "The Social Geography of Rural Revolt at the Beginning of the French Revolution." *American Sociological Review* 50: 761–81.

Masters, Roger D. 1968. *The Political Philosophy of Rousseau*. Princeton: Princeton University Press.

Matz, F. 1973. "The Maturity of Minoan Civilization." In *The Cambridge Ancient History*, vol. II, part 1. *History of the Middle East and the Aegean Region c. 1800–1380 BC*. Cambridge: Cambridge University Press.

McCrone, Donald J. and Charles F. Cnudde. 1967. "Toward a Communications Theory of Democratic Political Development." *American Political Science Review* 61: 72–79.

McCullagh, P. and J. A. Nelder. 1989. *Generalized Linear Models*. New York: Chapman and Hall.

McDonald, James B. 1984. "Some Generalized Functions for the Size Distribution of Income." *Econometrica* 52: 647–63.

McDowall, David *et al.* 1980. *Interrupted Time Series Analysis*. Beverly Hills, Sage.

McLuhan, Herbert M. 1962. *The Gutenberg Galaxy: The Making of Typographic Man.* Toronto: University of Toronto Press.

McNulty, M. L., M. A. O. Ayeni, M. O. Filani, and G. O. Olaore. 1984. "Access to Rural Services in Nigeria." In *Rural Public Services: International Comparisons,* eds. Richard E. Lonsdale and Gyorgy Enyedi. Boulder, CO: Westview Press.

Merton, Robert K. 1968. "The Matthew Effect in Science." *Science* 159: 56–63.

—— 1973. "The Normative Structure of Science." In *The Sociology of Science: Theoretical and Empirical Investigations.* Chicago: University of Chicago Press.

Meyer, John W., Francisco O. Ramirez, R. Rubinson, and John Boli-Bennett. 1979. "Educational Revolution, 1950–1970." In *National Development and the World System: Educational, Economic and Political Change, 1950–1970,* eds. John W. Meyer and Michael T. Hannan. Chicago: University of Chicago Press.

Meyer, John W., Francisco O. Ramirez, and Y. N. Soysel. 1992. "World Expansion of Mass Education, 1870–1980." *Sociology of Education* 65: 128–40.

Midlarsky, Manus I. 1988. "Rulers and the Ruled: Patterned Inequality and the Onset of Mass Political Violence." *American Political Science Review* 82: 491–509.

—— 1992a. "The Origins of Democracy in Agrarian Society: Land Inequality and Political Rights." *Journal of Conflict Resolution* 36: 454–77.

—— 1992b. "Reversing the Causal Arrow: Domestic and International Sources of Early Democracy." Paper presented at The International Workshop on Environment, Technology, and Democracy. Institute of Political Science, University of Maria Curie-Skodowska, Lublin, Poland.

—— 1995. "Environmental Influences on Democracy: Aridity, Warfare, and a Reversal of the Causal Arrow." *Journal of Conflict Resolution* 39: 224–62.

—— Forthcoming. *The Evolution of Inequality: War, State Survival, and Democracy in Comparative Perspective.* Stanford: Stanford University Press.

Miller, Nicholas R. 1983. "Pluralism and Social Choice." *American Political Science Review* 77: 734–47.

Milligan, Glenn W. and Martha C. Cooper. 1985. "An Examination of Procedures for Determining the Number of Clusters in a Data Set." *Psychometrika* 50: 159–79.

Mintz, Alex and Nehemia Geva. 1993. "Why Don't Democracies Fight Each Other?: An Experimental Study." *Journal of Conflict Resolution* 37: 484–503.

Moaddel, Manssor. 1994. "Political Conflict in the World Economy: A Cross-National Analysis of Modernization and World System Theories." *American Sociological Review* 59: 276–303.

Moon, Bruce E. 1991. *The Political Economy of Basic Human Needs.* Ithaca: Cornell University Press.

Moon, Bruce E. and William J. Dixon. 1985. "Politics, the State, and Basic Human Needs: A Cross-National Study." *American Journal of Political Science* 29: 661–94.

Moore, Barrington, Jr. 1966. *Social Origins of Dictatorship and Democracy.* Boston: Beacon Press.

Muller, Edward N. 1985. "Income Inequality, Regime Repressiveness, and Political Violence." *American Sociological Review* 50: 47–61.

—— 1988. "Democracy, Economic Development, and Income Inequality." *American Sociological Review* 53: 50–68.

—— 1989. "Democracy and Inequality (Reply to Weede)." *American Sociological Review* 54: 868–71.

—— 1995a. "Economic Determinants of Democracy." *American Sociological Review* 60: 966–82.

—— 1995b. "Income Inequality and Democratization: Reply to Bollen and Jackman." *American Sociological Review* 60: 990–6.

Muller, Edward N. and Mitchell A. Seligson. 1987. "Inequality and Insurgency." *American Political Science Review* 81: 425–51.

—— 1994. "Civic Culture and Democracy: The Question of Causal Relationships." *American Political Science Review* 88: 635–52.

Murdock, George P. and Caterina Provost. 1980. "Measurement of Cultural Complexity." In *Cross-Cultural Samples and Codes*, eds. Herbert Barry III and Alice Schlegel. Pittsburgh: University of Pittsburgh Press.

Murdock, George P. and Douglas R. White. 1980. "Standard Cross-Cultural Sample." In *Cross-Cultural Samples and Codes*, eds. Herbert Barry III and Alice Schlegel. Pittsburgh: University of Pittsburgh Press.

Murrell, Peter. 1992. "Evolutionary and Radical Approaches to Reform." *Economics of Planning* 25: 79–95.

Murrell, Peter and Mancur Olson. 1991. "The Devolution of Centrally Planned Economies." *Journal of Comparative Economics* 15: 239–65.

Myers, Fred R. 1986. *Pintupi Country, Pintupi Self: Sentiment, Place and Politics among Western Desert Aborigines.* Washington: Smithsonian Institution Press.

Naím, Moisés. 1994. "Latin America: The Second Stage of Reform." *Journal of Democracy* 5: 32–48.

Naughton, Barry. 1995. *Growing Out of the Plan: Chinese Economic Reform, 1978–1993.* New York: Cambridge University Press.

Nee, Victor. 1991. "Social Inequalities in Reforming State Socialism: Between Redistribution and Markets in China." *American Sociological Review* 56: 267–82.

—— 1992. "Organizational Dynamics of Market Transition: Hybrid Forms, Property Rights, and Mixed Economy in China." *Administrative Science Quarterly* 37: 1–27.

Nee, Victor and Peng Lian. 1994. "Sleeping with the Enemy: A Dynamic Model of Declining Political Commitment in State Socialism." *Theory and Society* 23: 253–96.

Nee, Victor and Su Sijin. 1996. "Institutions, Social Ties and Commitment in China's Corporatist Transformation." In *Reforming Asian Socialism: The Growth of Market Institutions*, eds. J. McMillan and B. Naughton. Ann Arbor: University of Michigan Press.

—— 1996. "The Emergence of a Market Society: Changing Mechanisms of Stratification in China." *American Journal of Sociology* 101: 908–49.

Nelson, Joan. 1994. "Overview: How Market Reforms and Democratic Consolidation Affect Each Other?" In *Intricate Links: Democratization and Market Reforms in Latin America and Eastern Europe*, ed. Joan Nelson. New Brunswick, NJ: Transaction Books, pp. 1–37.

Nemeth, R. J. and D. A. Smith. 1985. "The Political Economy of Contrasting Urban Hierarchies in South Korea and the Philippines." In *Urbanization in the World Economy*, ed. Michael Timberlake. New York: Academic Press.

Neubauer, Deane E. 1967. "Some Conditions of Democracy." *American Political Science Review* 61: 1002–9.

Nissen, Hans J. 1988. *The Early History of the Ancient Near East: 9000–2000 BC*, trans. Elizabeth Lutzeier and Kenneth Northcott. Chicago: University of Chicago Press.

Nolan, Patrick and Gerhard Lenski. 1985. "Technoeconomic Heritage, Patterns of Development, and the Advantage of Backwardness." *Social Forces* 64: 341–58.

North, Douglass C. 1981. *Structure and Change in Economic History*. New York: Norton.

Nygard, Fredrik and Arne Sandstrom. 1981. *Measuring Income Inequality*. Stockholm: Almquist and Wiksell.

Oates, Joan. 1977. "Mesopotamian Social Organization: Archaeological and Philological Evidence." In *The Evolution of Social Systems*, eds. J. Friedman and M. J. Rowlands. London: Duckworth.

O'Donnell, Guillermo A. 1978. "Reflections on the Patterns of Change in the Bureaucratic-Authoritarian State." *Latin American Research Review* 13: 3–38.

—— 1979. *Modernization and Bureaucratic-Authoritarianism*. Berkeley: Institute of International Studies.

—— 1988. *Bureaucratic Authoritarianism: Argentina, 1966–1973, in Comparative Perspective*. Berkeley: University of California Press.

—— 1993. "On the State, Democratization and Some Conceptual Problems: A Latin American View with Glances at Some Post-Communist Countries." *World Development* 21: 1355–69.

—— 1994. "Delegative Democracy." *Journal of Democracy* 5: 55–69.

OECD-ILO. 1993. *Structural Change in Central and Eastern Europe: Labour Market and Social Policy Implications*.

Offe, Claus. 1991. "Capitalism by Democratic Design? Democratic Theory Facing the Triple Transition in East Central Europe." *Social Research* 58: 865–92.

Oi, Jean. 1990. "The Fate of the Collective after the Commune." In *Chinese Society on the Eve of Tiananmen*, eds. D. Davis and E. F. Vogel. Cambridge, MA: Council on East Asian Studies.

—— 1992. "Fiscal Reform and the Economic Foundation of Local State Corporatism in China." *World Politics* 45: 99–126.

Olsen, M. E. 1968. "Multivariate Analysis of National Political Development." *American Sociological Review* 33: 699–712.

Olson, Mancur, Jr. 1963. "Rapid Growth as a Destabilizing Force." *Journal of Economic History* 23: 529–52.

—— 1982. *The Rise and Decline of Nations*. New Haven: Yale University Press.

—— 1993. "Dictatorship, Democracy, and Development." *American Political Science Review* 87: 567–76.

Oppenheim, A. Leo. 1977. *Ancient Mesopotamia*, rev. edn. Chicago: University of Chicago Press.

Ost, David. 1992. "Labor and Societal Transition." *Problems of Communism* 41: 48–51.

Parkin, Frank. 1971. *Class Inequality and Political Order*. New York: Praeger.

Parpia, Banoo. 1994. "Socioeconomic Determinants of Food and Nutrient Intakes in Rural China." Doctoral dissertation, Department of Sociology, Cornell University.

Parsons, Talcott. 1977. *The Evolution of Societies*, ed. Jackson Toby. Englewood Cliffs, NJ: Prentice-Hall.

Paukert, Felix. 1973. "Income Distribution at Different Levels of Development: A Survey of Evidence." *International Labour Review* 108: 97–125.

Paxton, Pamela. 1995. "Women in National Legislatures: A Cross National Analysis." Unpublished manuscript.

Payne, James L. 1989. *Why Nations Arm*. Oxford: Basil Blackwell.

Peng, Yusheng. 1992. "Wage Determination in Rural and Urban China: A Comparison of Public and Private Industrial Sectors." *American Sociological Review* 57: 198–213.

Peterson, Wallace C. 1994. *Silent Depression: The Fate of the American Dream*. New York: W. W. Norton.

Pitkin, Hanna. 1967. *The Concept of Representation*. Berkeley: University of California Press.

Poggi, Gianfranco. 1978. *The Development of the Modern State: A Sociological Introduction*. Stanford: Stanford University Press.

Polanyi, Karl. 1957. *The Great Transformation: The Political and Economic Origins of our Time*. Boston: Beacon Books.

Prosterman, Roy L. and Jeffrey M. Riedinger. 1987. *Land Reform and Democratic Development*. Baltimore: Johns Hopkins University Press.

Przeworski, Adam. 1991. *Democracy and the Market: Political and Economic Reforms in Eastern Europe and Latin America*. Cambridge: Cambridge University Press.

Przeworski, Adam, ed. 1995. *Sustainable Democracy*. Cambridge: Cambridge University Press.

Przeworski, Adam, Michael Alvarez, José A. Cheibub, and Fernando Limongi. 1996. "What Makes Democracies Endure?" *Journal of Democracy* 7: 39–55.

Prezworski, Adam and Fernando Limongi. 1993. "Political Regimes and Economic Growth." *Journal of Economic Perspectives* 7: 51–70.

Przeworski, Adam and Henry Teune. 1970. *The Logic of Comparative Social Inquiry*. New York: Wiley.

Psacharopoulos, George. 1973. *Returns to Education: An International Comparison*. San Francisco, CA: Jossey-Bass.

Putnam, Robert D. 1993. *Making Democracy Work: Civic Traditions in Modern Italy*. Princeton: Princeton University Press.

—— 1996. "The Strange Disappearance of Civic America." *The American Prospect* 24: 34–48.

Pye, Lucian W. 1966. *Aspects of Political Development: An Analytic Study*. Boston: Little, Brown.

—— 1990. "Political Science and the Crisis of Authoritarianism." *American Political Science Review* 84: 3–19.

Qian Yingyi and Chenggang Xu. 1993. "Why China's Economic Reforms Differ: The M-Form Hierarchy and Entry/Expansion of the Non-State Sector." *The Economics of Transition* 1: 135–70.

Ramirez, Francisco O. and John Boli. 1987. "The Political Construction of Mass Education: European Origins and Worldwide Institutionalization." *Sociology of Education* 60: 2–17.

Ravenhill, John. 1986a. "A Rejoinder." *Comparative Political Studies* 19: 275–6.

—— 1986b. "Inequality in the Third World: A Reexamination." *Comparative Political Studies* 19: 259–68.

Rawls, John. 1971. *A Theory of Justice*. Cambridge, MA: Harvard University Press.

Ray, James L. 1995. *Democracy and International Conflict: An Evaluation of the Democratic Peace Proposition*. Columbia, SC: University of South Carolina Press.

Remmer, Karen. 1990. "Democracy and Economic Crisis: The Latin American Experience." *World Politics* 42: 315–35.

Remmer, Karen and Gilbert Merckx. 1982. "Bureaucratic-Authoritarianism Revisited." *Latin American Research Review* 17: 3–40.

Renfrew, Colin. 1972. *The Emergence of Civilization: The Cyclades and the Aegean in the Third Millennium BC* London: Methuen.

—— 1979. *Before Civilization*. Cambridge: Cambridge University Press.

—— 1982. "Polity and Power: Interaction, Intensification and Exploitation." In *An Island Polity: The Archaeology of Exploitation in Melos*, eds. Colin Renfrew and Malcolm W. Wagstaff. Cambridge: Cambridge University Press.

Richardson, Lewis F. 1960. *Statistics of Deadly Quarrels*. Pittsburgh: Boxwood.

Ridington, R. 1988. "Knowledge, Power and the Individual in Subarctic Hunting Society." *American Anthropology* 90: 98–110.

Roberts, K. 1985. "Democracy and the Dependent Capitalist State in Latin America." *Monthly Review* 37: 12–26.

Roeder, Philip. 1985. "Do New Soviet Leaders Really Make a Difference? Rethinking the 'Succession Connection.' " *American Political Science Review* 79: 958–76.

—— 1986. "The Effects of Leadership Succession in the Soviet Union." *American Political Science Review* 80: 219–24.

Rogers, Everett M. 1983. *Diffusion of Innovations*, 3rd edn. London: Free Press.

Rona-tas, Akos. 1994. "The First Shall be Last? Entrepreneurship and Communist Cadres in the Transition from Socialism." *American Journal of Sociology* 100: 40–69.

Ross, Marc H. 1981. "Socioeconomic Complexity, Socialization, and Political Differentiation: A Cross-Cultural Study." *Ethos* 9: 217–47.

—— 1983. "Political Decision-Making and Conflict: Additional Cross-Cultural Codes and Scales." *Ethnology* 22: 169–92.

—— 1986. "Female Political Participation: A Cross-Cultural Explanation." *American Anthropologist* 88: 843–58.

Rostow, Walt W. 1960. *The Stages of Economic Growth: A Non-Communist Manifesto.* Cambridge: Cambridge University Press.

Rozelle, Scott. 1994. "Stagnation without Equity: Changing Patterns of Income and Inequality in China's Post-Reform Rural Economy." *Journal of Comparative Economics* 19: 362–91.

Rubinson, Richard. 1976. "The World-Economy and the Distribution of Income within States: A Cross-National Study." *American Sociological Review* 41: 638–59.

Rubinson, Richard and Dan Quinlan. 1977. "Democracy and Social Inequality: A Reanalysis." *American Sociological Review* 42: 611–23.

Rueschemeyer, Dietrich, Evelyne H. Stephens, and John D. Stephens. 1992. *Capitalist Development and Democracy.* Chicago: University of Chicago Press.

Rummel, Rudolph J. 1983. "Libertarianism and International Violence." *Journal of Conflict Resolution* 27: 27–71.

Russett, Bruce M. 1964. "Inequality and Instability: The Relation of Land Tenure to Politics." *World Politics* 16: 442–54.

—— 1993. *Grasping the Democratic Peace: Principles for a Post-Cold War World.* Princeton: Princeton University Press.

Russett, Bruce M., Hayward Alker, Karl Deutsch, and Harold Lasswell. 1964. *World Handbook of Political and Social Indicators.* New Haven: Yale University Press.

Russett, Bruce M., Carol R. Ember, and Melvin Ember. 1993. "The Democratic Peace in Nonindustrial Societies." In *Grasping the Democratic Peace: Principles for a Post-Cold War World*, by Bruce Russett (with the collaboration of William Antholis, Carol R. Ember, Melvin Ember, and Zeev Maoz). Princeton: Princeton University Press.

Russett, Bruce M., Christopher Layne, David E. Spiro, and Michael W. Doyle. 1995. "The Democratic Peace." *International Security* 19: 164–84.

Rustow, Dankwart A. 1967. *A World of Nations.* Washington, DC: Brookings.

—— 1970. "Transitions to Democracy." *Comparative Politics* 2: 337–63.

Sabloff, Jeremy. 1990. *The New Archaeology and the Ancient Maya.* New York: Scientific American Library.

Sanders, William T. and Barbara J. Price. 1968. *Mesoamerica: The Evolution of a Civilization.* New York: Random House.

Sartori, Giovanni. 1994. *Comparative Constitutional Engineering.* New York: New York University Press.

—— 1995. "How Far Can Free Government Travel?" *Journal of Democracy* 6: 101–11.

Savishinsky, Joel S. 1974. *On the Trail of the Hare.* New York: Gordon and Breach.

Sawyer, Malcolm. 1976. "Income Distribution in OECD Countries." *OECD Economic Outlook: Occasional Studies* July: 3–36.

Schamis, Hector E. 1991. "Reconceptualizing Latin American Authoritarianism in the 1970s: From Bureaucratic-Authoritarianism to Neoconservatism." *Comparative Politics* 23: 201–20.

Schmitter, Philippe and Terry Karl. 1994. "The Conceptual Travels of Transitologists and Consolidologists: How Far to the East Should They Attempt to Go?" *Slavic Review* 53: 173–85.

Schooler, C. 1976. "Serfdom's Legacy: An Ethnic Continuum." *American Journal of Sociology* 81: 1265–81.

Schweller, Randall L. 1992. "Domestic Structure and Preventive War: Are Democracies More Pacific?" *World Politics* 44: 235–69.

Scott, James C. 1976. *The Moral Economy of the Peasant: Rebellion and Subsistence in Southeast Asia*. New Haven: Yale University Press.

Sealey, Raphael. 1987. *The Athenian Republic: Democracy or the Rule of Law?* University Park: Pennsylvania State University Press.

Shin, D. C. 1994. "On the Third Wave of Democratization: A Synthesis and Evaluation of Recent Theory and Research." *World Politics* 47: 135–70.

Shirk, Susan L. 1993. *The Political Logic of Economic Reform in China*. Berkeley: University of California Press.

Shostak, Marjorie. 1981. *Nisa: The Life and Words of a !Kung Woman*. Cambridge, MA: Haward University Press.

Shugart, Matthew and John Carey. 1992. *Presidents and Assemblies*. Cambridge: Cambridge University Press.

Sík, Endre. 1994. "From the Multicoloured to the Black and White Economy: The Hungarian Second Economy and the Transformation." *International Journal of Urban and Regional Research* 18: 46–70.

Simmel, Georg. 1971. "Group Expansion and the Development of Individuality." In *Georg Simmel: On Individuality and Social Forms*, ed. D. N. Levine. Chicago: University of Chicago Press.

Simpson, Miles. 1972. "Authoritarianism and Education: A Comparative Approach." *Sociometry* 35: 223–34.

—— 1990. "Political Rights and Income Inequality: A Cross-National Test." *American Sociological Review* 55: 682–93.

—— 1993a. "Political Power Versus Ecological-Evolutionary Forces: What are the Proximal Sources of National Income Distribution?" *Social Forces* 71: 797–806.

—— 1993b. "The Social Origins of Democracy: A Cross National Study." Paper presented at the 31st International Congress of the International Institute of Sociology, Paris, France.

Sirowy, Larry and Alex Inkeles. 1991. "The Effects of Democracy on Economic Growth and Inequality: A Review." In *On Measuring Democracy*, ed. Alex Inkeles. New Brunswick, NJ: Transaction Publishers

Sivard, Ruth Leger. 1985. *Woman . . . A World Survey*. Washington, DC: World Priorities.

Skidmore, Thomas E. 1977. "The Politics of Economic Stabilization in Postwar Latin America." In *Authoritarianism and Corporatism in Latin America*, ed. James M. Malloy. Pittsburgh: University of Pittsburgh Press.

Smith, Adam. 1776. *The Wealth of Nations*. Middlesex, England: Penguin.

Snyder, David and Edward L. Kick. 1979. "Structural Position in the World System and Economic Growth, 1955–1970: A Multiple-Network Analysis of Transnational Interactions." *American Journal of Sociology* 84: 1096–1126.

Spencer, Herbert. 1852, [1972]. "Population and Progress." In *Herbert Spencer:*

On Social Evolution, ed. John D. Y. Peel. Chicago: University of Chicago Press.

—— 1876. *The Principles of Sociology*. London: Williams and Norgram.

Spiro, David E. 1994. "The Insignificance of the Liberal Peace." *International Security* 19: 50–81.

Spring, David. 1977. "Landed Elites Compared." In *European Landed Elites in the Nineteenth Century*, ed. David Spring. Baltimore: Johns Hopkins University Press.

Sprout, Harold and Margaret Sprout. 1962. *Foundations of International Politics*. Princeton, NJ: Van Nostrand.

Staniszkis, Jadwiga. 1991. *The Dynamics of the Breakthrough in Eastern Europe: The Polish Experience*. Berkeley and Los Angeles: University of California Press.

Stark, David. 1996. "Recombinant Property in East European Capitalism." *American Journal of Sociology* 101: 993–1027.

Starr, Harvey. 1991. "International System." *Journal of Conflict Resolution* 35: 356–81.

Starr, Harvey and Benjamin A. Most. 1978. "A Return Journey: Richardson, 'Frontiers' and Wars in the 1946–1965 Era." *Journal of Conflict Resolution* 22: 441–67.

Stern, Fritz. 1977. "Prussia." In *European Landed Elites in the Nineteenth Century*, ed. David Spring. Baltimore: Johns Hopkins University Press.

Stimson, James A. 1985. "Regression in Space and Time: A Statistical Essay." *American Journal of Political Science* 29: 915–47.

Stokes, Randall G. and Andy B. Anderson. 1990. "Disarticulation and Human Welfare in Less Developed Countries." *American Sociological Review* 55: 63–74.

Stone, Elizabeth C. and Paul Zimansky. 1995. "The Tapestry of Power in a Mesopotamian City." *Scientific American* 272 (4): 118–23.

Stone, Lawrence. 1969. "Literacy and Education in England." *Past and Present* 2: 69–139.

Strehlow, T. G. H. 1970. "Geography and the Totemic Landscape in Central Australia: A Functional Study." In *Australian Aboriginal Anthropology*, ed. Ronald M. Berndt. Nedlands: University of Western Australia Press.

Strouse, James C. and Richard P. Claude. 1976. "Empirical Comparative Rights Research: Some Preliminary Tests of Development Hypotheses." In *Comparative Human Rights*, ed. Richard P. Claude. Baltimore: Johns Hopkins University Press, pp. 51–67.

Summers, Robert and Alan Heston. 1984. "Improved International Comparisons of Real Product and its Composition: 1950–1980." *Review of Income and Wealth* 30: 207–62.

—— 1988. "A New Set of International Comparisons of Real Product and Price Levels Estimates for 130 Countries, 1950–1985." *Review of Income and Wealth* 34: 1–25.

Sussman, L. R. 1980. "Freedom of the Press: Problems on Restructuring the Flow of International News." In *Freedom in the World, 1980*, ed. Raymond D. Gastil. New York: Freedom House, pp. 53–98.

—— 1981. "Freedom of the Press: A Personal Account of the Continuing

Struggle." In *Freedom in the World, 1981*, ed. Raymond D. Gastil. Westport, CT: Greenwood Press, pp. 57–78.

—— 1982. "The Continuing Struggle for Freedom of Information." In *Freedom in the World, 1982*, ed. Raymond D. Gastil. Westport, CT: Greenwood Press, pp. 109–19.

Swanson, Guy E. 1967. *Religion and Regime: A Sociological Account of the Reformation.* Ann Arbor: University of Michigan Press.

Szelenyi, Ivan. 1978. "Social Inequalities in State Socialist Redistributive Economies." *International Journal of Comparative Sociology* 19: 63–87.

Szelenyi, Ivan and Robert Manchin. 1987. "Social Policy under State Socialism." In *Stagnation and Renewal in Social Policy*, eds. Gosta Esping-Anderson, Lee Rainwater, and Martin Rein. White Plains, NY: M. E. Sharpe.

Taagepera, Rein and Matthew Shugart. 1989. *Seats and Votes.* New Haven: Yale University Press.

Tarrow, Sidney. 1994. *Power in Movement: Social Movements, Collective Action, and Politics.* Cambridge: Cambridge University Press.

Taylor, Charles L. and Michael C. Hudson. 1972. *World Handbook of Political and Social Indicators*, 2nd edn. New Haven: Yale University Press.

Taylor, Charles L. and David A. Jodice. 1983. *World Handbook of Political and Social Indicators*, 3rd edn, 2 vols. New Haven: Yale University Press.

Thomas, G. M. and J. W. Meyer. 1986. "The Expansion of the State." *Annual Review of Sociology* 10: 461–82.

Thompson, E. P. 1966. *The Making of the English Working Class.* New York: Vintage Books.

Thurow, Lester C. 1970. "Analyzing the American Income Distribution." Papers and Proceedings, *American Economics Association* 60: 261–9.

Tilly, Charles. 1978. *From Mobilization to Revolution.* Reading, MA: Addison-Wesley.

—— 1986. *The Contentious French.* Cambridge, MA: Harvard University Press.

—— 1990. *Coercion, Capital, and European States, AD 990–1990.* Cambridge, MA: Basil Blackwell.

Timberlake, Michael. 1987. "World-System Theory and the Study of Comparative Urbanization." In *The Capitalist City: Global Restructuring and Community Politics*, eds. Michael P. Smith and Joe R. Feagin. Oxford: Basil Blackwell, pp. 37–65

Timberlake, Michael and K. R. Williams. 1984. "Dependence, Political Exclusion, and Government Repression: Some Cross-National Evidence." *American Sociological Review* 49: 141–6.

Tocqueville, Alexis de. 1945. *Democracy in America*, vols. 1 and 2. New York: Vintage Books.

—— 1955. *The Old Regime and the French Revolution.* New York: Doubleday.

Todaro, Michael. 1969. "A Model of Labor Migration and Urban Development in Less Developed Countries." *American Economic Review* 59: 138–48.

Tonnies, Ferdinand. 1963. *Community and Society.* Trans. C. P. Loomis. New York: Harper and Row.

Tóth, István J. 1992. "Gazdasági szervezetek és érdekérvén yesítési módszerek (elsõ megközelítés)." Unpublished manuscript, Budapest.

Trent, J. S. and L. L. Medsker. 1969. *High School and Beyond: A Psychosociological Study of 10,000 High School Graduates*. San Francisco, CA: Jossey-Bass.

Turner, Jonathan H. 1993. *Classical Sociological Theory: A Positivist's Perspective*. Chicago: Nelson-Hall.

United Nations. 1993. *UN Statistical Yearbook 1990–91*.

United Nations Industrial Development Organization (UNIDO). 1988. *Industry and Development: Global Report 1988–89*. Vienna.

Urbán László. 1991. "Why was the Hungarian Transition Exceptionally Peaceful?" In *Democracy and Political Transformation: Theories and East-Central European Realities*, ed. György Szoboszlai. Budapest: Hungarian Political Science Association, pp. 303–9.

Valenzuela, Samuel and Arturo Valenzuela. 1978. "Modernization and Dependency: Alternative Perspectives in the Study of Latin American Development." *Comparative Politics* 10: 535–57.

Van Ginnekan, Wouter. 1976. *Rural and Urban Income Inequalities*. Geneva: International Labour Office.

Vanhanen, Tatu. 1977. *Power and the Means of Power: A Study of 119 Asian, European, American and African States, 1850–1979*. Ann Arbor: Published for the Center for the Study of Developing Societies by University Microfilm International.

—— 1984. *The Emergence of Democracy: A Comparative Study of 119 States, 1850–1979*. Helskinki: The Finnish Society of Sciences and Letters.

—— 1990. *The Process of Democratization: A Comparative Study of 147 States, 1980–88*. New York: Crane Russak.

—— 1992. "Social Constraints of Democratization." In *Strategies of Democratization*, ed. Tatu Vanhanen. Washington: Crane Russak.

Vogt, Evon Z. 1971. "The Genetic Model and Maya Cultural Development." In *Desarrollo Cultural de los Mayas*, 2nd edn, eds. Evon Z. Vogt and Aberto Ruz L. Universidad Nacional Autónoma de México, Centro de Estudios Mayas.

Voszka, Eva. 1992. "Not Even the Contrary is True: The Transfigurations of Centralization and Decentralization." *Acta Oeconomica* 44: 77–94.

Walder, Andrew G. 1990. "Economic Reform and Income Inequality in Tianjin, 1976–1986." In *Chinese Society on the Eve of Tiananmen*, eds. Debra Davis and Ezra Vogel. Cambridge, MA: Harvard Contemporary China Series, Council on East Asian Studies.

—— 1995. "Career Mobility and the Communist Political Order." *American Sociological Review* 60: 309–28.

Wallerstein, Immanuel. 1974. *The Modern World-System*, New York: Academic Press.

Wallerstein, Michael. 1980. "The Collapse of Democracy in Brazil: Its Economic Determinants." *Latin American Research Review* 15: 3–40.

Walton, John. 1989. "Debt, Protest, and the State in Latin America." In *Power and Popular Protest: Latin American Social Movements*, ed. Susan Eckstein, 299–328. Berkeley: University of California Press.

Walton, John and David Seddon. 1994. *Free Markets and Food Riots: The Politics of Global Adjustment*. Oxford: Blackwell.

Wan, Henry Jr. 1994. "The Market Transition in Taiwan: Any Relevance to the PRC?" In *The Economic Transformation of South China: Reform and Development in the Post-Mao Era*, co-ed. Thomas P. Lyons. Cornell East Asia Series, no. 70. Ithaca: East Asia Program.

Ward, Michael D. 1978. *The Political Economy of Distribution: Equality versus Inequality*. New York: Elsevier.

Warren, Peter. 1989. *The Aegean Civilizations*, 2nd edn. Oxford: Equinox.

Waterbury, John. 1989. "The Political Management of Economic Adjustment and Reform." In *Fragile Conditions: The Politics of Economic Adjustment*, ed. Joan Nelson. New Brunswick, NJ: Transaction Books, pp. 39–57.

Weber, Max. 1958. *The Protestant Ethic and the Spirit of Capitalism*. Trans. Talcott Parsons. New York: Scribner.

Webster, Thomas B. L. 1969. *Everyday Life in Classical Athens*. New York: G. P. Putnam's Sons.

Weede, Erich. 1980. "Beyond Misspecification in Sociological Analyses of Income Inequality." *American Sociological Review* 45: 497–501.

—— 1982. "The Effects of Democracy and Socialist Strength on the Size Distribution of Income." *International Journal of Sociology* 23: 151–65.

—— 1990. "Democracy, Party Government and Rent-Seeking as Determinants of Distributional Inequality in Industrial Societies." *European Journal of Political Research* 18: 515–33.

Weede, Erich and Horst Tiefenbach. 1981a. "Correlates of the Size Distribution of Income and Cross-National Analyses." *Journal of Politics* 43: 1029–41.

—— 1981b. "Rejoinder." *International Studies Quarterly* 25: 289–93.

—— 1981c. "Some Recent Explanations of Income Inequality: An Evaluation and Critique." *International Studies Quarterly* 25: 255–82.

Weingast, Barry R. 1993. "The Economic Role of Political Institutions." *Working Papers on the Transitions from State Socialism*. No. 93.8, Mario Einaudi Center for International Studies, Cornell University, Ithaca, New York.

White, Harrison C. 1981. "Where Do Markets Come From?" *American Journal of Sociology* 87: 517–47.

Whiting, John W. M. 1954. "The Cross-Cultural Method." In *Handbook of Social Psychology*, vol. I, ed. Gardner Lindzey. Cambridge, MA: Addison-Wesley.

Whyte, Martin K. 1978. *The Status of Women in Preindustrial Societies*. Princeton: Princeton University Press.

Willetts, R. F. 1965. *Ancient Crete: A Social History from Early Times until the Roman Occupation*. London: Routledge.

Wilmsen, Edwin N. 1989. *Land Filled With Flies: A Political Economy of the Kalahari*. Chicago: University of Chicago Press.

Wilson, Scott. 1994. "Peasants into Villagers: Social Networks and Power Relations in Contemporary Shanghai Villages." Doctoral dissertation, Department of Government, Cornell University.

Wittfogel, Karl A. 1957. *Oriental Despotism: A Comparative Study of Total Power*. New Haven: Yale University Press.

Woodburn, James. 1982. "Egalitarian Societies." *Man* 17: 431–51.

Woodcock, George. 1977. *Peoples of the Coast: The Indians of the Pacific Northwest.* Bloomington: Indiana University Press.

World Bank. 1978. *Rural Employment and Nonfarm Employment.* Washington, DC: World Bank.

—— 1980. *World Development Report 1980.* New York: Oxford University Press.

—— 1984a. *World Development Report 1984.* New York: Oxford University Press.

—— 1984b. *World Tables Vol. II: Social Indicators.* Washington, DC: World Bank.

—— 1985. *World Development Report 1985.* New York: Oxford University Press.

—— 1987a. *Social Indicators of Development.* Washington, DC: World Bank.

—— 1987b. *World Development Report 1987.* New York: Oxford University Press.

—— 1990. *World Tables, 1989–90.* Baltimore: Johns Hopkins University Press.

—— 1991. *The Challenge of Development. World Development Report 1991.* New York: Oxford University Press.

—— 1992. *World Tables, 1992.* Baltimore: Johns Hopkins University Press.

—— 1994. *World Data 1994: World Bank Indicators on CD-ROM.* Washington, DC: World Bank.

Wright, R. 1992. "Islam and Democracy." *Foreign Affairs* 71(3): 131–45.

Wrightson, Keith. 1982. *English Society: 1580–1680.* New Brunswick: Rutgers University Press.

Zaslavsky, Victor. 1994. "From Redistribution to Marketization: Social and Attitudinal Change in Post-Soviet Russia." In *The New Russia: Troubled Transformation,* ed. Gail Lapidus. Boulder, CO: Westview Press.

Zhao, Renwei. 1993. "Three Features of the Distribution of Income during the Transition to Reform." In *The Distribution of Income in China,* eds. K. Griffin and R. Zhao. New York: St. Martin's Press.

Zhu, Ling. 1990. *Rural Reform and Peasant Income in China.* London: Macmillan Press.

Zhu, Xiangdong and Jiangwu Wen. 1990. "Nonmin Shouru Chayi Yanjiu" [A Study of Differentials in Peasant Income] *Tongji Yanjiu [Statistical Studies]* 4: 48–52.

Zolo, Danilo. 1992. *Democracy and Complexity: A Realist Approach.* University Park: Pennsylvania State University Press.

Zwick, J. 1984. "Militarism and Repression in the Philippines." In *The State as Terrorist: The Dynamics of Government Violence and Repression,* eds. Michael Stohl and George A. Lopez. Westport, CT: Greenwood Press, pp. 123–42.

Index

DATE DUE

GAYLORD			PRINTED IN U.S.A.